The
Incredibly Indispens

Web

Directory

The
Incredibly Indispensable
Web
Directory
3rd edition

CLIVE AND BETTINA ZIETMAN

Published by Kogan Page

in association with

DAILY EXPRESS

www.thomweb.co.uk
THOMSON
Directories

Publishers' note

Every possible effort has been made to ensure that the information contained in this book is accurate at the time of going to press and neither the publishers nor the authors can accept responsibility for any errors or omissions, however caused. No responsibility for loss or damage occasioned to any person acting, or refraining from action, as a result of the material in this publication can be accepted by the editor, the publisher or the authors.

First published in 2000
Second edition 2000
Third edition 2001

Apart from any fair dealing for the purposes of research or private study, or criticism or review, as permitted under the Copyright, Designs and Patents Act 1988, this publication may only be reproduced, stored or transmitted, in any form or by any means, with the prior permission in writing of the publishers, or in the case of reprographic reproduction in accordance with the terms and licences issued by the CLA. Enquiries concerning reproduction outside these terms should be sent to the publishers at the undermentioned address:

Kogan Page Limited
120 Pentonville Road
London N1 9JN

Kogan Page (US) Limited
163 Central Avenue, Suite 4
Dover, NH 03820, USA

Kogan Page website: www.kogan-page.co.uk

Daily Express website: www.express.co.uk

© Clive and Bettina Zietman, 2001

The right of Clive and Bettina Zietman to be identified as the author of this work has been asserted by him in accordance with the Copyright, Designs and Patents Act 1988.

British Library Cataloguing in Publication Data

A CIP record for this book is available from the British Library.

ISBN 0 7494 3617 4

Cover design by Marcus Perry
Typeset by Bibliocraft Ltd, Dundee
Printed and bound in Great Britain

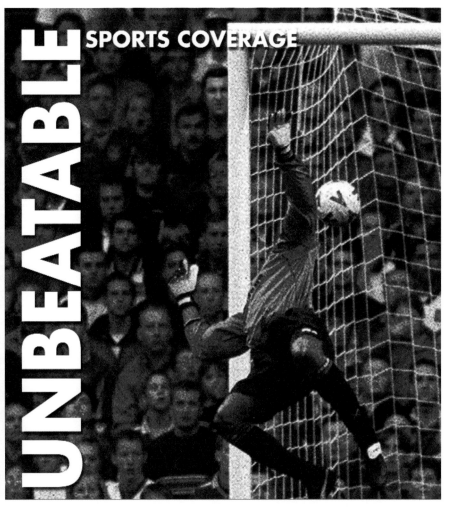

arts & entertainment

actors & actresses...3
art 4
ballet...5
clubs...6
comedy..6
events...7
fashion..8
film...9
funding, organisations & regulation 12
literature...13
magazines & websites...13
magicians 14
music..14
professional bodies 22
promotors & directors 23
radio 23
stadia & concert halls..25
television...26
theatre 28
tickets 31

business

advertising 35
automotive...35
aviation 35
chambers of commerce 35
chemicals 36
couriers...36
electrical & technological 37
energy..37
engineering 37
finance 37
food, beverage & tobacco...41
ftse 100 companies..41
insurance 43
leisure 43
livery companies & guilds...44
magazines & websites..44
manufacturing..45
materials & construction...45
media...45
metals & mining...46
model agencies 46
office supplies & services..46
paper & packaging 47
pharmaceutical 47
printing & publishing..48
private investigators 49

professional bodies 49
professional bodies & associations 49
professions 50
real estate 51
recruitment 51
retail 52
services 52
shipping & shipbuilding 52
standards 53
stock & commodity exchanges & financial listings 53
telecommunications 54
trade associations 54
trades unions 55
transport 56
us corporations 56
utilities 58

children

cartoon characters 63
clubs & activities 63
computer games 63
days out 64
film & television 64
games & toys 65
homework & revision 66
magazines, books & authors 66
theatre 67
websites 67

education, training & research

agriculture 71
art & architecture 71
ballet, drama & music 71
books, magazines & websites 72
business & law 72
complementary health 73
educational organisations 73
medical & dental 73
postgraduate & research 74
pre-school 74
professional associations 74
schools 74
sport 75
students 75
tuition & part-time learning 75
universities 75
veterinary schools 78

environment

agriculture 83

architecture..83
construction...83
government 84
green issues 84
landscape..84
preservation...85
transport 86

food & drink

breweries 89
chefs1 89
clubs & associations..90
famous brands 90
fast food 94
food & drink online 94
food marketing 94
magazines & websites...94
restaurants & bars 95
supermarkets...96
trade associations 96
whisky..96
wine 98

government

armed forces 101
embassies 101
foreign governments..102
international organisations..105
law 105
legal institutions abroad 106
monarchy...106
overseas territories & crown dependencies 107
people..107
political parties 107
post offices...108
pressure groups 108
professional associations 109
research councils 109
uk government 109

healthcare

ancillary services 125
animal health 125
complementary...125
dentistry...126
government agencies 126
health authorities 126
hospitals, clinics & nhs trusts..127
journals, magazines & websites 128
medicine & surgery..129

nursing & midwifery 130
pharmacy 130
psychiatry & psychology 130
research 131
vision 131

help!

ambulance services 135
breakdown services 135
charities & helplines 135
consumer problems 138
fire & rescue services 139
funeral services 139
police 139
watchdogs & ombudsmen 140

hobbies & leisure

astrology 143
ballooning 143
birds 143
boating 143
bodybuilding 143
bridge 143
chess 144
climbing 144
collecting 144
cookery 145
country pursuits 145
dancing 145
fishing 145
flying 146
football 146
gambling 146
games 147
gardening 147
genealogy 147
handicraft 148
homebrew 148
horse riding 148
karting 149
metal detecting 149
miscellaneous clubs & associations 149
models 149
music 150
outdoor pursuits 150
parachuting 150
pets 150
photography 151
ten pin bowling 152

living

cars...155
dating agencies 157
disabilty 158
driving schools 158
family life 158
hairdressers, beauty salons & image consultants........158
health & fitness 158
home life..159
magazines & websites...162
military associations 163
motorcycles...163
new age 164
religion 164
retirement 165
weddings 165

museums, libraries & information

encyclopaedias..169
history..169
libraries 169
maps..170
museums 170
opinion polls & market research.................................173
phone numbers 173
professional bodies & associations 173
reference..173
weather..174

news & information

news 177
newspapers 177
professional bodies & associations 183

personal finance

banks & building societies..187
credit cards 188
insurance 188
investment funds 190
magazines & websites..191
mortgages 192
professional bodies 192
stockbrokers..192

places

angola..197
argentina..197
australia 197
austria..197

bangladesh 197
belgium 198
brazil 198
britain 198
cameroon 204
canada 204
caribbean 204
channel islands 204
china 205
cyprus 205
denmark 205
egypt 205
falkland islands 205
finland 205
france 206
gambia 206
germany 206
ghana 206
gibraltar 206
greece 206
hungary 206
iceland 207
india 207
ireland 207
israel 207
italy 207
japan 207
jordan 208
kenya 208
korea 208
kuwait 208
lebanon 208
liechtenstein 208
luxembourg 208
malaysia 208
maldives 208
malta 209
mauritius 209
mexico 209
monaco 209
morocco 209
nepal 209
netherlands 209
new zealand 209
norway 209
pacific islands 210
pakistan 210
philippines 210
portugal 210
romania 210

russia 210
serbia 210
seychelles 210
singapore 210
south africa 210
spain 210
sweden 211
switzerland 211
thailand 212
tibet 212
tunisia 212
turkey 212
uganda 212
united arab emirates 212
usa 212
venezuela 213
web cams 213

science & nature

astronomy 217
conservation 217
magazines & websites 218
societies & institutions 218
zoos 219

shopping

antiques & auctions 223
beds & bedding 223
books 223
china & glass 223
clothes 224
computers & electrical 228
cosmetics & perfumes 230
department stores 231
flooring 231
flowers 231
furniture & upholstery 231
gifts & stationery 235
healthcare, beauty & personal hygiene 235
home entertainment 236
home improvements & products 237
jewellers 238
kitchens & appliances 238
lighting 239
luggage 239
magazines & websites 239
markets & malls 239
mother & baby 240
music, games & video 240
photography 241

shoes & accessories 241
specialist.. 241
sports & outdoor 242
tobacco 242
toys.. 242
trade associations 243
wallcovering.. 243
watches 243

sport

american football... 247
athletics 247
badminton 247
baseball 247
basketball 247
bowls 247
boxing.. 248
canoeing... 248
combat 248
cricket.. 248
cycling 249
darts 249
fencing... 249
football... 250
golf.. 251
gymnastics 252
handball 252
hockey 252
horseracing... 252
inline & roller skating 254
international games 254
korfball... 254
magazines & websites.. 254
motor racing 254
netball.. 255
personalities 255
polo.. 256
promotion & education.. 256
rounders 256
rowing.. 256
rugby 257
sailing & watersports 258
show jumping 259
snooker & billiards... 259
softball... 259
sportswear & equipment 259
squash 260
sub-aqua 261
swimming 261
table tennis... 261

target sports 261
tennis 261
volleyball 262
weightlifting & strength 262
winter sports 262
wrestling 262

technology

cable 265
computers 265
internet companies 266
internet service providers 266
magazines & websites 267
search engines 267
telecommunications 268
web censors 269

travel

airlines 273
airports 276
bus companies 277
car hire 278
ferries 278
hotels 280
magazines & websites 280
parking 282
professional bodies & trade associations 282
resorts 282
trains 282
travel agents, tour operators & cruises 283

preface to the 3rd edition

This edition has been considerably revised and expanded and now covers over 10,000 household names on the web while the new, fully searchable CD Rom gives you instant access via your browser to all the sites featured in the book.

the top household names on the internet

clive & bettina zietman

People who surf the web seem to enjoy the mere process of wandering aimlessly through different websites. Although surfing can be a fun hobby, this book has been written for people who know that the information or institution is out there, they want to go straight to it but do not know how. In other words, it is designed to give those who are frustrated and fazed by the Internet a portable, friendly guide through the maze. For anyone who has spent hours on their computer boosting BT's profits but getting nowhere with the simplest search, this non-technical and straightforward directory is the answer.

This directory is different from all others. It is aimed at all UK users who are frustrated with the Web generally, in particular the failing of search engines. It is ideal for beginners, non-surfers, families, researchers and business users. It is a cherry-picked selection of household names on the Web, chosen from an essentially British perspective. Be it Tom Cruise or the Inland Revenue, the BBC or Nesquik, this book contains them all. It is a neat and crystal-clear list of official household names, familiar to everyday UK users.

For those who wish to go directly to the sites for Buckingham Palace, Aintree Racecourse or British Airways this book will be incredibly indispensable. It is not cluttered with the weird or the obscure. It is not dominated by American sites, nor does it contain anything but official sites supported by well-known companies and institutions. The Tate gallery, Battersea Dogs Home and Tesco are in. The Utah Elvis Appreciation Society and Klingon Dictionary are out. The websites listed are self-explanatory and thus the book does not contain commentary or descriptions. Roald Dahl, Oxford University, 10 Downing Street and Barclays Bank need no introduction.

searching the web

People who have just bought a computer may not be familiar with the mystique, language and workings of the Internet. Because the Internet was born and has grown in an unstructured and largely unregulated fashion it can be very difficult to navigate. Most people search the Web by inserting keywords into search engines. The search engines produce lists of websites (often in no particular order) which are triggered by the selected word. Say, for example, you are looking for the Imperial War

Museum's website. By inserting the words 'imperial', 'war' and 'museum' into a search engine, you may, with luck, be led in the right direction. Often however you will be led astray. Why?

There is a skill in using search engines. This is a skill which mere mortals don't necessarily possess. People who spend their lives working with computers assume that everyone in the world thinks like they do. The truth is that they don't.

Even the most powerful and sophisticated search engines only cover about 15% of all websites.

Search engines are not human brains. They therefore do not think like the human brain, in particular they do not think like yours. Although you know what you are looking for, the search engine may well have very different ideas.

It is so easy to set up a website that the Web has already become full to the point of overflowing with websites of dire quality. The search engines find it hard to sift the wheat from the chaff.

Different search engines have different rules about refining searches. To use a particular search engine properly you have to learn the rules.

Even the choice of search engine is overwhelming. There are scores of search engines and some are better at searching particular subjects. At the last count, there were approximately 4,000 in existence. Which search engine to use can be mystifying.

Although the Web is a wonderful source of information and search engines can do the trick, there is an alternative. If you know the precise company or institution you are looking for, it is far easier and quicker to go straight to it by typing in the web address. All computers linked to the Internet have an address box. Type in the address, press enter on your keyboard and you will be taken directly to your chosen destination. YOU DO NOT NEED TO USE A SEARCH ENGINE. This book enables you to circumvent the search engines completely if the website you are looking for is listed here.

Please note that not every famous name has a website. For example, only new films seem to have official websites. Films that pre-date the Internet do not. Similarly, many large institutions have not yet caught up with the Internet age. Some have sites under construction and others may well have changed their website address between the time this book was compiled and the date of publication. When companies are taken over or merge, this also tends to affect the website address. To some extent this book is aiming at a moving target and future editions will incorporate as many additions and changes as possible.

If for any reason you feel that a household name deserves inclusion in the next edition of the book – or if you have any other comments – please email your suggestions to update@householdnames.co.uk

- actors & actresses
- art
- ballet
- clubs
- comedy
- events
- fashion
- film
- funding, organisations & regulation
- literature
- magazines & websites
- magicians
- music
- professional bodies
- promotors & directors
- radio
- stadia & concert halls
- television
- theatre
- tickets

actors & actresses

Adam Sandler
www.adamsandler.com

Alicia Silverstone
www.alicia-silverstone.net

Alyssa Milano
www.alyssa.com

Anna Friel
www.netshopuk.co.uk/annafriel

Anthony Hopkins
www.nasser.net/hopkins

Antonio Banderas
www.antoniobanderasfans.com

Arnold Schwarzenegger
www.schwarzenegger.com

Audrey Hepburn
www.audreyhepburn.com

Ava Gardner
www.avagardner.org

Ben Affleck
www.affleck.com

Bob Hope
www.bobhope.com

Bruce Lee
www.brucelee.org.uk

Burl Ives
www.burlives.com

Cameron Diaz
www.cameron-diaz.com

Carrie Fisher
www.carriefisher.com

Cary Grant
www.carygrant.co.uk

Cheryl Ladd
www.cherylladd.com

Christian Bale
www.christianbale.org

Claire Danes
www.claire-danes.com

Clint Eastwood
www.clinteastwood.net

Courteney Cox
www.courteneycox.net

Craig Charles
www.craigcharles.co.uk

Daniel Day-Lewis
www.danielday.org

David Boreanaz
www.celebrityblvd.com/davidboreanaz

David Schwimmer
www.davidschwimmer.net

Don Johnson
www.donjohnson.com

Doris Day
www.dorisday.com

Errol Flynn
www.errolflynn.net

Ewan McGregor
www.ewanspotting.com

Gail Porter
www.gail-porter-world.co.uk

George Clooney
www.georgeclooney.org

Gillian Anderson
http://gaws.ao.net

Gwyneth Paltrow
www.gwyneth.cjb.net

Harold Lloyd
www.haroldlloyd.com

Harrison Ford
www.harrison-ford.net

Helena Bonham-Carter
www.helena-bonham-carter.com

Ian McKellen
www.mckellen.com

Ingrid Pitt
www.pittofhorror.com

Jack Ryder
www.jackryder.cjb.net

Jim Carrey
www.jimcarreyonline.com

Jimmy Stewart
www.jimmy.org

Joseph Smith
www.joesmith.com

Kate Winslet
www.kate-winslet.org

Keanu Reeves
www.keanunet.com

Kelly Brook
www.kellybrookonline.com

Kevin Spacey
www.spacey.com

Kristen Johnston
www.kristenjohnston.net

Leonard Nimoy
www.nimoy.com

Leonardo di Caprio
www.leonardodicaprio.com

Martin Lawrence
www.martin-lawrence.com

Matt Damon
www.mattdamon.com

Meg Ryan
www.megryan.net

Melanie Griffith (Fan Club)
www.antoniobanderasfans.com/melanie_griffith

Melissa Joan Hart
www.melissa-joan-hart.com

Nicolas Cage
www.cage-cave.avalon.hr

Nicole Kidman (Fan Club)
www.nicolekidman.org

Pamela Anderson Lee
www.pamelaandersonlee.com

Paul Nicholls
www.paul-nicholls.com

Robson Green
www.robsongreen.com

Roy Rogers
www.royrogers.com

Sandra Bullock
www.sandra.com

Sheree J Wilson
www.shereejwilson.com

Stephen Collins
www.stephencollins.com

Thomas Dolby
www.thomas-dolby.com

Timothy Dalton
www.timothydalton.com

Tom Cruise (Fan Club)
www.tomcruise.fans.net

Tony Curtis
www.tonycurtis.com

Tony Hancock (Fan Club)
www.staff.ncl.ac.uk/nigel.collier/index2.html

Tori Spelling
www.tori-spelling.com

Val Kilmer
http://vkn.com

Wes Craven
www.wescraven.com

Will Smith
www.willsmith.net

William Shatner
www.williamshatner.com

Winona Ryder
www.winonaryder.org

art

Artists

Andy Warhol
www.warholstore.com

Clarice Cliff
www.claricecliff.co.uk

Cynthia Lennon
www.cynthialennon.co.uk

Escher
www.worldofescher.com

Gilbert & George
www.gilbertandgeorge.co.uk

Pablo Picasso
www.clubinternet.com/picasso

Associations & Institutes

Arts Council
www.artscouncil.org.uk

Arts Council of Northern Ireland
www.artscouncil-ni.org

Arts Council of Wales
www.ccc-acw.org.uk

Association of Art Historians
www.gold.ac.uk/aah

Association of Illustrators
www.aoi.co.uk

British Arts Festivals Association
www.artsfestivals.co.uk

English Regional Arts Boards
www.arts.org.uk

Institute of Contemporary Arts
www.ica.org.uk

London Arts Board
www.arts.org.uk/directory/regions/london

National Acrylic Painters Association
www.artarena.force9.co.uk/napa

National Art Library
www.nal.vam.ac.uk

National Portraiture Association
www.natportrait.com

North West Arts Board
www.arts.org.uk/directory/regions/north_west

Northern Arts Board
www.arts.org.uk/directory/regions/northern

Northern Ireland Film Commission
www.nifc.co.uk

RSA
www.rsa.org.uk

Scottish Arts Council
www.sac.org.uk

South West Arts Board
www.swa.co.uk

Southern Arts Board
www.arts.org.uk/directory/regions/southern

Galleries & Exhibitions

Aberdeen Art Gallery
www.aagm.co.uk

Andrew Logan Museum of Sculpture
www.andrewlogan.com

Ashmolean Museum
www.ashmol.ox.ac.uk

Birmingham Museum & Art Gallery
www.birmingham.gov.uk/bmag

Blackheath Gallery
www.blackheath-gallery.co.uk

City Art Gallery, Southampton
www.southampton.gov.uk/leisure/arts

Courtauld Institute
www.courtauld.ac.uk

Dean Gallery
www.natgalscot.ac.uk

Dove Cottage (The Wordsworth Museum)
www.dovecott.demon.co.uk

Edinburgh City Art Centre
www.edinburgh.gov.uk/city_art_centre/web/cac

Guernsey Museum & Art Gallery
www.museum.guernsey.net

Hatton Gallery, Newcastle-upon-Tyne
www.ncl.ac.uk/hatton

Hatton Gallery, Tyne & Wear
www.ncl.ac.uk/hatton

Hayward Gallery
www.hayward-gallery.org.uk

Henry Moore Foundation
www.henry-moore-fdn.co.uk/hmf

Holburne Museum of Art
www.bath.ac.uk/holburne

Hunterian Art Gallery
www.gla.ac.uk/museum

Hunterian Art Gallery, Glasgow
www.gla.ac.uk/museum/artgall

Ikon Gallery, Birmingham
www.ikon-gallery.co.uk

Inverleith House, Edinburgh
www.rbge.org.uk/inverleith-house

Khalili Collections
www.khalili.org

Letchworth Museum and Art Gallery
www.fleck.freeserve.co.uk/nhms/let/letmg.html

Maidstone Museum & Art Gallery
www.museum.maidstone.gov.uk

Manchester City Art Galleries
www.u-net.com/set/mcag/cag.html

Marlborough Fine Art
www.marlboroughfineart.com

Museum of Modern Art, Oxford
www.moma.org.uk

National Art Library
www.nal.vam.ac.uk

National Gallery
www.nationalgallery.org.uk

National Gallery of Scotland
www.natgalscot.ac.uk

National Museum of Photography, Film & Television
www.nmpft.org.uk

National Museums & Galleries of Wales
www.nmgw.ac.uk

National Portrait Gallery
www.npg.org.uk

Norwich Gallery
www.nsad.ac.uk/gallery

Photographers' Gallery
www.photonet.org.uk

Redfern Gallery
www.redfern-gallery.co.uk

Royal Academy
www.royalacademy.org.uk

Scottish Gallery, Edinburgh
www.scottish-gallery.co.uk

Serpentine Gallery
www.serpentinegallery.org

Tate Gallery
www.tate.org.uk

Tate Gallery, St Ives
www.tate.org.uk/stives

Tunbridge Wells Museum and Art Gallery
www.tunbridgewells.gov.uk/museum

Turner House Gallery
www.nmgw.ac.uk/th/thghome.html

University Gallery, Leeds
www.leeds.ac.uk/library/spcoll/gallery

Wallace Collection
www.demon.co.uk/heritage/wallace

White Cube Gallery
www.whitecube.com

Whitworth Art Gallery, Manchester
www.whitworth.man.ac.uk

William Morris Gallery
www.lbwf.gov.uk/wmg

York City Art Gallery
www.york.gov.uk/heritage/museums

ballet

American Ballet Theatre
www.abt.org

5

Australian Ballet
www.australianballet.com.au

Birmingham Royal Ballet
www.brb.org.uk

Bolshoi Ballet
www.bolshoi.ru

Continental Ballet
www.continentalballet.com

Copenhagen International Ballet
www.koelpin.com

English National Ballet
www.ballet.org.uk

Frankfurt Ballet
www.frankfurt-ballett.de

Hamburg Ballet
www.hamburgballett.de

Hong Kong Ballet
www.hkballet.com

Kirov Ballet
www.kirovballet.com

London Junior Ballet
www.londonjuniorballet.cwc.net

Moscow Flying Ballet
www.flying-ballet.com

National Ballet of Canada
www.nationalballet.ca

New York City Ballet
www.nycballet.com

Northern Ballet Theatre
www.nbt.co.uk/nbt

Rambert Dance Company
www.rambert.co.uk

Royal Ballet
www.royalballet.org

Royal Ballet School
www.royal-ballet-school.org

Sadler's Wells
www.sadlers-wells.com

Scottish Ballet
www.scottishballet.co.uk

clubs

Cavern
www.cavernclub.co.uk

Jazz Café
www.jazzcafe.co.uk

Ministry of Sound
www.ministryofsound.co.uk

Nightclub Network
www.nightclub.com

Roadhouse
www.roadhouse.co.uk

Ronnie Scott's
www.ronniescotts.co.uk

Scala
www.scala-london.co.uk

Stringfellows
www.stringfellows.co.uk

UK Clubs
www.ukclubs.co.uk

comedy

Abbott & Costello (Fan Club)
www.city-net.com/abbottandcostellofc

Attila the Stockbroker
www.attilathestockbroker.com

BBC Comedy Zone
www.comedyzone.beeb.com

Ben Elton
www.ben-elton.com

Comedy Store
www.thecomedystore.co.uk

Comic Relief
www.comicrelief.org.uk

Dame Edna
www.dame-edna.com

Danny La Rue
www.dannylarue.com

Dilbert
www.unitedmedia.com/comics/dilbert

Eddie Izzard
www.izzard.com

Fascinating Aida
www.fascinating-aida.co.uk

French and Saunders
www.frenchandsaunders.com

George Formby
www.georgeformby.co.uk

Graham Norton
www.grahamnorton.co.uk

Jongleurs
www.jongleurs.com

Laurel & Hardy
www.laurel-and-hardy.com

Lee & Herring
www.leeandherring.com

Monty Python Online
www.pythonline.com

Morecambe & Wise
www.morecambeandwise.co.uk

Penn & Teller
www.sincity.com

Reeves & Mortimer
www.come.to/vicandbob

Rowan Atkinson
www.hsn.dk/rowan

events

Aldeburgh Productions
www.aldeburgh.co.uk

Arts Worldwide
www.artsworldwide.org.uk

BAFTA Awards
www.bafta.org

Berlin International Film Festival
www.berlinale.de

Birmingham International Film and
Television Festival
www.film-tv-festival.org.uk

Blues & Roots Music Festival
www.bluesfest.com.au

Booker Prize
www.bookerprize.co.uk

Brighton Festival
www.brighton-festival.org.uk

Brit Awards
www.brits.co.uk

British Arts Festivals Association
www.artsfestivals.co.uk

British Federation of Festivals for Music,
Dance and Speech
www.festivals.demon.co.uk

Buxton Festival
www.buxtonfestival.freeserve.co.uk

Cambridge Folk Festival
www.cam-folkfest.co.uk

Cannes Film Festival
www.festival-cannes.fr

City of London Festival
www.city-of-london-festival.org.uk

Covent Garden Festival
www.cgf.co.uk

Crufts Dog Show
www.crufts.org.uk

Dance Umbrella
www.danceumbrella.co.uk

Edinburgh Festival
www.edinburghfestivals.co.uk

Edinburgh Fringe Festival
www.edfringe.com

European Festivals Association
www.euro-festival.net

Fleadh Festival
www.fleadhfestival.com

Glasgow International Jazz Festival
www.jazzfest.co.uk

Glastonbury Festival
www.glastonbury-festival.co.uk

Glyndebourne
www.glyndebourne.com

Greenwich & Docklands Festival
www.festival.org

Grosvenor House Art & Antiques Fair
www.grosvenor-antiquesfair.co.uk

Henley Festival
www.henley-festival.co.uk

Ideal Home Show
www.idealhomeshow.co.uk

International Festival of Chocolate
www.chocfest.com

International Film Festival of Wales
www.iffw.co.uk

International Musical Eisteddfod
www.international-eisteddfod.co.uk

International Workshop Festival
www.i-w-f.demon.co.uk

Just For Laughs - International Comedy
Festival (Montreal)
www.hahaha.com

Laurence Olivier Awards
www.officiallondontheatre.co.uk/olivier

Leeds International Film Festival
www.sensei.co.uk/liff

Lichfield Festival
www.lichfieldfestival.org

London Art Week
http://londonart.co.uk

London Fashion Week
www.londonfashionweek.co.uk

London Festival of Literature
www.theword.org.uk

London Film Festival
www.lff.org.uk

London International Festival of Theatre
www.lift-info.co.uk

London International Mime Festival
www.mimefest.co.uk

London Open House
www.londonopenhouse.demon.co.uk

London Parade
www.londonparade.co.uk

London String of Pearls Golden Jubilee
Festival
www.stringofpearls.org.uk

Lord Mayor's Show
www.lord-mayors-show.org.uk

Los Angeles Film Festival
www.laiff.com

Millennium Experience
www.dome2000.co.uk

Montreux Jazz Festival
www.montreuxjazz.com

Moscow State Circus
www.moscowstatecircus.co.uk

Motor Show
www.motorshow.co.uk

Music Festivals UK
www.aloud.com/festival.shtml

Music Festivals Worldwide
www.festivals.com

Notting Hill Carnival
www.nottinghillcarnival.net.uk

Oscars
www.oscar.com

Promenade Concerts
www.bbc.co.uk/proms

Raindance Film Showcase
www.raindance.co.uk

Reading Festival
www.readingfestival.co.uk

Royal Highland Games
www.braemargathering.org

Sundance Film Festival
www.sundance.org

Thames Festival
www.thamesfestival.org

Tony Awards
www.tonys.org

Toronto International Film Festival
www.bell.ca/toronto/filmfest

Welsh International Film Festival
www.iffw.co.uk

Whitbread Book Awards
www.whitbreadbookawards.co.uk

Womad
www.womad.org

fashion

Agnes B
www.agnesb.fr

Alberta Ferretti
www.albertaferretti.it

Alexander McQueen
www.alexandermcqueen.net

Armani
www.armaniexchange.com

Caprice
www.caprice-supermodel.com

Cartier
www.cartier.com

Cerruti
www.cerruti.net

Chanel
www.chanel.fr

Charles Jourdan
www.charles-jourdan.com

Chloe
www.chloesdesigns.com

Christian Lacroix
www.christian-lacroix.fr

Cindy Crawford
www.cindy.com

Cindy Margolis
www.cindymargolis.com

Claude Montana
www.claudemontana.net

Claudia Schiffer
www.claudiaschiffer.com

Dolce & Gabbana
www.dolcegabbanaonline.com

Energie
www.energie.it

Escada
www.escada.com

Esprit
www.esprit.com

Fashion Café
www.fashion-cafe.com

Fashion UK
www.fuk.co.uk

Ferragamo
www.salvatoreferragamo.com

Fiorelli
www.fiorelli.com

Fiorucci
www.fioruccisafetyjeans.com

Fruit Of The Loom
www.fruit.com

Ghost
www.ghost.co.uk

Gianfranco Ferre
www.gianfrancoferre.com

Givenchy
www.givenchy.fr

Gucci
www.gucci.com

Guess
www.guess.com

Helmut Lang
www.helmutlang.com

Hugo Boss
www.hugo.com

Iman
www.i-iman.com

Jean-Paul Gaultier
www.jpgaultier.fr

John Galliano
www.area.co.uk/galliano_b.html

Joop
www.joop.com

Jordache
www.jordache.com

Kate Moss
www.facescafe.com/kate

Kookai
www.kookai.fr

Krizia
http://modaitalia.net/krizia/index.htm

La Perla
www.laperla.com

Lacoste
www.lacoste.fr

Lancome
www.lancome.com

Louis Vuitton
www.vuitton.com

Maharishi
www.emaharishi.com

Mr Python
www.mrpython.com

Paul Smith
www.paulsmith.co.uk

Prada
www.prada.com

Rodier
www.rodier.tm.fr

Samantha Fox
www.samfox.com/foxy

Sisley
www.sisley.com

Sonia Rykiel
www.sonia-rykiel.com

Ted Baker
www.tedbaker.co.uk

Tommy Hilfiger
www.tommy.com

Trussardi
www.trussardi.it

Yves Saint Laurent
www.yslonline.com

Zandra Rhodes
www.zandrarhodes.com

film

Cinemas

ABC
www.abc.cinemas.co.uk

Apollo
www.apollocinemas.co.uk

Caledonian
www.caledoniancinemas.co.uk

Cinemark
www.cinemark.com

Cineworld
www.cineworld.co.uk

Circle
www.circlecinemas.co.uk

Empire
www.empireonline.co.uk

Imax
www.imax.com

Odeon
www.odeon.co.uk

Pathe
www.pathe.co.uk

Picture House
www.picturehouse-cinemas.co.uk

Queen's Film Theatre, Belfast
www.qub.ac.uk/qft

Reeltime
www.reeltime-cinemas.co.uk

Robins
www.robinscinemas.co.uk

Roxy
www.roxycinema.co.uk

Scott
www.scottcinemas.co.uk

Screen
www.screencinemas.co.uk

Showcase
www.showcasecinemas.co.uk

UCI
www.uci-cinemas.co.uk

Virgin
www.virgin.net/cinema

Warner
www.warnervillage.co.uk

West Coast
www.westcoastcinemas.co.uk

Films

Alien Resurrection
www.alien-resurrection.co.uk

American Beauty
www.americanbeauty-thefilm.com

American Psycho
www.americanpsycho.com

Angela's Ashes
www.angelasashes.com

As Good As It Gets
www.spe.sony.com/movies/asgoodasitgets

Austin Powers
www.austinpowers.com

The Avengers
www.the-avengers.com

Back to the Future
www.bttf.com

Batman & Robin
www.batman-robin.com

The Beach
www.virgin.net/thebeach

Bicentennial Man
http://studio.go.com/movies/bicentennialman

Billy Elliot
www.billyelliot.net

Blair Witch Project
www.blairwitch.co.uk

The Bone Collector
www.thebonecollector.com

Boogie Nights
www.boogie-nights.com

Carry On
www.carryonline.com

Celebrity
www.miramax.com/celebrity

Chicken Run
www.chickenrun.co.uk

Dancer in the Dark
http://dancerinthedark.co.uk

East is East
www.eastiseast.co.uk

Elizabeth
www.elizabeth-themovie.com

End of Days
www.end-of-days.com

End of the Affair
www.spe.sony.com/movies/endoftheaffair

Entrapment
www.foxmovies.com/entrapment

Eyes Wide Shut
www.eyeswideshut.com

Godzilla
www.godzilla.com

Gone in 60 Seconds
www.gonein60seconds.com

The Governess
www.spe.sony.com/classics/governess

Grease
www.greasemovie.com

Hannibal
www.mgm.com/hannibal

Hideous Kinky
www.kwfc.com/filmography/hideouskinky.shtml

High Fidelity
www.studio.go.com/movies/highfidelity

Hilary & Jackie
www.octoberfilms.com/hilary-jackie

Honest
www.honestthemovie.com

Independence Day
www.id4.com

Jackie Brown
www.jackiebrown.co.uk

James Bond
www.jamesbond.com

Jerry Maguire
www.jerrymaguire.com

Julien Donkey-boy
www.juliendonkeyboy.com

The King & I
www.thekingandi.com

Lock, Stock & Two Smoking Barrels
www.lockstock2barrels.com

Lost in Space
www.dangerwillrobinson.com

Men In Black
www.meninblack.com

Midsummer Night's Dream
www.fox.co.uk/midsummer

Mission Impossible
www.missionimpossible.com

The Mummy
www.themummy.com

My Dog Skip
http://mydogskip.warnerbros.com

Nightmare on Elm Street
www.elmstreet.co.uk

Notting Hill
www.notting-hill.com

Oscar Wilde
www.oscarwilde.com

The Out-of-Towners
www.outoftowners.com

The Patriot
www.thepatriot.com

The Perfect Storm
www.perfectstorm.net

The Phantom Menace
www.starwars.com/episode-i

Pokemon
www.pokemonthemovie.com

The Postman
www.thepostman.com

Prince of Egypt
www.prince-of-egypt.com

Psycho
www.universalstudios.com/home/psycho

The Road to Eldorado
www.roadtoeldorado.com

Rocky Horror Picture Show
www.rockyhorror.com

Rugrats Movie
www.rugratsmovie.com

Rules of Engagement
www.rulesmovie.com

Runaway Bride
www.runawaybride.com

The Saint
www.thesaint.com

Saving Private Ryan
www.rzn.com/pvt.ryan

Scream 3
www.scream3.com

Shakespeare in Love
www.miramax.com/shakespeareinlove

Sleepy Hollow
www.sleepyhollowthemovie.co.uk

Snatch
www.snatch-the-movie.com

South Park The Movie
www.southparkmovie.com

Star Wars
www.starwars.com

Stuart Little
www.stuartlittle.com

The Talented Mr. Ripley
www.talentedmrripley.com

Tarzan (Disney's)
www.tarzan.co.uk

There's Something About Mary
www.aboutmary.com

Thin Red Line
www.thethinredline.co.uk

The Thomas Crown Affair
www.mgm.com/thethomascrownaffair

Time Code
www.timecode2000.com

Titanic
www.titanicmovie.com

Tomorrow Never Dies
www.tomorrowneverdies.com

Toy Story 2
http://disney.go.com/worldsofdisney/toystory2

Trainspotting
www.miramax.com/trainspotting

Tumbleweeds
www.tumbleweeds-movie.com

Turbo: A Power Rangers Movie
www.powerrangersturbo.com

Viva Rock Vegas
www.vivarockvegas.com

Waterworld: Quest for the Mariner
www.mca.com/unicity/waterworld

Wild Wild West
www.wildwildwest.net

Wizard of Oz
www.thewizardofoz.com

The World is Not Enough
www.jamesbond.com/bond19

You've Got Mail
www.youvegotmail.com

Organisations

Academy of Motion Picture Arts & Sciences
www.oscars.org

American Film Institute
www.afionline.org

Association of Motion Picture Sound
www.amps.net

BAFTA
www.bafta.org

British Board of Film Classification
www.bbfc.co.uk

British Film Commission
www.britfilmcom.co.uk

British Film Institute
www.bfi.org.uk

British Films Catalogue
www.britfilms.com

British Screen Finance
www.britishscreen.co.uk

British Universities Film and Video Council
www.bufvc.ac.uk

British Video Association
www.bva.org.uk

Cinema Organ Society
www.cinema-organs.org.uk

Cinema Theatre Association
www.cinema-theatre.org.uk

Directors' Guild of Great Britain
www.dggb.co.uk

London Film and Video Development Agency
www.lfvda.demon.co.uk

Moving Image Society
www.bksts.com

New Producer's Alliance
www.npa.org.uk

Producers Alliance for Cinema and Television
www.pact.co.uk

Production Companies & Studios

Bollywood
www.bollywood.org.uk

Buena Vista International
www.bvimovies.com

Castle Rock
www.castle-rock.com

Columbia Tristar
www.spe.sony.com/movies

Dimension Films
www.dimensionfilms.com

Disney
www.disney.com/disneypictures

Ealing - NTFS
www.ealingstudios.co.uk

Elstree
www.elstreefilmstudios.co.uk

FilmFour
www.filmfour.com

Fine Line Features
www.flf.com

HDS
www.hds-studios.com

Hollywood
www.hollywood.com

Leavesden
www.leavesdenstudios.com

Lucas Film
www.lucasfilm.com

MCA Universal
www.mca.com

MGM
www.mgm.com

Miramax
www.miramax.com

New Line
www.newline.com

October Films
www.octoberfilms.com

Orion
www.orionpictures.com

Paramount
www.paramount.com/motionpicture

Pathé
www.pathé.co.uk

Picture Palace Productions
www.picturepalace.com

Polygram Video
www.polygramvideo.co.uk

Sony Pictures Entertainment
www.spe.sony.com

Steven Spielberg Dreamworks
www.spielberg-dreamworks.com

Teddington
www.teddington.co.uk

Three Mills Island
www.threemills.com

20th Century Fox UK
www.fox.co.uk

United International Pictures
www.uip.com

Universal
www.universalstudios.com

Universal Pictures
www.universalpictures.com

Walt Disney
www.disney.go.com/studiooperations

Warner Bros
www.movies.warnerbros.com

West Freugh
www.backlot.co.uk/westfreugh

funding, organisations & regulation

American Film Foundation
www.americanfilmfoundation.com

Arts Council for England
www.artscouncil.org.uk

Arts Council for Wales
www.ccc-acw.org.uk

Association of Professional Theatre for Children and Young People
www.apt.org.uk

British Academy of Dramatic Combat
www.badc.co.uk

British Copyright Council
www.britishcopyright.org.uk

Broadcasting Standards Commission
www.bsc.org.uk

Community Development Foundation
www.cdf.org.uk

Community Media Association
www.commedia.org.uk

Copyright Licensing Agency
www.cla.co.uk

Crafts Council
www.craftscouncil.org.uk

Department for Culture, Media & Sport
www.culture.gov.uk

Digital Arts Development Agency
www.da2.org.uk

Film & Video Umbrella
www.beyond2000.co.uk/umbrella

Foundation for Art & Creative Technology
www.fact.co.uk

Freeform Arts Trust
www.freeform.org.uk

Heritage Lottery Fund
www.hlf.org.uk

Independent Television Commission
www.itc.co.uk

Independent Theatre Council
www.itc-arts.org

International Arts Bureau
www.international-arts.org

International Thespian Society
www.etassoc.org

Media Trust
www.mediatrust.org

Millennium Commission
www.millennium.gov.uk

Museums and Galleries Commission
www.museums.gov.uk

National Campaign for the Arts
www.ecna.org/nca

National Council for Voluntary Organisations
www.vois.org.uk/ncvo

National Endowment for Science,
Technology and the Arts (NESTA)
www.nesta.org.uk

National Foundation for Youth Music
www.youthmusic.org.uk

National Lottery Charities Board
www.nlcb.org.uk

New Opportunities Fund
www.nof.org.uk

Scottish Arts Council
www.sac.org.uk

literature

Ambit Magazine
www.ambit.co.uk

Anne Frank
www.annefrank.com

Arthur C Clarke
www.acclarke.co.uk

Arvon Foundation
www.arvonfoundation.org

Book Trust
www.booktrust.org.uk

Danielle Steel
www.daniellesteel.com

Douglas Adams
www.douglasadams.com

Fay Weldon
www.tile.net/weldon

Helen Keller
www.hki.org/helen.html

Ian Fleming
www.ianfleming.org

John Grisham
www.jgrisham.com

John Steinbeck
www.steinbeck.org

Ken Follett
www.ken-follett.com

Lewis Carroll
www.lewiscarroll.org/carroll

London Review of Books
www.lrb.co.uk

Margaret Drabble
www.tile.net/drabble

PG Wodehouse (Fan Club)
www.serv.net/~camel/wodehouse

Poetry Book Society
www.poetrybooks.co.uk

Poetry Review
www.poetrysoc.com

Rudyard Kipling
www.kipling.org.uk

Shakespeare Birthplace Trust
www.shakespeare.org.uk

Stephen King
www.stephenking.com

magazines & websites

Amateur Stage
www.uktw.co.uk/amstage

Art Guide
www.artguide.org.uk

Art Libraries of UK & Ireland
http://arlis.nal.vam.ac.uk

Art Review
www.art-review.co.uk

Arts Business
www.arts-business.co.uk

BBC Music
www.bbcworldwide.com/musicmagazine

BBC Music Magazine
www.bbcmusicmagazine.beeb.com

Cable Guide
www.cableguide.co.uk

Casting Weekly
www.ndirect.co.uk/~castingw

Circa
www.recirca.com

Dotmusic
www.dotmusic.com

G-Wizz
www.g-wizz.net

Galleries Magazine
www.artefact.co.uk

Gramophone Magazine
www.gramophone.co.uk

Hitchhikers Guide to the Galaxy
www.h2g2.com

International Directory of Art Libraries
http://iberia.vassar.edu/ifla-idal

International Movie Database
www.imdb.com

Live Art Magazine
http://art.ntu.ac.uk/livemag

Media Week
www.mediaweek.co.uk

MP3
www.mp3.com

New Musical Express
www.nme.com

Official London Theatre
www.officiallondontheatre.co.uk

Opening Line
www.openingline.co.uk

Popcorn
www.popcorn.co.uk

Q
www.qonline.co.uk

Radio Times
www.radiotimes.co.uk

Rolling Stone
www.rollingstone.com

Route On-line
www.route-online.com

Satellite World
www.satelliteworld.demon.co.uk

SceneOne
www.sceneone.co.uk

Screen International
www.screendaily.com

Spotlight Casting Directory
www.spotlightcd.com

The Stage
www.thestage.co.uk

Teletext
www.teletext.co.uk

Theatre
www.uktw.co.uk/theatremag

Time
www.time.com

Time Out
www.timeout.com

TV Times
www.tvtimes.co.uk

Ultimate Band List
www.ubl.com

Variety
www.variety.com

Warner ESP (Music Catalogue)
www.warneresp.co.uk

World Wide Arts Resources
www.world-arts-resources.com

magicians

David Copperfield
www.dcopperfield.com

Paul Daniels
www.pauldaniels.co.uk

Penn & Teller
www.sincity.com

music

Artists

A-ha
www.a-ha.net

A1
www.a1-online.com

Abba
www.abbasite.com

AC/DC
www.elektra.com/retro/acdc

Adam Ant
www.adam-ant.net

Aerosmith
www.aerosmith.com

Alanis Morisette
www.alanismorisette.com

Alice Cooper
www.alicecoopershow.com

All Saints
www.theallsaints.com

America
www.venturahighway.com

Animals
www.animals.mcmail.com

Anne Murray
www.annemurray.com

Another Level
www.anotherlevel.co.uk

Aqua
www.aqua.dk

Atomic Kitten
www.atomickitten.co.uk

Atomic Rooster
www.atomicrooster.com

Aztec Camera
www.killermontstreet.com

B*Witched
www.b-witched.com

B-52's
www.repriserec.com/theb52s

B52's
www.theb52s.com

Backstreet Boys
www.backstreetboys.com

Bananarama
www.bananaramaweb.com

Barbra Streisand
www.barbra-streisand.com

Barclay James Harvest
www.bjharvest.co.uk

Barry Manilow
www.manilow.com

BB King
www.bbking.com

Be-Bop Deluxe
http://billnelson.com/bebopdeluxe/main.htm

Beach Boys
www.beach-boys.com

Beastie Boys
www.beastieboys.com

Beatles
www.beatles.com

Beautiful South
www.beautifulsouth.co.uk

Beck
www.beck.com

Bee Gees
www.beegees.net

Bellamy Brothers
www.bellamybros.com

Belle & Sebastian
www.jeepster.co.uk/belleandsebastian

Big Brother and the Holding Company
www.bbhc.com/bigbrother.htm

Big Country
www.bigcountry.co.uk

Billie Piper
www.billie.co.uk

Billy Idol
www.billyidol.com

Billy Joel
www.billyjoel.com

Bjork
www.bjork.co.uk/bjork

Bjorn Again
www.demon.co.uk/bjornagain

Black Sabbath
www.black-sabbath.com

Blondie
www.blondie.net

Blur
www.blur.co.uk

Bob Dylan
www.bobdylan.com

Bob Marley
www.bobmarley.com

Bob Seger
www.segerbob.com

Bon Jovi
www.bonjovi.com

Boy George
www.boy.george.net

Boyzone
www.boyzone.co.uk

Britney Spears
www.britneyspears.co.uk

Bruce Springsteen
www.brucespringsteen.net

Buzzcocks
www.buzzcocks.com

Cardigans
www.cardigans.net

Cat Stevens
www.catstevens.co.uk

Catatonia
www.catatonia.com

Celine Dion
www.celineonline.com

Charlie Parker
www.charlieparker.com

Chemical Brothers
www.algonet.se/~inftryck/chemical

Cher
www.cher.com

Chicago
www.chirecords.com

Chopin
www.chopin.org

Chris De Burgh
www.cdeb.com

Chris Isaak
www.repriserec.com/chrisisaak

Christina Aguilera
www.christina-aguilera.com

Clash
www.westwaytotheworld.com

Cleopatra
www.cleopatramusic.com

Cliff Richard
www.cliffrichard.org

Cocteau Twins
www.cocteautwins.com

Coldplay
www.coldplay.com

Corrs
www.corrs.com

Crosby, Stills, Nash & Young
www.csny.net

Craig David
www.craigdavid.co.uk

Cranberries
www.the-cranberries.net

Crash Test Dummies
www.crashtestdummies.com

Culture Club
www.cultureclub.net

Cure
www.thecure.com

Dannii Minogue
www.dannii.com

David Bowie
www.davidbowie.com

David Cassidy
www.davidcassidy.com

David Essex
www.davidessex.4orce.com/themain.htm

David Knopfler
www.knopfler.com

Dean Friedman
www.deanfriedman.com

Deep Purple
www.deep-purple.com

Del Amitri
www.delamitri.com

Depeche Mode
www.depechemode.com

Des'ree
www.desree.co.uk

Destiny's Child
www.destinyschild.com

Diana Ross
www.dianaross.com

Divine Comedy
www.thedivinecomedy.com

Dixie Chicks
www.dixiechicks.com

Dolly Parton
www.dolly.net

Donny & Marie Osmond
www.donnyandmarie.com

Doobie Brothers
www.doobiebros.com

Doors
www.thedoors.com

Duran Duran
www.duranduran.com

Dwight Yoakam
www.wbr.com/nashville/dwightyoakam

E-17
www.msite.sk/e-17

Elton John
www.eltonjohn.com

Elvis Costello
www.elvis-costello.com

Elvis Presley
www.elvis-presley.com

Emerson Lake & Palmer
www.emersonlakepalmer.com

Eminem
www.eminem.com

Emma Bunton
www.emma-lee-bunton.com

Enigma
http://enigma.kaizo.org

Enya
www.repriserec.com/enya

Eric Clapton
www.repriserec.com/ericclapton

Everything But The Girl
www.ebtg.com

Fairport Convention
www.fairportconvention.co.uk

Faith Hill
www.faithhill.com

Fatboy Slim
www.normancook.cjb.net

Five
www.5ive.co.uk

Forever Brandy
www.foreverbrandy.com

Frank Sinatra
www.sinatra.com

Fugees
www.fugees.net

Gabrielle
www.gabrielle.co.uk

Garbage
www.garbage.com

Gary Barlow
www.garybarlow.mcmail.com

Genesis
www.genesis-web.com

George Benson
www.georgebenson.com

George Harrison
www.allthingsmustpass.com

George Michael
www.aegean.net

Geri Halliwell
www.gerihalliwell.co.uk

Gerry Marsden & the Pacemakers
www.gerrymarsden.com

Glen Campbell
www.glencampbellshow.com

Glen Miller Orchestra
www.glennmillerorchestra.com

Glitter Band
www.glitterband.fsnet.co.uk

Gloria Estefan
www.gloriafan.com

Golden Earring
www.golden-earring.nl

Grateful Dead
www.dead.net

Greg Lake
www.greglake.com

Guns N' Roses
www.geffen.com/gunsnroses

Hall & Oates
www.hallandoates.org.uk

Hanson
www.hansonline.com

Harry Connick Jr
www.hconnickjr.com

Hawkwind
www.hawkwind.com

Heaven 17
www.heaven17.com

Henry Purcell
www.bl.uk/exhibitions/purcell

Hollies
www.hollies.co.uk

Honeyz
www.honeyz.co.uk

Hootie & the Blowfish
www.hootie.com

Howard Jones
www.howardjones.com

Ian Dury
www.iandury.co.uk

Iron Maiden
www.ironmaiden.co.uk

Isaac Hayes
www.isaachayes.com

Isley Brothers
http://sonymusic.com/artists/theisleybrothers

Jamiroquai
www.jamiroquai.co.uk

Janet Jackson
www.friendsofjanet.com

Jean Michel Jarre
www.jeanmicheljarre.com

Jeff Beck
www.epicrecords.com/jeffbeck

Jennifer Lopez
www.jenniferlopez.com

Jethro Tull
www.j-tull.com

Jewel
www.jeweljk.com

Jimi Hendrix
www.jimi-hendrix.com

JJ72
www.jj72.com

Jo Dee Messina
www.jodeemessina.com

Joan Armatrading
www.joanarmatrading.com

Joan Baez
www.baez.woz.org

Joe Brown
www.joebrown.co.uk

Joe Diffle
www.joediffie.com

Joe Jackson
www.joejackson.com

Johnny Cash
www.johnnycash.com

Jon Bon Jovi
www.jonbonjovi.com

Joni Mitchell
www.jonimitchell.com

Joy Division
www.wbr.com/joydivision

Judy Tzuke
www.tzuke.com

Julian Cope
www.juliancope.com

Julian Lennon
www.julianlennon.com

Julie Felix
www.herebedragons.co.uk

Julio Inglesias
www.julioiglesias.net

Kajagoogoo
www.kajagoogoo.com

Kavana
www.c3.vmg.co.uk/kavana

KC & the Sunshine Band
www.heykcsb.com

kd lang
www.kdlang.com

Kenny Rogers
www.kennyrogers.net

Kinks
http://kinks.it.rit.edu/okfc

Kiss
www.kissonline.com

Korn
www.korn.com

Kula Shaker
www.kulashaker.co.uk

Kylie Minogue
www.kylie.com

LeAnn Rimes
www.rimestimes.com

Led Zeppelin
www.led-zeppelin.com

Lenny Kravitz
www.virginrecords.com/kravitz

Leonard Bernstein
www.leonardbernstein.com

Leonard Cohen
www.leonardcohen.com

Level 42
www.level42.com

Levellers
www.levellers.co.uk

Lighthouse Family
www.lighthousefamily.wildcardrecords.co.uk

Lightning Seeds
www.lightningseeds.com

Limahl
www.limahl.co.uk

Limp Bizkit
www.limpbizkit.com

Lou Reed
www.loureed.org

Luther Vandross
www.epicrecords.com/luthervandross

Lynyrd Skynyrd
www.superstars.com/skynyrd

Macy Gray
www.macygray.com

Madness
www.madness.co.uk

Madonna
www.wbr.com/madonna

Mandy Moore
www.mandymoore.com

Manic Street Preachers
www.manics.co.uk

Mansun
www.mansun.co.uk

Marc Almond
www.marcalmond.co.uk

Mariah Carey
www.mcarey.com

Marillion
www.marillion.com

Marilyn Manson
www.marilynmanson.net

Mark Knofler
www.mark-knopfler-news.co.uk

Mark Knopfler
www.neck-and-neck.com

Martine McCutcheon
www.martinemccutcheon.com

Mary Chapin Carpenter
www.sonymusic.com/labels/nashville/mcc

Mary J Blige
www.mjblige.com

Massive Attack
www.massiveattack.co.uk

Mavericks
www.themavericks.com

Meat Loaf
www.meatloaf-oifc.com

Melanie C
www.northern-star.co.uk

Metallica
www.metclub.com

Michael Bolton
www.michaelbolton.com

Michael Jackson
www.mjnet.com

Michael Nyman
www.december.org/nyman

Mike Oldfield
www.mikeoldfield.org

Miles Davis
www.miles-davis.com

Moody Blues
www.moodyblues.co.uk

Morrissey
www.morrissey.co.uk

Natalie Imbruglia
www.natalie-imbruglia.co.uk

Neil Diamond
www.sonymusic.com/artists/neildiamond

Neneh Cherry
www.nenehweb.com

911
http://c3.vmg.co.uk/911

Nitty Gritty Dirt Band
www.nittygritty.com

Norman Greenbaum
www.spiritinthesky.com

Oasis
www.oasisinet.com

Ocean Colour Scene
www.oceancolourscene.com

Olivia Newton John
www.onlyolivia.com/onj.html

Osmonds
www.osmond.com

Ozzy Osbourne
www.ozzy.com

Patsy Cline
www.patsy.nu

Paul Young
www.paul-young.com

Paula Abdul
www.undermyspell.com

Pet Shop Boys
www.petshopboys.co.uk

Peter Andre
www.amws.com.au/a/andre-peter

Peter Gabriel
www.geffen.com/gabriel

Peter Tork
www.petertork.com

PJ Harvey
www.pjh.org

Placebo
www.placebo.co.uk

Placido Domingo
www.placido-domingo.com

Pogues
www.pogues.com

Portishead
www.portishead.co.uk

Prince
www.love4oneanother.com

Prodigy
www.theprodigy.co.uk

Public Enemy
www.public-enemy.com

Puff Daddy
www.puffdaddy.com

Pulp
www.rise.co.uk/pulp

Queen
www.queen-fip.com

Quincy Jones
www.wbr.com/quincyjones

Radiohead
www.radiohead.co.uk

Ralph Vaughan Williams
www.cs.qub.ac.uk/~j.collis/rvw.html

Ramones
www.officialramones.com

Ray Charles
www.raycharles.com

REM
www.wbr.com/rem

Ricky Martin
www.rickymartin.com

Ringo Starr
www.ringotour.com

Robbie Williams
www.robbiewilliams.co.uk

Rod Stewart
www.wbr.com/rodstewart

Roger Daltrey
www.rogerdaltrey.net

Roger Waters
www.roger-waters.com

Roger Whittaker
www.rogerwhittaker.com

Rolf Harris
www.rolfharris.com

Rolling Stones
www.the-rolling-stones.com

Ronan Keating
www.ronankeating.net

Roy Orbison
www.orbison.com

Roy Wood
www.roywood.com

S Club 7
www.sclub7.co.uk

Sarah McLachlan
www.sarahmclachlan.com

Seal
www.wbr.com/seal

Searchers
www.the-searchers.co.uk

Shania Twain
www.shania-twain.com

Sheena Easton
www.sheenaeaston.com

Sheryl Crow
www.sherylcrow.com

Shola Ama
www.shola-ama.com

Simon & Garfunkel
www.sonymusic.com/artists/simonandgarfunkel

Sinead O'Connor
www.sinead-oconnor.com

Sixpence None the Richer
www.sixpence-ntr.com

Smashing Pumpkins
www.smashing-pumpkins.net

Smokey Robinson & the Miracles (Fan Club)
www.edgenet.net/smokey_miracles

Sparks
www.sparksofficialwebsite.com

Spice Girls
www.virginrecords.com/spicegirls/index2.html

Spinal Tap
www.spinaltap.com

Squeeze
www.squeezefan.com

Status Quo
www.statusquo.co.uk

Stephen Sondheim
www.sondheim.com

Steps
www.stepsofficial.com

Stereophonics
www.stereophonics.co.uk

Stevens Shakin
www.shaky.net

Stevie Nicks
www.nicksfix.com

Sting
www.sting.com

Suede
www.suede.co.uk

Supergrass
www.supergrass.com

Supertramp
www.supertramp.com

Suzanne Vega
www.vega.net

Tammy Wynette
www.tammywynette.com

Tears for Fears
www.music.sony.com/music/artistinfo/tearsfo
fears

Texas
www.texas.uk.com

Tina Turner
www.tina-turner.com

Tom Jones
www.tomjones.com

Tom Petty
www.tompetty.com

Toni Braxton
www.tonibraxton.net

Tony Bennett
www.tonybennett.net

Tori Amos
www.tori.com

Travis
www.travisonline.com

Tricky
www.trickyonline.com

Trisha Yearwood
www.mca-nashville.com/trishayearwood

Turtles
www.theturtles.com

U2
www.island.co.uk/u2

UB 40
www.ub40-dep.com

Ultravox
www.ultravox.org.uk

Van Halen
www.van-halen.com

Vanessa Mae
www.vanessa-mae.org

Vengaboys
www.vengaboys.com

Verve
www.the-raft.com/theverve

Village People
www.villagepeople-official.com

Westlife
www.westlife.co.uk

Wet Wet Wet
www.wetwetwet.co.uk

Whitney Houston
www.whitney-houston.co.uk

Will Smith
www.willsmith.net

Willie Nelson
www.a2bmusic.com/willienelson/index.html

Wishbone Ash
www.wishboneash.com

Wyclef
www.wyclef.com

Opera

English National Opera
www.eno.org

Grand Opera House Belfast
www.goh.co.uk

La Scala
http://lascala.milano.it

London Opera Players
www.operaplayers.co.uk

Royal Opera House
www.royaloperahouse.org

Welsh National Opera
www.wno.org.uk

Orchestras

Adelaide Symphony Orchestra
www.aso.com.au

Ambache
www.ambache.co.uk

Association of British Orchestras
www.abo.org.uk

BBC Philharmonic Orchestra
www.bbc.co.uk/orchestras/philharmonic

BBC Symphony
www.bbc.co.uk/orchestras/so

Berlin Philharmonic
www.berlin-philharmonic.com

Birmingham Contemporary Music Group
www.bcmg.org.uk

Boston Symphony
www.bso.org

Chicago Symphony
www.chicagosymphony.org

City of Birmingham Symphony Orchestra
www.cbso.co.uk

Israel Philharmonic
www.ipo.co.il

Liverpool Philharmonic
www.rlps.merseyworld.com

London Metropolitan
www.lmo.co.uk

London Philharmonic
www.lpo.co.uk

London Symphony
www.lso.co.uk

Los Angeles Philharmonic
www.laphil.org

National Association of Youth Orchestras
www.nayo.org.uk

New York Philharmonic
www.nyphilharmon.org

New Zealand Symphony Orchestra
www.nzso.co.nz

Northern Sinfonia
www.ndirect.co.uk/~nsinfonia

Philharmonia
www.philharmonia.co.uk

Royal Liverpool Philharmonic Orchestra
http://rlps.merseyworld.com

Royal Philharmonic
www.rpo.co.uk

Royal Scottish National
www.scot-art.org/rsno

Seattle Symphony
www.seattlesymphony.org

Toronto Symphony
www.orchestra.on.ca

Vienna Philharmonic
www.vienna.at/philharmoniker/vph

Vienna Symphony
www.weiner-symphoniker.at

Organisations

British Music Information Centre
www.bmic.co.uk

British Phonographic Industry
www.bpi.co.uk

Music Industries Association
www.mia.org.uk

National Foundation for Youth Music
www.youthmusic.org.uk

Performing Rights Society
www.prs.co.uk

Sonic Arts Network
www.sonicartsnetwork.org

Record Companies

A&M
www.amrecords.com

Arista
www.aristarec.com

Atlantic
www.atlantic-records.com

Beggars Banquet
www.beggars.com

Chandos
www.chandos-records.com

Columbia
www.columbiarecords.com

Creation
www.creation.co.uk

Decca
www.decca.com

ECM
www.ecmrecords.com

EMI Chrysalis
www.emichrysalis.co.uk

Epic
www.epicrecords.com

Geffen
www.geffen.com

Grapevine
www.grapevine-label.co.uk

HMV
www.hmv.co.uk

Hyperion
www.hyperion-records.co.uk

Island
www.island.co.uk

Legacy Recordings
www.legacyrecordings.com

MCA
www.mcarecords.com

Mercury
www.mercuryrecords.com

Ministry of Sound
www.ministryofsound.co.uk

Naxos & Marco Polo
www.hnh.com

Nimbus
www.nimbus.ltd.uk

Parlophone
www.parlophone.co.uk

Polydor
www.polydor.co.uk

Polygram
www.polygram.com

QED Productions
www.qed-productions.com

Sony
www.sonymusic.co.uk

Sony Classical
www.sonyclassical.com

Telstar
www.telstar.co.uk

Tower
www.towerrecords.co.uk

21st Century Music
www.21stcentury.co.uk

Universal Music Group
www.umusic.com

Virgin
www.virginrecords.co.uk

Warner Bros
www.wbr.com

Studios

Abbey Road Studios
www.abbeyroad.co.uk

RAK Recording Studios
www.rakstudios.co.uk

professional bodies

Association of British Theatre Technicians
www.abtt.org.uk

Association of Mouth & Foot Painting Artist
Worldwide
www.amfpa.com

British Society of Master Glass Painters
www.bsmgp.org.uk

Cartoonists' Guild
www.pipemedia.net/cartoons

Directors' Guild of Great Britain
www.dggb.co.uk

Equity British Actors' Union
www.equity.org.uk

Fine Art Trade Guild
www.fineart.co.uk

Guild of Film Production Accountants &
Financial Administrators
www.gfpa.org.uk

Guild of Television Cameramen
www.gtc.org.uk

Incorporated Society of Musicians
www.ism.org

London Association of Art & Design
Education
www.laade.org

Magic Circle
www.themagiccircle.co.uk

Piano Tuners' Association
www.pianotuner.org.uk

Producers Alliance for Cinema & Television
www.pact.co.uk

Production Managers' Association
www.pma.org.uk

Society of Authors
www.writers.org.uk/society

Society of Television Lighting Directors
www.stld.org.uk

Writers' Guild of Great Britain
www.writers.org.uk/guild

promotors & directors

Directors' Guild of Great Britain
www.dggb.co.uk

Raymond Gubbay
www.raymond-gubbay.co.uk

Robert Stigwood Organisation
www.rsogroup.com

Stephen Berkoff
www.east-productions.demon.co.uk

radio

AFRICA

Egypt Government Information Service
www.sis.gov.eg

SAFM (Johannesburg)
www.safm.co.za

ANTARCTICA

Anetstation
www.anetstation.com

ASIA

China Radio International (Beijing)
www.cri.com.cn/english

Radio Nepal
www.catmando.com/news/radio-nepal

RTHK (Hong Kong)
www.rthk.org.hk

AUSTRALASIA

873 2GB (Sydney)
www.2gb.com

Fresh FM (Adelaide)
www.fresh.fm.net.au

Radio Australia (Melbourne)
www.abc.net.au/ra

EUROPE

Pioneer (Munich)
www.radiopioneer.com

Vatican Radio
www.vatican.va/news_services/radio

Voice of Russia
www.vor.ru/index_eng.html

XFM (Dublin)
www.isis.ie/xfm

Programmes

Archers (Fan Club)
www.archers-addicts.com

UK

Atlantic
www.atlantic252.com

Bath FM
www.bathfm.uk.com

BBC Asian Network
www.bbc.co.uk/england/asiannetwork

BBC Essex
www.bbc.co.uk/england/essex

BBC GMR (Manchester)
www.bbc.co.uk/england/gmr

BBC Hereford & Worcester
www.bbc.co.uk/england/herefordworcester

BBC Local Radio
www.bbc.co.uk/england/radindex.shtml

BBC Radio 1
www.bbc.co.uk/radio1

BBC Radio 2
www.bbc.co.uk/radio2

BBC Radio 3
www.bbc.co.uk/radio3

BBC Radio 4
www.bbc.co.uk/radio4

BBC Radio 5
www.bbc.co.uk/radio5

BBC Radio Berkshire
www.bbc.co.uk/england/thamesvalley

BBC Radio Bristol
www.bbc.co.uk/england/radiobristol

BBC Radio Cambridgeshire
www.bbc.co.uk/england/radiocambridgeshire

BBC Radio Cleveland
www.bbc.co.uk/england/radiocleveland

BBC Radio Cornwall
www.bbc.co.uk/england/radiocornwall

BBC Radio Coventry and Warwickshire
www.bbc.co.uk/england/coventrywarwickshire

BBC Radio Cumbria
www.bbc.co.uk/england/radiocumbria

BBC Radio Cymru
www.bbc.co.uk/cymru

BBC Radio Derby
www.bbc.co.uk/england/radioderby

BBC Radio Devon
www.bbc.co.uk/england/radiodevon

BBC Radio Guernsey
www.bbc.co.uk/england/radioguernsey

BBC Radio Gloucestershire
www.bbc.co.uk/england/radiogloucestershire

BBC Radio Humberside
www.bbc.co.uk/england/radiohumberside

BBC Radio Jersey
www.bbc.co.uk/england/radiojersey

BBC Radio Kent
www.bbc.co.uk/england/radiokent

BBC Radio Lancashire
www.bbc.co.uk/england/radiolancashire

BBC Radio Leeds
www.bbc.co.uk/england/radioleeds

BBC Radio Leicester
www.bbc.co.uk/england/radioleicester

BBC Radio Lincolnshire
www.bbc.co.uk/england/radiolincolnshire

BBC Radio Merseyside
www.bbc.co.uk/england/radiomerseyside

BBC Radio Newcastle
www.bbc.co.uk/england/radionewcastle

BBC Radio Norfolk
www.bbc.co.uk/england/radionorfolk

BBC Radio Northampton
www.bbc.co.uk/england/radionorthampton

BBC Radio Nottingham
www.bbc.co.uk/england/radionottingham

BBC Radio Sheffield
www.bbc.co.uk/england/radiosheffield

BBC Radio Shropshire
www.bbc.co.uk/england/radioshropshire

BBC Radio Solent
www.bbc.co.uk/england/radiosolent

BBC Radio Stoke
www.bbc.co.uk/england/radiostoke

BBC Radio Suffolk
www.bbc.co.uk/england/radiosuffolk

BBC Radio Wales
www.bbc.co.uk/wales

BBC Radio WM
www.bbc.co.uk/england/radiowm

BBC Radio York
www.bbc.co.uk/england/radioyork

BBC Somerset Sound
www.bbc.co.uk/england/radiobristol

BBC Southern Counties
www.bbc.co.uk/england/southerncounties

BBC Three Counties Radio
www.bbc.co.uk/england/threecounties

BBC Wiltshire Sound
www.bbc.co.uk/england/wiltshiresound

BBC World Service
www.bbc.co.uk/worldservice

Beacon FM (Shropshire)
www.beaconfm.co.uk

Beacon FM (Wolverhampton)
www.beaconfm.co.uk

BRMB FM (Birmingham)
www.brmb.co.uk

Cambridge Red
www.redradio.com

Capital FM (London)
www.capitalfm.com

Capital Gold (London)
www.capitalgold.co.uk

Century 105 (North West)
www.century105.com

Century 106 (Nottingham)
www.century106.com

Channel 103FM (Channel Islands)
www.channel103.com

Classic FM
www.classicfm.co.uk

Classic Gold
www.classicgold828.co.uk

Classic Gold Amber
www.amber.radio.co.uk

Clyde
www.radioclyde.co.uk

Cool FM (Belfast)
www.coolfm.co.uk

County Sound (Surrey)
www.countysound.co.uk

Essex FM
www.essexfm.co.uk/new

Forth FM (Edinburgh)
www.radioforth.co.uk

Fox FM (Oxford)
www.foxfm.co.uk

Fresh Air FM
www.freshairfm.co.uk

Galaxy 105 (Yorkshire)
www.galaxy105.co.uk

Galaxy Radio
www.galaxyradio.co.uk

GWR FM
www.gwrfm.musicradio.com

Hallam FM (Sheffield)
www.hallamfm.co.uk

Invicta FM (Kent)
www.invictafm.com

Island FM (Guernsey)
www.islandfm.guernsey.net

Isle of Wight Radio
www.iwradio.co.uk

Jazz FM (London)
www.jazzfm.com

Kiss FM (London)
www.kissfm.co.uk

Lantern FM (Devon)
www.lanternnet.co.uk

LBC (London)
www.lbc.co.uk

Lincs FM (Lincolnshire)
www.lincsfm.co.uk

Magic AM (Yorkshire)
www.magicam.co.uk

Manx Radio
www.manxradio.com

Medway FM (Kent)
www.medwayfm.com

Metro FM (Newcastle)
www.metrofm.co.uk

New Atlantic 252
www.atlantic252.co.uk

News Direct (London)
www.newsdirect.co.uk

Ocean FM
www.oceanfm.com

Operadio
www.operadio.com

Orchard FM
www.orchardfm.co.uk

Oxygen FM
www.oxygen.demon.co.uk

Pirate FM
www.piratefm102.co.uk

Plymouth FM
www.plymouthsound.com

Power FM
www.powerfm.com

Radio Caroline
www.radiocaroline.co.uk

Radio City 96.7 (Liverpool)
www.yourliverpool.com/radiocity

Red Dragon FM
www.reddragonfm.co.uk

Red Dragon FM (Cardiff)
www.reddragonfm.co.uk

Signal Radio FM
www.signalradio.com

Spire FM
www.spirefm.co.uk

Talk Radio
www.talk-radio.co.uk

Talk Sport
www.talksport.net

Victory FM (Portsmouth)
www.radiovictory.co.uk

Virgin Radio
www.virginradio.com

Voice of America
www.voa.gov

XFM
www.xfm.co.uk

USA

KIIS FM (Los Angeles)
www.kiisfm.com

Mountain 103.7 (Washington)
www.kmtt.com

New Orleans Channel
www.southernmusic.net/orleansthisweek.htm

WFNX (Boston)
www.fnxradio.com

WNYC (New York)
www.wnyc.org

stadia & concert halls

Aberdeen Exhibition & Conference Centre
www.aecc.co.uk

Aberystwyth Arts Centre
www.aber.ac.uk/~arcwww

Barbican
www.barbican.org.uk

Birmingham Hippodrome
www.birminghamhippodrome.co.uk

Birmingham NEC
www.nec.co.uk

Bridgewater Hall, Manchester
www.bridgewater-hall.co.uk

Brighton Centre
www.brightoncentre.co.uk

Earls Court Olympia
www.eco.co.uk

Hackney Empire
www.hackneyempire.co.uk

London Arena
www.londonarena.co.uk

Manchester G-Mex
www.gmex.co.uk

Mean Fiddler
www.meanfiddler.com

National Indoor Arena
www.nia-birmingham.co.uk

Ocean Music Venue
www.ocean.org.uk

Royal Albert Hall
www.alberthall.co.uk

Royal Opera House
www.royaloperahouse.org

Sheffield Arena
www.sheffield-arena.co.uk

South Bank Centre
www.sbc.org.uk

Wembley
www.wembley.co.uk

television

Channels

ABC
www.abc-tv.net

Anglia
www.angliatv.co.uk

BBC
www.bbc.co.uk

BBC News
www.news.bbc.co.uk

Border
www.border-tv.com

Bravo
www.bravo.co.uk

Carlton
www.carltontv.co.uk

Carlton Select
www.carltonselect.com

Central
www.centraltv.co.uk

Challenge TV
www.challengetv.co.uk

Channel 4
www.channel4.co.uk

Channel 5
www.channel5.co.uk

Channel Television
www.channeltv.co.uk

God Channel
www.godnetwork.com

CNN
www.cnn.com

Discovery
www.discovery.com

Disney Channel
www.disneychannel.co.uk

Euro TV
www.eurotv.com

FilmFour
www.filmfour.com

Golf Channel
www.thegolfchannel.com

Grampian
www.grampiantv.co.uk

Granada
www.granada.tv.co.uk

Granada Plus
www.gplus.co.uk

Granada Sky Broadcasting
www.gsb.co.uk

HTV
www.htv.co.uk

ITV
www.itv.co.uk

Living
www.livingtv.co.uk

LWT
www.lwt.co.uk

Meridian
www.meridiantv.co.uk

MTV
www.mtv.co.uk

NBC
www.nbc.com

ONDigital
www.ondigital.co.uk

S4C (Wales)
www.s4c.co.uk

Sci-Fi Channel
www.scifi.com

Scottish Television
www.stv.co.uk

Sky
www.sky.co.uk

UTV (Ulster)
www.utvlive.com

Web TV
www.webtv.com

West Country
www.westcountry.co.uk

Critics

Victor Lewis-Smith
www.lewis-smith.com

Organisations

Emmys (Academy of Television Arts & Sciences)
www.emmys.org

Producers Alliance for Cinema and Television
www.pact.co.uk

Royal Television Society
www.rts.org.uk

Personalities

Anthea Turner
www.anthea-turner.co.uk

Cilla Black
www.cillablack.com

David Copperfield
www.dcopperfield.com

Des O'Connor
www.des-oconnor.com

Graham Norton
www.grahamnorton.co.uk

Jonathan Dimbleby
www.jonathandimbleby.co.uk

Zoe Ball
www.zoeball.net

Production Companies

Aardman Animations
www.aardman.com

Addictive Television
www.addictive.com

Ginger Media Group
www.ginger.com

Hat Trick Productions
www.hat-trick.co.uk

Mentorn
www.mentorn.co.uk

Mersey Television Company
www.merseytv.com

Programmes

Alan Partridge
www.alan-partridge.co.uk

Ally McBeal
www.ally-mcbeal.com

Babylon 5
http://babylon5.warnerbros.com

Baywatch
www.baywatchtv.com

BBC Comedy Zone
www.comedyzone.beeb.com

BBC Schools
www.bbc.co.uk/education/schools

Beverly Hills 90210
www.helicon7.com/90210

Bewitched
www.bewitched.net

Big Breakfast
www.bigbreakfast.channel4.com

The Bill
www.thebill.com

Blind Date
www.blinddate.co.uk

Brookside
www.brookie.com

Buffy the Vampire Slayer
www.buffyslayer.com

Bugs
www.bugs.co.uk

Cagney & Lacey
http://w3.one.net/~voyager/candl.html

Challenge Anneka
www.mentorn.co.uk/challenge

Changing Rooms
www.bbc.co.uk/changingrooms

Channel 4 Schools
www.schools.channel4.com

Charlie's Angels
www.charliesangels.com

Chicago Hope
www.geocities.com/TelevisionCity/6025

Cold Feet
www.coldfeetonline.co.uk

Coronation Street
www.coronationstreet.co.uk

Dawson's Creek
www.dawsons-creek.com

Dempsey & Makepeace
www.dempseyandmakepeace.de

Dr Quinn Medicine Woman
www.drquinn.com

Due South
www.duesouth.com

Eastenders
www.bbc.co.uk/eastenders

Emmerdale
www.emmerdale.co.uk

ER
www.ertv.com

The Fast Show
www.comedyzone.beeb.com/fastshow

Frasier
www.frasier.mcmail.com

Friends
www.friends.warnerbros.com

Gardeners' World
www.gardenersworld.beeb.com

Gladiators
www.lwt.co.uk/gladiators

GMTV
www.gmtv.co.uk

Have I Got News For You
www.haveigotnewsforyou.com

Hawaii Five-O
www.mjq.net/fiveo

Hill Street Blues
www.net-hlp.com/hsb

Holby City
www.bbc.co.uk/holbycity

Holiday
www.takeoff.beeb.com

Hollyoaks
www.merseytv.com/hollyoaks.com

Home & Away
www.homeandaway.seven.com.au

Horizon
www.bbc.co.uk/horizon

Jerry Springer Show
www.universalstudios.com/tv/jerryspringer

Kavanagh QC
www.kavanaghqc.co.uk

Knight Rider
www.knight-rider.com

League of Gentlemen
www.roystonvasey.co.uk

London Tonight
www.londontonight.co.uk

Lost in Space
www.lostinspacetv.com

Men Behaving Badly
www.menbehavingbadly.com

Monty Python
www.montypython.net

Mr Bean
www.mrbean.co.uk

Neighbours
www.neighbours.com

Northern Exposure
www.netspace.org/~moose/moose.html

NYPD Blue
www.nypdblue.com

Oprah Winfrey
www.oprahshow.com

Peak Practice
www.peakpractice.co.uk

Planet of the Apes
www.foxhome.com/planetoftheapes

The Prisoner
www.the-prisoner-6.freeserve.co.uk

Railway Children
http://therailwaychildren.carlton.com

Red Dwarf
www.reddwarf.co.uk

The Saint
www.saint.org

Seinfeld
www.seinfeld.com

South Park
www.southpark.co.uk

Space 1999
www.space1999.net

Star Trek
www.startrek.com

Stars In Their Eyes
www.starsintheireyes.co.uk

Starsky & Hutch
www.spe.sony.com/tv/shows/sgn/sh

The Sweeney
www.thesweeney.com

Talk TV
www.talktv.co.uk

TFI Friday
www.tfifriday.com

They Think It's All Over
www.talkback.co.uk/theythink

This Morning
www.g-wizz.net/thismorning

Today's the Day
www.mentorn.co.uk/tdd

Tomorrow's World
www.bbc.co.uk/tw

Tomorrow's World Plus
www.twplus.beeb.com

Top Gear
www.topgear.beeb.com

Top of the Pops
www.totp.beeb.com

Who Wants to be a Millionaire?
www.phone-a-friend.com

Wish You Were Here?
www.wishyouwerehere.com

World at War
www.theworldatwar.com

World in Action
www.world-in-action.co.uk

X-Files
www.fox.com/thexfiles

theatre

Companies

NTC Touring Theatre Company
www.ntc-touringtheatre.co.uk

Quicksilver Theatre Company
www.quicksilvertheatre.org

Rocket Theatre Company
www.rockettheatre.co.uk

Soho Theatre Company
www.sohotheatre.com

Tara Arts
www.tara-arts.com

Productions

Art
www.dewynters.com/art

Beautiful Game
www.beautifulgamemusical.com

Buddy Holly Story
www.mpcgroup.co.uk/buddy

Carousel
www.shubert.com/carousel.html

Cats
www.reallyuseful.com/cats

Chicago
www.chicagothemusical.com

Doctor Dolittle
www.doctordolittle.co.uk

Evita
www.thenewevita.com

Fosse the Musical
www.fosse.uk.com

Grease
www.grease-tour.com

Houdini The Musical
www.houdinithemusical.com

Jekyll & Hyde
www.jekyll-hyde.com

The King and I
www.kingandi.co.uk

Les Miserables
www.lesmis.com

Lord of the Dance
www.lordofthedance.com

Mamma Mia!
www.mamma-mia.com

Miss Saigon
www.miss-saigon.com

My Fair Lady
www.tcfhe.com/myfairlady

Notre Dame de Paris
www.notredameusa.com

Phantom of the Opera
www.thephantomoftheopera.com

Riverdance
www.riverdance.com

Rocky Horror Picture Show
www.rockyhorror.com

Saturday Night Fever
www.nightfever.co.uk

Spend, Spend, Spend
www.spendspendspend.net

Starlight Express
www.starlightexpress.co.uk

Tap Dogs
www.tapdogs.com

Theatres

ADC Theatre, Cambridge
www.adc-theatre.cam.ac.uk

Almeida
www.almeida.co.uk

Bloomsbury Theatre
www.ucl.ac.uk/bloomsburytheatre

Brighton Centre
www.brightoncentre.co.uk

Bristol Old Vic
www.bristol-old-vic.co.uk

Chapter, Cardiff
www.chapter.org

Chichester Festival Theatre
www.cft.org.uk

Citizens Theatre, Glasgow
www.citz.co.uk

Corn Exchange, Cambridge
www.cambridge.gov.uk/cornex.htm

De Montfort Hall, Leicester
www.demontforthall.co.uk

Derngate Theatre, Northampton
www.ntt.org.uk

Donmar Warehouse
www.donmar-warehouse.com

Eden Court Theatre, Inverness
www.edencourt.uk.com

Empire Theatre, Sunderland
www.newsnorth.com/empire/default.html

Everyman Theatre
www.everymantheatre.com

Everyman Theatre, Cheltenham
www.everyman.u-net.com

Everyman Theatre, Liverpool
http://everyman.merseyworld.com

Festival Theatre, Chichester
www.cft.org.uk

Festival Theatre, Edinburgh
www.eft.co.uk

Gaiety Theatre Isle of Man
www.iom.com/gaietytheatre

Gateway Theatre, Chester
www.gateway-theatre.org

Gilded Balloon, Edinburgh
www.gilded-balloon.co.uk

Grand Opera House, Belfast
www.gohbelfast.com

Grand Theatre, Leeds
www.leeds.gov.uk/grandtheatre

Grand Theatre, Wolverhampton
www.grandtheatre.co.uk

Hackney Empire
www.hackneyempire.co.uk

Hampstead Theatre
www.hampstead-theatre.co.uk

Haymarket, Basingstoke
www.haymarket.org.uk

Hexagon, Reading
www.reading.gov.uk/hexagon

Hippodrome, Birmingham
www.birmingham-hippodrome.co.uk

Hoxton Hall
www.hoxtonhall.dabsol.co.uk

Kenneth More Theatre, Ilford
http://members.aol.com/kmtheatre

Komedia Theatre, Brighton
www.brighton.co.uk/listings/komedia

Landmark, Ilfracombe
www.northdevontheatres.org.uk/landmark

Library Theatre, Manchester
www.libtheatreco.org.uk

Lyric Studio Theatre
www.lyric.co.uk

Lyric Theatre, Belfast
www.lyrictheatre.co.uk

Milton Keynes Theatre and Gallery
www.mktgc.co.uk

Minack Theatre, Porthcurno
www.minack.com

New Victoria Theatre, Stoke on Trent
www.uktw.co.uk/info/newvic.htm

North Wales Theatre, Llandudno
www.nwtheatre.co.uk

Nuffield Theatre, Lancaster
www.lancs.ac.uk/users/nuffield

Open Air Theatre Regent's Park
www.open-air-theatre.org.uk

Pavilion Theatre, Glasgow
www.paviliontheatre.co.uk

Phoenix Arts, Leicester
www.phoenix.org.uk

Pitlochry Festival Theatre
www.pitlochry.org.uk

Playhouse Theatre, Derby
www.derbyplayhouse.demon.co.uk

Playhouse Theatre, Oxford
www.oxfordplayhouse.co.uk

Playhouse, Edinburgh
www.gold.co.uk/playhouse.html

Playhouse, Liverpool
www.playhouse.org

Playhouse, Nottingham
www.nottinghamplayhouse.co.uk/playhouse

Really Useful Theatres
www.rutheatres.com

Regent, Ipswich
www.ipswich-ents.co.uk/regent

Royal Centre, Nottingham
www.netpresence.co.uk/royalcentre

Royal Court Theatre
www.royal-court.org.uk

Royal Exchange Theatre Company
www.royalexchange.co.uk

Royal Exchange Theatre, Manchester
www.royalexchange.co.uk

Royal Lyceum Theatre, Edinburgh
www.infoser.com/infotheatre/lyceum

Royal National Theatre
www.nt-online.org.uk

Royal Shakespeare Company Theatre
www.rsc.org.uk

Royal Theatre, Northampton
www.northamptonshire.co.uk/royal.theatre

The Royal, Hanley
www.webfactory.co.uk/theroyal

Sadler's Wells
www.sadlers-wells.com

Scarlet Theatre
www.scarlettheatre.co.uk

Shakespeare's Globe
www.shakespeares-globe.org

Stephen Joseph Theatre, Scarborough
www.sjt.uk.com

Stoll Moss Theatres
www.stoll-moss.com

Theatre Royal, Bury St Edmunds
www.theatreroyal.org

Theatre Royal, Glasgow
www.theatreroyalglasgow.com

Traverse Theatre, Edinburgh
www.traverse.co.uk

Tron Theatre, Glasgow
www.tron.co.uk

Unicorn Theatre for Children
www.unicorntheatre.com

Warehouse Theatre, Croydon
www.live-uk.com/warehouse_theatre

Watford Theatre
www.watfordtheatre.co.uk

West Yorkshire Playhouse, Leeds
www.wyp.co.uk

Wimbledon Theatre
www.uktw.co.uk/info/wimbledon.htm

York Theatre Royal
www.theatre-royal-york.co.uk

Yvonne Arnaud Theatre, Guildford
www.yvonne-arnaud.co.uk

tickets

Albemarle of London
www.albemarle-london.com

BBC Ticket Unit
www.bbc.co.uk/tickets

First Call
www.first-call.co.uk

Global Tickets
www.globaltickets.com

Group Line
www.groupline.com

Hot Tickets Direct
www.hotticketsdirect.com

Keith Prowse
www.keithprowse.co.uk

Lashmars
www.londontheatre.co.uk/lashmars

Lastminute.com
www.lastminute.com

London Theatre Bookings
www.londontheatrebookings.com

Mayflower
www.mayflower.org.uk

Really Useful Theatres
www.stoll-moss.com

Society of Ticket Agents & Retailers
www.s-t-a-r.org.uk

Theatre Tokens
www.theatretokens.com

Ticketmaster
www.ticketmaster.co.uk

Tickets Online
www.tickets-online.co.uk

Ticketweb
www.ticketweb.co.uk

Wembley
www.wembleyticket.com

West End Theatre Bookings
www.uktickets.co.uk

What's On Stage
www.whatsonstage.com

Need to

track down

a business

in a hurry?

advertising ●

automotive ●

aviation ●

chambers of commerce ●

chemicals ●

couriers ●

electrical & technological ●

energy ●

engineering ●

finance ●

food, beverage & tobacco ●

ftse 100 companies ●

insurance ●

leisure ●

livery companies & guilds ●

magazines & websites ●

manufacturing ●

materials & construction ●

media ●

metals & mining ●

model agencies ●

office supplies & services ●

paper & packaging ●

pharmaceutical ●

printing & publishing ●

private investigators ●

professional bodies ●

professional bodies
& associations ●

professions ●

real estate ●

recruitment ●

retail ●

services ●

shipping & shipbuilding ●

standards ●

stock & commodity
exchanges & financial listings ●

telecommunications ●

trade associations ●

trades unions ●

transport ●

us corporations ●

utilities ●

www.thomweb.co.uk
THOMSON
Directories™

Need to

track down

a business

in a hurry?

advertising

Abbott Mead Vickers
www.amvbbdo.co.uk

Addison Wesley Longman
www.awl.com

Advertising Age
www.adage.com

Bartle Bogle Hegarty
www.bbh.co.uk

Bates Dorland
www.bates-dorland.co.uk

Beer Davies
www.beerdavies.co.uk

BMP DDB
www.bmp.co.uk

Charles Barker
www.cbarker.co.uk

CHJS
www.chjs.co.uk

Dewynters
www.dewynters.com

DMBB
www.dmbb.com

Dryden Brown
www.dryden.co.uk

Duckworth Finn Grub Waters
www.dfgw.co.uk

FCB
www.fcb.com

Grey
www.grey.co.uk

HHCL
www.hhcl.com

J Walter Thompson
www.jwtworld.com

Joslin Shaw
www.joshaw.co.uk

Leo Burnett
www.leoburnett.com

Lowe Howard Spink
www.lowehoward-spink.co.uk

McCann Erickson
www.mccann.com

Paling Walters Targis
www.palingwalters.com

Poulter
www.poulter.co.uk

RDW
www.zebra.co.uk/ctd/rdwa

Saatchi & Saatchi
www.saatchi-saatchi.com

Young & Rubicam
www.yandr.com

automotive

Dennis
www.dennis-group.co.uk

Henlys
www.henlys.com

Inchcape
www.inchcape.com

Kwik-Fit
www.kwik-fit.com

Lex Service
www.lex.co.uk

Motor Vehicle Repairers' Association
www.mvra.com

Retail Motor Industry Federation
www.rmif.co.uk

aviation

Aviation Industry Group
www.ai-group.co.uk

Aviation Today
www.aviationtoday.com

chambers of commerce

British

Aberdeen
www.aberdeenchamber.co.uk

Bedfordshire
www.bedschamber.co.uk

Birmingham
www.bci.org.uk

Bradford
www.bradford-cbr-of-trade.freeserve.co.uk

British
www.britishchambers.org.uk

Cambridge
www.cambridgechamber.co.uk

Central & West Lancashire
www.lancschamber.co.uk

Central Scotland
www.central-chamber.co.uk

Dorset
www.wdi.co.uk/dcci

East of England
www.go-eastern.gov.uk

Exeter
www.exeter-chamber-of-commerce.co.uk

Guernsey
www.industry.guernsey.net

Liverpool
www.liverpoolchamber.org.uk

Manchester
www.manccitecbl.org.uk/mcrcci

North Derbyshire
www.derbyshire.org/chamber

Northern Ireland
www.nicci.co.uk

Oxford
www.oxlink.co.uk/coc

Plymouth
www.plymouth-chamber.co.uk

Rotherham
www.rccte.org.uk

Shropshire
www.shropshire-chamber.co.uk

Somerset
www.somerset.businesslink.co.uk

Southern Derbyshire
www.sdccte.com

Suffolk
www.suffolkchamber.co.uk

Thames Valley
www.thamesvalleychamber.co.uk

Wolverhampton
www.wton-chamber.co.uk

York & North Yorkshire
www.york.chamber.co.uk

Foreign

American
www.uschamber.org

Association of European Chambers of Commerce
www.eurochambre.be

Austrian
www.wk.or.at

Dutch
www.nbcc.demon.co.uk

Singaporean
www.asianconnect.com/sicc/home.shtml

chemicals

AGA Group
www.aga.com

BOC
www.boc.com

British Biotech
www.britbio.co.uk

Burmah Castrol
www.burmah-castrol.com

Celltech Chiroscience
www.celltech.co.uk

Imperial Chemical Industries
www.ici.com

Laporte
www.laporteplc.com

couriers

Amtrak
www.amtrak.co.uk

Arrow Express
www.arrow-express.co.uk

Business Post
www.business-post.com

City Link
www.city-link.co.uk

Crossflight
www.crossflight.co.uk

DHL
www.dhl.co.uk

Federal Express
www.fedex.com

Five Ways Express
www.5ways.mcmail.com

International Association of Air Travel Couriers
www.aircourier.co.uk

Lynx
www.lynx.co.uk

Mercury
www.mercurycourier.com

Moves
www.moves.co.uk

Parcel Force
www.parcelforce.co.uk

Post Office
www.consignia.com

Royal Mail
www.royalmail.co.uk

Securicor-Omega
www.securicor.co.uk

Sprint
www.sprintexpress.co.uk

TNT
www.tnt.co.uk

UPS
www.ups.com

World Courier
www.worldcourier.com

electrical & technological

Cookson Group
www.cooksongroup.co.uk

Danka Business Systems
www.danka.com

Eidos
www.eidos.com

Invensys
www.invensys.com

Logica
www.logica.com

Lynx Group
www.lynx-group.co.uk

Misys
www.misys.co.uk

Parity Group
www.parity.co.uk

Psion
www.psion.com

QXL.com
www.qxl.com

Racal Electronics
www.racal.com

Sage
www.sage.com

Scoot.com
www.scoot.com

Sema Group
www.semagroup.com

Smiths Industries
www.smiths-industries.com

Surf Control

www.surfcontrol.com

energy

AgipPetroli
www.agippetroli.it/uk/index.html

BP Amoco
www.bpamoco.com

British-Borneo Oil & Gas
www.british-borneo.co.uk

Burmah Castrol
www.burmah-castrol.com

Chevron
www.chevron.com

Conoco
www.conoco.com

Enterprise Oil
www.entoil.com

Exxon (Esso)
www.exxon.com

Gulf
www.gulfoil.com

Lasmo
www.lasmo.com

Mobil
www.mobil.co.uk

Premier Oil
www.premier-oil.com

Shell Transport & Trading Company
www.shell.com

Texaco
www.texaco.co.uk

Total
www.total.com

Xerox
www.xerox.com

engineering

Arup
www.arup.com

Babcock International
www.babcock.co.uk

Rolls Royce
www.rolls-royce.com

Shipbuilders and Shiprepairers Association
www.ssa.org.uk

finance

Foreign

ABN AMRO, Netherlands
www.abnamro.nl

ABSA Bank, South Africa
www.absa.co.za

Agricultural Bank of China
www.abocn.com

Allied Bank, South Africa
www.absa.co.za

American National Bank
www.accessanb.com

American Savings Bank
www.asbhawaii.com

Arab Bank
www.arabbank.com

Asian Development Bank
www.adb.org

Australia and New Zealand Banking Group
www.anz.com

Banca Commerciale Italiana
www.bci.it

Banca d'Italia
www.bancaditalia.it

Banco Central Do Brasil
www.bcb.gov.br

Banco de España
www.bde.es

Banco de Portugal
www.bportugal.pt

Bangkok Bank, Thailand
www.bbl.co.th

Bank Austria
www.bankaustria.com

Bank of America
www.bankamerica.com

Bank of Baharian and Kuwait
http://bbkonline.com

Bank of Baroda
www.bankofbaroda.com

Bank of Canada
www.bank-banque-canada.ca

Bank of China
www.bank-of-china.com

Bank of Cyprus
www.bankofcyprus.com

Bank of Estonia
www.ee/epbe/en

Bank of Finland
www.bof.fi

Bank of Greece
www.bankofgreece.gr

Bank of Hawaii
www.boh.com

Bank of India
www.webindia.com/boi

Bank of Ireland
www.bankofireland.ie

Bank of Israel
www.bankisrael.gov.il

Bank of Japan
www.boj.or.jp/en

Bank of Kuwait & the Middle East
www.bkme.com

Bank of Latvia
www.bank.lv

Bank of Lebanon
www.bdl.gov.lb

Bank of Lithuania
www.lbank.lt

Bank of Mexico
www.banxico.org.mx

Bank of Montreal
www.bmo.com

Bank of Moscow
www.mmbank.ru

Bank of Mozambique
www.bancomoc.mz

Bank of New York
www.bankofny.com

Bank of Papua New Guinea
www.bankpng.gov.uk

Bank of Portugal
www.bportugal.bt

Bank of Russia
www.cbr.ru

Bank of Slovenia
www.bsi.si

Bank of Thailand
www.bot.or.th

Bank of Tokyo
www.btm.co.jp

Bank of Wales
www.bankofwales.co.uk

Bank of Zambia
www.boz.zm

Bankers Trust, New York
www.bankerstrust.com

Bankgesellschaft Berlin
www.bankgesellschaft.de/en_index.html

Banque Centrale du Luxembourg
www.bcl.lu

Banque de France
www.banque-france.fr

Banque Nationale de Belgique
www.bnb.be

Banque Nationale de Paris
www.bnp.fr

Bermuda Monetary Authority
www.bma.bm

Bulgarian National Bank
www.bnb.bg

Canada Trust
www.canadatrust.com

Central Bank of Armenia
www.cba.am

Central Bank of Barbados
www.centralbank.org.bb

Central Bank of Bosnia
www.cbbh.gov.ba

Central Bank of Chile
www.bcentral.cl

Central Bank of China
www.cbc.gov.tw

Central Bank of Cyprus
www.centralbank.gov.cy

Central Bank of Iceland
www.sedlabanki.ias

Central Bank of India
www.centralbankofindia.co.in

Central Bank of Ireland
www.centralbank.ie

Central Bank of Jordan
www.cbj.gov.jo

Central Bank of Kenya
www.africaonline.co.ke/cbk

Central Bank of Malta
www.centralbankmalta.com

Central Bank of Swaziland
www.centralbank.sz

Central Bank of the Netherlands Antilles
http://centralbank.an

Central Bank of the Republic of Indonesia
www.bi.go.id

Central Bank of the Republic of Turkey
www.tcmb.gov.tr

Central Bank of the Russian Federation
www.cbr.ru

Central Bank of Trinidad & Tobago
www.central-bank.org.tt

Central Bank of Uruguay
www.bcu.gub.uy

Central Reserve Bank of El Salvador
www.bcr.gob.sv

Chase Manhattan
www.chase.com

Citibank
www.citibank.com

Commonwealth Bank of Australia
www.commbank.com.au

Credit Agricole, France
www.credit-agricole.fr

Creditanstalt
www.creditanstalt.co.at

Croatian National Bank
www.hnb.hr/sadr.htm

Czech National Bank
www.cnb.cz/en

Danmarks Nationalbank
www.nationalbanken.dk/uk

De Nederlandsche Bank
www.dnb.nl

Deutsche Bank
http://public.deutsche-bank.de

Deutsche Bundesbank
www.bundesbank.de

Dresdner Kleinwort Benson
www.dresdnerkb.com

Eastern Caribbean Bank
www.eccb-centralbank.org

European Central Bank
www.ecb.int

Federal Reserve Bank, San Francisco
www.frbsf.org

Fidelity Federal Savings Bank
www.fidfed.com

First Chicago
www.bankone.com

ForeningsSparbanken (Swedbank)
www.foreningssparbanken.se

Fuji Bank, Japan
www.fujibank.co.jp/eng

Grindlays Private Banking
www.pb.grindlays.com

Gulf International Bank
www.gibonline.com

ING Bank, Netherlands
www.ingbank.nl

Istituto di Credito Sammarinese
www.isc.sm

J P Morgan & Co.
www.jpmorgan.com

Jordan National Bank
www.ahli.com

JP Morgan
www.jpmorgan.com

Muslim Commercial Bank, Pakistan
www.mcb.com.pk

National Australia Bank
www.national.com.au

National Bank of Bahrain
www.nbbonline.com

National Bank of Egypt
www.nbe.com.eg

National Bank of Moldova
www.bnm.org

National Bank of New Zealand
www.nbnz.co.nz

National Bank of the Republic of Macedonia
www.nmrm.gov.mk

National Commercial Bank, Saudi Arabia
www.ncb.com.sa

Oesterreichische Nationalbank (Austria)
www.oenb.co.at/oenb

Ottoman Bank, Turkey
www.ottomanbank.com.tr/english

Philippine National Bank
www.philnabank.com

Punjab National Bank, India
http://exploreindia.com/pnb

Rabobank, Netherland
www.rabobank.nl

Reserve Bank of Australia
www.rba.gov.au

Reserve Bank of India
www.rbi.org.in

Reserve Bank of New Zealand
www.rbnz.govt.nz

Reykjavík Savings Bank, Iceland
www.spron.is

Rindal Sparebank, Norway
www.rindalsbanken.no

Schweizerische Nationalbank (Switzerland)
www.snb.ch

Scotiabank
www.scotiabank.com

Standard Chartered Bank
www.stanchart.com

State Bank of India
www.sbi.co.in

Sumitomo Bank
www.sumitomobank.co.jp/eng

Suomen Pankki (Finland)
www.bof.fi

Sveriges Riksbank (Sweden)
www.riksbank.se

Swiss National Bank
www.snb.ch

Unibank, Denmark
www.unibank.dk

Union Bank of Switzerland
www.ubs.com

Wells Fargo
www.wellsfargo.com

Wells Fargo Bank, USA
www.wellsfargo.com

World Bank
www.worldbank.org

UK

Abbey National
www.abbeynational.plc.uk

Agricultural Credit Bureau
www.lltps.co.uk/acb

Alliance & Leicester
www.alliance-leicester.co.uk

Arab Banking Corporation
www.arabbanking.com

Bank of England
www.bankofengland.co.uk

Bank of Scotland
www.bankofscotland.co.uk

Banking Liaison Group
www.bankingliaison.co.uk

British Venture Capital Association
www.bvca.co.uk

Charterhouse Bank
www.charterhouse.co.uk/homebank

Citibank
www.citibank.co.uk

Close Brothers Group
www.cbcf.com

Coinco International
www.coinco.co.uk

Halifax
www.halifax.co.uk

Lloyds TSB Group
www.lloydstsbgroup.co.uk

M & G Group
www.mandg.co.uk

National Westminster Bank
www.natwestgroup.com

Northern Rock
www.nrock.co.uk

Perpetual
www.perpetual.co.uk

Provident Financial
www.providentfinancial.co.uk

Royal Bank of Scotland
www.royalbankscot.co.uk

Salomon Smith Barney
www.sbil.co.uk

Schroders
www.schroders.com

Standard Chartered Bank
www.stanchart.com

3i Group
www.3igroup.com

UBS
www.ubs.co.uk/privatebanking

Woolwich
www.woolwich.co.uk

food, beverage & tobacco

Allied Domecq
www.allieddomecq.co.uk

Associated British Foods
www.abf.co.uk

Bass Brewers
www.bass-brewers.com

Booker
www.booker-plc.com

British Sugar
www.britishsugar.co.uk

Cadbury Schweppes
www.cadburyschweppes.com

Dairy Crest
www.dairycrest.co.uk

Diageo
www.diageo.com

Express Dairies
www.express-dairies.co.uk

Gallaher
www.gallaher-group.com

Geest
www.geest.com

Grant & Cutler
www.grant-c.demon.co.uk

Hazlewood Foods
www.hazlewoodfoods.com

Highland Distillers
www.grouse.com

Hillsdown Holdings
www.hillsdown.com

Imperial Tobacco
www.imperial-tobacco.com

Northern Foods
www.northern-foods.co.uk

Scottish & Newcastle
www.scottish-newcastle.com

Tate & Lyle
www.tate-lyle.co.uk

Traidcraft
www.traidcraft.co.uk

Unigate
www.unigate.plc.uk

Unilever
www.unilever.com

United Biscuits
www.unitedbiscuits.co.uk

United Distillers & Vintners
www.diageo.com/udv.html

ftse 100 companies

Abbey National
www.abbeynational.co.uk

Alliance & Leicester
www.alliance-leicester.co.uk

Allied Domecq
www.allieddomecqplc.com

Amvescap
www.amvescap.com

Asda
www.asda.co.uk

Associated British Foods
www.abf.co.uk

AstraZeneca
www.astrazeneca.com

BAA
www.baa.co.uk

Bank of Scotland
www.bankofscotland.co.uk

Barclays
www.barclays.co.uk

Bass
www.bass.co.uk

Billiton
www.billiton.com

BOC
www.boc.com

Boots
www.boots-plc.com

BP Amoco
www.bpamoco.com

British Aerospace
www.bae.co.uk

British Airways
www.british-airways.com

British Energy
www.british-energy.com

British Gas
www.bgplc.com

British Telecom
www.bt.com

BSkyB
www.sky.co.uk

Cable & Wireless
www.cwplc.com

Cadbury Schweppes
www.cadburyschweppes.com

Carlton
www.carltonplc.co.uk

Centrica
www.centrica.co.uk

CGU
www.cgu-insurance.net

Colt
www.colt-telecom.co.uk

Compass
www.compass-group.com

Daily Mail
www.dmgt.co.uk

Diageo
www.diageo.com

Dixons
www.dixons-group-plc.co.uk

Emap
www.emap.com/plc

EMI
www.emigroup.com

Energis
www.energis.co.uk

GEC
www.gec.com

GKN
www.gknplc.com

Glaxo Wellcome
www.glaxowellcome.co.uk

Granada
www.granada.co.uk

Guardian Royal Exchange
www.gre-group.com

GUS
www.gusplc.com

Halifax
www.halifax.co.uk

Hanson
www.hansonplc.com

Hays
www.hays.co.uk

HSBC
www.hsbcgroup.com

ICI
www.ici.com

Imperial Tobacco
www.imperial-tobacco.com

Invensys
www.invensys.com

Kingfisher
www.kingfisher.co.uk

Ladbroke
www.ladbrokegroup.com

Land Securities
www.propertymall.com/landsecurities

Legal & General
www.landg.com

Lloyds TSB
www.lloydstsb.co.uk

Marks & Spencer
www.marks-and-spencer.co.uk

Misys
www.misys.co.uk

National Grid
www.ngc.co.uk

National Power
www.national-power.com

NatWest
www.natwestgroup.com

Norwich Union
www.norwichunion.co.uk

Orange
www.uk.orange.net

P & O
www.p-and-o.com

Pearson
www.pearson.com

Powergen
www.pgen.com

Prudential
www.prudentialcorporation.com

Railtrack
www.railtrack.co.uk

Reckitt and Colman
www.reckittandcolman.com

Rentokil Initial
www.rentokil-initial.com

Reuters
www.reuters.com

Rio Tinto
www.riotinto.com

Rolls Royce
www.rolls-royce.com

Royal & Sun Alliance
www.royalsunalliance.co.uk

Royal Bank of Scotland
www.royalbankscot.co.uk

Sainsburys
www.j-sainsbury.co.uk

Schroders
www.schroders.co.uk

Scottish and Newcastle
www.scottish-newcastle.com

Scottish and Southern Energy
www.scottish-southern.co.uk

Scottish Power
www.scottishpower.plc.uk

Securicor
www.securicor.com

Sema
www.semagroup.com

Severn Trent
www.severn-trent.com

Shell
www.shell.com

SmithKline Beecham
www.sb.com

Smiths Industries
www.smiths-industries.com

South African Breweries
www.sab.co.za

Stagecoach
www.stagecoachholdings.com

Standard Chartered Bank
www.standard.com

Telewest
www.telewest.co.uk

Tesco
www.tesco.co.uk

Thames Water
www.thames-water.com

3i Group
www.3igroup.com

Unilever
www.unilever.com

United News and Media
www.unm.com

United Utilities
www.unitedutilities.com

Vodafone
www.vodafone.co.uk

Whitbread
www.whitbread.co.uk

Woolwich
www.woolwich.co.uk

WPP
www.wpp.com

insurance

Association of Insurers & Risk Managers
www.airmic.com

British Insurance and Investment Brokers'
Association (BIIBA)
www.biiba.org.uk

CGU
www.cguplc.com

Hiscox
www.hiscox.com

Independent Insurance
www.independent-insurance.co.uk

Jardine Lloyd Thompson
www.jltgroup.com

Legal & General
www.legal-and-general.co.uk

Lloyd's of London
www.lloyds.com

London International Insurance and
Reinsurance Market Association (LIRMA)
www.lirma.co.uk

Norwich Union
www.norwich-union.com

Prudential
www.prudential.co.uk

Royal & Sun Alliance
www.royalsunalliance.com

Standard Life Assurance Company
www.standardlife.com

Sun Life and Provincial Holdings
www.axa.co.uk

Unionamerica Holdings
www.unionamerica.com

Willis Corroon Group
www.williscorroon.com

leisure

Airtours
www.airtours.com

Camelot Group
www.camelotplc.com

Compass Group
www.compass-group.com

Esporta
www.esporta.co.uk

First Choice Holidays
www.firstchoiceholidaysplc.com

Granada Group
www.granada.co.uk

Hilton Group
www.hiltongroup.com

J D Wetherspoon
www.jdwetherspoon.co.uk

Manchester United
www.manutd.com

PizzaExpress
www.pizzaexpress.co.uk

Rank
www.rank.com

Scottish & Newcastle
www.scottish-newcastle.com

Swallow Group
www.vaux-group.co.uk

Thistle Hotels
www.thistlehotels.com

Thomas Cook Group
www.thomascook.com

Thomson Travel Group
www.thomson-holidays.com

Whitbread
www.whitbread.co.uk

livery companies & guilds

Company of Water Conservators
www.waterlco.co.uk

Guild of Air Pilots and Air Navigators
www.gapan.org

Mercer's Company
www.mercers.co.uk

Worshipful Collection of Clock Makers
www.clockmakers.org

Worshipful Company of Bakers
www.bakers.co.uk

Worshipful Company of Barbers
www.barbers.org.uk

Worshipful Company of Carpenters
www.thecarpenterscompany.co.uk

Worshipful Company of Curriers
www.btinternet.com/~kestrels

Worshipful Company of Engineers
www.engineerscompany.org.uk

Worshipful Company of Fan Makers
www.fanmakers.co.uk

Worshipful Company of Farriers
www.wcf.org.uk

Worshipful Company of Framework Knitters
www.frameworkknitters.co.uk

Worshipful Company of Goldsmiths
www.thegoldsmiths.co.uk

Worshipful Company of Grocers
www.grocershall.co.uk

Worshipful Company of Information Technologists
www.wcit.org.uk

Worshipful Company of Ironmongers
www.ironhall.co.uk

Worshipful Company of Makers of Playing Cards
www.epcs.mcmail.com/worshipful.html

Worshipful Company of Marketors
www.marketors.fsnet.co.uk

Worshipful Company of Professional Turners
www.rpturners.co.uk

Worshipful Company of Scientific Instrument Makers
www.wcsim.co.uk

Worshipful Company of Spectaclemakers
www.spectaclemakers.com

Worshipful Company of Stationers and Newspaper Makers
www.stationers.org

Worshipful Company of Upholders
www.upholders.co.uk

Worshipful Company of Wax Chandlers
www.waxchandlershall.co.uk

Worshipful Company of World Traders
www.world-traders.org

Worshipful Society of Apothecaries
www.apothecaries.org

magazines & websites

Accountancy
www.accountancymag.co.uk

Accountancy Age
www.accountancyage.co.uk

Banker
www.thebanker.com

Business Week
www.businessweek.com

Campaign
www.campaignlive.com

Economist
www.economist.co.uk

Euromoney
www.euromoneydirectory.com

European Business Forum
www.europeanbusinessforum.com

Farmers Weekly
www.fwi.co.uk

Forbes
www.forbes.com

Harvard Business Review
www.hbsp.harvard.edu/groups/hbr

Investment Week
www.invweek.co.uk

Law Society Gazette
www.lawgazette.co.uk

Lloyd's List
www.llplimited.com

Marketing
www.marketing.haynet.com

Media Week
www.mediaweek.co.uk

Retail Week
www.retailing.co.uk

Reuters Money Network
www.moneynet.com

Yahoo Finance
http://biz.yahoo.com

manufacturing

Anti-Counterfeiting Group
www.a-cg.com

Arjo Wiggins Appleton
www.paperpoint.co.uk

Avon Rubber
www.avonrubber.co.uk

Berisford
www.berisford.co.uk

Britax International
www.britax.com

Coats Viyella
www.coats-viyella.com

Courtaulds
www.courtaulds.com

First Technology
www.firsttech.co.uk

FKI
www.fki.co.uk

GKN
www.gknplc.com

Laird
www.laird-plc.com

Morgan Crucible
www.morgancrucible.com

Pilkington
www.pilkington.com

Reckitt Benckiser
www.reckitt.com

TI
www.tigroup.com

Tomkins
www.tomkins.co.uk

TT
www.ttgroup.com

Weir
www.weir.co.uk

materials & construction

AAF Industries
www.aaf.co.uk

Barratt Developments
www.ukpg.co.uk/barratt

Bellway
www.bellway.co.uk

Berkeley Group
www.berkeleygroup.com

BICC
www.bicc.com

Blue Circle
www.bluecircle.co.uk

Bovis Construction
www.bovis.com

Bryant Group
www.bryant.co.uk

Caradon
www.caradon.com

Costain
www.costain.com

George Wimpey
www.wimpey.co.uk

Hanson
www.hansonplc.com

John Laing
www.john-laing.com

Persimmon
www.persimmon.plc.uk

Readymix
www.readymix.com

Rockwool
www.hardrock.co.uk

Rugby Group
www.rugbygroup.co.uk

Shanks
www.shanks.co.uk

Tarmac
www.tarmac.co.uk

Taylor Woodrow
www.taywood.co.uk

Travis Perkins
www.travisperkins.co.uk

Vibroplant
www.vibroplant.com

media

British Sky Broadcasting
www.sky.co.uk

Capital Radio
www.capitalradio.plc.uk

Carat
www.carat.com

Carlton Communications
www.carltonplc.co.uk

Daily Mail & General Trust
www.dmgt.co.uk

Flextech
www.flextech.co.uk

Johnston Press
www.johnstonpress.co.uk

Newsquest
www.newsquest.co.uk

Reed Elsevier
www.reed-elsevier.com

Reuters
www.reuters.com

Scottish Media Group
www.scottishmedia.com

United News & Media
www.unm.com

Virgin
www.virgin.com

metals & mining

Anglo American
www.angloamerican.co.uk

Bodycote International
www.bodycote.com

Corus Group
www.corusgroup.com

Johnson Matthey
www.matthey.com

Metal Bulletin
www.metalbulletin.plc.uk

Rio Tinto
www.riotinto.com

model agencies

Elisabeth Smith
www.elisabethsmith.co.uk

Elite
www.elitepremier.com

Models 1
www.models1.co.uk

Scallywags
www.scallywags.co.uk

Storm
www.stormmodels.com

office supplies & services

Bigron
www.bigron.co.uk

The Cartridge Company
www.inkjet-supplies-cartridges.co.uk

Conqueror
www.conqueror.com

Cucumberman
www.cucumberman.com

Filofax
www.filofax.com

Ikon
www.ikon.com

Kall Kwik
www.kallkwik.co.uk

NCR
www.ncr.com

Office World
www.officeworld.co.uk

Pilot Pens
www.pilotpen.co.uk

Pitney Bowes
www.pitneybowes.com/uk

Prontaprint
www.prontaprint.co.uk

Regus
www.regus.com

Ricoh
www.ricoh.com

Ryman
www.ryman.co.uk

Spicers
www.spicersnet.com

Tibbett & Britten
www.tibbet-britten.com

Viking
www.viking-direct.co.uk

Wordflow
www.wordflow.co.uk

paper & packaging

Abbey Corrugated
www.abbeycorrugated.co.uk

Bunzl
www.bunzl.com

David S Smith
www.davidssmith.com

Rexam
www.rexam.co.uk

Tetrapak
www.tetrapak.com

pharmaceutical

Abbott
www.abbott.com

Allergan
www.allergan.com

Amersham International
www.amersham.co.uk

Asta Medica
www.astamedica.com

AstraZeneca
www.astrazeneca.com

Aventis
www.aventis.com

BASF
www.basf.com

Bayer
www.bayer.com

Bristol Myers Squibb
www.bms.com

Dura
www.durapharm.com

Eli Lilly
www.lilly.com

Fischer
www.dr-fischer.com

Glaxo Wellcome
www.glaxowellcome.com

Hoechst
www.hoechst.com

Johnson & Johnson
www.jnj.com

Medeva
www.medeva.co.uk

Merck
www.merck.com

Monsanto
www.monsanto.com

Novartis
www.novartis.com

Novo Nordisk
www.novo.dk

Nycomed Amersham
www.amersham.co.uk

Organon
www.organon.com

Pfizer
www.pfizer.com

Roche
www.roche.com

Schering-Plough
www.schering-pl.it

Searle
www.monsanto.com

Shire Pharmaceuticals Group
www.shiregroup.com

SmithKline Beecham
www.sb.com

Solvay
www.solvay.com

Takeda
www.takedapharm.com

3M
www.3m.com

UniChem
www.unichem.co.uk

Warner Lambert
www.warner-lambert.com

printing & publishing

Associated News
www.associatednewspapers.co.uk

Blackwell
www.blackwellpublishers.co.uk

Bloomsbury
www.bloomsbury.com

Butterworth Heinemann
www.bh.com

Butterworths
www.butterworths.co.uk

Cambridge University Press
www.cup.cam.ac.uk

DC Thomson
www.dcthomson.co.uk

Dorling Kindersley
www.dk.com

Earthscan
www.earthscan.co.uk

Eastern Counties Newspapers
www.ecn.co.uk

Express Newspapers
www.expressnewspapers.co.uk

Ginn
www.ginn.co.uk

Harper Collins
www.harpercollins.co.uk

Heinemann
www.heinemann.co.uk

HMSO
www.hmso.gov.uk

Hodder & Stoughton
www.hodder.co.uk

Kogan Page
www.kogan-page.co.uk

Macmillan
www.macmillan.co.uk

McGraw-Hill
www.mcgraw-hill.co.uk

Metro
www.metro-books.demon.co.uk

Miller Freeman
www.mfplc.co.uk

Minerva Press
www.minerva-press.co.uk

News International
www.newscorp.com

Orbit
www.orbitbooks.co.uk

Osborne Books
www.osbornebooks.co.uk

Oxford University Press
www.oup.co.uk

Paragon
www.paragon.co.uk

Pearson
www.pearson.co.uk

Penguin
www.penguin.co.uk

Puffin
www.puffin.co.uk

Random House
www.randomhouse.co.uk

Reed
www.reedbusiness.com

Rough Guides
www.roughguides.com

Simon & Schuster
www.simonsays.com

St Ives
www.st-ives.co.uk

Sweet & Maxwell
www.smlawpub.co.uk

Thomson
www.thomson.com

Thorsons
www.thorsons.com

Time Warner
www.timeinc.com

Trinity Mirror
www.trinity.plc.uk

Usborne Publishing
www.usborne.com

Western Newspapers
www.westpress.co.uk

Wiley
www.wiley.com

private investigators

Association of British Investigators
www.uklegal.com/abi

Carratu
www.carratu.com

Dun & Bradstreet
www.dnb.com

Institute of Professional Investigators
www.ipi.org.uk

International Federation of Associations of Private Investigators
www.i-k-d.com

Nationwide Investigations Group
www.nig.co.uk

professional bodies

British Airline Pilots Association
www.balpa.org.uk

professional bodies & associations

Academy of Experts
www.academy-experts.org

Accounting Standards Body
www.asb.org.uk

Advertising Association
www.adassoc.org-uk

Agricultural Engineers Association
www.aea.uk.com

Association of Accounting Technicians
www.aat.co.uk

Association of Chartered Certified Accountants
www.acca.co.uk

Association of Consulting Engineers
www.acenet.co.uk

Association of Corporate Treasurers
www.corporate-treasurers.co.uk

Association of Fundraising Consultants
www.afc.org.uk

Association of International Accountants
www.a-i-a.org.uk

Association of Investment Trust Companies
www.aitc.co.uk

Association of Personal Injury Lawyers
www.apil.com

Association of Private Client Investment Managers & Stockbrokers
www.apcims.org

Association of Qualitative Research Practitioners
www.aqrp.co.uk

Association of Unit Trusts & Investment Funds (AUTIF)
www.investmentfunds.org.uk

British Association of Professional Draftsmen
www.drafter.co.uk

British Women Pilots' Association
www.bwpa.demon.co.uk

British Women Racing Drivers Club
www.autolinkuk.co.uk/bwrdc

Charted Institute of Environmental Health Officers
www.cieh.org.uk/cieh

Chartered Institute of Marketing
www.cim.co.uk

Chartered Institute of Patent Agents
www.cipa.org.uk

Chartered Institute of Public Finance & Accountancy
http://cipfa.sift.co.uk

Chartered Institute of Taxation
www.tax.org.uk

Chartered Institute of Transport
www.citrans.org.uk

European Central Securities Depositories Association
www.ecsda.com

Factors & Discounters Association
www.factors.org.uk

Financial Accounting Standards Board
www.fasb.org

Financial Reporting Council
www.frc.org.uk

Hotel & Catering International Management Association
www.hcima.org.uk

Incorporated Society of British Advertisers
www.isba.org.uk

Institute of Chartered Accountants
www.icaew.co.uk

Institute of Chartered Accountants of Scotland
www.icas.org.uk

Institute of Chartered Engineers
www.ice.org.uk

Institute of Financial Accountants
www.ifa.org.uk

Institute of Internal Auditors
www.iia.org.uk

Institute of Practitioners in Advertising
www.ipa.co.uk

International Federation of Accountants
www.ifac.org

Law Society
www.law-services.org.uk

London Investment Bank Association
www.liba.org.uk

Securities Institute
www.securities-institute.org.uk

Society of Authors
www.writer.org.uk/society

Society of Freelance Editors and Proofreaders
www.sfep.demon.co.uk

Society of Indexers
www.socind.demon.co.uk

Society of Insolvency Practitioners
www.spi.org.uk

Society of Investment Professionals
www.iimr.org.uk

Writers' Guild of Great Britain
www.writers.org.uk/guild

professions

Accountants

Arthur Andersen
www.arthurandersen.com

Baker Tilly
www.bakertilly.co.uk

BDO Stoy Hayward
www.bdo.co.uk

Blick Rothenberg
www.blickrothenberg.com

Deloitte & Touche
www.deloitte-touche.co.uk

Ernst & Young
www.ey.com

Fraser Williams
www.fraser-williams.com

Grant Thornton
www.grant-thornton.co.uk

Hacker Young
www.hackeryoung.co.uk

Haines Watts
www.hwca.com

Hamlyns
www.hamlyns.co.uk

Hays Allan
www.haysallan.com

Horwath Clark Whitehill
www.clarkwhitehill.com

Hughes Allen
www.hughes-allen.co.uk

Kidsons Impey
www.kidsons.co.uk

KPMG
www.kpmg.co.uk

Levy Gee
www.levygee.co.uk

Mazars Neville Russell
www.mazars-nr.co.uk

Moores Rowland
www.moores-rowland.co.uk

Pannell Kerr Forster
www.pkf.com

PricewaterhouseCoopers
www.pwcglobal.com

Robson Rhodes
www.robsonrhodes.com

Solicitors

Allen & Overy
www.allenovery.com

Baker & McKenzie
www.bakerinfo.com

Barlow Lyde & Gilbert
www.blg.co.uk

Beachcroft Stanleys
www.beachcroft.co.uk

Berwin Leighton
www.berwinleighton.com

Bird & Bird
www.twobirds.com

Brodies
www.brodies.co.uk

Cameron McKenna
www.cmck.com

Clifford Chance
www.cliffordchance.com

Collyer Bristow
www.collyer-bristow.co.uk

Coudert Brothers
www.coudert.com

Davies Arnold Cooper
www.dac.co.uk

Denton Hall
www.dentonhall.com

Dibb Lupton Alsop
www.dibbluptonalsop.co.uk

DJ Freeman
www.djfreeman.co.uk

Edge & Ellison
www.edge.co.uk

Eversheds
www.eversheds.com

Fenwick Elliot
www.fenwickelliott.co.uk

Field Fisher Waterhouse
www.ffwlaw.com

Freshfields
www.freshfields.com

Gouldens
www.gouldens.com

Harbottle & Lewis
www.harbottle.co.uk

Herbert Smith
www.herbertsmith.com

Jeffrey Green Russell
www.jgrweb.com

Lawrence Graham
www.lawgram.com

Linklaters
www.linklaters.com

Llewelyn Zietman
www.llz.co.uk

Lovell White Durrant
www.lovellwhitedurrant.com

MacFarlanes
www.macfarlanes.com

Maclay Murray & Spens
www.maclaymurrayspens.co.uk

McGrigor Donald
www.mcgrigors.com

Nabarro Nathanson
www.nabarro.com

Nicholson Graham Jones
www.ngj.co.uk

Norton Rose
www.nortonrose.com

Olswang
www.olswang.co.uk

Paisner & Co
www.paisner.co.uk

Pinsent Curtis
www.pinsent-curtis.co.uk

Shoosmiths
www.shoosmiths.co.uk

Simkins Partnership
www.simkins.com

Simmons & Simmons
www.simmons-simmons.com

Slaughter & May
www.slaughterandmay.com

Taylor Joynson Garrett
www.tjg.co.uk

Theodore Goddard
www.theogoddard.com

real estate

Canary Wharf Group
www.canarywharf.com

Great Portland Estates
www.gpe.co.uk

Land Securities
http://propertymall.com/landsecurities

Slough Estates
www.sloughestates.com

recruitment

Agencies

Adecco
www.adecco.co.uk

Blue Arrow
www.bluearrow.co.uk

Brook Street
www.brookstreet.co.uk

Hays
www.hays-ap.com

Manpower
www.manpower.co.uk

Michael Page
www.michaelpage.com

Pareto Law
www.paretolaw.co.uk

RCR International
www.rcri.co.uk

Reed
www.reed.co.uk

Select Appointments
www.selectgroup.com

Talisman
www.talismanretail.co.uk

Job Listings

BBC
www.bbc.co.uk/jobs

Big Blue Dog
www.bigbluedog.com

Guardian
www.jobsunlimited.co.uk

Job Hunter
www.jobhunter.co.uk

Jobs Unlimited
www.jobsunlimited.co.uk

Monster
www.monster.co.uk

Stepstone
www.stepstone.co.uk

Top Jobs
www.topjobs.net

Total Jobs
www.totaljobs.com

Yahoo! Classifieds
uk.classifieds.yahoo.com/uk/emp

retail

Arcadia
www.arcadia.co.uk

Asda
www.asda.co.uk

Body Shop
www.the-body-shop.com

Boots
www.boots-plc.com

Debenhams
www.debenhams.co.uk

Dixons
www.dixons-group-plc.co.uk

Great Universal Stores
www.gusplc.co.uk

House of Fraser
www.hofbi.co.uk

Iceland
www.iceland.co.uk

J Sainsbury
www.j-sainsbury.co.uk

JJB Sports
www.jjb.co.uk

John Lewis Partnership
www.john-lewis-partnership.co.uk

Kingfisher
www.kingfisher.co.uk

Marks & Spencer
www.marks-and-spencer.com

MFI Furniture
www.mfigroup.co.uk

Next
www.next.co.uk

Safeway
www.safeway.co.uk

Selfridges
www.selfridges.co.uk

Somerfield
www.somerfield.co.uk

Storehouse
www.storehouse.co.uk

Tesco
www.tesco.co.uk

WH Smith
www.whsmithgroup.com

Wm. Morrison Supermarkets
www.morrisons.plc.uk

Wolsey
www.wolsey.com

services

Accenture (Andersen Consulting)
www.accenture.com

Association of Exhibition Organisers
www.aeo.org

Avis Europe
www.avis-europe.com

British Franchise Association
www.franchise.org.uk

British Security Association
www.bsia.co.uk

Capita Group
www.capitagroup.co.uk

Chartered Institute of Marketing
www.cim.co.uk

Chartered Institute of Purchasing & Supply
www.cips.org

Christie's International
www.christies.com

Confederation of British Industry
www.cbi.org.uk

De La Rue
www.delarue.com

Federation of Small Business
www.fsb.org.uk

Hays
www.hays-plc.com

Insitute of Export
www.export.org.uk

Photo-Me International
www.photo-me.co.uk

Rentokil
www.rentokil.co.uk

Rentokil Initial
www.rentokil-initial.com

Tempus Group
www.tempusgroup.co.uk

Williams
www.williams-plc.com

shipping & shipbuilding

BP Marine
www.bpmarine.com

Fairplay
www.fairplay.co.uk

Geest Line
www.geestline.co.uk

Harland and Wolff Holdings PLC
www.harland-wolff.com

Harrison Line
www.harrisons.co.uk

Institute of Chartered Shipbrokers
www.ics.org.uk

Maersk Company
www.maersk.co.uk

Medway Ports
www.medwayports.com

Norman Shipping Group
www.norman.co.uk

Port of Kawasaki
www.city.kawasaki.jp/english

Port of Antwerp
www.portofantwerp.be

Port of Bordeaux
www.bordeaux-port.fr

Port of Larne
www.portoflarne.co.uk

Port of Liverpool
www.portofliverpool.co.uk

Port of London
www.portoflondon.co.uk

Port of Marseilles
www.marseillesportservices.com

Port of Montreal
www.port-montreal.com

Port of Oostende
www.portofoostende.be

Port of Osaka
www.optc.or.jp

Port of Quebec
www.portquebec.ca

Port of Reykjavik
www.rvk.is/hofnin

Port of Zeebrugge
www.zeebruggeport.be

standards

Qualifications and Curriculum Authority
www.qca.org.uk

Qualifications for Industry
www.qfi.co.uk

stock & commodity exchanges & financial listings

America
www.amex.com

Amsterdam
www.aex.nl

Australia
www.asx.com.au

Baltic Exchange
www.balticexchange.co.uk

Berlin
www.berlinerboerse.de

Bermuda
www.bsx.com

Brussels
www.stockexchange.be

Bucharest
www.bvb.ro

Cayman
www.csx.com.ky

Chicago
www.chicagostockex.com

Dow Jones
www.dowjones.com

EASDAQ
www.easdaq.be

Frankfurt
www.exchange.de

Helsinki
www.hse.fi

Hong Kong
www.sehk.com.hk

International Petroleum Exchange (IPE)
www.ipe.uk.com

Johannesburg
www.jse.co.za

LIFFE
www.liffe.com

Lisbon
www.bvl.pt

London
www.londonstockex.co.uk

London Clearing House
www.lch.co.uk

London Metal Exchange
www.lme.co.uk

Madrid
www.bolsamadrid.es

Montreal
www.me.org

NASDAQ
www.nasdaq.com

New York
www.nyse.com

Paris
www.bourse-de-paris.fr

Stockholm
www.xsse.se

Switzerland
www.swx.ch

Taiwan
www.tse.com.tw

Tokyo
www.tse.or.jp

Toronto
www.tse.com

Vancouver
www.vse.ca

Warsaw
www.gpw.com.pl

telecommunications

British Telecommunications
www.bt.com

Cable & Wireless
www.cwplc.com

COLT Telecom Group
www.colt-telecom.com

Energis
www.energis.co.uk

Freeserve
www.freeserve.net

Marconi
www.marconi.com

Orange
www.orange.co.uk

Telewest Communications
www.telewest.co.uk

Vodafone AirTouch
www.vodafone-airtouch-plc.com

trade associations

Association for Consultants & Trainers
www.act-assn.dircon.co.uk

Association for Information Management
www.aslib.co.uk

Association of Car Fleet Operators
www.bizjet.com/fleet

Association of Direct Labour Organisation
www.adlo.org.uk

Association of European Travel Agents International
www.aeta.co.uk

Association of Independent Tour Operator
www.aito.co.uk

Association of Master Upholsters & Soft Furnishers
www.upholsterers.co.uk

Association of National Tourist Offices
www.tourist-offices.org.uk

Association of Plastic Manufacturers
www.apme.org

Association of Play Industries
www.playindustries.org

Association of Residential Letting Agents
www.arla.co.uk

Association of Suppliers to the British Clothing Industry
www.ntu.ac.uk/fas/asbci

Association of Suppliers to the Furniture Industry
www.asfi.org

Balloon Association
www.nabas.co.uk

Booksellers Association
www.booksellers.org.uk

British Aerosol Manufacturers Association
www.bama.co.uk

British Antique Furniture Restorers Association
www.bafra.org.uk

British Apparel and Textile Confederation
www.batc.co.uk

British Association of Picture Libraries
www.bapla.org.uk

British Contract Furnishing Association
www.bcfa.org.uk

British Furniture Manufacturers
www.bfm.org.uk

British Healthcare Trades Association
www.bhta.com

British Jewellers Association
www.bja.org.uk

British Marine Industries Federation
www.marinedata.co.uk/bmif

British Office Systems and Stationery Federation
www.bossfed.co.uk

British Printing Industries Federation
www.bpif.org.uk

British Toy & Hobby Association
www.btha.co.uk

Butlers Guild
www.butlersguild.com

Federation of Recruitment and Employment Services
www.fres.co.uk

Federation of the Electronics Industry
www.fei.org.uk

Giftware Association
www.giftware.org.uk

Grain and Feed Trade Association (GAFTA)
www.gafta.com

Independent Financial Advisers Association (IFA Association)
www.ifaa.org.uk

Independent Publishers Guild
www.ipg.uk.com

Institute of Building Control
www.building-control.org

Institute of Packaging
www.iop.co.uk

Institute of Paper
www.instpaper.org.uk

Institute of Printing
www.globalprint.com/uk/iop

Institute of the Motor Industry
www.motor.org.uk

International Association for the Protection of Industrial Property
www.aippi.org

Kitchen Specialists Association
www.ksa.co.uk

National Association of Goldsmiths
www.on-lineappraiser.com

National Association of Paper Merchants
www.napm.org.uk

National Housing Federation
www.housing.org.uk

Newspaper Society
www.newspapersoc.org.uk

Periodical Publishers Association
www.ppa.co.uk

Printmakers Council
www.printmaker.co.uk/pmc

Scottish Newspaper Publishers Association
www.snpa.org.uk

Screen Printers Association
www.martex.co.uk

Shipbuilders & Shiprepairers Association
www.ssa.org.uk

Tobacco Manufacturers' Association
www.the-tma.org.uk

UK Aromatherapy Practitioners & Suppliers
www.fragrant.demon.co.uk/ukaromas.html

trades unions

Amalgamated Engineering & Electrical (AEEU)
www.aeew.org.uk

Associated Society of Locomotive Engineers & Fireman
www.aslef.org.uk

Association of University Teachers
www.aut.org.uk

Broadcasting Entertainment Cinematograph and Theatre Union (BECTU)
www.bectu.org.uk

Communications Workers Union (CWU)
www.cwu.org

Graphic and Printworkers Union (GPMU)
www.gpmu.org.uk

Institution of Professionals Managers and Specialists (IPMS)
www.ipms.org.uk

International Federation of Chemical, Energy, Mine & General Workers Unions
www.icem.org

Knitting, Footwear & Textile Workers (KFAT)
www.kfat.org.uk

Musicians Union
www.musiciansunion.org.uk

National Association of School Masters Union of Women Teachers (NASUWT)
www.teachersunion.org.uk

National Union of Journalists (NUJ)
www.gn.apc.org/media/nuj.html

National Union of Teachers (NUT)
www.teachers.org.uk

Public and Commercial Services Union
www.ptc.org.uk

Transport & General Workers Union
www.tgwu.org.uk

Transport Salaried Staffs Association
www.tssa.org.uk

TUC
www.tuc.org.uk

Union of Shop, Distributive & Allied Workers (USDAW)
www.poptel.org.uk/usdaw

Unison
www.unison.org.uk

transport

ARRIVA
www.arriva.co.uk

Associated British Ports
www.abports.co.uk

BAA
www.baa.co.uk

British Airways
www.british-airways.com

Chamber of Shipping
www.british-shipping.org

Eurotunnel
www.eurotunnel.co.uk

FirstGroup
www.firstgroup.com

Go-Ahead
www.go-ahead.com

Lloyds Register
www.lr.org

Mersey Docks & Harbour Company
www.merseydocks.co.uk

National Express
www.nationalexpress.co.uk

NFC
www.nfc.co.uk

Ocean
www.oceangroup.uk.com

Railtrack
www.railtrack.co.uk

Road Haulage Association
www.rha.net

Sea Containers
www.seacontainers.com

Stagecoach Holdings
www.stagecoachholdings.com

us corporations

AlliedSignal
www.alliedsignal.com

Amerada Hess
www.hess.com

American Electric Power
www.aep.com

American Express
www.americanexpress.com

American Home Products
www.ahp.com

American Standard
www.americanstandard.com

Amoco
www.bpamoco.com

Apple
www.apple.com

AT&T
www.att.com

BankAmerica Corp.
www.bankamerica.com

Barnes & Noble
www.barnesandnoble.com

Bell Atlantic
www.bell-atl.com

Black & Decker
www.blackanddecker.com

Boeing
www.boeing.com

CBS
www.cbs.com

Cendant
www.cendant.com

Chase Manhattan Corp.
www.chase.com

Chevron
www.chevron.com

Chubb
www.chubb.com

Coca-Cola
www.thecoca-colacompany.com

Colgate-Palmolive
www.colgate.com

Computer Associates
www.compusa.com

Continental Airlines
www.flycontinental.com

Delta Airlines
www.delta-air.com

Dow Chemical
www.dow.com

Du Pont
www.dupont.com

Eastman Kodak
www.kodak.com

Electronic Data Systems
www.eds.com

Eli Lilly
www.lilly.com

Exxon
www.exxon.com

Federal Express
www.fedex.com

Ford Motor
www.ford.com

General Electric
www.ge.com

General Mills
www.generalmills.com

General Motors
www.gm.com

Goodyear
www.goodyear.com

Hershey Foods
www.hersheys.com

Hewlett Packard
www.hewlett-packard.com

Hilton Hotels
www.hilton.com

Honeywell
www.honeywell.com

Intel
www.intel.com

J C Penney
www.jcpenney.com

Johnson & Johnson
www.jnj.com

JP Morgan
www.jpmorgan.com

Kelloggs
www.kelloggs.com

Kimberly-Clark
www.kimberly-clark.com

Lockheed Martin
www.lockheedmartin.com

Manpower
www.manpower.com

McDonald's
www.mcdonalds.com

McGraw-Hill
www.mcgraw-hill.com

Merck
www.merck.com

Merrill Lynch
www.ml.com

Microsoft
www.microsoft.com

Monsanto
www.monsanto.com

Morgan Stanley Dean Witter Discover
www.deanwitterdiscover.com

NCR
www.ncr.com

Nickelodeon
www.nick.com

Occidental Petroleum
www.oxy.com

Paramount Pictures
www.paramount.com

PepsiCo
www.pepsico.com

Pfizer
www.pfizer.com

Pharmacia & Upjohn
www.pharmacia.se

Philip Morris
www.pmdocs.com

Proctor & Gamble
www.pg.com

Quaker Oats
www.quakeroats.com

Reader's Digest Association
www.readersdigest.com

RJR Nabisco Holdings
www.rjrnabisco.com

Rockwell International
www.rockwell.com

Sara Lee
www.saralee.com

Schering-Plough
www.sch-plough.com

Sears Roebuck
www.sears.com

Texas Instruments
www.ti.com

Time Warner
www.pathfinder.com/corp

Union Carbide
www.unioncarbide.com

Union Pacific
www.up.com

Unisys
www.unisys.com

United Airlines
www.ual.com

United Parcel Service
www.ups.com

United Technologies
www.utc.com

Viacom
www.viacom.com

Wal-Mart
www.wal-mart.com

Walt Disney
www.disney.go.com

Warner-Lambert
www.warner-lambert.com

Whirlpool
www.whirlpool.com

Xerox
www.xerox.com

utilities

Anglian Water
www.anglianwater.co.uk

BG
www.bg-group.com

British Energy
www.british-energy.com

British Nuclear Fuels
www.bnfl.co.uk

Centrica
www.centrica.co.uk

Eastern
www.eastern.co.uk

Kelda
www.keldagroup.com

National Grid
www.ngc.co.uk

National Power
www.national-power.com

Pennon Group
www.pennon-group.co.uk

Powergen
www.pgen.com

Scottish & Southern Energy
www.scottish-southern.co.uk

Scottish Power
www.scottishpower.plc.uk

Severn Trent
www.severn-trent.com

Thames Water
www.thames-water.com

United Utilities
www.unitedutilities.com

Viridian Group
www.viridiangroup.co.uk

cartoon characters ●

clubs & activities ●

computer games ●

days out ●

film & television ●

games & toys ●

homework & revision ●

magazines, books & authors ●

theatre ●

websites ●

children

SurfControl®

The Filtering Company

www.surfcontrol.com

cartoon characters

Asterix
www.asterix.tm.fr

Batman
www.batman.com

Beavis and Butthead
www.beavis-butthead.com

Bugs Bunny
www.cartoonnetwork.com/bugs

Captain America
www.winghead.org

Captain Marvel
http://shazam.imginc.com

Casper
www.harvey.com/comics/04/index.shtml

Daffy Duck
www.cartoonnetwork.com/daffy

Danger Mouse
www.dangermouse.org

Dick Tracy
http://dicktracy.comicspage.com

Dilbert
www.unitedmedia.com/comics/dilbert

Doonesbury
www.doonesbury.com

Dumbo
www.disney.go.com

Felix the Cat
www.felixthecat.com

Flash Gordon
www.kingfeatures.com/features/comics/fgordon/about.htm

Flintstones
http://members.optushome.com.au/webrock

Fred Basset
http://fredbasset.comicspage.com

Garfield
www.garfield.com

Hagar the Horrible
www.kingfeatures.com/comics/hagar

Inspector Gadget
www.inspector-gadget.net

Marmaduke
www.unitedmedia.com/comics/marmaduke

Noggin The Nog
www.nogginthenog.co.uk

Pokemon
www.pokemon.com

Popeye
www.kingfeatures.com/features/comics/popeye/about.htm

Road Runner
www.itr.qc.ca/~mario/roadrunner.htm

Scooby Doo
www.cartoonnetwork.com/scooby

Simpsons
www.thesimpsons.com

Spiderman
www.kingfeatures.com/comics/spiderman

Teenage Mutant Ninja Turtles
www.ninjaturtles.com

Tom and Jerry
http://tomandjerrythemovie.warnerbros.com

X-men
www.x-men.com

clubs & activities

Boys' Brigade
www.boys-brigade.org.uk

Crusaders
www.crusaders.org.uk

Duke of Edinburgh Award
www.theaward.org

Girl Guides
www.guides.org.uk

National Rounders Association
http://rounders.punters.co.uk

Ocean Youth Trust
www.oyc.org.uk

Pony Club
www.pony-club.org.uk

Roald Dahl Club
www.roalddahlclub.com

ScoutNet
www.scoutnet.org.uk

Scouts
www.scoutbase.org.uk

Sea Cadets
www.btinternet.com/~sailmaster

Tumbletots
www.tumbletots.com

computer games

Console Domain
www.consoledomain.com

Nintendo
www.nintendo.com

PlayStation
www.playstation.com

Sega
www.sega.com

Sega Dreamcast
www.dreamcast-europe.com

days out

Adventure Island
www.adventureisland.co.uk

Alton Towers
www.alton-towers.co.uk

American Adventure Theme Park
www.adventureworld.co.uk

Babbacombe Model Village
www.babbacombemodelvillage.co.uk

Barry Island Pleasure Park
www.pleasurepark.co.uk

Bekonscot Model Village
www.bekonscot.org.uk

Bingham's Park Farm
www.binghams.co.uk

Blackpool Pleasure Beach
www.bpbltd.com

Blackpool Tower
www.blackpool.gov.uk/tower.htm

Brighton Palace Pier
www.brightonpier.co.uk

Cedarpoint
www.cedarpoint.com

Chessington World of Adventure
www.chessington.co.uk

Crealy Park
www.crealy.co.uk

Dome
www.dome2000.co.uk

Drayton Manor
www.draytonmanor.co.uk

Eureka!
www.eureka.org.uk

Fantasy Island
www.fantasyisland.co.uk

Flambards Village
www.flambards.co.uk

Football World
www.football-world.co.uk

Great Yarmouth Pleasure Beach
www.pleasure-beach.co.uk

Harbour Park
www.harbourpark.com

Heron's Brook
www.herons-brook.co.uk

Kidsnet
www.kidsnet.co.uk

Kidstravel
www.kidstravel.co.uk

Lands End
www.landsend-landmark.co.uk

Legoland
www.legoland.co.uk

Lightwater Valley
www.lightwatervalley.co.uk

Louden Castle
www.loudencastle.co.uk

Lowther Leisure & Wildlife Park
www.lowtherpark.co.uk

Oakwood Park
www.oakwood-leisure.com

Plan It For Kids
www.planit4kids.com

Pleasure Island
www.pleasure-island.co.uk

Pleasureland
www.pleasureland.uk.com

Secret Bunker St Andrews
www.secretbunker.co.uk

Southend on Sea Pier
www.digitalessex.com/pages/southend/index.shtml

Thorpe Park
www.thorpepark.co.uk

Wicksteed Park
www.wicksteedpark.co.uk

film & television

Animal Zone
www.bbc.co.uk/animalzone

Antz
www.antz.com

Art Attack
www.artattack.co.uk

Barney
www.barneyonline.com

Batman & Robin
www.batman-robin.com

BBC Schools
www.bbc.co.uk/education/schools

Bill Nye the Science Guy
www.disney.com/disneytelevision/billnye

Blue Peter
www.bbc.co.uk/bluepeter

Bob the Builder
www.bobthebuilder.org

The Borrowers
www.britfilms/detail/?film=BF00100533118

Bug's Life
www.abugslife.com

Cartoon Network
www.cartoon-network.co.uk

CBBC
www.bbc.co.uk/cbbc

Channel 4 Schools
www.schools.channel4.com

CITV
www.itv.co.uk/citv

Clangers
www.clangers.co.uk

Close Shave
www.aardman.com/wallaceandgromit/films/acloseshave

Dennis the Menace
www.kingfeatures.com/comics/dennis.gif

Discovery Channel
www.discovery.com

Disney Channel
www.disneychannel.co.uk

Fairy Tale
www.fairytalemovie.com

Flash Gordon
www.kingfeatures.com/comics/flashg.gif

4Learning
www.4learning.co.uk

Fox Kids
www.foxkids.co.uk

Garfield
www.garfield.com

Hercules
www.herc.co.uk

Hyperlinks
www.bbc.co.uk/hyperlinks

Little Mermaid
www.thelittlemermaid.com

Live & Kicking
www.bbc.co.uk/kicking

Mighty Morphin' Power Rangers
www.foxkids.com/power_rangers

Mulan
www.mulan.com

Munsters
www.munsters.com

Muppets
www.muppets.com

Muppets from Space
www.muppetsfromspace.com

Newsround
www.bbc.co.uk/newsround

Nickelodeon
www.nicktv.co.uk

Pokemon the First Movie
www.pokemonthemovie.com

Popeye
www.kingfeatures.com/comics/popeye

Rugrats
www.cooltoons.com/shows/rugrats

Rugrats the Movie
www.nick.com/rugrats.tin

Sabrina the Teenage Witch
www.paramount.com/tvsabrina

Sesame Street
www.sesamestreet.com

Simpsons
http://thesimpsons.com

Star Trek
www.startrek.com

Star Wars
www.starwars.com

Tarzan
www.tarzan.co.uk

Teddy Bears
www.theteddybears.com

Teletubbies
www.teletubbies.com

Thunderbirds
www.thunderbirdsonline.com

Top of the Pops
www.totp.beeb.com

Tweenies
www.bbc.co.uk/education/tweenies

Universal Studios
www.universalstudios.com

Wallace & Gromit
www.aardman.com

Warner Bros
www.kids.warnerbros.com

Wombles
www.mikebatt.com/wombles

Xena Warrior Princess
www.mca.com/tv/xena

games & toys

Airfix Models
www.airfix.com

Barbie
www.barbie.com

Beanie Babies
www.ty.com

Brio
www.brio.co.uk

Cluedo
www.cluedo.com

Corgi
www.corgi.co.uk

Crayola
www.crayola.com

Fisher Price
www.fisher-price.com

Furbys
www.furbys.co.uk

Hasbro
www.hasbro.com

Hasbro Interactive
www.hasbro-interactive.com

Hornby
www.hornby.co.uk

Knex
www.knex.co.uk

Lego
www.lego.com

Little Tikes
www.rubbermaid.com/littletikes

Matchbox
www.matchboxtoys.com

Mattel
www.mattel.com

Meccano
www.meccano.co.uk

Monopoly
www.monopoly.com

Mr Potato Head
www.mrpotatohead.com

Panini
www.panini.co.uk

Playmobil
www.playmobil.de

Pokemon
www.pokemon.com

Quadro
www.quadro-toys.co.uk

Scalextric
www.scalextric.co.uk

Scrabble
www.scrabble.com

Tomy
www.tomy.co.uk

Trivial Pursuits
www.trivialpursuit.com

Young Embroiderers
www.hiraeth.com/ytg

homework & revision

A-levels
www.a-levels.co.uk

Bitesize Revision
www.bbc.co.uk/education/revision

BJ Pinchbeck Homework Helper
www.bjpinchbeck.com

Freeserve Revision
www.freeserve.net/education/examrevision

GCSE Answers
www.gcse.com

GCSE Bitesize Revision
www.bbc.co.uk/education/gcsebitesize

Homework Elephant
www.homeworkelephant.free-online.co.uk

Homework High
www.homeworkhigh.com

Learn
www.learn.co.uk

Learn Free
www.learnfree.co.uk

LineOne Learning
www.lineone.net/learning

Minimus
www.minimus-etc.co.uk

NRICH Primary Maths (University of Cambridge)
www.nrich.maths.org.uk/primary

S-Cool
www.s-cool.co.uk

Schools Online (Science)
www.shu.ac.uk/schools/sci/sol/contents.htm

Thunk.com
www.thunk.com

Topmarks
www.topmarks.co.uk

magazines, books & authors

Anne Fine
www.annefine.co.uk

Beano
www.beano.co.uk

Beatrix Potter
www.peterrabbit.co.uk

Bright Sparks (Junior Mensa Magazine)
www.mensa.org.uk/mensa/junior/magazine.html

British Arthur Ransome Society
www.arthur-ransome.org

Children's Book Council
www.cbcbooks.org

DC Comics
www.dccomics.com

Dorling Kindersley
www.dk.com

Dr Seuss
www.seussville.com

Enid Blyton
www.blyton.com

Eric Carle
www.eric-carle.com

Flash Gordon
www.kingfeatures.com/comics/fgordon

Girl Talk
www.girl-talk.com

Girl's World
www.agirlsworld.com

Goosebumps
www.scholastic.com/goosebumps

Hagar the Horrible
www.kingfeatures.com/comics/hagar

HarperCollins Childrens Books
www.harperchildrens.com

Harry Potter
www.harrypotter.com

Judy Blume
www.judyblume.com

Marvel Comics
www.marvelcomics.com

Miffy
www.miffy.co.uk

Mr Men
www.mrmen.net

National Geographic for Kids
www.nationalgeographic.com/kids

Paddington Bear
www.paddingtonbear.co.uk

Right Start
www.rightstartmagazine.co.uk

Roald Dahl
www.roalddahl.org

Snoopy
www.snoopy.com

Spider Man
www.kingfeatures.com/comics/spiderman

Thomas the Tank Engine
www.thomasthetankengine.com

Tintin
www.tintin.be

Watership Down
www.watershipdown.net

Willie Wonka
www.wonka.com

Winnie the Pooh
www.winniethepooh.co.uk

theatre

Mersey Young Peoples Theatre
www.mypt.uk.com

National Association of Youth Theatre
www.nayt.org.uk

Polka Children's Theatre
www.polkatheatre.com

Puppeteers Company
www.puppco.demon.co.uk

QuickSilver
www.ecna.org/qsilver

websites

Alfy
www.alfy.co.uk

AOL UK Kid's Channel
www.aol.co.uk/channels/kids

Ask Jeeves for Kids
www.ajkids.com

Beanie Babies Official Club
www.beaniebabyofficialclub.com

Bonus.com
www.bonus.com

Brain Teaser
www.brain-teaser.com

Bullying
www.bullying.co.uk

Bullying (BBC)
www.bbc.co.uk/education/bully

Carnegie Museum - Discovery Room
www.carnegiemuseums.org/cmnh/exhibits/permanent/discovery.html

ChildLine
www.childline.org.uk

Compuserve Kids
www.compuserve.com/gateway/kids

Cooking for Kids
www.learnfree.co.uk/cookingforkids/html

Disney Interactive
www.disney.co.uk/disneyinteractive

EcoKids
www.bytesize.com/ecokids

Enchanted Learning
www.enchantedlearning.com

Eplay
www.eplay.com

Galaxy Kids
www.galaxykids.co.uk

How Stuff Works
www.howstuffworks.com

The Junction
www.thej.co.uk

Kids' Almanac
www.kids.infoplease.com

Kids' Crosswords
www.kidcrosswords.com

Kids' Jokes
www.kidsjokes.com

McVities Jaffa Cakes
www.jaffacakes.co.uk

Microsoft Kids
www.microsoft.com/kids

Pooh Corner
www.pooh-corner.com

Pupil Line
www.pupiline.net

Puzzle Up
www.puzzleup.com

RSPCA Kid's Stuff
www.rspca.org.uk/content/kids_stuff.html

Surf Control

www.surfcontrol.com

Warner Bros Kid's Page
www.kids.warnerbros.com

Yahoo! Games
www.games.yahoo.com

Yahooligans!
www.yahooligans.com

agriculture ●

art & architecture ●

ballet, drama & music ●

books, magazines & websites ●

business & law ●

complementary health ●

educational organisations ●

medical & dental ●

postgraduate & research ●

pre-school ●

professional associations ●

schools ●

sport ●

students ●

tuition & part-time learning ●

universities ●

veterinary schools ●

education, training & research

agriculture

Royal Agricultural College
www.royagcol.ac.uk

Scottish Agricultural College
www.sac.ac.uk

art & architecture

Architectural Association School of
Architecture
www.arch-assoc.org.uk

Courtauld Institute
www.courtauld.ac.uk

Glasgow School of Art
www.gsa.ac.uk

Hull School of Architecture
www.humber.ac.uk/arc

Institute of Contemporary Art
www.ica.org.uk

London College of Printing
www.linst.ac.uk/lcp

National Society for Education in Art and
Design
www.nsead.org

National Training Organisation for Arts and
Entertainment (Metier)
www.metier.org.uk

Royal College of Art
www.rca.ac.uk

Ruskin School of Drawing & Fine Art
www.ruskin-sch.ox.ac.uk

Slade
www.ucl.ac.uk/slade

Surrey Institute of Art & Design
www.surrart.ac.uk

ballet, drama & music

Arts Educational London Schools
www.artsed.co.uk

Associated Board of the Royal Schools of
Music
www.abrsm.ac.uk

Birmingham School of Speech & Drama
www.bssd.ac.uk/bssd

Bristol Old Vic Theatre School
www.oldvic.drama.ac.uk

Brit School
www.brit.croydon.sch.uk

Central School of Speech & Drama
www.cssd.ac.uk

Cygnet Training Theatre (Exeter)
www.drama.ac.uk/cygnet.html

Dance School of Scotland
www.scottishballet.co.uk/school/school.htm

De Montfort University
www.dmu.ac.uk

Drama Centre London
http://dcl.drama.ac.uk

East 15 Acting School
http://east15.ac.uk

Elmhurst School for Dance & Performing
Arts
www.elmhurstdance.co.uk

English National Ballet School
www.en-ballet.co.uk/school

Guildhall School of Music & Drama
www.guildhall.drama.ac.uk

Jeremy Whelan
www.jeremy-whelan-acting.com

John Moore's University
www.livjm.ac.uk/university/courses/dance.htm

Lee Strasberg
www.strasberg.com

Liverpool Institute for Performing Arts
www.lipa.ac.uk

London Academy of Music & Dramatic Art
(LAMDA)
www.lamda.org.uk

London Contemporary Dance School
www.theplace.org.uk/html/nav/edfr.htm

London International Film School
www.lifs.org.uk

Manchester Metropolitan University, School
of Theatre
www.artdes.mmu.ac.uk

Mountview Theatre School
www.mountview.ac.uk

National Council for Drama Training
www.ncdt.co.uk

National Film & Television School
www.nftsfilm-tv.ac.uk

North of England College of Dance
www.zebra.co.uk/necd

Northern School of Contemporary Dance
www.nscd.ac.uk

Oxford School of Drama
http://oxford.drama.ac.uk

Queen Margaret College, School of Drama
(Edinburgh)
www.drama.ac.uk/queenm.html

Rambert School
www.brunel.ac.uk/faculty/arts/rambert

Roehampton Institute of Dance
www.roehampton.ac.uk/academic/arts&hum/dance/dance.html

Rose Bruford College of Speech & Drama
www.bruford.ac.uk

Royal Academy of Dramatic Art (RADA)
www.rada.org

Royal Academy of Music
www.ram.ac.uk

Royal Ballet School
www.royal-ballet-school.org.uk

Royal College of Music
www.rcm.ac.uk

Royal Northern College
www.rncm.ac.uk

Royal Scottish Academy of Music & Drama
www.rsamd.ac.uk

Trinity College of Music
www.tcm.ac.uk

University of Surrey
www.surrey.ac.uk/dance

Webber Douglas Academy of Dramatic Art
www.drama.ac.uk/webberd.html

Welsh College of Music & Drama
www.welsh.drama.ac.uk

books, magazines & websites

@School
www.atschool.co.uk

BBC Education
www.bbc.co.uk/education

BT Teaching Awards
www.teachingawards.com

Bullying
www.bullying.co.uk

Education Show
www.education-net.co.uk

Floodlight
www.floodlight.co.uk

Good Schools Guide
www.goodschoolsguide.co.uk

Guide to UK Boarding Schools
www.boarding-schools.com

Incorporated Association of Preparatory Schools
www.iaps.org.uk

Independent Schools Directory
www.indschools.co.uk

Independent Schools Information Service
www.isis.org.uk

Learn
www.learn.co.uk

Maths Maze
www.mathsyear2000.co.uk

National Curriculum
www.nc.uk.net

National Grid for Learning
www.ngfl.gov.uk

Nelson Books
www.nelson.co.uk

On Course
www.oncourse.co.uk

Qualifications & Curriculum Authority
www.qca.org.uk

RM
www.rm.com

Scottish Qualifications Authority
www.sqa.org.uk

Special Educational Needs
www.dfee.gov.uk/sen/senhome.htm

Student Life
www.student-life-magazine.co.uk

Student World
www.student-world.com

Times Educational Supplement
www.tes.co.uk

Times Higher Educational Supplement
www.thesis.co.uk

Times Literary Supplement
www.the-tls.co.uk

business & law

Aberdeen Business School
www.abs.ac.uk

BPP Law School
www.bpp.com

College of Law
www.lawcol.org.uk

London Business School
www.lbs.lon.ac.uk

Manchester Business School
www.mbs.ac.uk

complementary health

Academy of Curative Hypnotherapists
www.ach.co.uk

British College of Naturopathy & Osteopathy
www.bcno.org.uk

British School of Homeopathy
www.homeopathy.co.uk

College of Integrated Chinese Medicine
www.cicm.org.uk

London College of Clinical Hypnosis
www.lcch.co.uk

London College of Traditional Acupuncture & Oriental Medicine
www.lcta.com

Royal College of Speech & Language Therapists
www.rcslt.org

educational organisations

General

Association of Recognised English Language Schools
www.arels.org.uk

Book Trust
www.booktrust.org.uk

Careers Research & Advisory Centre
www.crac.org.uk

Careers Services National Association
www.careers-uk.com

Careers Services Unit
www.prospects.csu.man.ac.uk

Civil Service College
www.open.gov.uk/college/cschome.htm

National Institute of Adult Continuing Education
www.niace.org.uk

National Literacy Trust
www.literacytrust.org.uk

On Course
www.oncourse.co.uk

Scottish Book Trust
www.scottishbooktrust.com

Scottish Council For Research In Education
www.scre.ac.uk

University of London Careers Service
www.careers.lon.ac.uk

Governing Bodies

British Association for Open Learning
www.baol.co.uk

British Educational Communications & Technology Agency (BECTA)
www.becta.org.uk

Central Council for Education and Training in Social Work
www.ccetsw.org.uk

City & Guilds Institute
www.city-and-guilds.co.uk

Higher Education Funding Council for England
www.hefce.ac.uk

Higher Education Funding Council for Scotland
www.shefc.ac.uk/shefc

Higher Education Funding Council for Wales
www.niss.ac.uk/education/hefcw

National Council for Drama Training
www.ncdt.co.uk

National Council for the Training of Journalists
www.nctj.com

Royal Institution of Great Britain
www.ri.ac.uk

Scottish Council for Educational Technology
www.scet.org.uk

Teacher Training Agency
www.teach-tta.gov.uk

Training & Enterprise Councils
www.tec.co.uk

UK Council for Graduate Education
www.wlv.ac.uk/ukcge

medical & dental

Eastman Dental Institute
www.eastman.ucl.ac.uk

Glasgow Caledonian University
www.fhis.gcal.ac.uk

Glasgow Dental School
www.gla.ac.uk/acad/dental

Imperial College of Science, Technology & Medicine
www.ic.ac.uk

King's College School of Medicine & Dentistry
www.smd.kcl.ac.uk

Liverpool School of Tropical Medicine
www.liv.ac.uk/lstm

London Hospital Medical College
www.lhmc.ac.uk

London School of Hygiene & Tropical Medicine
www.lshtm.ac.uk

Royal College of Paediatrics & Child Health
www.rcpch.ac.uk

Royal College of Physicians
www.rcplondon.ac.uk

Royal College of Psychiatrists
www.rcpsych.ac.uk

Royal Free & University College Medical School
www.rfc.ucl.ac.uk

St Bartholomew's & The Royal London School of Medicine & Dentistry
www.mds.qmw.ac.uk

St George's Hospital Medical School
www.sghms.ac.uk

United Medical & Dental Schools of King's, Guy's & St Thomas' Hospitals
www.umds.ac.uk

University of Aberdeen
www.bms.abdn.ac.uk

University of Birmingham School of Medicine
www.medweb.bham.ac.uk

University of Hull
www.hull.ac.uk/hull/health_ps

University of Nottingham
www.nottingham.ac.uk/schools-index.html

University of Southampton
www.medschool.soton.ac.uk

University of Wales, Cardiff
www.uwcm.ac.uk

postgraduate & research

Greenwich Maritime Institute
www.nri.org/gmi

Nuffield Trust
www.nuffieldtrust.org.uk

Royal Academy of Engineers
www.raeng.org.uk

Royal Institute of International Affairs
www.riia.org

Society of Antiquaries
www.sal.org.uk

Tenovus
www.tenovus.org.uk

pre-school

Montessori Foundation
www.montessori.org

Norland Nanny School
www.norland.co.uk

professional associations

Association of Christian Teachers
www.christian-teachers.org

Association of University Administrators
www.aua.ac.ul

schools

Independent

American Community Schools
www.acs-england.co.uk

Gabbitas Guide to Independent Schools
www.gabbitas.net

Incorporated Association of Preparatory Schools
www.iaps.org.uk

Independent Schools Directory
www.indschools.co.uk

Independent Schools Information Service
www.isis.org.uk

Public

Ampleforth
www.ampleforth.org.uk

Benenden
www.benenden.kent.sch.uk

Cheltenham College
www.cheltcoll.gloucs.sch.uk

Dulwich College
www.dulwich.org.uk

Eton College
www.etoncollege.com

Gordonstoun
www.gordonstoun.org.uk

King's
www.ksw.org.uk

Manchester Grammar
www.mgs.org

Millfield
www.millfield.somerset.sch.uk

Oundle
www.oundleschool.org.uk

Roedean
www.roedean.co.uk

Rugby
www.rugby-school.co.uk

Shrewsbury
www.shrewsbury.org.uk

St Paul's
www.stpauls.co.uk

Stowe
www.stowe.co.uk

Uppingham
www.uppingham.co.uk

Westminster
www.westminster.org.uk

Winchester College
www.wincoll.ac.uk

Wrekin College
www.wrekin-college.salop.sch.uk

sport

United States Sports Academy
www.sport.ussa.edu

students

Camp America
www.campamerica.co.uk

National Union of Students
www.nus.org.uk

Student Life Magazine
www.student-life-magazine.co.uk

Student UK
www.studentuk.com

University & Colleges Admissions Service
www.ucas.ac.uk

tuition & part-time learning

Floodlight
www.floodlight.co.uk

Institut Francais
www.institut.ambafrance.org.uk

Kumon Maths
www.kumon.co.uk

Learn Direct
www.learndirect.co.uk

Lifelong Learning (DfEE)
www.lifelonglearning.co.uk

Linguaphone
www.linguaphone.co.uk

National Literacy Trust
www.literacytrust.org.uk

National Organisation for Adult Learning
www.niace.org.uk

Oncourse
www.oncourse.co.uk

University of the Third Age
www.u3a.org.uk

Workers' Educational Association
www.wea.org.uk

universities

Aberdeen
www.abdn.ac.uk

Abertay Dundee
www.abertay-dundee.ac.uk

Aberystwyth
www.aber.ac.uk

American International University
www.richmond.ac.uk

Aston
www.aston.ac.uk

Bangor
www.bangor.ac.uk

Bath
www.bath.ac.uk

Birkbeck College London
www.bbk.ac.uk

Birmingham
www.birmingham.ac.uk

Bournemouth
www.bournemouth.ac.uk

Bradford
www.brad.ac.uk

Brighton
www.bton.ac.uk

Bristol
www.bris.ac.uk

Brunel
www.brunel.ac.uk

Buckinghamshire Chilterns University College
www.buckscol.ac.uk

Cambridge
www.cam.ac.uk

Canterbury Christ Church University College
www.cant.ac.uk

Cardiff
www.cf.ac.uk

Central Lancashire
www.uclan.ac.uk

City
www.city.ac.uk

Coventry
www.coventry.ac.uk

Cranfield
www.cranfield.ac.uk

De Montfort
www.dmu.ac.uk

Derby
www.derby.ac.uk

Dundee
www.dundee.ac.uk

Durham
www.dur.ac.uk

East London
www.uel.ac.uk

Edinburgh
www.ed.ac.uk

Essex
www.essex.ac.uk

Exeter
www.exeter.ac.uk

Glamorgan
www.glam.ac.uk

Glasgow
www.gla.ac.uk

Glasgow Caledonian University
www.gcal.ac.uk

Goldsmiths College London
www.goldsmiths.ac.uk

Greenwich
www.greenwich.ac.uk

Guildhall London
www.lgu.ac.uk

Heriot-Watt
www.hw.ac.uk

Hertfordshire
www.herts.ac.uk

Huddersfield
www.hud.ac.uk

Hull
www.hull.ac.uk

Imperial College
www.ic.ac.uk

Keele
www.keele.ac.uk

Kent
www.ukc.ac.uk

King's College London
www.kcl.ac.uk

Kingston-upon-Thames
www.kingston.ac.uk

Lancaster
www.lancs.ac.uk

Leeds
www.leeds.ac.uk

Leeds Metropolitan
www.lmu.ac.uk

Leicester
www.leicester.ac.uk

Lincolnshire & Humberside
www.ulh.ac.uk

Liverpool
www.liv.ac.uk

London
www.lon.ac.uk

London Business School
www.lbs.ac.uk

London Guildhall
www.lgu.ac.uk

London School of Economics
www.lse.ac.uk

Loughborough
www.lut.ac.uk

Luton
www.luton.ac.uk

Manchester
www.man.ac.uk

Manchester Metropolitan
www.mmu.ac.uk

Middlesex
www.mdx.ac.uk

Napier
www.napier.ac.uk

Newcastle
www.ncl.ac.uk

North London
www.unl.ac.uk

Northumbria
www.unn.ac.uk

Nottingham
www.nott.ac.uk

Nottingham Trent
www.ntu.ac.uk

Open University
www.open.ac.uk

Oxford
www.ox.ac.uk

Oxford Brookes
www.brookes.ac.uk

Paisley
www.paisley.ac.uk

Plymouth
www.plym.ac.uk

Portsmouth
www.port.ac.uk

Queen Mary & Westfield College London
www.qmw.ac.uk

Queen's
www.qub.ac.uk

Reading
www.reading.ac.uk

Robert Gordon
www.rgu.ac.uk

Royal Holloway London
www.rhbnc.ac.uk

Salford
www.salford.ac.uk

Sheffield
www.shef.ac.uk

Sheffield Hallam
www.shu.ac.uk

South Bank
www.sbu.ac.uk

Southampton
www.soton.ac.uk

St Andrews
www.st-and.ac.uk

St Mark & St John
www.marjon.ac.uk

Staffordshire
www.staffs.ac.uk

Stirling
www.stir.ac.uk

Strathclyde
www.strath.ac.uk

Sunderland
www.sunderland.ac.uk

Surrey
www.surrey.ac.uk

Sussex
www.sussex.ac.uk

Swansea
www.swan.ac.uk

Teeside
www.tees.ac.uk

Thames Valley
www.tvu.ac.uk

Ulster
www.ulst.ac.uk

University College London
www.ucl.ac.uk

Wales Institute
www.uwic.ac.uk

Warwick
www.warwick.ac.uk

West of England
www.uwe.ac.uk

Westminster
www.wmin.ac.uk

Wolverhampton
www.wlv.ac.uk

York
www.york.ac.uk

Australia

Australian National University
www.anu.edu.au

Canberra Institute of Technology
www.cit.act.edu.au

Central Queensland University
www.cqu.edu.au

Northern Territory University
www.ntu.edu.au

University of Adelaide
www.adelaide.edu.au

University of Melbourne
www.unimelb.edu.au

University of New South Wales
www.unsw.edu.au

University of Queensland
www.uq.edu.au

University of South Australia
www.unisa.edu.au

University of Southern Queensland
www.usq.edu.au

University of Sydney
www.usyd.edu.au

University of Tasmania
http://info.utas.edu.au

University of Western Australia
www.uwa.edu.au

Canada

University of Alberta
www.ualberta.ca

New Zealand

Auckland University of Technology
www.aut.ac.nz

University of Auckland
www.auckland.ac.nz

University of Canterbury
www.canterbury.ac.nz

University of Otago
www.otago.ac.nz

United States

Arizona State University
www.asu.edu

California State University
www.csuchico.edu

Colorado State University
www.colostate.edu

Florida State University
www.fsu.edu

Harvard University
www.harvard.edu

Indiana University
www.indiana.edu

Iowa State University
www.iastate.edu

Kansas University
www.ukans.edu

Massachusetts Institute of Technology
www.mit.edu

Michigan State University
www.msu.edu

Minnesota State University
www.msus.edu

Mississippi State University
www.msstate.edu

New York University
www.nyu.edu

North Dakota University
www.nodak.edu

Ohio State University
www.ohio-state.edu

Oklahoma State University
www.okstate.edu

Oregon State University
www.orst.edu

Pennsylvania State University
www.psu.edu

Princeton University
www.princeton.edu

San Diego State University
www.sdsu.edu

San Jose State University
www.sjsu.edu

Smithsonian Institution
www.si.edu

Stanford University
www.stanford.edu

UC Berkeley
www.berkeley.edu

UCLA
www.ucla.edu

University of Arizona
www.arizona.edu

University of Chicago
www.uchicago.edu

University of Colorado
www.colorado.edu

University of Delaware
www.udel.edu

University of Georgia
www.uga.edu

University of Idaho
www.uidaho.edu

University of Illinois
www.uiuc.edu

University of Iowa
www.uiowa.edu

University of Maryland
www.umd.edu

University of Michigan
www.umich.edu

University of Minnesota
www.umn.edu

University of Missouri-Columbia
www.missouri.edu

University of Oregon
www.uoregon.edu

University of Pennsylvania
www.upenn.edu

University of Southern California
www.usc.edu

University of Texas
www.utexas.edu

University of Utah
www.utah.edu

University of Virginia
www.virginia.edu

University of Washington
www.washington.edu

University of Wisconsin-Madison
www.wisc.edu

Washington State University
www.wsu.edu

Yale University
www.yale.edu

veterinary schools

Bristol
www.bris.ac.uk/depts/vetsci/wel.htm

Cambridge
www.vet.cam.ac.uk

Dublin
www.ucd.ie/~vetmed

Edinburgh
www.vet.ed.ac.uk

Glasgow
www.gla.ac.uk/acad/facvet

Liverpool
www.liv.ac.uk/vets/vethome.html

Royal College of Veterinary Surgeons (London)
www.rcvs.org.uk

Royal Veterinary College (London)
www.rvc.ac.uk

agriculture ●

architecture ●

construction ●

government ●

green issues ●

landscape ●

preservation ●

transport ●

environment

agriculture

Country Landowners' Association
www.cla.org.uk

Dalgety Arable
www.dalgety.co.uk

East of England Agricultural Society
www.eastofengland.org.uk

Farmers Weekly Interactive
www.fwi.co.uk

Farmers' Union of Wales
www.fuw.org.uk

Home Grown Cereals Authority
www.hgca.co.uk

Institute for Animal Health
www.iah.bbsrc.ac.uk

Institute of Arable Crops Research
www.iacr.bbsrc.ac.uk

Institute of Food Research
www.ifrn.bbsrc.ac.uk

John Innes Centre
www.jic.bbsrc.ac.uk

Milk Marque
www.milkmarque.com

National Institute of Agricultural Botany
www.niab.com

Royal Agricultural Society
www.rase.org.uk

Royal Bath & West Society
www.bathandwest.co.uk

Royal Highland and Agricultural Society of Scotland
www.rhass.org.uk

Royal Ulster Agricultural Society
www.ruas.co.uk

Royal Welsh Agricultural Society
www.rwas.co.uk

Soil Association
www.soilassociation.org

Tenant Farmers Association
www.tenant-farmers.org.uk

Yorkshire Agricultural Society
www.yas.co.uk

architecture

Archinet
www.archinet.co.uk

Architects Journal
www.ajplus.co.uk

Architectural Heritage
www.eup.ed.ac.uk/journals/architectural

Architectural Heritage Fund
www.ahfund.co.uk

Architectural Review
www.arplus.com

Architecture Centre, Bristol
www.arch-centre.demon.co.uk

Architecture Foundation
www.architecturefoundation.org.uk

Architecture Week
www.archweek.co.uk

Architecturelink
www.architecturelink.org.uk

Association for Environment Conscious Building
www.aecb.net

Civic Trust
www.civictrust.org.uk

Commission for Architecture & the Built Environment (CABE)
www.cabe.org.uk

Commonwealth Association of Architects
www.archexchange.org

Frank Lloyd Wright
www.wrightplus.com

Guild of Architectural Ironmongers (GAI)
www.martex.co.uk/gai/index.htm

International Union of Architects
www.uia-architectes.org

Pevsner Architectural Guides
www.pevsner.co.uk

RIAS, Scotland
www.rias.org.uk

RIBA Publications
www.ribabookshop.com

Royal Institute of British Architects
www.riba.org

Society of Architectural Historians of Great Britain
www.sahgb.org.uk

Stirling Prize
www.ribaawards.co.uk

Twentieth Century Society
www.c20society.demon.co.uk

World Architecture
www.world-architecture.co.uk

construction

Association of Consulting Engineers
www.acenet.co.uk

Association of Project Management
www.apm.org.uk

BEPAC
www.bepac.dmu.ac.uk

British Construction Industry Awards
www.bciawards.org.uk

Concrete Society
www.concrete.org.uk

Construction Industry Board
www.ciboard.org.uk

Construction Industry Council
www.cic.org.uk

Construction Industry Research and
Information Association
www.ciria.org.uk

Energy-Efficient Building Association
www.eeba.org

European Construction Institute
www.eci-online.org

Housing Forum
www.thehousingforum.org.uk

Institution of Civil Engineers
www.ice.org.uk

National Homebuilder Awards
www.nationalhomebuilder.com

Steel Construction Institute
www.steel-sci.org

Urban Design Alliance
www.udal.org.uk

government

Countryside Agency
www.countryside.gov.uk

Countryside Council for Wales
www.ccw.gov.uk

Department of Environment, Transport & the
Regions
www.detr.gov.uk

English Nature
www.english-nature.org.uk

Environment Agency Wales
www.environment-agency.wales.gov.uk

GRID - Global Resource Information
Database (United Nations)
www.grida.no

Ministry of Agriculture, Fisheries & Food
www.open.gov.uk/maff

National Heritage
www.culture.gov.uk/heritage

Natural Environment Research Council
www.nerc.ac.uk

Royal Commission on Historical
Manuscripts
www.hmc.gov.uk

Royal Commission on the Ancient and
Historical Monuments of Scotland
www.rcahms.gov.uk

Royal Commission on the Ancient and
Historical Monuments of Wales
www.rcahmw.org.uk

Scottish Environment Protection Agency
www.sepa.org.uk

Town & Country Planning Association
www.tcpa.org.uk

green issues

Action for the Environment
www.groundwork.org.uk

British Wind Energy Association
www.bwea.com

Can-Do Community Recycling
www.fraserburgh.org.uk/cando

Centre for Alternative Technology
www.cat.org.uk

Conservation Foundation
www.conservationfoundation.co.uk

Countryside Council for Wales
www.ccw.gov.uk

Countryside Foundation
www.countrysidefoundation.org.uk

Countryside Foundation for Education
www.countrysidefoundation.org.uk

Countryside Watch
www.countrysidewatch.co.uk

Earthwatch
www.uk.earthwatch.org

Energy Saving Trust
www.est.org.uk

Friends of the Earth
www.foe.co.uk

Friends of the Earth Scotland
www.foe-scotland.org.uk

Game Conservancy Trust
www.game-conservancy.org.uk

Going for Green
www.gfg.iclnet.co.uk

Greenpeace International
www.greenpeace.org

Waste Watch
www.wastewatch.org.uk

landscape

Alliance for Historic Landscape Preservatic
www.mindspring.com/~ahlp

Arboricultural Association
www.trees.org.uk

Association of Gardens Trusts
www.btinternet.com/~gardenstrusts

Association of National Park and
Countryside Voluntary Wardens
www.naturenet.net/orgs/acvw

Field Magazine
www.thefield.co.uk

Historic Gardens Foundation
www.historicgardens.freeserve.co.uk

International Society of Arboriculture
www.ag.uiuc.edu/~isa

Landscape Design Trust
www.landscape.co.uk

Landscape Institute
www.l-i.org.uk

Moorland Association
www.cla.org.uk/moorland

National Arborist Association
www.natlarb.com

National Countryside Show
www.countrysideshow.co.uk

Royal Forestry Society
www.rfs.org.uk

Rural Development Council
www.rdc.org.uk

Tree Register
www.tree-register.org

Trees for Life
www.treesforlife.org.uk

preservation

Antiquity Journal
http://intarch.ac.uk/antiquity

Architectural Heritage Society of Scotland
www.ahss.org.uk

Assemblage Archaeology Journal
www.shef.ac.uk/~assem

Association for Industrial Archaeology
www.twelveheads.demon.co.uk/aia.htm

Association for the Protection of Rural
Scotland
www.aprs.org.uk

Association of Archaeological Illustrators &
Surveyors
www.aais.org.uk

Association of Local Government
Archaeological Officers
www.algao.org.uk

British Archaeology Magazine
www.britarch.ac.uk/ba/ba.html

British Trust for Conservation Volunteers
www.btcv.org.uk

Construction History Society
www.construct.rdg.ac.uk/chs

Council for British Archaeology
www.britarch.ac.uk

Current Archaeology Magazine
www.archaeology.co.uk

Ecclesiological Society
www.ecclsoc.org

English Heritage
www.english-heritage.org.uk

European Association of Archaeologists
www.e-a-a.org

Historic Chapels Trust
www.hct.org.uk

Historic Houses Association
www.historic-houses-assn.org

Institute of Field Archaeologists
www.archaeologists.net

Institution of Historic Building Conservation
www.ihbc.org.uk

Landmark Trust
www.landmarktrust.co.uk

Museum of London Archaeology Service
www.molas.org.uk

National Trust
www.nationaltrust.org.uk

National Trust for Scotland
www.nts.org.uk

Open Churches Trust
www.merseyworld.com/faith/html_file
/octhead.htm

Regeneration Through Heritage
www.bitc.org.uk/rth

RESCUE (British Archaeology Trust)
www.rescue-archaeology.freeserve.co.uk

River Thames Society
www.riverthamessociety.org.uk

Royal Highland Education Trust
www.rhet.rhass.org.uk

Royal Society for Nature Conservation
www.rsnc.org

Society for the Protection of Ancient
Buildings
www.spab.org.uk

United Kingdom Institute for Conservation
www.ukic.org.uk

York Archaeological Trust
www.pastforward.co.uk

transport

Environmental Transport Association
www.eta.co.uk

Sustrans
www.sustrans.org.uk

breweries •

chefs •

clubs & associations •

famous brands •

fast food •

food & drink online •

food marketing •

magazines & websites •

restaurants & bars •

supermarkets •

trade associations •

whisky •

wine •

breweries

Abbey Ales
www.abbeyales.co.uk

Amstel
www.amstel.com

Badger
www.breworld.com/badger

Bass Ale
www.bassale.com

Beamish Brewery
www.aardvark.ie/beamish

Beck's
www.becks-beer.com

Blacksheep
www.blacksheep.co.uk

Boddingtons
www.boddingtons.com

Brains
www.sabrain.co.uk

Budweiser
www.budweiser.com

Budweiser Budvar
www.budweiser.cz

Caffrey's
www.caffreys.ie

Carlsberg
www.carlsberg.co.uk

Cobra
www.cobrabeer.com

Corona
www.corona.com

Duvel
www.duvel.be

Felinfoel
www.felinfoel-brewery.com

Firkin
www.firkins.co.uk

Foster's
www.fostersbeer.com

Freedom
www.freedombrew.com

Fuller's
www.fullers.co.uk

Grolsch
www.grolsch.com

Guinness
www.guinness.ie

Heineken
www.heineken.com

Holsten
www.holsten.de

HP Bulmer
www.bulmer.com

JD Wetherspoon
www.jdwetherspoon.co.uk

Kronenbourg
www.k1664.co.uk

Labatt's
www.labatt.com

Maclay Thistle
www.maclay.com

Marston's
www.breworld.com/marstons

Merrydown
www.merrydown.plc.uk

Miller Lite
www.millerlite.com

Molson
www.molson.com

Morland
www.morland.co.uk

Morrells
www.morrells.co.uk

Newcastle Brown
www.broonale.co.uk

Ridleys
www.ridleys.co.uk

Rolling Rock
www.rollingrock.co.uk

Ruddles
www.ruddles.co.uk

Scrumpy Jack
www.scrumpyjack.com

Shepherd Neame
www.shepherd-neame.co.uk

Singha
www.singha.com

Strongbow
www.strongbow.com

Thwaites
www.thwaites.co.uk

Vaux Breweries
www.vaux-breweries.co.uk

Woodfordes
www.woodfordes.co.uk

Wychwood Brewery
www.wychwood.co.uk

Young's
www.youngs.co.uk

chefs

Albert Roux
www.albertroux.co.uk

Anton Mosiman
www.mosiman.com

Craft Guild of Chefs
www.chefpoint.co.uk

Delia Smith
www.deliaonline.com

Lindsay Bareham
www.thisislondon.com/lindsaybareham

Raymond Blanc
www.manoir.co.uk

clubs & associations

British Meat
www.meatmatters.com

British Nutrition Foundation
www.nutrition.org.uk

CAMRA (Campaign for Real Ale)
www.camra.org.uk

Chocolate Society
www.chocolate.co.uk

Circle of Wine Writers
www.circleofwinewriters.org

Guild of Food Writers
www.gfw.co.uk

National Pork Producers Council
www.nppc.org

Slow Food
www.slowfood.com

Vegan Society
www.vegansociety.com

Vegetarian Society
www.vegsoc.org

famous brands

Absolut Vodka
www.absolutvodka.com

After Eights
www.aftereights.co.uk

Anchor Foods
www.anchorfoods.com

Asian Home Gourmet
www.asianhomegourmet.com

Bacardi
www.bacardi.com

Bahlsen
www.bahlsen.co.uk

Baileys
www.baileys.com

Baxters
www.baxters.co.uk

Beefeater
www.beefeater.co.uk

Ben & Jerry's
www.benjerry.co.uk

Bendicks of Mayfair
www.bendicks.co.uk

Bensons Crisps
www.bensons-crisps.co.uk

Birds Eye Walls
www.birdseye.com

Blue Dragon
www.bluedragon.co.uk

Boaters Coffee
www.boaters.co.uk

Boost
www.boost.co.uk

Brannigans
www.brannigans.co.uk

Budweiser
www.budweiser.com

Buitoni
www.buitoni.co.uk

Cadbury's
www.cadbury.co.uk

Campbell's
www.campbellsoup.com

Captain Morgan Rum
www.rum.com

Celebrations
www.celebrations365.com

Chiltern Hills
www.chilternhills.co.uk

Clipper Teas
www.clipper-teas.com

Coca-Cola
www.cocacola.com

Courvoisier
www.courvoisier.com

Crème Egg
www.cremeegg.co.uk

Crunchie
www.crunchie.co.uk

Cuervo
www.cuervo.com

Culpeper
www.culpeper.co.uk

Danepak
www.danepak.co.uk

Danone
www.danone.com

Delifrance
www.delifrance.com

Douwe Egberts
www.douwe-egberts.co.uk

Dr Pepper
www.drpepper.com

Drambuie
www.drambuie.co.uk

Evian
www.evian.com

Finlandia Vodka
www.finlandia-vodka.com

Fishermans Friends
www.fishermansfriend.co.uk

Fresh Food Company
www.freshfood.co.uk

Frosties
www.frosties.co.uk

Fyffes
www.fyffes.com

Gerber Foods
www.gerberfoods.com

Godiva
www.godiva.com

Gourmet World
www.gourmet-world.co.uk

Grahams Port
www.grahams-port.com

Grand Marnier
www.grand-marnier.com

Haagen Dazs
www.haagen-dazs.com

Haribo
www.haribo.com

Harmonie
www.harmonie.co.uk

Harveys of Bristol
www.harveysbc.com

Heinz
www.heinz.co.uk

Homepride
www.homepride.co.uk

Horizon Foods
www.horizonfoods.com

Hula Hoops
www.hulahoops.co.uk

I Can't Believe It's Not Butter
www.tasteyoulove.com

Irn Bru
www.irn-bru.co.uk

Jaffa Cakes
www.jaffacakes.co.uk

Jelly Belly
www.jellybelly.com

Jersey Royals
www.jerseyroyals.co.uk

Kellogg's
www.kelloggs.co.uk

Kenco
www.kencocoffee.co.uk

Kerrygold
www.kerrygold.co.uk

Kinder Surprise
www.kindersurprise.co.uk

Kit-Kat
www.kitkat.co.uk

Kraft
www.kraftfoods.com

Lavazza
www.lavazza.com

Lift
www.lifttea.co.uk

Loch Fyne
www.loch-fyne.com

Lucozade
www.lucozade.co.uk

Mackies
www.mackies.co.uk

Malibu
www.malibu-rum.com

Mars
www.mars.com

Mini Heroes
www.miniheroes.co.uk

Moet & Chandon
www.moet.com

Moy Park
www.moypark.co.uk

Muller
www.muller.co.uk

Natco Spices
www.natco-foods.co.uk

Nescafe
www.nescafe.co.uk

Nesquik
www.nesquik.co.uk

Nestle
www.nestle.co.uk

Nimble
www.nimblebread.co.uk

Nutrasweet
www.nutrasweet.com

Old Speckled Hen
www.oldspeckledhen.co.uk

Olivetum Olive Oil
www.olivetum.com

Peperami
www.peperami.com

Pepsi
www.pepsi.co.uk

Pernod-Ricard
www.pernod-ricard.fr

Perrier
www.perrier.com

Pillsbury
www.pillsbury.com

Plymouth Gin
www.plymouthgin.com

Poppets
www.poppets.com

Primebake
www.primebake.co.uk

Pro Plus
www.proplus.co.uk

Quaker Oats
www.quakeroatmeal.com

Quorn
www.quorn.com

Rank Hovis
www.rankhovis.co.uk

Remy Martin
www.remy.com

Ridgways
www.ridgways.co.uk

Rivella
www.rivella.co.uk

Rombouts
www.rombouts.co.uk

Ryvita
www.ryvita.co.uk

Sara Lee
www.saraleebakery.com

Schwartz Herbs
www.schwartz.co.uk

Schweppes
www.schweppes.com

Sharwood's
www.sharwoods.com

Silver Spoon
www.silverspoon.co.uk

Slush Puppy
www.slushpuppy.co.uk

Smint
www.smint.co.uk

Smirnoff
www.smirnoff.com

Snickers
www.snickers.com

Southern Comfort
www.southerncomfort.com

Spam
www.spam.com

St Ivel
www.st-ivel.co.uk

Sunny Delight
www.sunnyd.com

Sweet Factory
www.sweet-factory.com

Sweet'N Low
www.sweetnlow.com

Tango
www.tango.co.uk

Tate & Lyle
www.tate-lyle.co.uk

Thorntons
www.thorntons.co.uk

Tia Maria
www.tiamaria.co.uk

Tiptree
www.tiptree.com

Tizer
www.tizer.co.uk

Twinings Tea
www.twinings.co.uk

Twix
www.twix.com

Typhoo
www.typhoo.com

Uncle Ben's
www.unclebens.com

Unigate
www.unigate.plc.uk

United Biscuits
www.unitedbiscuits.co.uk

Utterly Butterly
www.utterly-butterly.co.uk

Van den Bergh Foods
www.vdbfoods.co.uk

Vichy
www.vichy.com

Virgin Cola
www.virgincola.co.uk

Volvic
www.volvic.co.uk

Walkers
www.walkers.co.uk

Wensleydale
www.wensleydale.co.uk

Whittard of Chelsea
www.whittard.com

Whitworths
www.whitworths.co.uk

Whole Earth
www.earthfoods.co.uk

Wotsits
www.wotsits.co.uk

Wrigley's
www.wrigley.com

Yakult
www.yakult.co.uk

Yeo Valley
www.yeo-organic.co.uk

Yogz
www.yogz.com

fast food

Burger King
www.burgerking.co.uk

Deliverance
www.deliverance.co.uk

Domino's Pizza
www.dominos.co.uk

Dunkin' Donuts
www.dunkindonuts.com

KFC
www.kfc.co.uk

Little Chef
www.little-chef.co.uk

McDonald's
www.mcdonalds.co.uk

Perfect Pizza
www.perfectpizza.co.uk

Pret A Manger
www.pret.com

Roadchef
www.roadchef.com

Room Service
www.roomservice.co.uk

Starbucks
www.starbucks.com

food & drink online

Betty's By Post (Harrogate)
www.bettysbypost.com

Bottoms Up
www.bottomsup.co.uk

Fortnum & Mason
www.fortnumandmason.co.uk

Grapeland
www.grapeland.uk.com

Harrods
www.harrods.com

Heinz Direct
www.heinz-direct.co.uk

Jane Asher Party Cakes
www.jane-asher.co.uk

Last Orders.com
www.lastorders.com

Le Gourmet Francais
www.gourmet2000.co.uk

Oddbins
www.oddbins.co.uk

Organics Direct
www.organicsdirect.com

Paxton & Whitfield
www.cheesemongers.co.uk

Price Offers
www.priceoffers.co.uk

Real Meat Company
www.realmeat.co.uk

Selfridges
www.selfridges.co.uk

Threshers
www.thresherwineshop.co.uk

Vegnet
www.vegnet.co.uk

Victoria Wine
www.victoriawine.co.uk

Whittards of Chelsea
www.whittard.com

Wine Cellar
www.winecellar.co.uk

food marketing

British Egg Information Service
www.britegg.co.uk

British Meat
www.britishmeat.org.uk

British Potato Council
www.potato.org.uk

Food from Britain
www.foodfrombritain.com

National Dairy Council
www.milk.co.uk

Tea Council
www.tea.co.uk

magazines & websites

BBC Food & Drink
www.bbc.co.uk/foodanddrink

Brewer
www.breworld.com/the_brewer

British Food Journal
www.mcb.co.uk/bfj.htm

Carlton Food Network
www.cfn.co.uk

Cooking Light
www.cookinglight.com

The Grocer
www.foodanddrink.co.uk

Oz Clarke
www.ozclarke.com

Pub Guide
www.licensee.co.uk

Wine Spectator
www.winespectator.com

Wine Today
www.winetoday.com

restaurants & bars

Aquarium
www.theaquarium.co.uk

Balls Brothers
www.ballsbrothers.co.uk

Bank
www.bankrestaurant.co.uk

Belgo
www.belgo-restaurants.co.uk

Benihana
www.benihana.co.uk

Bibendum
www.bibendum.co.uk

Blue Elephant
www.blueelephant.com

Blue Print Café
www.conran.co.uk/restaurants/blueprint

Café Rouge
www.caferouge.co.uk

Cantina Del Ponte
www.conran.co.uk/restaurants/cantina

Chez Gerard
www.santeonline.co.uk/chezgerard/index.htm

Corney & Barrow
www.corney-barrow-winebars.co.uk

Fashion Café
www.fashion-cafe.com

Fatty Arbuckle's
www.fatty-arbuckles.co.uk

Fish!
www.fishdiner.co.uk

Football Football
www.footballfootball.com

Greenhouse
www.capital-london.net/greenhouse/index.html

Hard Rock Café
www.hardrock.com

Harry Ramsden's
www.harryramsdens.co.uk

Jazz Café
www.jazzcafe.co.uk

Le Pont de la Tour
www.conran.co.uk/restaurants/lepont

Leith's
www.leiths.com

Moshi Moshi
www.moshimoshi.co.uk

Nando's Chickenland UK
www.nandos.co.uk

Offshore
www.offshore.co.uk

People's Palace
www.capital-london.net/peoples-palace/index.html

Pharmacy
www.outpatients.co.uk

Pizza Express
www.pizzaexpress.co.uk

Pizza Hut
www.pizzahut.com

Planet Hollywood
www.planethollywood.com

Porters
www.porters.uk.com

Prism
www.prismrestaurant.com

Rainforest Café
www.rainforestcafe.com

Red Fort
www.redfort.co.uk

Ritz
www.theritzhotel.co.uk/restaurant

Rock Garden
www.rockgarden.co.uk

Rules
www.rules.co.uk

Sardis
www.sardis.com

Savoy Grill
www.savoy-group.co.uk/savoy/dining/savoy_grill.html

Sticky Fingers
www.stickyfingers.co.uk

Veeraswamy
www.veeraswamy.com

Wagamama
www.wagamama.com

Waterside Inn
www.waterside-inn.co.uk

Wiltons
www.wiltons.co.uk

Yo! Sushi
www.yosushi.co.uk

supermarkets

Aldi
www.aldi-stores.co.uk

Asda
www.asda.co.uk

Budgens
www.budgens.co.uk

Co-op
www.co-op.co.uk

Iceland
www.iceland.co.uk

Londis
www.londis.co.uk

Marks & Spencer

www.marksandspencer.com

Morrisons
www.morrisons.plc.uk

Safeway
www.safeway.co.uk

Sainsburys
www.jsainsbury.co.uk

Savacentre
www.savacentre.co.uk

Somerfield
www.somerfield.co.uk

Spar
www.spar.co.uk

Tesco
www.tescodirect.com

Waitrose
www.waitrose.co.uk

trade associations

Allied Brewers Traders Association
www.breworld.com/abta

Brewers & Licensed Retailers Association
www.blra.co.uk

British Sandwich Association
www.martex.co.uk/bsa

Catering Equipment Distributors Association
www.ceda.co.uk

Consortium of Caterers and Administration in Education
www.fairtry.ndirect.co.uk/ccaeduc

Federation of Bakers
www.bakersfederation.org.uk

Gin & Vodka Association of Great Britain
www.ginvodka.org

Institute of Brewing
www.breworld.com/iob

Institute of Food Research
www.ifrn.bbsrc.ac.uk

Institute of Food Science and Technology
www.ifst.org

International Brewers' Guild
www.breworld.com/brewersguild

National Association of Catering Butchers
www.haighs.com/nacb.htm

National Association of Master Bakers
www.masterbakers.co.uk

National Farmers' Union
www.nfu.org.uk

National Federation of Fish Friers
www.federationoffishfriers.co.uk

National Pasta Association
www.ilovepasta.org

National Soft Drink Association
www.nsda.org

Restaurant Association
www.ragb.co.uk

Scotch Whisky Association
www.scotch-whisky.org.uk

Traidcraft Exchange
www.traidcraft.co.uk

Worshipful Company of Bakers
www.bakers.co.uk

whisky

Adelphi Distillery
www.highlandtrail.co.uk

Ardbeg
www.ardbeg.com

Arran
www.arranwhisky.com

Ballantines
www.ballantines.com

Bowmore
www.bowmorescotch.com

Chivas
www.chivas.com

Cragganmore
www.scotch.com

Dalwhinnie
www.scotch.com

Dew of Ben Nevis
www.bennevis.co.uk

Edradour
www.edradour.co.uk

Famous Grouse
www.famousgrouse.com

Glen Moray
www.glenmoray.com

Glen Ord
www.glenord.com

Glencoe
www.bennevis.co.uk

Glenfarclas
www.glenfarclas.co.uk

Glenfiddich
www.glenfiddich.com

Glengoyne
www.glengoynedistillery.co.uk

Glenkinchie
www.scotch.com

Glenlivet
www.glenlivet.com

Glenmorangie
www.glenmorangie.com

Glenturret
www.glenturret.com

Gordon & MacPhail
www.gordonandmacphail.com

Highland Park
www.highlandpark.co.uk

Islay
www.islaywhisky.com

J & B
www.jbscotch.com

Jack Daniels
www.jackdaniels.co.uk

Jim Beam
www.jimbeam.com

Johnny Walker
www.scotch.com

Lagavulin
www.scotch.com

Laphroaig
www.laphroaig.com

Macallan
www.themacallan.com

Oban
www.scotch.com

Scotch Whisky Heritage Centre
www.whisky-heritage.co.uk

Seagram
www.seagram.com

Talisker
www.scotch.com

Whisky Shop
www.whiskyshop.com

wine

Berry Bros & Rudd
www.berry-bros.co.uk

Bodegas Faustino
www.bodegasfaustino.com

Bordeaux Direct
www.bordeauxdirect.co.uk

Cranwick
www.cranwick.com

Hardys
www.hardys-wines.com

International Wine Challenge
www.intwinechallenge.co.uk

Jacobs Creek
www.jacobscreek.com

Laytons
www.laytons.co.uk

Lindemans
www.lindemans.co.uk

Orgasmic Wines
www.orgasmicwines.com

Vinopolis
www.evinopolis.com

Virgin Wines
www.virginwines.com

armed forces ●

embassies ●

foreign governments ●

international organisations ●

law ●

legal institutions abroad ●

monarchy ●

overseas territories & crown dependencies ●

people ●

political parties ●

post offices ●

pressure groups ●

professional associations ●

research councils ●

uk government ●

government

armed forces

Air Training Corps (ATC)
www.open.gov.uk/atc

Army Records Office
www.army.mod.uk/army/contact/army_ro.htm

British Army
www.army.mod.uk

RAF Careers
www.raf-careers.raf.mod.uk

Royal Air Force
www.raf.mod.uk

Royal Air Forces Association
www.rafa.org.uk

Royal Auxillary Air Force
www.rauxaf.mod.uk

Royal Marines
www.royal-marines.mod.uk

Royal Navy
www.royal-navy.mod.uk

Royal Navy Careers
www.royal-navy.mod.uk/careers

Territorial Army
www.army.mod.uk/army/recruit/ta

embassies

British Embassies Abroad

Australia
www.uk.emb.gov.au

Azerbaijan
www.intrans.baku.az/british

Bahrain
www.ukembassy.gov.bh

Belgium
www.british-embassy.be

Bulgaria
www.british-embassy.bg

Cameroon
http://britcam.org

Canada
www.bis-canada.org

Cyprus
www.britain.org.cy

Czech Republic
www.britain.cz

Denmark
www.britishembassy.dk

European Union
http://ukrep.fco.gov.uk

Fiji
www.ukinthepacific.bhc.org.fj

Finland
www.ukembassy.fi

France
www.amb-grandbretagne.fr

Germany
www.britischebotschaft.de

Greece
www.british-embassy.gr

Hong Kong
www.britishconsulate.org.hk

India
www.ukinindia.org

Indonesia
www.british-emb-jakarta.or.id

Israel
www.britemb.org.il

Italy
www.britain.it

Japan
www.uknow.or.jp/uk_now/index_e.html

Jordan
www.britain.org.jo

Lebanon
www.britishembassy.org.lb

Mexico
www.embajadabritanica.com.mx

Netherlands
www.britishembassy.org.lb

New Zealand
www.brithighcomm.org.nz

Norway
www.britain.no

Poland
www.it.com.pl/britemb

Singapore
www.britain.org.sg

South Africa
www.britain.org.za

Sweden
www.britishembassy.com

Switzerland
www.british-embassy-berne.ch

Tunisia
www.british-emb.intl.tn

Ukraine
www.britemb-ukraine.net

United Arab Emirates
www.britain-uae.org

United Nations
www.ukun.org

USA
www.britainusa.com

Venezuela
www.britain.org.ve

Foreign Embassies & Consulates in the UK

Algerian
www.consalglond.u-net.com

American
www.usembassy.org.uk

Argentinian
www.argentine-embassy-uk.org.uk

Australian
www.australia.org.uk

Austrian
www.bmaa.gv.at/embassy/uk

Belgian
www.belgium-embassy.co.uk

Brazilian
www.brazil.org.uk

Canadian
www.canada.org.uk

Chilean
www.demon.co.uk/echileuk

Chinese
www.chinese-embassy.org.uk

Costa Rican
www.embcrlon.demon.co.uk

Czech
www.cz.mzv

Danish
www.denmark.org.uk

Egyptian
www.egypt-embassy.org.uk

Estonian
www.estonia.gov.uk

Finnish
www.finemb.org.uk

French
www.ambafrance.org.uk

German
www.german-embassy.org.uk

Indian
www.hcilondon.org

Iranian
www.iran-embassy.org.uk

Israeli
www.israel-embassy.org.uk

Italian
www.embitaly.org.uk

Jamaican
www.jhcuk.com

Japanese
www.embjapan.org.uk

Jordanian
www.jordanembassyuk.gov.jo

Luxembourg
www.luxembourg.co.uk

Mexican
www.embamex.co.uk

New Zealand
www.newzealandhc.org.uk

Norwegian
www.norway.org.uk

Peruvian
www.peruembassy-uk.com

Philippines
www.philemb.demon.co.uk

Polish
www.poland-embassy.org.uk

Portuguese
www.portembassy.gla.ac.uk

Russian
www.britemb.msk.ru

Slovenian
www.embassy-slovenia.org.uk

South African
www.southafricahouse.com

Spanish
www.spanishembassy.org.uk

Swedish
www.swedish-embassy.org.uk

Swiss
www.swissembassy.org.uk

Tanzanian
www.tanzania-online.gov.uk

Thai
www.thaiconsul-uk.com

Turkish
www.turkishembassy-london.com

Venezuelan
www.venezlon.demon.co.uk

foreign governments

Albanian
http://president.gov.al

Algerian
www.gga.dz/dwww/english

Andorran
www.andorra.ad/govern

Angolan
www.angola.org

Argentinian
www.senado.gov.ar

Australian
www.fed.gov.au

Australian Parliament
www.aph.gov.au

Austrian
www.parlinkom.gv.at

Bangladeshi
www.bangladeshonline.com/gob

Barbadan
www.barbados.gov.bb

Belarussian
www.president.gov.by/eng

Belgian
www.belgium.fgov.be

Bolivian
www.congreso.gov.bo

Botswanan
www.gov.bw

Brazilian
www.brasil.gov.br

Brunei
www.brunei.gov.bn

Bulgarian
www.govrn.bg

Burkina Faso
www.primature.gov.bf

Canadian
www.canada.gc.ca

Chilean
www.presidencia.cl

Chinese
www.gov.cn

Costa Rican
www.casapres.go.cr

Croatian
www.sabor.hr

Cypriot
www.pio.gov.cy

Czech
www.vlada.cz

Danish
www.folketinget.dk

Dominican
www.presidencia.gov.do

Dutch
www.parlement.nl

Egyptian
www.presidency.gov.eg

Estonian
www.vm.ee/eng

Finnish
www.edus.kunta.fi

French
www.assemblee-nat.fr

Gambian
www.gambia.com

German
www.government.de

German (Parliament)
www.bundesregierung.de

Greek
www.mpa.gr

Hong Kong
www.info.gov.hk

Hungarian
www.mkogy.hu

Icelandic
www.althingi.is

Indian Government
www.indiagov.org

Indonesian
www.dpr.go.id

Iranian
www.president.ir

Irish
www.irlgov.ie

Israeli
www.info.gov.il

Israeli (Foreign Affairs)
www.israel.org

Italian
http://english.camera.it

Jamaica
www.cabinet.gov.jm

Japanese
www.kantei.go.jp

Jordanian
www.parliament.gov.jo/english

Kenyian
www.kenyaweb.com/kenyagov

Korean
www.assembly.go.kr

Kuwaiti
www.kna.org.kw

Latvian
www.mfa.gov.lv

Lebanese
www.lp.gov.lb/english

Liberian
www.liberiaemb.org

Liechtenstein
www.firstlink.li/regierung

Luxembourg
www.chd.lu

Malaysian
www.parlimen.gov.my

Maltese
www.manet.mt

Mauritanian
www.mauritania.mr

Mexican
www.senado.gob.mx

Mongolian
www.pmis.gov.mn

Mozambiqui
www.mozambique.mz

New Zealand
www.govt.nz

Norwegian
www.stortinget.no

Omani
www.omanet.com

Pakistani
www.pak.gov.pk/govt

Panamanian
www.presidencia.gob.pa

Peruvian
www.congreso.gob.pe

Philippino
www.ops.gov.ph

Polish
www.poland.pl

Portuguese
www.parlamento.pt

Romanian
www.guv.ro/english

Russian
www.gov.ru

Russian (Parliament)
www.duma.ru

Senegalese
www.primature.sn

Sierra Leonian
www.sierra-leone.gov.sl

Singaporean
www.gov.sg

Slovakian
www.government.gov.sk

South African
www.polity.org.za/gnu

South Korean
www.cwd.go.kr/english

Spanish
www.la-moncloa.es

Swaziland
www.swazi.com/government

Swedish
www.royalcourt.se/eng

Swiss
www.admin.ch

Tanzanian
www.bungetz.org

Thai
www.parliament.go.th

Togan
www.republicoftogo.com

Trinidad & Tobagan
www.ttparliament.org

Tunisian
www.ministeres.tn

Turkish
www.tbmm.gov.tr

Turkish Cypriot
www.cm.gov.nc.tr

Ukranian
www.rada.kiev.ua

United Arab Emirates
www.uae.gov.ae

Uruguayan
www.parlamento.gub.uy

USA - CIA
www.cia.gov

USA - Congress
www.congress.org

USA - FBI
www.fbi.gov

USA - House of Representatives
www.house.gov

USA - Republican National Committee
www.rnc.org

USA - Senate
www.senate.gov

USA - Supreme Court
www.uscourts.gov

USA - White House
www.whitehouse.gov

Uzbekistani
www.gov.uz

Vatican
www.vatican.va

Venezuelan
www.parlamento.gov.ve

Yemenite
www.yemeninfo.gov.ye

Yugoslavian
www.gov.yu

Zambian
www.statehouse.gov.zm

international organisations

Amnesty International
www.amnesty.org

Arctic Council
www.arctic-council.org

Commonwealth Secretariat
www.thecommonwealth.org

Council of Europe
www.coe.fr

European Central Bank
www.ecb.int

European Commission
www.europa.eu.int

European Court of Justice
www.curia.eu.int/en

European Investment Bank
www.eib.eu.int

European Monetary Union
www.europeanmovement.ie/emu.htm

European Parliament
www.europarl.eu.int

European Trade Union Confederation
www.etuc.org

European Union
www.europa.eu.int

G8
www.g7.utoronto.ca

Institute of World Politics
www.iwp.edu

International Albert Schweitzer Foundation
www.schweitzer.org

International Atomic Energy Agency
www.iaea.org

International Crisis Group
www.intl-crisis-group.org

International Maritime Organisation
www.imo.org

International Monetary Fund
www.imf.org

International Red Cross
www.icrc.org

NATO
www.nato.int

Organisation for Economic Co-operation & Development (OECD)
www.oecd.org

Organisation of Petroleum Exporting Countries (OPEC)
www.opec.org

Royal Commonwealth Society
www.rcint.org

Smithsonian Institution
www.si.edu

UNESCO
www.unesco.org

UNICEF (United Nations Children's Fund)
www.unicef.org

United Nations
www.un.org

World Bank
www.worldbank.org

World Health Organisation
www.who.int

World Meteorological Organisation
www.wmo.ch

World Trade Organisation
www.wto.org

law

Advisory, Conciliation & Arbitration Service
www.acas.org.uk

Bar Council
www.barcouncil.org.uk

Civil Justice Council
www.open.gov.uk/civjustice

Court Service of England & Wales
www.courtservice.gov.uk

Criminal Cases Review Commission
www.ccrc.gov.uk

Criminal Justice System
www.criminal-justice-system.gov.uk

Crown Prosecution Service
www.cps.gov.uk

Employment Appeal Tribunal
www.employmentappeals.gov.uk

European Court of Human Rights
www.echr.cue.int

European Court of Justice
http://europa.eu.int/cj/en

HM Land Registry
www.open.gov.uk/landreg/home.htm

International Court of Justice
www.icj-cij.org

Law Society of England & Wales
www.lawsoc.org.uk

Law Society of Scotland
www.lawscot.org.uk

Legal Aid
www.legal-aid.gov.uk

Lord Chancellor's Department
www.open.gov.uk/lcd

Magistrates' Association
www.magistrates-association.org.uk

Official Solicitor's Department
www.offsol.demon.co.uk

Scottish Courts Service
www.scotcourts.gov.uk

Serious Fraud Office
www.sfo.gov.uk

Society for Computers & Law
www.scl.org

Youth Justice Board
www.youth-justice-board.gov.uk

legal institutions abroad

Australia
www.fedcourt.gov.au

Brazil
www.trt10.gov.br

Canada
www.courts.gov.bc.ca

Chile
www.lakota.clara.net/derechos/dissidence.htm

Croatia
www.croadria.com/zupsudbj

Egypt
www.us.sis.gov.eg/online/html/ol0412a.htm

Hong Kong
www.info.gov.hk/index_e.htm

India
www.supremecourtofindia.com

Ireland
www.local.ie/society_and_government/government/law

Israel
www.court.gov.il

Japan
www.courts.go.jp

Jordan
www.nic.gov.jo

Kenya
www.kenyastatehouse.go.ke/organisation/sect-judiciary.htm

Korea
www.scourt.go.kr/menu_eng.html

Malaysia
www.mahkamah.gov.my

Mexico
http://info.juridicas.unam.mx

New Zealand
www.courts.govt.nz

Pakistan
www.pakistanbiz.com/pakistan/judiciary.html

Phillipines
www.supremecourt.gov.ph

Singapore
www.gov.sg/judiciary/supremect

Turkey
www.turkey.org/politics/p_judici.htm

USA
www.uscourts.gov

monarchy

European

Belgium
http://belgium.fgov.be/monarchie

Liechtenstein
www.news.li/fam/fam.htm

Monaco
www.monaco.mc/monaco

Netherlands
www.koninklijkhuis.nl

Sweden
www.royalcourt.se/eng/index.html

General

Crown Estate
www.crownestate.co.uk

Middle & far East

Brunei
http://brunei.sultanate.com

Jordan
www.kinghussein.gov.jo/rfamily_left.html

Thailand
www.escati.com/king_of_thailand.htm

Royal Family

Diana, Princess of Wales (Obituary)
www.royal.gov.uk/start.htm

HM Queen Elizabeth
www.royal.gov.uk/family/hmqueen

HM Queen Elizabeth, Queen Mother
www.royal.gov.uk/family/mother

HRH Duke of York
www.royal.gov.uk/family/york

HRH Earl of Wessex
www.royal.gov.uk/family/edward

HRH Prince of Wales
www.princeofwales.gov.uk

HRH Prince Philip, Duke of Edinburgh
www.royal.gov.uk/family/philip

HRH Princess Alexandra
www.royal.gov.uk/family/alex.htm

HRH Princess Margaret
www.royal.gov.uk/family/margaret.htm

HRH Princess Royal
www.royal.gov.uk/family/royal

TRH Duke & Duchess of Kent
www.royal.gov.uk/family/kent1.htm

TRH Princess Alice, Duchess of Gloucester
& the Duke & Duchess of Gloucester
www.royal.gov.uk/family/gloucs.htm

Royal Palaces

Balmoral
www.royal.gov.uk/palaces/balmoral.htm

Buckingham Palace
www.royal.gov.uk/palaces/bp.htm

Frogmore House
www.royal.gov.uk/palaces/frogmore.htm

Holyroodhouse
www.royal.gov.uk/palaces/holyrood.htm

Kensington Palace
www.royal.gov.uk/palaces/kengsingt.htm

Sandringham House
www.royal.gov.uk/palaces/sandring.htm

St James's Palace
www.royal.gov.uk/palaces/stjamess

Windsor Castle
www.royal.gov.uk/palaces/windsor.htm

overseas territories & crown dependencies

Falklands Islands Government
www.falklands.gov.fk

Isle of Man Government
www.gov.im

people

George W Bush
www.georgewbush.com

political parties

British

Communist Party
www.myspace.co.uk/cp-of-britain/

Conservative Party
www.tory.org.uk

Democratic Unionist Party, Northern Ireland
www.dup.org.uk

Green Party, England & Wales
www.greenparty.org.uk

Green Party, Scotland
www.scottishgreens.org.uk

Green Party, Wales
www.walesgreenparty.org.uk

Labour Party
www.labour.org.uk

Liberal Democratic Party
www.libdems.org.uk

Natural Law Party
www.natural-law-party.org.uk

Plaid Cymru, Wales
www.plaid-cymru.wales.com

Progrssive Unionist Party
www.pup.org

Scottish Liberal Democratic Party
www.scotlibdems.org.uk

Scottish Nationalist Party
www.snp.org.uk

Sinn Fein, Northern Ireland
www.sinnfein.ie

Social & Democratic Labour Party, Northern Ireland
www.sdlp.ie

Socialist Party
www.socialistparty.org.uk

Ulster Democratic Party
www.udp.org/main.html

Ulster Unionist Party
www.uup.org

Foreign

African National Congress, South Africa
www.anc.org.za

Christian Democratic Party, Netherlands
www.cda.nl

Communist Party, Russian Federation
www.kprf.ru/eng/htm/eng.htm

Communist Party, USA
www.cpusa.org

Democratic Party, Australia
www.democrats.org.au

Democratic Party, USA
www.democrats.org

International Socialist Organisation
www.internationalsocialist.org

Labour Party, Australia
www.alp.org.au

Labour Party, New Zealand
www.labour.org.nz

Labour Party, Norway
www.dna.no/internett/foreignlenglish

Liberal Democratic Party, Japan
www.jimin.or.jp/jimin/english

Liberal Party, Australia
www.liberal.org.au

Liberal Party, Canada
www.liberal.ca

National Congress, India
www.indiancongress.org

National Party, New Zealand
www.national.org.nz

Nationalist Party, Vietnam
www.vietquoc.com

People's Party, Pakistan
www.ppp.org.pk

Reform Party
www.reformparty.org

Republican Movement, Australia
www.republic.org.au

Republican Party, Ireland
www.fiannafail.ie

Republican Party, USA
www.rnc.org

Social Democratic Party, Germany
www.spd.de/english

United Democratic Front, Nigeria
www.udfn.com

United National Party, Sri Lanka
www.lanka.net/lisl2/yellow/unp

post offices

Consignia
www.consignia.com

Guernsey
http://post-office.guernsey.net

Ireland
www.anpost.ie

Isle of Man
www.gov.im/postoffice

Jersey
www.jerseypost.com

Post Office
www.postoffice.co.uk

Post Office Counters
www.postoffice-counters.co.uk

Royal Mail
www.royalmail.co.uk

pressure groups

Adam Smith Institute
www.adamsmith.org.uk

Amnesty International
www.amnesty.org.uk

ASH
www.ash.org.uk

Association of British Counties
www.abcounties.co.uk

Association of British Drivers
www.abd.org.uk

Bruges Group
www.eurocritic.demon.co.uk

Campaign Against Censorship of the Internet in Britain
www.liberty.org.uk/cacib

Campaign for an English Parliament
www.englishpm.demon.co.uk

Campaign for Dark Skies
www.dark-skies.freeserve.co.uk

Campaign for Freedom of Information
www.cfoi.org.uk

Campaign for Nuclear Disarmament (CND)
www.cnduk.org

Campaign for Press & Broadcasting Freedom
www.cpbf.org.uk

Campaign for Safe E-Commerce Legislatic
www.stand.org.uk

Campaign for Shooting
www.foresight-cfs.org.uk

Charter 88
www.charter88.org..uk

Country Landowners Association
www.cla.org.uk

Crimestoppers
www.crimestoppers-uk.org

Democracy Movement
www.democracy-movement.org.uk

Electoral Reform Society
www.electoral-reform.org.uk

Fabian Society
www.fabian-society.org.uk

Fireworks Safety Campaign
www.fireworksafety.co.uk

Free Britain
www.freebrit.demon.co.uk

Friends of the Earth
www.foe.co.uk

Going for Green
www.gfg.iclnet.co.uk

Greenpeace International
www.greenpeace.org

League Against Cruel Sports
www.league.uk.com

Liberty (National Council for Civil Liberties)
www.liberty-human-rights.org.uk

London Cycling Campaign
www.lcc.org.uk

National Pure Water Association
www.npwa.freeserve.co.uk

Portman Group
www.portman-group.org.uk

Privacy International
www.privacyinternational.org

Searchlight
www.s-light.demon.co.uk

Silent Majority
www.silentmajority.co.uk

UK Independence Party
www.independenceuk.org.uk

Vegetarian Society
www.vegsoc.org

Voluntary Euthanasia Society
www.ves.org.uk

professional associations

Association of Directors of Social Services
www.adss.org.uk

Association of First Division Civil Servants
www.fda.org.uk

research councils

Biotechnology and Biological Sciences
www.bbsrc.ac.uk

Council for the Central Laboratory
www.cclrc.ac.uk

Economic and Social Research Council
www.esrc.ac.uk

Engineering and Physical Sciences
www.epsrc.ac.uk

Medical
www.mrc.ac.uk

Natural Environment Research Council
www.nerc.ac.uk

Particle Physics and Astronomy
www.pparc.ac.uk

uk government

Government Agencies

Advisory, Conciliation & Arbitration Service
www.acas.org.uk

Air Accident Investigation Branch
www.open.gov.uk/aaib

Arts Council
www.artscouncil.org.uk

Audit Commission
www.audit-comm.gov.uk

Benefits Agency
www.dss.gov.uk/ba

British Council
www.britcoun.org

British Railways Board
www.brb.gov.uk

British Trade International
www.brittrade.com

British Waterways Board
www.british-waterways.org

Central Computer & Telecommunications
Agency (CCTA)
www.ccta.gov.uk

Central Office of Information
www.coi.gov.uk

Centre for Policy Studies
www.cps.org.uk

Charity Commission
www.charity-commission.gov.uk

Child Support Agency
www.dss.gov.uk/csa

Citizens' Charter
www.open.gov.uk/charter

Commission for Architecture & the Built
Environment (CABE)
www.cabe.org.uk

Commission for Racial Equality
www.cre.gov.uk

Commonwealth War Graves Commission
www.cwgc.org

Communicable Disease Surveillance Centre
www.open.gov.uk/cdsc

Companies House
www.companieshouse.gov.uk

Contributions Agency
www.dss.gov.uk/ca

Crafts Council
www.craftscouncil.org.uk

Crown Prosecution Service (CPS)
www.cps.gov.uk

Data Protection Register
www.dpr.gov.uk

Design Council
www.design-council.org.uk

Driver & Vehicle Licensing Agency (DVLA)
www.open.gov.uk/dvla

Driving Standards Agency (DSA)
www.dsa.gov.uk

Employment Service
www.employmentservice.gov.uk

Enterprise Zone
www.enterprisezone.org.uk

Equal Opportunities Commission
www.eoc.org.uk

Equality Commission for Northern Ireland
www.equality.org.uk

Forestry Commission of Great Britain
www.forestry.gov.uk

Government Communications Headquarters
(GCHQ)
www.gchq.gov.uk

Government Information Service
www.open.gov.uk

Health & Safety Executive
www.hse.gov.uk

Highways Agency
www.highways.gov.uk

HM Customs & Excise
www.hmce.gov.uk

HM Land Registry
www.landreg.gov.uk

HM Prison Service
www.open.gov.uk/prison/prisonhm

HM Stationery Office
www.hmso.gov.uk

HM Treasury Euro Site
www.euro.gov.uk

Housing Corporation
www.housingcorp.org.uk

Inland Revenue
www.inlandrevenue.gov.uk

Insolvency Service
www.insolvency.gov.uk

Institute for Fiscal Studies
www.ifs.org.uk

Law Commission
www.open.gov.uk/lawcomm

Local Government Association
www.lga.gov.uk

Medical Devices Agency
www.medical-devices.gov.uk

Medicines Control Agency
www.open.gov.uk/mca

MI5
www.mi5.gov.uk

Museums & Galleries Commission
www.cornucopia.org.uk

National Association of Citizens Advice
Bureaux
www.nacab.org.uk

National Audit Office
www.nao.gov.uk

National Criminal Intelligence Service
www.ncis.co.uk

National Disability Council
www.disability-council.gov.uk

National Grid for Learning
www.ngfl.gov.uk

National Health Service
www.nhs50.nhs.uk

National Institute for Social Work
www.nisw.org.uk

National Playing Fields Association
www.npfa.co.uk

National Rivers Authority
www.highway57.co.uk/tvbc/tbnra.html

New Deal
www.newdeal.gov.uk

Occupational Pensions Regulatory Author
www.opra.gov.uk

Office of Technology
www.dti.gov.uk/ost

Official Publications
www.ukop.co.uk

Ordnance Survey
www.ordsvy.gov.uk

Parliamentary Monitoring and Information
Service
www.pamis.gov.uk

Passport Agency
www.ukpa.gov.uk

Planning Inspectorate
www.open.gov.uk/pi/pihome

Port of London Authority
www.portoflondon.co.uk

Post Office
www.postoffice.co.uk

Public Record Office
www.pro.gov.uk

Regional Arts Boards of England
www.arts.org.uk

Royal Mint
www.royalmint.com

Stationery Office
www.tsonline.co.uk

Teacher Training Agency
www.teach-tta.gov.uk

Trade UK
www.tradeuk.com

Trading Standards Central
www.tradingstandards.gov.uk

Traffic Committee for London
www.tcfl.gov.uk

Transport for London
www.transportforlondon.gov.uk

United Kingdom Hydrographic Office
www.hydro.gov.uk

Vehicle Inspectorate
www.via.gov.uk

Wales Information Society
www.wis.org.uk

Women's National Commission
www.thewnc.org.uk

Government Departments

Cabinet Office
www.cabinet-office.gov.uk

Crown Estates
www.crownestate.co.uk

Culture, Media & Sport
www.culture.gov.uk

Department for Work, Family and Pensions
www.dss.gov.uk

Department of Education for Northern Ireland
www.deni.gov.uk

Department of the Environment for Northern Ireland
www.doeni.gov.uk

Department of Work & Pensions
www.dwp.gov.uk

Education & Skills
www.dfes.gov.uk

Environment, Food & Rural Affairs
www.defra.gov.uk

Foreign & Commonwealth Office
www.fco.gov.uk

Health
www.doh.gov.uk

HM Treasury
www.hm-treasury.gov.uk

Home Office
www.homeoffice.gov.uk

International Development
www.dfid.gov.uk

Lord Chancellor's Department
www.open.gov.uk/lcd

Ministry of Defence
www.mod.uk

National Heritage
www.heritage.gov.uk

Northern Ireland Office
www.nio.gov.uk

Trade & Industry
www.dti.gov.uk

Transport, Local Government & the Regions
www.dtlr.gov.uk

Local Government

Aberdeen
www.aberdeencity.gov.uk

Aberdeenshire
www.aberdeenshire.gov.uk

Adur
www.adur.co.uk

Alnwick
http://alnwick.northumberland.gov.uk

Amber Valley
http://public.ambervalley.gov.uk

Anglesey
www.anglesey.gov.uk

Angus
www.angus.gov.uk

Antrim
www.antrim.gov.uk

Ards
www.ards-council.gov.uk

Argyll & Bute
www.argyll-bute.gov.uk

Armagh
www.armagh.gov.uk

Arun
www.arun.gov.uk

Ashfield
www.ashfield.gov.uk

Ashford
www.ashford.gov.uk

Aylesbury
www.aylesburyvaledc.gov.uk

Babergh
www.babergh-south-suffolk.gov.uk

Ballymoney
www.ballymoney.gov.uk

Banbridge
www.banbridge.com

Banbury
www.banburytown.co.uk

Barking & Dagenham
www.barking-dagenham.gov.uk

Barnet
www.barnet.gov.uk

Barnsley
www.barnsley.gov.uk

Barrow-in-Furness
www.barrowbc.gov.uk

Basildon
www.basildon.gov.uk

Basingstoke
www.basingstoke.gov.uk

Bassetlaw
www.bassetlaw.gov.uk

Bath
www.bathnes.gov.uk

Bedford
www.bedford.gov.uk

Bedfordshire
www.bcclgis.gov.uk

Belfast
www.belfastcity.gov.uk

Berwick-upon-Tweed
www.berwick-upon-tweed.gov.uk

Bexley
www.bexley.gov.uk

Birmingham
www.birmingham.gov.uk

Blaby
www.blaby.gov.uk

Blackburn
www.blackburn.gov.uk

Blackpool
www.blackpool.gov.uk

Blyth Valley
www.blythvalley.gov.uk

Bolsover
www.bolsover.gov.uk

Bolton
www.bolton.gov.uk

Boston
www.boston.gov.uk

Bournemouth
www.bournemouth.gov.uk

Bracknell Forest
www.bracknell-forest.gov.uk

Bradford
www.bradford.gov.uk

Braintree
www.braintreedc.demon.co.uk

Breckland
www.breckland.gov.uk

Brent
www.brent.gov.uk

Brentwood
www.brentwood-council.gov.uk

Bridgend
www.bridgend.gov.uk

Brighton & Hove
www.brighton-hove.gov.uk

Bristol
www.bristol-city.gov.uk

Broadland
www.broadland.gov.uk

Bromley
www.bromley.gov.uk

Bromsgrove
www.bromsgrove.gov.uk

Broxbourne
www.broxbourne.gov.uk

Broxtowe
www.broxtowe.gov.uk

Buckinghamshire
www.buckscc.gov.uk

Burnley
www.burnley.gov.uk

Bury
www.bury.gov.uk

Caerphilly
www.caerphilly.gov.uk

Calderdale
www.calderdale.gov.uk

Cambridge
www.cambridge.gov.uk

Cambridgeshire
www.camcnty.gov.uk

Camden
www.camden.gov.uk

Cannock
www.cannockchasedc.gov.uk

Canterbury
www.canterbury.gov.uk

Caradon
www.caradon.gov.uk

Cardiff
www.cardiff.gov.uk

Carlisle
www.carlsile-city.gov.uk

Carmarthenshire
www.carmarthenshire.gov.uk

Carrick
www.carrick.gov.uk

Carrickfergus
www.carrickfergus.org

Castle Morpeth
www.castlemorpeth.gov.uk

Castlereagh
www.castlereagh.gov.uk

Ceredigion
www.ceredigion.gov.uk

Chard
www.chard.gov.uk

Charnwood
www.charnwoodbcgov.uk

Chelmsford
www.chelmsfordbcgov.uk

Cheltenham
www.cheltenham.gov.uk

Cherwell
www.cherwell-dc.gov.uk

Cheshire
www.cheshire.gov.uk

Chester
www.chestercc.gov.uk

Chester le Street
www.chester-le-street.gov.uk

Chesterfield
www.chesterfieldbc.gov.uk

Chicester
www.chichester.gov.uk

Chiltern
www.chiltern.gov.uk

Christchurch
www.christchurch.gov.uk

Clackmannan
www.clacs.gov.uk

Colchester
www.colchester.gov.uk

Coleraine
www.colerainebc.gov.uk

Congleton
www.congleton.gov.uk

Conwy
www.conwy.gov.uk

Cookstown
www.cookstown.gov.uk

Copeland
www.copelandbc.gov.uk

Cornwall
www.cornwall.gov.uk

Corporation of London
www.cityoflondon.gov.uk

Cotswold
www.cotswold.gov.uk

Coventry
www.coventry.gov.uk

Craigavon
www.craigavon.gov.uk

Craven
www.cravendc.demon.co.uk

Crawley
www.crawley.gov.uk

Crewe & Nantwich
www.crewe-nantwich.gov.uk

Croydon
www.croydon.gov.uk

Cumbria
www.cumbria.gov.uk

Dacorum
www.dacorum.gov.uk

Darlington
www.darlington.gov.uk

Daventry
www.daventrydc.gov.uk

Denbighshire
www.denbighshire.gov.uk

Derby
www.derby.gov.uk

Derbyshire
www.derbyshire.gov.uk

Derbyshire Dales
www.derbeyshiredaes.gov.uk

Derry
www.derrycity.gov.uk

Derwentside
www.derwentside.gov.uk

Devizes
www.devizes-tc.gov.uk

Devon
www.devon-cc.gov.uk

Doncaster
www.doncaster.gov.uk

Dorset
www.dorset-cc.gov.uk

Dover
www.dover.gov.uk

Down
www.downdc.gov.uk

Dudley
www.dudley.gov.uk

Dumfries & Galloway
www.dumgal.gov.uk

Dunbarton
www.west-dunbarton.gov.uk

Dundee
www.dundeecity.gov.uk

Dungannon
www.dungannon.gov.uk

Durham (City)
www.durhamcity.gov.uk

Durham (County)
www.durham.gov.uk

Ealing
www.ealing.gov.uk

Easington
www.easington.gov.uk

East Ayrshire
www.east-ayrshire.gov.uk

East Devon
www.east-devon.gov.uk

East Dorset
www.eastdorsetdc.gov.uk

East Dunbartonshire
www.e-dunbarton.org.uk

East Grinstead
www.egnet.co.uk/egtc

East Hampshire
www.easthants.gov.uk

East Hertfordshire
www.eastherts.gov.uk

East Lindsey
www.e-lindsey.gov.uk

East Lothian
www.eastlothian.gov.uk

East Northamptonshire
www.east-northamptonshire.gov.uk

East Renfrewshire
www.eastrenfrewshire.gov.uk

East Riding
www.east-riding-of-yorkshire.gov.uk

East Sussex
www.eastsussexcc.gov.uk

Eastbourne
www.eastbourne.org/council

Eastleigh
www.eastleigh.gov.uk

Eden
www.eden.gov.uk

Edinburgh
www.edinburgh.gov.uk

Elmbridge
www.elmbridge.gov.uk

Enfield
www.enfield.gov.uk

Epping Forest
www.eppingforestdc.gov.uk

Epsom
www.epsom-ewell.gov.uk

Erewash
www.erewash.gov.uk

Essex
www.essexcc.gov.uk

Exeter
www.exeter.gov.uk

Falkirk
www.falkirk.gov.uk

Fareham
www.fareham.gov.uk

Felixstowe
www.felixstowe.gov.uk

Fenland
www.fenland.gov.uk

Fermanagh
www.fermanagh.gov.uk

Fife
www.fife.gov.uk

Flintshire
www.flintshire.gov.uk

Forest Heath
www.forest-heath.gov.uk

Forest of Dean
www.fdean.gov.uk

Fylde
www.fylde.gov.uk

Gateshead
www.gatesheadmbc.gov.uk

Gedling
www.gedling.gov.uk

Glasgow
www.glasgow.gov.uk

Gloucester
www.glos-city.gov.uk

Gloucestershire
www.gloscc.gov.uk

Godalming
www.godalming-tc.gov.uk

Gosport
www.gosport.gov.uk

Gravesham
www.gravesham.gov.uk

Great Yarmouth
www.great-yarmouth.gov.uk

Greater London Assembly & Mayor of London
www.london.gov.uk

Greenwich
www.greenwich.gov.uk

Guildford
www.guildford.gov.uk

Gwynedd
www.gwynedd.gov.uk

Hackney
www.hackney.gov.uk

Halton
www.halton-borough.gov.uk

Hambleton
www.hambleton.gov.uk

Hammersmith & Fulham
www.lbhf.gov.uk

Hampshire
www.hants.gov.uk

Harborough
www.harborough.gov.uk

Haringey
www.haringey.gov.uk

Harlow
www.harlow.gov.uk

Harrogate
www.harrogate.gov.uk

Harrow
www.harrowlb.demon.co.uk

Hart
www.hart.gov.uk/dc

Hartlepool
www.hartlepool.gov.uk

Hastings
www.hastings.gov.uk

Havant
www.havant.gov.uk

Havering
www.havering.gov.uk

Herefordshire
www.herefordshire.gov.uk

Hertfordshire
www.hertscc.gov.uk

Hertsmere
www.hertsmere.gov.uk

High Peak
www.highpeak.gov.uk

Highland
www.highland.gov.uk

Hillingdon
www.hillingdon.gov.uk

Horsham
www.horsham.gov.uk

Hounslow
www.hounslow.gov.uk

Huntingdonshire
www.huntsdc.gov.uk

Hyndburn
www.hyndburnbc.gov.uk

Ipswich
www.ipswich.gov.uk

Isle of Wight
www.isleofwight.gov.uk

Islington
www.islington.gov.uk

Jersey
www.jersey.gov.uk

Kennet
www.kennet.gov.uk

Kensington & Chelsea
www.rbkc.gov.uk

Kent
www.kent.gov.uk

Kerrier
www.kerrier.gov.uk

Kettering
www.kettering.gov.uk

Kings Lynn & West Norfolk
www.west-norfolk.gov.uk

Kingston-upon-Hull
www.hullcc.gov.uk

Kingston-upon-Thames
www.kingston.gov.uk

Kirklees
www.kirkleesmc.gov.uk

Knowsley
www.knowsley.gov.uk

Lambeth
www.lambeth.gov.uk

Lancashire
www.lancashire.gov.uk

Lancaster
www.lancaster.gov.uk

Larne
www.larne.com

Leeds
www.leeds.gov.uk

Leicester
www.leicester.gov.uk

Leicestershire
www.leics.gov.uk

Lewes
www.lewes.gov.uk

Lewisham
www.lewisham.gov.uk

Lichfield
www.lichfield.gov.uk

Lincoln
www.lincoln-info.org.uk

Lincolnshire
www.lincolnshire.gov.uk

Lisburn
www.lisburn.gov.uk

Litchfield
www.litchfield.gov.uk

Liverpool
www.liverpool.gov.uk

Londonderry
www.derrycity.gov.uk

Luton
www.luton.gov.uk

Macclesfield
www.macclesfield.gov.uk

Magherafelt
www.magherafelt.gov.uk

Maidstone
www.digitalmaidstone.co.uk

Maldon
www.maldon.gov.uk

Manchester
www.manchester.gov.uk

Mansfield
www.mansfield.gov.uk

Medway
www.medway.gov.uk

Melton
www.melton.gov.uk

Mendip
www.mendip.gov.uk

Merthyr Tydfil
www.merthyr.gov.uk

Merton
www.merton.gov.uk

Mid Bedfordshire
www.midbeds.gov.uk

Mid Devon
www.middevon.gov.uk

Mid Suffolk
www.mid-suffol-dc.gov.uk

Mid-Sussex
www.midsussex.gov.uk

Middlesbrough
www.middlesbrough.gov.uk

Midlothian
www.midlothian.gov.uk

Milton Keynes
www.miltonkeynes.gov.uk

Mole Valley
www.mole-valley.gov.uk

Monmouthshire
www.monmouthshire.gov.uk

Moray
www.moray.gov.uk

Moyle
www.moyle-council.org

Neath Port Talbot
www.neath-porttalbot.gov.uk

New Forest
www.nfdc.gov.uk

Newark
www.newark.gov.uk

Newcastle-under-Lyme
www.newcastle-staffs.gov.uk

Newcastle-upon-Tyne
www.newcastle.gov.uk

Newham
www.newham.gov.uk

Newport
www.newport.gov.uk

Newtonabbey
www.newtonabbey.gov.uk

Norfolk
www.norfolk.gov.uk

North Ayrshire
www.north-ayrshire.gov.uk

North Cornwall
www.ncdc.gov.uk

North Devon
www.northdevon.gov.uk

North Dorset
www.north-dorset.gov.uk

North Down
www.north-down.gov.uk

North East Derbyshire
www.ne-derbyshire.gov.uk

North East Lincolnshire
www.nelinks.gov.uk

North Hertfordshire
www.nhdc.gov.uk

North Kesteven
www.oden.co.uk

North Lanarkshire
www.northlan.gov.uk

North Lincolnshire
www.northlincs.gov.uk

North Norfolk
www.north-norfolk.gov.uk

North Shropshire
www.nshropshire.gov.uk

North Somerset
www.n-somerset.gov.uk

North Tyneside
www.northtyneside.gov.uk

North Warwickshire
www.warwickshire.gov.uk

North West Leicestershire
www.nwleicsdc.gov.uk

North Wiltshire
www.northwilts.gov.uk

North Yorkshire
www.northyorks.gov.uk

Northampton
www.northampton.gov.uk

Northamptonshire
www.northamptonshire.gov.uk

Northumberland
www.northumberland.gov.uk

Norwich
www.norwich.gov.uk

Nottingham
www.nottinghamcity.gov.uk

Nottinghamshire
www.nottscc.gov.uk

Oadby
www.oadby-wigston.gov.uk

Oldham
www.oldham.gov.uk

Oxford
www.oxford.gov.uk

Oxfordshire
www.oxfordshire.gov.uk

Pembrokeshire
www.pembrokeshire.gov.uk

Pendle
www.pendle.gov.uk

Penwith
www.penwith.gov.uk

Perth & Kinross
www.pkc.gov.uk

Peterborough
www.peterborough.gov.uk

Plymouth
www.plymouth.gov.uk

Poole
www.poole.gov.uk

Portsmouth
www.portsmouthcc.gov.uk

Powys
www.powys.gov.uk

Preston
www.preston.gov.uk

Reading
www.reading.gov.uk

Redbridge
www.redbridge.gov.uk

Redcar & Cleveland
www.redcar-cleveland.gov.uk

Redditch
www.redditchbc.gov.uk

Reigate & Banstead
www.reigate-banstead.gov.uk

Renfrewshire
www.renfrewshire.gov.uk

Rhondda-Cynon-Taff
www.rhondda-cynon-taff.gov.uk

Ribble Valley
www.ribblevalley.gov.uk

Richmond
www.richmond.gov.uk

Richmondshire
www.richmondshire.gov.uk

Rochdale
www.rochdale.gov.uk

Rochester-upon-Medway
www.rochester.gov.uk

Rochford
www.rochford.gov.uk

Rother
www.rother.gov.uk

Rotherham
www.rotherham.gov.uk

Runnymede
www.runnymede.gov.uk

Rushcliffe
www.rushcliff.gov.uk

Rushmore
www.rushmore.gov.uk

Rutland
www.rutland.gov.uk

Ryedale
www.ryedale.gov.uk

Salford
www.salford.gov.uk

Salisbury
www.salisbury.gov.uk

Sandwell
www.sandwell.gov.uk/smbc

Scarborough
www.scarborough.gov.uk

Scottish Borders
www.scotborders.gov.uk

Sedgefield
www.sedgefield.gov.uk

Sefton
www.sefton.gov.uk

Selby
www.selby.gov.uk

Sevenoaks
www.sevenoaks.gov.uk

Sheffield
www.sheffield.gov.uk

Shepway
www.shepway.gov.uk

Shetland Islands
www.shetland.gov.uk

Shrewsbury & Atchham
www.shrewsbury-atcham.gov.uk

Shropshire
www.shropshire-cc.gov.uk

Slough
www.slough.gov.uk

Solihull
www.solihull.gov.uk

Somerset
www.somerset.gov.uk

South Ayrshire
www.south-ayrshire.gov.uk

South Bedfordshire
www.southbeds.gov.uk

South Buckinghamshire
www.southbucks.gov.uk

South Cambridgeshire
www.scambs.gov.uk

South Gloucestershire
www.southglos.gov.uk

South Hams
www.south-hams-dc.gov.uk

South Holland
www.sholland.gov.uk

South Kesteven
www.skdc.com

South Lanarkshire
www.southlanarkshire.gov.uk

South Norfolk
www.south-norfolk.gov.uk

South Northamptonshire
www.southnorthants.gov.uk

South Oxfordshire
www.southoxon.gov.uk

South Ribble
www.south-ribblebc.gov.uk

South Shropshire
www.southshropshire.gov.uk

South Somerset
www.southsomerset.gov.uk

South Staffordshire
www.sstaffs.gov.uk

South Tyneside
www.s-tyneside-mbc.gov.uk

Southampton
www.southampton.gov.uk

Southend on Sea
www.southend.gov.uk

Southwark
www.southwark.gov.uk

Spelthorne
www.spelthorne.gov.uk

St Albans
www.stalbans.gov.uk

St Edmundsbury
www.stedmundsbury.gov.uk

St Helens
www.sthelens.gov.uk

Stafford
www.staffordbc.gov.uk

Staffordshire
www.staffordshire.gov.uk

Sterling
www.sterling.gov.uk

Stevenage
www.stevenage.gov.uk

Stockport
www.stockportmbc.gov.uk

Stockton-on-Tees
www.stockton-bc.gov.uk

Stoke-on-Trent
www.stoke.gov.uk

Strabane
www.strabanedc.org.uk

Stroud
www.stroud.gov.uk

Suffolk
www.suffolkcc.gov.uk

Sunderland
www.sunderland.gov.uk

Surrey
www.surreycc.gov.uk

Surrey Heath
www.surreyheath.gov.uk

Sutton
www.sutton.gov.uk

Swale
www.swale.gov.uk

Swansea
www.swansea.gov.uk

Swindon
www.swindon.gov.uk

Tameside
www.tameside.gov.uk

Tamworth
www.finditin-tamworth.co.uk/index2.htm

Tandridge
www.tandridgedc.gov.uk

Taunton Deane
www.tauntondeane.gov.uk

Teesdale
www.teesdale.gov.uk

Teignbridge
www.teignbridge.gov.uk

Telford & Wrekin
www.telford.gov.uk

Tendring
www.tendringdc.gov.uk

Test Valley
www.testvalley.gov.uk

Tewksbury
www.tewksburybc.gov.uk

Thannet
www.thannet.gov.uk

Three Rivers
www.3rivers.gov.uk

Thurrock
www.thurrock.gov.uk

Tonbridge & Malling
www.tmbc.gov.uk

Torbay
www.torbay.gov.uk

Torfaen
www.torfaen.gov.uk

Torridge
www.torridge.gov.uk

Tower Hamlets
www.towerhamlets.gov.uk

Trafford
www.trafford.gov.uk

Tunbridge Wells
www.tunbridgewells.gov.uk

Tynedale
www.tynedale.gov.uk

Uttlesford
www.uttlesford.gov.uk

Vale of Glamorgan
www.valeofglamorgan.gov.uk

Vale Royal
www.valeroyal.gov.uk

Wakefield
www.wakefield.gov.uk

Walsall
www.walsall.gov.uk

Waltham Forest
www.lbwf.gov.uk

Wandsworth
www.wandsworth.gov.uk

Wansbeck
www.wansbeck.gov.uk

Warrington
www.warrington.gov.uk

Warwickshire
www.warwickshire.gov.uk

Watford
www.watford.gov.uk

Waveney
www.waveney.gov.uk

Waverley
www.waverley.gov.uk

Wealden
www.wealden.gov.uk

Wear Valley
www.wearvalley.gov.uk

Wellingborough
www.wellingborough.gov.uk

Welwyn Hatfield
www.welhat.gov.uk

West Berkshire
www.westberks.gov.uk

West Devon
www.wdbc.gov.uk

West Dorset
www.westdorset-dc.gov.uk

West Dunbartonshire
www.west-dunbarton.gov.uk

West Oxfordshire
www.westoxon.gov.uk

West Sussex
www.westsussex.gov.uk

West Wiltshire
www.west-wiltshire-dc.gov.uk

Western Isles
www.w-isles.gov.uk

Westminster
www.westminster.gov.uk

Weymouth & Portland
www.weymouth.gov.uk

Wigan
www.wiganmbc.gov.uk

Wiltshire
www.wiltshire.gov.uk

Winchester
www.winchester.gov.uk

Windsor & Maidenhead
www.rbwm.gov.uk

Wirral
www.wirral.gov.uk

Woking
www.woking.gov.uk

Wokingham
www.wokingham.gov.uk

Wolverhampton
www.wolverhampton.gov.uk

Worcester
www.cityofworcester.gov.uk

Worcestershire
www.worcestershire.gov.uk

Worthing
www.worthing.gov.uk

Wrexham
www.wrexham.gov.uk

Wychavon
www.wychavon.gov.uk

Wycombe
www.wycombe.gov.uk

Wyre
www.wyrebc.gov.uk

Wyre Forest
www.wyreforestdc.gov.uk

York
www.york.gov.uk

Parliament

General Election
www.election.co.uk

House of Commons
www.parliament.uk/commons/hsecom.htm

House of Lords
www.publications.parliament.uk/pa/ld/ldho-me.htm

Isle of Man
www.tynwald.isle-of-man.org.im

Northern Ireland Assembly
www.ni-assembly.gov.uk

Parliament
www.parliament.uk

Scottish Parliament
www.scotland.gov.uk

States of Jersey
www.jersey.gov.uk

Welsh Assembly
www.wales.gov.uk

What you see is what you ge

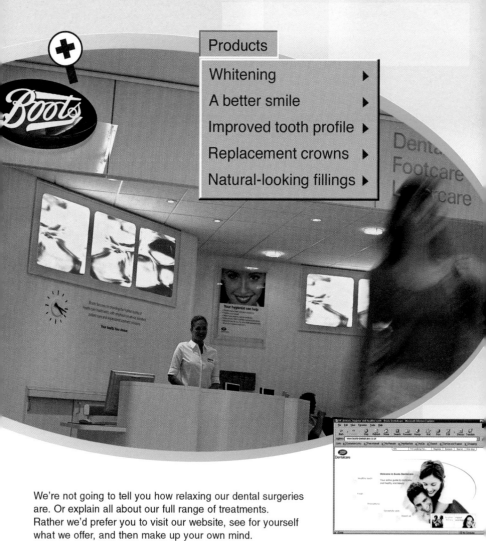

Products

Whitening ▶

A better smile ▶

Improved tooth profile ▶

Replacement crowns ▶

Natural-looking fillings ▶

We're not going to tell you how relaxing our dental surgeries are. Or explain all about our full range of treatments. Rather we'd prefer you to visit our website, see for yourself what we offer, and then make up your own mind.

After browsing through our full list of prices, looking at our range of cosmetic services and taking a virtual visit of one of our high street surgeries, we're confident you'll find that we really do offer a refreshingly modern approach to dentistry. And if you need any more convincing, why not check out one of our money-saving online promotions.

The above image shows an example of a Boots Dentalcare reception.

www.boots-dentalcare.co.uk

Dentalca

ancillary services •
animal health •
complementary •
dentistry •
government agencies •
health authorities •
hospitals, clinics & nhs trusts •
journals, magazines & websites •
medicine & surgery •
nursing & midwifery •
pharmacy •
psychiatry & psychology •
research •
vision •

healthcare

Dentalcare

www.boots-dentalcare.com

Visit the dentist **before**
you visit the denti

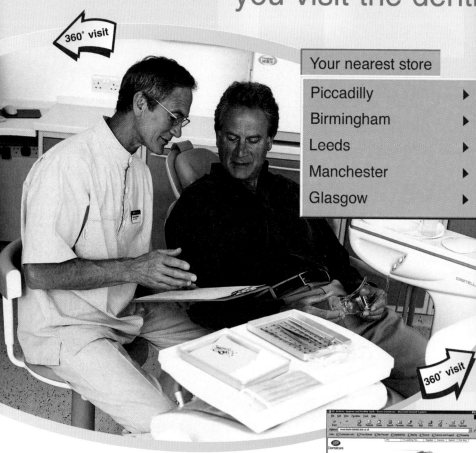

360° visit

Your nearest store

Piccadilly ▶
Birmingham ▶
Leeds ▶
Manchester ▶
Glasgow ▶

360° visit

Modern. Clean. Comfortable. Relaxing. Enjoyable even.

We can harp on for ages about just how different an experience you can look forward to at Boots Dentalcare. The best way to convince you, however, is simply to invite you to visit our website and take a virtual tour from the comfort of your home or office.

Just a quick look will persuade you that we really are a different kind of dentist. One that suits your lifestyle, with longer, worker-friendly opening hours and an approach that puts you and your needs first. So, visit today and judge for yourself our treatment room, reception area, prices, promotions, treatments and services.

www.boots-dentalcare.co.uk

Dentalca

ancillary services

Anthony Nolan Bone Marrow Trust
www.anthonynolan.com

Association of Professional Ambulance Personnel
www.apap.org.uk

British Association of Emergency Medical Technicians
www.baemt.org.uk

British Blood Transfusion Service
www.bbts.org.uk

British Healthcare Trade Association
www.bhta.com

British Organ Donor Society
www.argonet.co.uk/body

British Safety Council
www.britishsafetycouncil.co.uk

British Toxicology Society
www.bts.org

Carers National Association
www.carersuk.demon.co.uk

Health Education Authority
www.hea.org.uk

Health Education Board of Scotland
www.hebs.scot.nhs.uk

Hospital Broadcasting Association
www.nahbo.demon.co.uk

Institute of Food Science & Technology
www.ifst.org

Medical Advisory Services for Travellers Abroad (MASTA)
www.masta.org

National Association of Health Authorities & Trusts
www.nahat.net

National Blood Service
www.bloodnet.nbs.nhs.uk

Nursing Homes Registry
www.nursinghomes.co.uk

Royal Institute of Public Health & Hygiene
www.riphh.org.uk

Scottish National Blood Transfusion Service
www.showscot.nhs.uk/snbts

Welsh Blood Transfusion Service
www.welsh-blood.org.uk

animal health

British Equine Veterinary Association
www.beva.org.uk

British Small Animal Veterinary Association
www.bsava.ac.uk

British Veterinary Association
www.bva.co.uk

British Veterinary Nursing Association
www.vetweb.co.uk/sites/bvna

National Office of Animal Health
www.noah.demon.co.uk

Royal College of Veterinary Surgeons
www.rcvs.org.uk

Society of Practising Veterinary Surgeons
www.spvs.org.uk

Veterinary Medicines Directorate
www.open.gov.uk/vmd

complementary

Academy of Curative Hypnotherapists
www.ach.co.uk

Alexander Technique
www.ati.com

Association of Reflexologists
www.aor.org.uk

Bach Flower Essences
www.nelsonbach.com/bachessences

British Acupuncture Council
www.acupuncture.org.uk

British Chiropractic Association
www.chiropractic-uk.co.uk

British Dietetic Association
www.bda.uk.com

British Homoeopathic Library
www.hom-inform.org

British Medical Acupuncture Society
www.medical-acupuncture.co.uk

British Osteopathic Association
www.osteopathy.org

British School of Homeopathy
www.homeopathy.co.uk

Canadian Chiropractic Association
www.ccachiro.org

Chartered Society of Physiotherapy
www.csphysio.org.uk

Chiropractors' Association of Australia
www.caa.com.au

College of Integrated Chinese Medicine
www.cicm.org.uk

Foundation for Traditional Chinese Medicine
www.demon.co.uk/acupuncture

General Chiropractic Council
www.gcc-uk.org

International Chiropractors Association
www.chiropractic.org

International Federation of Aromatherapists
www.ifa.org.au

National Institute of Ayurvedic Medicine
www.niam.com

Osteopathic Information Service
www.osteopathy.org.uk

Register of Chinese Herbal Medicine
www.rchm.co.uk

Royal College of Speech & Language Therapists
www.rcslt.org

Society of Chiropodists & Podiatrists
www.feetforlife.org

Society of Teachers of the Alexander Technique
www.stat.org.uk

Trepanation Trust
www.trepanation.com

dentistry

Boots Dental Care

www.boots-dentalcare.com

British Dental Association
www.bda-dentistry.org.uk

British Dental Health Foundation
www.dentalhealth.org.uk

British Dental Trade Association
www.bdta.org.uk

British Endodontic Society
www.derweb.ac.uk/bes

British Homeopathic Dental Association
www.bhda.org

British Society for Restorative Dentistry
www.derweb.ac.uk/bsrd

British Society of Dentistry for the Handicapped
www.bsdh.org.uk

Denplan
www.denplan.co.uk

Dental Anxiety & Phobia Association
www.healthyteeth.com

Dental Practice Board
www.dentanet.org.uk

General Dental Council
www.gdc-uk.org

National Dentists Directory
www.nationaldirectories.net

National Radiological Protection Board
www.nrpb.org.uk

government agencies

Association of British Healthcare Industries
www.abhi.org.uk

Institute of Health Service Management
www.ihm.org.uk

Medical Devices Agency
www.medical-devices.gov.uk

Medicines Control Agency
www.open.gov.uk/mca

NHS Confederation
www.nhsconfed.net

health authorities

Avon
www.avon.nhs.uk

Barking & Havering
www.bhha.org.uk

Birmingham
www.birminghamhealth.org.uk

Bradford
www.braford-ha.nhs.uk

Buckinghamshire
www.buckshealth.com

Cambridge & Huntingdon
www.cambs-ha.nhs.uk

Cornwall & Isles of Scilly
www.cornwallhealth.org.uk

Croydon
www.carelink.info-com.com

Doncaster
www.donhlth.demon.co.uk

Dorset
www.dorset.swest.nhs.uk

Dudley
www.dudleyha.demon.co.uk

Ealing, Hammersmith & Hounslow
www.ehh-ha.nthames.nhs.uk

East Kent
www.ekent-ha.sthames.nhs.uk

East London & The City
www.elcha.co.uk

East Surrey
www.surreyweb.org.uk/esha

East Sussex, Brighton & Hove
www.esbhhealth.ndirect.co.uk

Enfield & Haringey
www.enhar-ha.org.uk

Gloucestershire
www.glos-health.org.uk

Grampian
www.show.scot.nhs.uk/ghb

Gwent
www.gwent-ha.wales.nhs.uk

Hillingdon
www.hhcu.demon.co.uk

Isle of Wight
www.iwha.swest.nhs.uk

Kingston & Richmond
www.krha.demon.co.uk

Lambeth, Southwark & Lewisham
www.lslha.nhs.uk

Leeds
www.leedshealth.org.uk

Leicestershire
www.leicester-ha.trent.nhs.uk

Liverpool
www.liverpool-ha.org.uk

Lothian
www.lothianhealth.scot.nhs.uk

Manchester
www.manchesterhealth.co.uk

Morecambe Bay
www.morecmbe-ha.nwest.nhs.uk

North & Mid Hampshire
www.hants.gov.uk/nmhha

North Cumbria
www.ncumbria.demon.co.uk

North Essex
www.ne-ha.nthames.nhs.uk

North Wales
www.nwi.co.uk/nwha/nwha.htm

North West Lancashire
www.nwlha.fsnet.co.uk

North Yorkshire
www.nyha.org.uk

Northamptonshire
www.northants-ha.anglox.nhs.uk

Portsmouth & South East Hampshire
www.portsha.hants.org.uk

Redbridge & Waltham Forest
www.rwf-ha.nthames.nhs.uk

Shropshire
www.shropshireha.wmids.nhs.uk

South and West Devon
www.sw-devon-ha.swest.nhs.uk

South Cheshire
www.scheshire-ha.nwest.nhs.uk

South Essex
www.nthames-health.tpmde.ac.uk

South Humber
www.southhumberha.org.uk

Southampton & South West Hampshire
www.sswhha.org.uk

St Helens & Knowsley
www.nhsconfed.net/knowsley

Wakefield
www.nhsconfed.net/wakefieldhealthauthority

Warwickshire
www.warwick-ha.wmids.nhs.uk

West Hertfordshire
www.wherts-ha.nthames.nhs.uk

West Surrey
www.surreyweb.org.uk/wsha

West Sussex
www.wsussex.health.org.uk

Worcestershire
www.phwhc.demon.co.uk

hospitals, clinics & nhs trusts

Complementary
Hale Clinic
www.haleclinic.com

NHS
Aberdeen Royal Infirmary
www.abdn-royal.com

Addenbrooke's
www.addenbrookes.org.uk

Alder Hey Children's Hospital
www.alderhey.org.uk

Ashworth
www.nhsconfed.net/ashworth/index.htm

Belfast Royal Hospitals
www.royalhospital.ac.uk

Blackpool Victoria
www.blackpool-victoria.nhs.uk

Bolton Hospice
www.boltonhospice.org

City Hospital, Birmingham
www.cityhospital.org.uk

Dartford & Gravesham
www.general-hospital.co.uk

Elizabeth Garrett Anderson
www.uclh.org/ega

Great Ormond Street
www.gosh.org.uk

Heatherwood & Wexham Park Hospitals
www.hwph-tr.fsnet.co.uk

127

Hope University
www.hop.man.ac.uk

Hospital for Tropical Diseases
www.uclh.org/htd

Leicester Royal Infirmary
www.lri.org.uk

Lifespan Healthcare
www.lifespan.org.uk

Middlesbrough General
www.southtees.northy.nhs.uk

Middlesex
www.uclh.org/mdx

Moorfields
www.moorfields.org.uk

National Hospital for Neurology &
Neurosurgery
www.uclh.org/nat

North Riding Infirmary
www.southtees.northy.nhs.uk

North Staffs Acute Psychiatric Unit
www.general-hospital.co.uk

Poole
www.poolehos.org

Queen Victoria, East Grinstead
www.queenvic.demon.co.uk

Royal Bournemouth
www.rbh.org.uk

Royal Brompton
www.rbh.nthames.nhs.uk

Royal Buckinghamshire
www.royalbucks.co.uk

Royal Infirmary of Edinburgh
www.show.scot.nhs.uk/rie

Royal Marsden
www.royalmarsden.org

Royal United Hospital Bath
www.ruh-bath.swest.nhs.uk

South Cleveland
www.southtees.northy.nhs.uk

Southampton University Hospitals
www.suht.nhs.uk

Southern General, Glasgow
www.general-hospital.co.uk

St Andrews Group
www.stah.org

Swindon
www.general-hospital.co.uk

UCL Hospitals
www.uclh.org

UCL Obstetric
www.uclh.org/obs

University College
www.uclh.org/uch

University Hospital of Wales
www.nhsconfed.net/universityhospitalofwales

Private

Betty Ford Center
www.bettyfordcenter.org

BMI Healthcare
www.bmihealth.co.uk

Bristol Cancer Help Centre
www.bristolcancerhelp.org

BUPA
www.bupa.co.uk

Cromwell
www.cromwell-hospital.co.uk

London Clinic
www.lonclin.co.uk

London Radiosurgical Centre
www.radiosurgery.co.uk

Marie Stopes Health Clinics
www.mariestopes.org.uk

Mayo Clinic
www.mayo.edu

Nuffield
www.nuffieldhospitals.org.uk

Partnerships in Care
www.partnershipsincare.co.uk

PPP Healthcare
www.ppphealthcare.co.uk

PPP/Columbia
www.columbiahealthcare.co.uk

Priory
www.thepriory-hospital.co.uk

St Martin's Healthcare
www.stmartins-healthcare.co.uk

Surgicare
www.surgicare.co.uk

journals, magazines & websites

British Journal of General Practice
www.rcgp.org.uk/rcgp/journal/index.asp

British Journal of Healthcare Management
www.bjhcm.com

British Journal of Nursing
www.britishjournalofnursing.com

British Medical Journal
www.bmj.com

British Nursing News
www.nurse-nurses-nursing.com/bnno.html

Evidence-Based Nursing
www.ebn.bmjjournals.com

Health Centre
www.healthcentre.org.uk

Health Service Journal
www.hsj.co.uk

Hospital Doctor
www.health-news.co.uk

Journal of Community Nursing
www.jcn.co.uk

Journal of Neonatal Nursing
www.neonatal-nursing.co.uk

Journal of Public Health Medicine
www.oup.co.uk/pubmed

Journal of the British Acupuncture Council
www.acupuncture.org.uk/ejom

Lancet
www.thelancet.com

Medic Direct
www.medicdirect.co.uk

Medisearch
www.medisearch.co.uk

Net Doctor
www.netdoctor.co.uk

NHS Digest
www.nhsdigest.org

NHS Direct
www.nhsdirect.nhs.uk

Nursing Standard
www.nursing-standard.co.uk

Nursing Times
www.nursingtimes.net

Portfolio of British Nursing
www.british-nursing.com

Positive Health
www.positivehealth.com

Practice Nursing
www.practicenursing.com

Pulse
www.epulse.co.uk

Reuters Health Information
www.reutershealth.com

medicine & surgery

American Medical Association
www.ama-assn.org

Anatomical Society
www.anatsoc.org.uk

Association of Clinical Pathologists
www.pathologists.org.uk

Association of Operating Department
Practitioners
www.aodp.org

Association of Police Surgeons
www.apsweb.org.uk

British Association of Accident & Emergency
Medicine
www.baem.org.uk

British Association of Paediatric Surgeons
www.baps.org.uk

British Association of Plastic Surgeons
www.baps.co.uk

British Fertility Society
www.britishfertilitysociety.org.uk

British Geriatrics Society
www.bgs.ord.uk

British Medical Association
www.bma.org.uk

British Psychological Society
www.bps.org.uk

Centre for Medicines Research
www.cmr.org

Chartered Institute of Environmental Health
www.cieh.org.uk

Clinical Trial Managers Association
www.ctma.org.uk

Diana, Princess of Wales Centre for
Reproductive Medicine
www.powc.org

General Medical Council
www.gmc-uk.org

Hospital Consultants & Specialists
Association
www.hcsa.com

Institute of Child Health
www.ich.bpmf.ac.uk

Medical Defence Union
www.the-mdu.com

Medical Protection Society
www.mps.org.uk

Medical Research Council
www.mrc.ac.uk

National Sports Medicine Institute
www.nsmi.org.uk

National Sports Medicine Institute of the UK
www.nsmi.org.uk

NHS Primary Care Group Alliance
www.nhsalliance.org

Physiological Society
www.physoc.org

Royal College of Anaesthetists
www.rcoa.ac.uk

Royal College of General Practitioners
www.rcgp.org.uk

Royal College of Obstetricians &
Gynaecologists
www.rcog.org.uk

Royal College of Physicians, Edinburgh
www.rcpe.ac.uk

Royal College of Surgeons, Edinburgh
www.rcsed.ac.uk

Royal College of Surgeons, England
www.rcseng.ac.uk

Royal Society of Medicine
www.roysocmed.ac.uk

nursing & midwifery

Active Birth Centre
www.activebirthcentre.com

Association for Improvements in Maternity
Services
www.aims.org.uk

Association of Radical Midwives
www.radmid.demon.co.uk

British Nursing Agencies
www.nursing-list.com

British Nursing Association
www.bna.co.uk

English National Board for Nursing,
Midwifery and Health Visiting
www.enb.org.uk

Federation of Independent Nursing
Agencies
www.fina-nursing.com

Florence Nightingale Foundation
www.florence-nightingale-foundation.org.uk

Foundation of Nursing Studies
www.fons.org

In-flight Nurses Association
www.gmb.dircon.co.uk/ifna

Infection Control Nurses Association
www.icna.co.uk

National Association of Theatre Nurses UK
www.natn.org.uk

National Board for Nursing, Midwifery and
Health Visiting for Northern Ireland
www.n-i.nhs.uk/nbni

National Board of Nursing, Midwifery and
Health Visiting in Scotland
www.nbs.org.uk

National HIV Nurses Association
www.fons.org/nhivna

NHS Nursing
www.doh.gov.uk/nursing.htm

Royal College of Nursing
www.rcn.org.uk

Royal College of Nursing Scotland
www.rcnscotland.org

United Kingdom Central Council for Nursing
Midwifery and Health Visiting
www.ukcc.org.uk

Welsh National Board for Nursing, Midwifery
and Health Visiting
www.wnb.org.uk

pharmacy

Association of British Pharmaceutical
Industry
www.abpi.org.uk

Association of the British Pharmaceutical
Industry
www.abpi.org.uk

Boots Pharmacists' Association
http://omnisbpa.members.beeb.net

British Association of European
Pharmaceutical Distributors
www.api.org.uk

British Pharmacopoeia
www.pharmacopoeia.org.uk

European Agency for the Evaluation of
Medicinal products
www.emea.eu.int

Medicines Control Agency
www.open.gov.uk/mca/mcahome.htm

National Pharmaceutical Association
www.npa.co.uk

Royal Pharmaceutical Society of Great
Britain
www.rpsgb.org.uk

Scottish Pharmaceutical General Council
www.spgc.org.uk

United Kingdom Medicines Information
Pharmacists Group
www.druginfozone.org

psychiatry & psychology

Association of Psychological Therapists
www.apt.uk.com

British Association for Behavioural &
Cognitive Psychotherapies
www.babcp.org.uk

British Association of Psychotherapists
www.bap-psychtherapy.org

British Psychological Society
www.bps.org.uk

Institute of Mental Health
www.imhl.com

Institute of Psychiatry
www.iop.kcl.ac.uk

Institute of Psychotherapy & Social Studies
www.ipss.dircon.co.uk

Manchester Institute of Psychotherapy
www.mcpt.co.uk

United Kingdom Council for Psychotherapy
www.psychotherapy.org.uk

research

AIDS Education & Research Trust
www.avert.com

Canadian Neuro-Optic Research Institute
www.cnri.edu

RAFT Institute
www.raft.ac.uk

Society for the Study of Fertility
www.ssf.org.uk

Tenovus
www.tenovus.org.uk

vision

Medical

British Ophthalmic Anaesthesia Society
www.boas.org

CIBAVision
www.cibavision.co.uk

College of Optometrists
www.college-optometrists.org

Opticians

Boots Opticians
www.bootsopticians.co.uk

David Clulow
www.davidclulow.com

Dolland & Aitchison
www.danda.co.uk

Eye Clinic
www.eye-clinic.co.uk

Specsavers
www.specsavers.com

20/20 Opticians
www.20-20.co.uk

Vision Express
www.visionexpress.co.uk

Zeiss Direct
www.zeiss-direct.co.uk

ambulance services ●

breakdown services ●

charities & helplines ●

consumer problems ●

fire & rescue services ●

funeral services ●

police ●

watchdogs & ombudsmen ●

help!

ambulance services

Ambulance Service Association
www.ambex.co.uk

Avon
www.avonambulance.org.uk

Berkshire
www.berkshire.nhs.uk/rbat

County Air Ambulance
www.ambulance.co.uk

Essex
www.essexambhq.demon.co.uk

Hampshire
www.nhsconfed.net/hampshireambulance

Lancashire
www.lancashireambulance.com

London
www.lond-amb.sthames.nhs.uk

Northern Ireland
www.n-i.nhs.uk/nias

Northumbria
www.quay.co.uk/northamb/nas.html

St John's Ambulance Brigade
www.london.sja.org.uk

Sussex
www.sxambs.sthames.nhs.uk/sast

breakdown services

AA
www.theaa.co.uk

Green Flag
www.greenflag.co.uk

RAC
www.rac.co.uk

charities & helplines

Animals

Animal Aid
www.animalaid.org.uk

Animal Health Trust
www.aht.org.uk

Animal Rescue
www.animalrescue.org.uk

Animal Samaritans
www.animalsamaritans.org.uk

AnimalKind
www.netcomuk.co.uk/~jcox

Battersea Dogs Home
www.dogshome.org

Blue Cross
www.thebluecross.org.uk

Brigitte Bardot Foundation
www.fondationbrigittebardot.fr/uk

British Horse Society
www.bhs.org.uk

Care for the Wild International
www.careforthewild.org.uk

Cats Protection League
www.cats.org.uk

Dian Fossey Gorilla Fund
www.gorillas.org

Donkey Sanctuary
www.thedonkeysanctuary.org.uk

International Animal Rescue
www.iar.org.uk

International Fund for Animal Welfare
www.ifaw.org

International League for the Protection of Horses
www.ilph.org

National Anti-Vivisection Society
www.navs.org

National Canine Defence League
www.ncdl.org.uk

National Pet Week
www.nationalpetweek.org.uk

PDSA
www.pdsa.org.uk

Royal Society for the Prevention of Cruelty to Animals (RSPCA)
www.rspca.org.uk

Royal Society for the Protection of Birds (RSPB)
www.rspb.org.uk

Save the Rhino
www.savetherhino.co.uk

VIVA
www.viva.org.uk

World Society for the Protection of Animals
www.wspa.org.uk

Children

Adoption Information Line
www.adoption.org.uk

Association for Families who have Adopted from Abroad
www.afaa.mcmail.com

Barnado's
www.barnados.org.uk

British Agencies for Adoption & Fostering
www.baaf.org.uk

Child Accident Prevention Trust
www.capt.org.uk

ChildLine
www.childline.org.uk

Children in Need
www.bbc.co.uk/cin

Children With Aids
www.cwac.org

Children's Society
www.the-childrens-society.org.uk

Contact a Family
www.cafamily.org.uk

Families Need Fathers
www.fnf.org.uk

First Cheque 2000
www.firstcheque2000.org.uk

Fostering Information Line
www.fostering.org.uk

Gingerbread
www.gingerbread.org.uk

Kidscape
www.kidscape.org.uk

Mensa Foundation for Gifted Children
www.mfgc.org.uk/mfgc

Missing Kids
www.missingkids.co.uk

National Society for the Prevention of
Cruelty to Children (NSPCC)
www.nspcc.org.uk

NCH
www.nch.org

NCH Action for Children
www.nchafc.org.uk

PACT
www.pactcharity.co.uk

Save the Children
www.savethechildren.org.uk

Variety Club of Great Britain
www.varietyclub.org.uk

Community

Action for Victims of Medical Accidents
www.avma.org.uk

Addaction
www.addaction.org.uk

Age Concern
www.ace.org.uk

British Association for Counselling
www.counselling.co.uk

Business in the Community
www.bitc.org.uk

Centrepoint
www.centrepoint.org.uk

Church Action on Poverty
www.church-poverty.org.uk

Citizens Advice Bureau
www.adviceguide.org.uk

Comic Relief
www.comicrelief.org.uk

Crisis
www.crisis.org.uk

Diana Memorial Fund
www.theworkcontinues.org

English-Speaking Union
www.esu.org

Gamblers Anonymous
www.gamblersanonymous.org.uk

Give As You Earn
www.giveasyouearn.org

Help the Aged
www.helptheaged.org.uk

Leonard Cheshire Foundation
www.lcf.org.uk

National Lotteries Charities Board
www.nclb.org.uk

Neighbourhood Watch
www.nwatch.org.uk

Nuffield Trust
www.nuffieldtrust.org.uk

Prince's Trust
www.princes-trust.org.uk

Relate
www.relate.org.uk

Rotary International
www.rotary.org

Royal National Institute for Deaf People
(RNID)
www.rnid.org.uk

Royal National Institute for the Blind (RNIE
www.rnib.org.uk

Royal National Lifeboat Institution (RNLI)
www.rnli.org.uk

Royal Society for the Prevention of
Accidents (ROSPA)
www.rospa.co.uk

Salvation Army
www.salvationarmy.org.uk

Samaritans
www.samaritans.org.uk

Shelter
www.shelter.org.uk

UK Firework Safety
www.eig.org.uk/fws

UK National Workplace Bullying Advice Lir
www.successunlimited.co.uk

Unison
www.unison.org.uk

VSO
www.vso.org.uk

Women's Aid
www.womensaid.org.uk

Education

Book Trust
www.booktrust.org.uk

British Association for Open Learning
www.baol.co.uk

British Dyslexia Association
www.bda-dyslexia.org.uk

Careers Services National Association
www.careers-uk.com

Raleigh International
www.raleighinternational.org

Scottish Book Trust
www.scottishbooktrust.com

Health

Ability
www.ability.org.uk

Action against Breast Cancer
www.aabc.org.uk

Action for Cancer Trust
www.actionforcancertrust.com

Action for ME
www.afme.org.uk

Action for Tinnitus Research
www.tinnitus-research.org

Action on Pre-eclampsia
www.apec.org.uk

Alcohol Concern
www.alcoholconcern.org.uk

Alcoholics Anonymous
www.alcoholics-anonymous.org

Alzheimer's Association
www.alz.org

Alzheimer's Disease Society
www.alzheimers.org.uk

Anorexia & Bulimia Care
www.anorexiabulimiacare.co.uk

Anthony Nolan Bone Marrow Trust
www.anthonynolan.com

Arachnoiditis Trust
www.merseyworld.com/arach

Arthritis Care
www.arthritiscare.org.uk

Association for International Cancer Research
www.aicr.org.uk

Association for Post-Natal Illness
www.apni.org

Association for Spina Bifida & Hydrocephalus
www.asbah.demon.co.uk

Bliss
www.bliss.org.uk

Bob Champion Cancer Trust
www.bobchampion.org.uk

Breast Cancer Campaign
www.bcc-uk.org

Breast Clinic
www.thebreastclinic.com

British Acoustic Neuroma Association
www.ukan.co.uk/bana

British Cardiac Society
www.cardiac.org.uk

British Diabetic Association
www.diabetes.org.uk

British Epilepsy Association
www.epilepsy.org.uk

British Heart Foundation
www.bhf.org.uk

Cancer Bacup
www.cancerbacup.org.uk

Cancer Research Fund
www.crc.org.uk

Centre for Recovery from Drug & Alcohol Abuse
www.recovery.org.uk

Council for Disabled Children
www.ncb.org.uk/cdc.htm

Crusaid
www.crusaid.org.uk

Depression Alliance
www.depressionalliance.org

Diabetes Insight
www.diabetic.org.uk

Disability Now
www.disabilitynow.org.uk

Disabled Living Foundation
www.dlf.org.uk

Downs Syndrome Association
www.dsa-uk.com

Ectopic Pregnancy Trust
www.ectopic.org.uk

Enuresis Resource & Information Centre
www.eric.org.uk

Epilepsy Research Foundation
www.erf.org.uk

Glaucoma Research Foundation
www.glaucoma.org

Institute for the Study of Drug Dependency
www.isdd.co.uk

King's Fund
www.kingsfund.org.uk

Leukaemia Research Fund
www.leukaemia-research.org.uk

Macmillan Relief
www.macmillan.org.uk

Marie Curie Cancer Care
www.mariecurie.org.uk

Mencap
www.mencap.org.uk

Meningitis Research Foundation
www.meningitis.org.uk

Mind
www.mind.org.uk

Miscarriage Association
www.the-ma.org.uk

Multiple Births Foundation
www.multiplebirths.org.uk

Multiple Sclerosis Society
www.mssociety.org.uk

Muscular Dystrophy Campaign
www.muscular-dystrophy.org

NACC
www.nacc.org.uk

National Addiction Centre
www.iop.kcl/ac.uk/iop/Departments/PsychMed/NAC/index.stn

National AIDS Trust
www.nat.org.uk

National Association for Premenstrual Syndrome
www.pms.org.uk

National Asthma Campaign
www.asthma.org.uk

National Autistic Society
www.oneworld.org/autism_uk

National Back Pain Association
www.backpain.org

National Deaf Children's Society
www.ndcs.org.uk

National Endometriosis Society
www.endo.org.uk

National Fertility Association
www.issue.co.uk

National Kidney Research Fund
www.nkrf.org.uk

National Meningitis Trust
www.meningitis-trust.org.uk

National Osteoporosis Society
www.nos.org.uk

Northern Ireland Chest, Heart & Stroke Association
www.nichsa.com

Nuffield Trust
www.nuffieldtrust.org

Paralinks
www.paralinks.net

Primary Immunodeficiency Association
www.pia.org.uk

Prostate Cancer
www.prostate-cancer.org.uk

Reach
www.reach.org.uk

Roy Castle Lung Cancer Foundation
www.roycastle.org

Scope
www.scope.org.uk

SIDS - Foundation
http://dspace.dial.pipex.com/fsid

Stillbirth & Neonatal Death Society
www.uk-sands.org

Stroke Association
www.stroke.org.uk

Terence Higgins Trust
www.tht.org.uk

World Federation of Haemophilia
www.wfh.org

Third World

Action Aid
www.oneworld.org/actionaid

Amnesty International
www.amnesty.org

Care International
www.care.org

Christian Aid
www.christian-aid.org.uk

Globalaid
www.globalaid.co.uk

Oxfam
www.oxfam.org.uk

Red Cross
www.redcross.org.uk

Sight Savers
www.sightsavers.org

consumer problems

British Standards Institution
www.bsi.org.uk

British Weights & Measures Association
www.british-weights-and-measures-association.co.uk

The Complainer
www.complainer.co.uk

Consumer Gateway (DTI)
www.consumer.gov.uk

Consumers in Europe Group
www.ceg.co.uk

European Agency of Information on
Consumer Affairs
www.euro-conso.org

Local Authorities Co-ordinating Body on
Food & Trading Standards
www.lacots.org.uk

National Association of Citizens Advice
Bureaux
www.nacab.org.uk

Trading Standards Office
www.tradingstandards.gov.uk

Watchdog
www.bbc.co.uk/watchdog

fire & rescue services

British Fire Service
www.fire.org.uk

Cheshire Fire Brigade
www.cheshirefire.co.uk

Cleveland Fire Brigade
www.clevelandfire.gov.uk

Coastguard Agency
www.coastguard.gov.uk

Fire Brigade Union
www.fbu-ho.org.uk

Gosport & Fareham Inshore Rescue Service
www.hants.gov.uk/gafirs

International Rescue Corps
www.ps2.com/irc

Maritime & Coastguard Agency
www.mcagency.org.uk

Mountain Rescue
www.mra.org

Royal Naval Lifeboat Institution
www.rnli.org.uk

Tyne & Wear Metropolitan Fire Brigade
www.twfire.org

West Sussex Fire Brigade
www.wsfb.co.uk

funeral services

British Institute of Embalmers
www.bie.org.uk

Co-operative Funeral Services
www.funeral-services.co.uk

National Association of Memorial Masons
www.namm.org.uk

Society of Allied & Independent Funeral
Directors
www.saif.org.uk

police

Association of Police Authorities
www.apa.police.uk

Avon & Somerset
www.avonandsomerset.police.uk

Bedfordshire
www.bedfordshire.police.uk

British Transport Police
www.btp.police.uk

Cheshire
www.cheshire.police.uk

City of London
www.cityoflondon.gov.uk/citypolice

Cleveland
www.cleveland.police.uk

Derbyshire
www.derbyshire.police.uk

Devon & Cornwall
www.devon-cornwall.police.uk

Durham
www.durham.police.uk

Dyfed & Powys
www.dyfed-powys.police.uk

Essex
www.essex.police.uk

Gloucestershire
www.gloucestershire.police.uk

Greater Manchester
www.gmp.police.uk

Hampshire
www.hampshire.police.uk

Hertfordshire
www.herts.police.uk

Humberside
www.humberside.police.uk

Interpol
www.interpol.com

Lancashire
www.lancashire.police.uk

Leicestershire
www.leics.police.uk

Lincolnshire
www.lincs.police.uk

Merseyside
www.merseyside.police.uk

Metropolitan Police
www.met.police.uk

National Crime Squad
www.nationalcrimesquad.police.uk

North Wales
www.north-wales.police.uk

Northamptonshire
www.norpol.com

Northumbria
www.northumbria.police.uk

Royal Ulster Constabulary
www.nics.gov.uk/ruc

Scotland
www.scottish.police.uk

South Wales
www.south-wales.police.uk

South Yorkshire
www.southyorks.police.uk

Staffordshire
www.staffordshire.police.uk

Suffolk
www.suffolk.police.uk

Surrey
www.surrey.police.uk

Sussex
www.sussex.police.uk

Thames Valley
www.thamesvalley.police.uk

West Mercia
www.westmercia.police.uk

West Midlands
www.west-midlands.police.uk

West Yorkshire
www.westyorkshire.police.uk

Wiltshire
www.wiltshire.police.uk

watchdogs & ombudsmen

Adjudicator's Office
www.open.gov.uk/adjoff/index.htm

Adult Learning Inspectorate
www.ali.gov.uk

Advertising Standards Authority
www.asa.org.uk

Banking Ombudsman
www.obo.org.uk

Broadcasting Standards Commission
www.bsc.org.uk

Data Protection Registrar
www.dataprotection.gov.uk

Drinking Water Inspectorate
www.dwi.detr.gov.uk

Estate Agents Ombudsman
www.oea.co.uk

Health Service Ombudsman
www.ombudsman.org.uk

Independent Complaints Reviewer to HM
Land Registry
www.icrev.demon.co.uk/icrbook.htm

Independent Television Commission
www.itc.org.uk

Insurance Ombudsman Bureau
www.theiob.org.uk

Jasper Griegson (The Complainer)
www.complainer.co.uk

Local Government Ombudsman
www.open.gov.uk/lgo

Northern Ireland Ombudsman
www.ombudsman.nics.gov.uk

OFFER (Electricity)
www.open.gov.uk/offer

Office for the Supervision of Solicitors
www.lawsociety.org.uk

Office of Fair Trading
www.oft.gov.uk

OFGAS (Gas)
www.ofgas.gov.uk

OFSTED (Teaching)
www.ofsted.gov.uk

OFTEL (Telecommunications)
www.oftel.org

OFWAT (Water)
www.open.gov.uk/ofwat

Parliamentary Ombudsman
www.ombudsman.org.uk

Press Complaints Commission
www.pcc.org.uk

Radio Authority
www.radioauthority.org.uk

Rail Users' Consultative Committees
www.rail-reg.gov.uk/rucc/rucindex.htm

Scottish Legal Services Ombudsman
www.scot-legal-ombud.org.uk

- astrology
- ballooning
- birds
- boating
- bodybuilding
- bridge
- chess
- climbing
- collecting
- cookery
- country pursuits
- dancing
- fishing
- flying
- football
- gambling
- games

- gardening
- genealogy
- handicraft
- homebrew
- horse riding
- karting
- metal detecting
- miscellaneous clubs & associations
- models
- music
- outdoor pursuits
- parachuting
- pets
- photography
- ten pin bowling

astrology

Astrological Association of Great Britain
www.astrologer.com/aanet

British Astrological & Psychic Society
www.bapsoc.co.uk

Jonathan Cainer
www.cainer.com

Russell Grant
www.russellgrant.com

ballooning

Adventure Balloons
www.adventureballoons.co.uk

British Association of Balloon Operators
www.babo.org.uk

Virgin Challenger
www.challenger.virgin.net

birds

African Bird Club
www.africanbirdclub.org

Association of Field Ornithologists
www.afonet.org

Bird On!
http://birdcare.com/birdon

Birds of Britain
www.birdsofbritain.co.uk

Birdwatch Magazine
www.birdwatch.co.uk

British Falconers Club
www.britishfalconersclub.co.uk

British Homing World
www.pigeonracing.com

British Ornithologists' Union
www.bou.org.uk

British Trust for Ornithology
www.birdcare.com

Budgerigar Society
www.budgerigarsociety.com

Budgerigar World
www.tuxford.dabsol.co.uk

Game Conservancy Trust
www.game-conservancy.org.uk

National Birds of Prey Centre
www.nbpc.co.uk

National Flying Club
www.nationalflyingclub.co.uk

Oriental Bird Club
www.orientalbirdclub.org

Parrot Society UK
www.theparrotsocietyuk.org

Racing Pigeon Magazine
www.racingpigeon.co.uk

Rare Breeding Birds Panel
www.indaal.demon.co.uk/rbbp.html

Royal Pigeon Racing Association
www.rpra-ne.demon.co.uk

UK Parrot Society
www.theparrotsocietyuk.org

boating

Association of Inland Navigation Authorities
www.aina.org.uk

Association of Waterways Cruising Clubs
www.penpont.demon.co.uk/awcchp.htm

Big Blue Boat Shows
www.bigblue.org.uk

British Waterways
www.britishwaterways.co.uk

Classic Motor Boat Association
www.cmba.classic-marine.co.uk

Inland Waterways Association
www.waterways.org.uk

National Association of Boat Owners
www.nabo.org.uk

UK Waterways Network
www.ukwaterways.net

bodybuilding

Flex Magazine
www.flexonline.com

International Federation of Body Builders
www.ifbb.com

Mens Fitness Magazine
www.mensfitness.com

Muscle & Fitness Magazine
www.muscle-fitness.com

Weider Nutrition
www.weider.ca

bridge

American Contract Bridge League
www.acbl.org

Bridge Today
www.bridgetoday.com/bt

Bridge World
www.bridgeworld.com

Canadian Bridge Federation
www.cbf.ca

English Bridge Union
www.ebu.co.uk

Israeli Bridge Federation
www.bridge.co.il

Northern Ireland Bridge Union
www.nibu.co.uk

Pakistan Bridge Federation
http://pbf.port5.com

Scottish Bridge Union
www.sbu.dircon.co.uk

South African Bridge Federation
www.sabf.co.za

Welsh Bridge Union
www.wbu.org.uk

World Bridge Federation
www.bridge.gr

chess

British Chess Federation
www.bcf.ndirect.co.uk

British Chess Magazine
www.bcmchess.co.uk

Garry Kasparov
www.clubkasparov.ru

Internet Chess Club
www.chessclub.com

London Chess Centre
www.chess.co.uk

Scottish Chess Association
www.users.globalnet.co.uk/~sca

This Week in Chess
www.chess.co.uk

World Chess Federation
www.fide.com

climbing

British Mountain Guides
www.bmg.org.uk

British Mountaineering Council
www.thebmc.co.uk

Mountain Rescue
www.mra.org

Mountain Sports Guide
www.mtn.co.uk

Mountaineering Council for Scotland
www.mountaineering-scotland.org.uk

Rockface
www.rockface.co.uk

Scottish Mountaineering Club
www.smc.org.uk/smc

144

Three Peaks Challenge
www.netdesktop.co.uk/3peaks

Welsh National Mountain Centre
www.pyb.co.uk

collecting

Cards

Cartophilic Society of Great Britain
www.cardclubs.ndirect.co.uk

English Playing Card Society
www.epcs.mcmail.com

International Playing Card Society
www.pagat.com/ipcs

Trade Card Collector's Association
www.tradecardcollectors.com

Coins

British Association of Numismatic Societie
www.coinclubs.freeserve.co.uk

Coin Dealer Directory
www.numis.co.uk

Coin News
www.coin-news.com

Coins & Antiquities Magazine
www.coins-and-antiquities.co.uk

Royal Numismatic Society
www.users.dircon.co.uk/~rns/index.html

Spink & Son
www.spink-online.com

World of Money
www.world-of-money.com

Miscellaneous

Airfix Collectors Club
www.djairfix.freeserve.co.uk

Antiquarian Horological Society
www.ahsoc.demon.co.uk

Armourer Magazine
www.armourer.u-net.com

Association of Bottled Beer Collectors
http://ourworld.compuserve.com/homepages/jo
n_mann/abbchome.htm

British Matchbox Label & Booklet Society
www.studenter.hb.se/~match/bml&bs

British Watch & Clock Collectors
Association
www.timecap.co.uk

UK Sucrologists Club
www.uksucrologistclub.org.uk

Stamps

Association of First Day Cover Collectors
www.gbfdc.co.uk

British Aerophilatelic Federation
www.btinternet.com/~baef

British Library Philatelic Collections
www.bl.uk/collections/philatelic

GB Philatelic Society
http://www.gbps.org.uk/

Hallmark Group
www.hallmark-group.co.uk

National Postal Museum
www.royalmail.co.uk/athome/stamps/museum.htm

Post Office
www.postoffice.co.uk

Robin Hood Stamp Company
www.robinhood-stamp.co.uk

Royal Philatelic Society London
www.rpsl.org.uk

Stanley Gibbons
www.stangib.com

UK Philatelic Museums & Libraries
www.gs.dial.pipex.com/museum3.htm

UK Stamp Fairs
www.stampdiary.com

cookery

Ballymaloe Cookery School
www.ballymaloe-cookery-school.ie

BBC Food & Drink
www.bbc.co.uk/foodanddrink

Fresh Food Cookbook
www.freshfood.co.uk/cookbook

Gourmet World
www.gourmetworld.co.uk

Leith's School of Food & Wine
www.leiths.com

Mosiman Academy
www.mosiman.com

Recipe World
www.recipe-world.com

Royal Thai Cookery School
www.rtsca.com

Tante Marie Cookery School
www.tantemarie.co.uk

country pursuits

British Association for Shooting & Conservation
www.basc.org.uk

British Falconers Club
www.users.zetnet.co.uk/bfc

British Field Sports Society
www.bfss.org

CLA Game Fair
www.countrypursuits.co.uk/cla.htm

Clay Pigeon Shooting Association
www.cpsa.co.uk

Countryside Alliance
www.countryside-alliance.org

Countrysports
www.countrysports.co.uk

Field Magazine
www.thefield.co.uk

National Association of Regional Game Councils
www.iol.ie/~nargc

National Association of Specialist Anglers
www.cygnet.co.uk/ukfw/nasa

Shooting Gazette
www.countrypursuits.co.uk

Sportsman's Association
www.sa-headquarters.freeserve.co.uk

Sportsman's Association (SAGBNI)
www.sportsmans-association.org

UK Practical Shooting Association
www.ukpsa.co.uk

Welsh Fishing & Trout Association
www.fishing-in-wales.com/wstaa

dancing

Ballroom Dancing Times
www.dancing-times.co.uk

DanceSport UK
www.dancesport.uk.com

Imperial Society of Teachers of Dancing (ISTD)
www.istd.org.uk

International Dance Sport Federation
www.idsf.net

International Dance Teachers Association (IDTA)
www.idta.co.uk

fishing

Angling Magazine
www.anglemag.freeserve.co.uk

Angling News
www.angling-news.co.uk

Bankside Fishing Tackle
www.banksidefishing.co.uk

Fishing UK
www.fishing.co.uk

Fishing World
www.fishing.org

Fly Dressers' Guild
www.the-fdg.org

Fly Fishing UK
www.flyfishuk.com

Gardner
www.gardnertackle.co.uk

Glasgow Angling Centre
www.fishingmegastore.com

Grayling Society
www.graylingsociety.org

Harrisons Rods
www.harrisonrods.co.uk

Maver
www.maver.co.uk

National Federation of Anglers
www.fire.org.uk/nfa

RMC Angling
www.rmcangling.co.uk

Salmon & Trout Association
www.salmon-trout.org

Scottish Anglers National Association
(SANA)
www.sana.org.uk

Sea Anglers Conservation Network
www.anglenet.co.uk

Specialist Anglers Conservation Group
www.anglersnet.co.uk/sacg

UK Angling Guide
http://uk-fishing.com

UK Fly Fishing & Tyers Federation
www.fly-fisherman.org.uk

flying

Aeroclub
www.aeroclub.net

Airspace Magazine
www.raes.org.uk

British Aerobatics Association
www.aerobatics.org.uk

British Disabled Flying Club
www.fly.to/bdfc

British Gliding Association
www.gliding.co.uk

British Microlight Aircraft Association
www.avnet.co.uk/bmaa

Civil Aviation Authority
www.caa.co.uk

Denham Aerodrome
www.egld.com

Flyer
www.flyer.co.uk

Pilot Magazine
www.pilotweb.co.uk

Red Arrows
www.raf.mod.uk/reds/redhome.html

World Air Sports Federation
www.fai.org

football

Ian St John's Soccer Camps
www.soccercamps.co.uk

Sunday Football League Directory
www.sunday-football.co.uk

Umbro International Football Festival
www.worldwidesoccer.co.uk

gambling

Blue Sq
www.bluesq.com

British Casino Association
www.british-casinos.co.uk

City Index
www.cityindex.co.uk

Greyhound Racing Board
www.thedogs.co.uk

IG Index
www.igindex.co.uk

Jamba (Carlton TV)
www.jamba.co.uk

Ladbrokes
www.ladbrokes.co.uk

Littlewoods Pools
www.littlewoods-pools.co.uk

Mecca Bingo Online
www.meccabingo.com

National Lottery
www.national-lottery.co.uk

Rank Leisure
www.rank.com

Sporting Index
www.sportingindex.com

Tote
www.tote.co.uk

UK Betting
www.ukbetting.com

Victor Chandler
www.victorchandler.com

William Hill
www.williamhill.co.uk

Zetters
www.zetters.co.uk

games

British Isles Backgammon Association
www.cottagewebs.co.uk/biba

Loquax
www.loquax.co.uk

Monopoly
www.monopoly.com

Scrabble
www.scrabble.com

Trivial Pursuit
www.trivialpursuit.com

gardening

Atco
www.atco.co.uk

Barnsdale Gardens (Geoff Hamilton)
www.barnsdalegardens.co.uk

BBC Ground Force
www.bbc.co.uk/groundforce

BBC Home Front in the Garden
www.bbc.co.uk/homefrontgarden

Birstall Garden Centre
www.birstall.co.uk

Black & Decker Online
www.blackanddecker.com

Chelsea Flower Show
www.rhs.org.uk/chelsea

Crocus
www.crocus.co.uk

Cyclamen Society
www.cyclamen.org

Florajac's
www.florajacs.co.uk

Flower & Plant Association
www.flowers.org.uk

Flymo
www.flymo.co.uk

Garden
www.igarden.co.uk

Garden History Society
www.gardenhistorysociety.org

Gardeners' World
www.gardenersworld.beeb.com

Hampton Court Palace Flower Show
www.rhs.org.uk/hamptoncourt

Hartland
www.hartland.co.uk

Hayter
www.hayter.co.uk

Herb Society
www.herbsociety.co.uk

Heritage Seed Library
www.hdra.org.uk/hsl

International Bulb Society
www.bulbsociety.com

Landscape Trust
www.landscape.co.uk

Levington
www.levington.co.uk

Miracle-Gro Online
www.miraclegro.com

National Garden Scheme
www.ngs.org.uk

National Gardens Scheme
www.ngs.org.uk

National Herb Centre
www.herbcentre.co.uk

New Eden
www.neweden.co.uk

Permaculture Association
www.permaculture.co.uk

Qualcast
www.qualcast.co.uk

Royal Horticultural Society
www.rhs.org.uk

Royal Horticultural Society Shop
www.grogro.com

Royal National Rose Society
www.roses.co.uk

Secretts
www.secretts.co.uk

Spear & Jackson
www.spear-and-jackson.com

Van Tubergen
www.vantubergen.co.uk

genealogy

Ancestry Research
www.ancestors.co.uk

British Heraldic Archive
www.kwtelecom.com/heraldry

Family Records Centre
www.pro.gov.uk/about/frc

Family Tree Magazine
www.family-tree.co.uk

Federation of Family History Societies
www.ffhs.org.uk

Gendex Genealogical Index
www.gendex.com

Genealogical Services Directory
www.genealogical.co.uk

General Register Office, Northern Ireland
www.nics.gov.uk/nisra/gro

General Register Office, Scotland
www.open.gov.uk/gros

GENUKI, UK & Ireland Geneology
www.genuki.org.uk

Institute of Heraldic & Genealogical Studies
www.ihgs.ac.uk

Irish Family History Foundation
www.mayo-ireland.ie/roots.htm

Mormons Family Search
www.familysearch.org

Public Record Office
www.pro.gov.uk

Scottish Genealogy Society
www.sol.co.uk/s/scotgensoc

Society of Genealogists
www.sog.org.uk

handicraft

Association of Guilds of Weavers, Spinners and Dyers
www.wsd.org.uk

Bead Society of Great Britain
http://members.delphi.com/britishbeads

Calligraphy & Lettering Arts Society
www.clas.co.uk

Ceramics Monthly
www.ceramicsmonthly.org

Classic Stitch
www.classicstitch.co.uk

Colour Craft Needlework
www.colour-craft.com

County Needlecraft
www.countyneedlecraft.com

Craft UK
www.craft-fair.co.uk

Crochet Design
www.crochet.co.uk

Embroiderers' Guild
www.embroiderersguild.org.uk

Glass Art Society
www.glassart.org

Guild of Silk Painters
www.silkpainters-guild.co.uk

Husqvarna
www.husqvarnastudio.co.uk

International Feltmakers Association
www.feltmakers.org.uk

Knitting Now
www.knittingnow.com

Knitting Today
www.knittingtoday.com

Lace Guild
www.laceguild.demon.co.uk

Lace Magazine
www.lacemagazine.com

Marquetry Society
www.marquetry.org

Quick and Easy Cross Stitch Magazine
www.futurenet.com/futureonline/magazines/magazine.asp?ID=39

Quilters' Guild of the British Isles
www.quiltersguild.org.uk

Quilting Directory
www.quiltingdirectory.co.uk

Rowan
www.rowanyarns.co.uk

Royal School of Needlework
www.royal-needlework.co.uk

Society of Scribes and Illuminators
www.calligraphy.org

Stoll UK
www.stolluk.co.uk

UK Cross Stitch Club
www.crossstitch.org

UK Stained Glass News
www.stainedglassnews.co.uk

Vogue Knitting
www.vogueknitting.com

homebrew

Breworld
www.breworld.com

Craft Brewing Association
www.breworld.com/cba

EDME
www.edme.com

horse riding

Association of British Riding Schools
www.equiworld.net/abrs

British Driving Society
www.britishdrivingsociety.co.uk

British Equestrian Trade Association
www.beta-uk.org

British Horse Society
www.bhs.org.uk

Endurance Horse and Pony Society
www.ehps.org.uk

Pony Club
www.pony-club.org.uk

Scottish Equestrian Magazine
www.thescottishequestrian.co.uk

Side Saddle Association
www.equiworld.com/ssa

karting

Association of British Kart Clubs
www.karting.co.uk/abkc

Association of Racing Kart Schools
www.arks.co.uk

British Superkart Association
www.superkart.mcmail.com

Challenge 2000
www.kartchallenge.com

Daytona
www.daytona.co.uk

UK Karting
www.karting.co.uk

metal detecting

C.Scope
www.cscope.co.uk

Detecnicks
www.detecnicks.co.uk

Federation of Independent Detectorists
www.detectorists.net

National Council for Metal Detecting
www.ncmd.freeserve.co.uk

UK Detector Net
www.ukdetectornet.co.uk

miscellaneous clubs & associations

Association of Woodturners of Great Britain
www.woodturners.co.uk

British Matchbox Label and Booklet Society
www.studenter.hb.se/~match/bml&bs

British Model Flying Association
www.bmfa.org

British Youth Council
www.byc.org.uk

Country Gentleman's Association
www.thecga.co.uk

Elgar Society
www.elgar.org

English Pool Association
www.epa.org.uk

Gunpowder Plot Society
www.gunpowder-plot.org

Historical Model Railway Society
www.hmrs.org.uk

Hovercraft Club of Great Britain
www.hovercraft.org.uk

Lighthouse Society of Great Britain
www.lsgb.co.uk

London Underground Railway Society
www.lurs.demon.co.uk

Mensa
www.mensa.org

National Federation of Young Farmers Clubs
www.nfyfc.org.uk

Paintball Zone
www.paintballzone.demon.co.uk

Radio Society of Great Britain
www.rsgb.org

Rotaract Club
www.rotaract.org.uk

Royal British Legion
www.britishlegion.org.uk

Tai Chi Union of Great Britain
www.eb61.dial.pipex.com

Tri-ang Model Railways
www.tri-ang.co.uk

United Kingdom Radio Society
www.ukrs.org

Women's Institute
www.nfwi.org.uk

Womens Royal Voluntary Service (WRVS)
www.wrvs.org.uk

YMCA
www.ymca.org.uk

Youth Clubs UK
www.youthclubs.org.uk

Youth Hostelling Association
www.yha.org.uk

models

Airfix
www.airfix.co.uk

Beatties
www.beatties.net

British Electric Flight Association
www.befa007.freeserve.co.uk

British Model Flying Association
www.bmfa.org

British Model Soldier Society
www.btinternet.com/~model.soldiers

Corgi
www.corgi.co.uk

Hannants
www.hannants.co.uk

Historical Model Railway Society
www.hmrs.org.uk

Hornby
www.hornby.co.uk

Model Yachting Association
www.ukmya.mcmail.com

Scalextric
www.scalextric.co.uk

Tri-ang Model Railways
www.tri-ang.co.uk

music

Akai
www.akai.com

Association of Blind Piano Tuners
www.uk-piano.org/abpt

Banks Music Publications
www.banksmusicpublications.cwc.net

Bluthners
www.bluthers.co.uk

Boosey & Hawkes
www.boosey.com

British Flute Society
www.bfs.org.uk

Chamberlain Music
www.chamberlainmusic.com

Chappells
www.uk-piano.org/chappell

Fender
www.fender.com

Gibson
www.gibson.com

Kemble Pianos
www.uk-piano.org/kemble

Marshall Amplification
www.marshallamps.com

Premier Percussion
www.premier-percussion.com

Sheet Music Direct
www.sheetmusicdirect.com

Steinway
www.steinway.com

Yamaha

www.yamaha.co.uk

outdoor pursuits

British Holiday & Home Parks Association
www.ukparks.com

British Orienteering Federation
www.cix.co.uk/~bof

British Walking Federation
www.bwf-ivv.org.uk

Camping & Caravanning Club
www.campingandcaravanningclub.co.uk

Camping & Outdoor Leisure Association
www.cola.org.uk

Camping UK Directory
www.camping.uk-directory.com

Caravan Club
www.caravanclub.co.uk

Compass Sport Magazine
www.compasssport.com

Cotswold Outdoor
www.cotswold-outdoor.co.uk

Duke of Edinburgh's Award Scheme
www.theaward.org

English Lakeland Ramblers
www.ramblers.com

Fell Runners Association
www.ae401.dial.pipex.com

Field & Trek
www.field-trek.co.uk

International Orienteering Federation
www.orienteering.org

National Caving Association
www.nca.org.uk

National Trails
www.nationaltrails.gov.uk

Ordnance Survey
www.ordsvy.gov.uk

Ramblers Association
www.ramblers.org.uk

parachuting

British Parachute Association
www.bpa.org.uk

Parachute Association of Ireland
http://indigo.ie/~pai

United States Parachute Association
www.uspa.org

pets

Cats

Cat World
www.catworld.co.uk

Cats Protection League
www.cats.org.uk

Feline Advisory Bureau
www.fabcats.org

Supreme Cat Show
www.chace.demon.co.uk

Whiskas Cat Food
www.petsource.com/whiskas

Dogs

Associated Sheep, Police and Army Dog Society
www.aspads.org.uk

Battersea Dogs Home
www.dogshome.org

Border Collie Trust
www.bctgb.freeserve.co.uk

British Dog Breeders Council
www.k9netuk.com/bdbc

Canine World
www.canineworld.com

Council of Docked Breeds
www.cdb.org

Crossbreed & Mongrel Club
www.crossbreed.freeserve.co.uk

Crufts
www.crufts.org.uk

Dog Club UK
www.dogclub.co.uk

Dogs Online
www.dogsonline.co.uk

Dogs Today
www.petspark.com/dogstoday

Dogs Worldwide
www.dogsworldwide.com

Fanciers Breeder Referral List
www.breedlist.com

Kennel Club
www.the-kennel-club.org.uk

National Canine Defence League
www.ncdl.org.uk

National Dogsitters
www.dogsit.com

National Puppy Register
www.findapup.net

Pedigree Petfoods
www.petcat.co.uk

Fish

British Aquatic Resource Centre
www.cfkc.demon.co.uk

British Cichlid Association
www.bca.zetnet.co.uk

British Killifish Association
www.bka.freeuk.com

British Koi Keepers' Society
www.bkks.co.uk

Practical Fishkeeping
www.aquarist.net/pfk

Water Web
www.vampire.free-online.co.uk

General

Animail
www.animail.co.uk

British Dragonfly Society
www.dragonflysoc.org.uk

British House Rabbit Association
www.houserabbit.co.uk

Insect World
www.insect-world.com

National Fancy Rat Society
www.nfrs.org

National Gerbil Society
www.gerbils.co.uk

National Hamster Council
www.hamsters-uk.org

Pet Cover
www.petcover.com

Pet Plan Insurance
www.petplan.co.uk

Pets Pyjamas.com
www.pets-pyjamas.co.uk

Rabbits Online
www.rabbitsonline.com

Rabbits UK
www.cs.cf.ac.uk/rabbits

Reptilian Online
www.reptilian.co.uk

Serpents Magazine
www.serpents.co.uk

Turtle World
www.downey288.freeserve.co.uk

UK Reptiles Online
www.ukreptiles.com

Vivarium Magazine
www.thevivarium.freeserve.co.uk

photography

Cameras & Equipment

Agfa
www.agfa.co.uk

Canon
www.canon.co.uk

151

Casio
www.casio.co.uk

Contax
www.contax.com

Epson
www.epson.com

Fuji Film
www.fujifilm.com

Kodak

www.kodak.co.uk

Konica
www.konica.com

Leica
www.leica-camera.com

Minolta
www.minolta.co.uk

Nikon
www.nikon.co.uk

Olympus
www.olympus-europa.com

Panasonic
www.panasonic.com

Pentax
www.pentax.co.uk

Polaroid
www.polaroid.com

Ricoh
www.ricoh-cameras.co.uk

Rollei
www.rollei.com

Samson
www.samson.com

Sigma
www.sigma-aldrich.com

Yashica
www.yashica.com

Magazines & Websites

Amateur Photography UK
www.amphot.co.uk

British Journal of Photography
www.bjphoto.demon.co.uk

Centre for Photographic Art
www.photography.org

Cheese Magazine
www.cheesemagazine.com

Classic Camera Magazine
www.marriott.u-net.com/ccm.htm

Digital Photography Review
http://photo.askey.net

Focus
www.focus-online.com

Royal Photographic Society
www.rps.org

UK Amateur Photograph
www.amphot.co.uk

Which Camera?
www.whichcamera.co.uk

ten pin bowling

British Ten Pin Bowling Association
www.shef.ac.uk/~sutbc/btba

SuperBowl
www.superbowl.co.uk

cars ●

dating agencies ●

disabilty ●

driving schools ●

family life ●

hairdressers, beauty salons & image consultants ●

health & fitness ●

home life ●

magazines & websites ●

military associations ●

motorcycles ●

new age ●

religion ●

retirement ●

weddings ●

living

cars

Accessories & Repairs

Allmake Motor Parts
www.allmakemotorparts.co.uk

Alpine Electronics
www.alpine1.com

Audioseek
www.audioseek.com

Autogas UK
www.autogas.co.uk

Autoglass
www.autoglass.co.uk

Britax
www.britax.co.uk

Car Parts World
www.carpartsworld.co.uk

Continental Tyres
www.conti.de

Cooper Tyre& Rubber Company
www.coopertire.com

Duckworth
www.duckworth.co.uk

Elite Registrations
www.elite-registrations.co.uk

Ferodo
www.ferodo.co.uk

Finelist
www.finelist.co.uk

Fleet Support Group
www.driversupport.demon.co.uk

Global Registrations
www.globalreg.co.uk

Halfords
www.halfords.co.uk

Hammerite
www.hammerite-automotive.com

KAGE
www.kage.ltd.uk

Kenwood
www.kenwood-electronics.co.uk

Kwik-Fit
www.kwik-fit.com

Michelin
www.michelin.com

Motor World
www.motor-world.co.uk

Motorola
www.mot.com

National Tyre Distributors Association
www.ntda.co.uk

National Tyres
www.national.co.uk

New Reg Personalised Registration Numbers
www.reg.co.uk

Parts Direct
www.partsdirect.co.uk

Pirelli
www.pirelli.co.uk

RAC Trackstar
www.ractrackstar.com

Registration Transfers
www.regtransfers.co.uk

Roaduser
www.roaduser.co.uk

Tracker
www.tracker-network.co.uk

Trafficmaster
www.trafficmaster.co.uk

Tyresave
www.tyresave.co.uk

UK Registrations
www.reg.co.uk

Unipart
www.unipart.co.uk

Buying, Selling & Auctions

Autobytel
www.autobyteluk.com

Autofinder
www.autofinder.net

British Car Auctions Group
www.bca-group.com

Fish4 Cars
www.fish4cars.co.uk

Jam Jar
www.jamjar.com

Lex Retail
www.lexretail.co.uk

Motor Auction Consortium
www.carworld.co.uk/auction/mac.htm

National Car Auctions
www.carworld.co.uk/auction/nca.htm

Scottish Car Auctions
www.scottishcarauctions.co.uk

UK Motor Vehicle Auctions
www.auctions.co.uk/cars

Magazines & Websites

Auto Exchange
www.autoexchange.co.uk

Auto Express
www.autoexpress.co.uk

Auto Trader
www.autotrader.co.uk

Autobytel
www.autobytel.co.uk

Autofinder
www.autofinder.net

Automobile Magazine
www.automobilemag.com

Automotive Body Repair News
www.abrn.com

Automotive Online
www.automotive-online.com

AutoWired
www.autowired.co.uk

BBC Top Gear
www.topgear.com

BMW Car
www.bmwcarmagazine.com

British Car Auctions
www.bca-group.com

Car
www.carmagazine.co.uk

CarNet
www.carnet.co.uk

Classic Car Directory
www.classicdirect.co.uk

Classic Car World
www.classiccarworld.co.uk

Classic Motor
www.classicmotor.co.uk

Drive
www.drive.com

Fleet NewsNet
www.automotive.co.uk

Haynes
www.haynes.co.uk

Learner Drivers UK
www.learners.co.uk

MG Enthusiast
www.mgcars.org.uk/mgmag

Motor World
www.motor-world.co.uk

Motoring UK
www.motoring-uk.co.uk

MotorTrader
www.motortrader.com

Power On Wheels
www.power-on-wheels.co.uk

ShopQ
www.shopq.co.uk

Top Gear
www.topgear.beeb.com

Tyre Trade News
www.tyretradenews.co.uk

Tyres-Online
www.tyres-online.co.uk

WhatCar?
www.whatcar.co.uk

Which? - Motoring
www.which.net/motoring

World Off Road
www.worldoffroad.com

Manufacturers

AC
www.accars.co.uk

Alfa Romeo
www.alfaromeo.com

Aston Martin
www.astonmartin.com

Audi
www.audi.co.uk

Bentley
www.rolls-royceandbentley.co.uk

BMW
www.bmw.co.uk

Bristol
www.bristolcars.co.uk

Cadillac
www.cadillaceurope.com

Caterham
www.caterham.co.uk

Chevrolet
www.chevrolet.com

Chrysler
www.chrysler.co.uk

Citroen
www.citroen.co.uk

Daewoo
www.daewoo.com

Dennis Group
www.dennis-group.co.uk

Ferrari
www.ferrari.com

Fiat
www.fiat.co.uk

General Motors
www.gm.com

Honda
www.honda.co.uk

Hyundai
www.hyundai-car.co.uk

Isuzo
www.isuzo.co.uk

Jaguar
www.jaguar.com/uk

Jeep
www.jeep.co.uk

Jensen
www.jensen-motors.com

Kia
www.kia.com

Lamborghini
www.lamborghini.it

Land Rover
www.landrover.co.uk

Lexus
www.lexus.co.uk

London Taxi
www.london-taxis.co.uk

Lotus
www.lotuscars.co.uk

Maserati
www.maserati.it/engquattroporte.htm

Mazda
www.mazda.co.uk

Mercedes Benz
www.mercedes-benz.co.uk

MG
www.mgcars.com

Mini
www.mini.co.uk

Mitsubishi
www.mitsubishi-cars.co.uk

Morgan
www.morgan-motor.co.uk

Nissan
www.nissan.co.uk

Opel
www.opel.com

Peugeot
www.peugeot.co.uk

Porsche
www.porsche.com

Proton
www.proton.co.uk

Renault
www.renault.co.uk

Rolls Royce
www.rolls-royceandbentley.co.uk

Rover
www.rovercars.com

Saab
www.saab.co.uk

SEAT
www.seat.com

Skoda
www.skoda-auto.com

Ssang Yong
www.ssangyong.co.kr/english/index.html

Subaru
www.subaru.co.uk

Suzuki
www.suzuki.co.uk

Toyota
www.toyota.co.uk

TVR
www.tvr-eng.co.uk

Vauxhall
www.vauxhall.co.uk

Volkswagen
www.vw.co.uk

Volvo
www.volvocars.volvo.co.uk

Westfield
www.westfield-sportscars.co.uk

Owners' Clubs

Aston Martin
www.amoc.org

Jensen
www.british-steel.org

Rolls Royce
www.rroc.org

Petrol

Esso
www.esso.co.uk

Mobil
www.mobil.co.uk

Shell
www.shell.com

Texaco
www.texaco.co.uk

TotalFinaElf
www.totalfinaelf.com

dating agencies

Dateline
www.dateline.co.uk

Drawing Down the Moon
www.drawingdownthemoon.co.uk

Executive Club
www.thematchmaker.co.uk

Sirius
www.clubsirius.com

disabilty

Shaw Trust
www.shaw-trust.org.uk

driving schools

BSM
www.bsm.co.uk

Institute of Advanced Motoring
www.iam.org.uk

UK Learner Drivers
www.learners.co.uk

family life

Advisory Centre For Education
www.ace-ed.org.uk

Association of Breastfeeding Mothers
http://home.clara.net/abm

BBC Parenting Resource
www.bbc.co.uk/education/health/parenting

Child of Achievement
www.childofachievement.co.uk

Community Hygiene Concern
www.chc.org

Families Need Fathers
www.fnf.org.uk

Family Planning Association
www.fpa.org.uk

La Leche League
www.lalecheleague.org

National Childbirth Trust
www.nct-online.org

Parent News
www.parents-news.co.uk

Parent Soup
www.parentsoup.com

Parentline
www.parentlineplus.org.uk

Serene
www.our-space.co.uk/serene.htm

hairdressers, beauty salons & image consultants

Andrew Collinge Hairdressing
www.andrewcollinge.com

Charles Worthington
www.cwlondon.com

Daniel Galvin
www.daniel-galvin.co.uk

Elizabeth Arden Red Door Salons
www.reddoorsalons.com

House of Colour
www.houseofcolour.co.uk

Jo Hansford
www.johansford.co.uk

Toni & Guy
www.toniandguy.co.uk

Vidal Sassoon
www.vidalsassoon.co.uk

health & fitness

British Naturist Society
www.british-naturist.org.uk

British Wheel of Yoga
www.bwy.org.uk

Cambridge Diet
www.cambridge-diet.co.uk

Cannons Health Clubs
www.cannons-health-clubs.co.uk

Champneys
www.champneys.com

David Lloyd Leisure
www.davidlloydleisure.co.uk

Esporta
www.esporta.co.uk

Forestmere Health Farm
www.forestmere.co.uk

Greens Health & Fitness
www.greensonline.co.uk

Harbour Club
www.harbourclub.co.uk

Henlow Grange Health Farm
www.henlowgrange.com

Holmes Place
www.holmesplace.co.uk

Nirvana Spa
www.nirvana-spa.co.uk

Pilates Foundation
www.pilatesfoundation.com

Pilates.co.uk
www.pilates.co.uk

Slimming World
www.slimming-world.co.uk

Sopwell House
www.sopwellhouse.co.uk

Weightwatchers
www.weightwatchers.com

home life

Cleaning & Laundry

Corby Press
www.corbypress.com

Finish
www.finish.co.uk

Persil
www.persil.co.uk

Scotchcare
www.scotchcare-services.co.uk

Sketchley
www.sketchley.co.uk

White Knight
www.white-knight.co.uk

Estate Agents

Bradford & Bingley
www.bb-ea.co.uk

Bushells
www.bushells.com

Chancellors
www.chancellors.co.uk

Chestertons
www.chestertons.co.uk

CityLet
www.citylet.com

Cluttons
www.cluttons.com

Connells
www.connells.co.uk

Copping Joyce
www.coppingjoyce.co.uk

Drivers Jonas
www.djonas.co.uk

Easier
www.easier.co.uk

Egerton
www.egertonproperty.co.uk

Felicity J Lord
www.fjlord.co.uk

Foxtons
www.foxtons.co.uk

Friend & Falcke
www.friendandfalcke.co.uk

General Accident
www.gaproperty.co.uk

Goldschmidt Howland
www.goldschmidt-howland.co.uk

Haart
www.haart.co.uk

Hamptons
www.hamptons.co.uk

Humberts
www.humberts.co.uk

Jackson-Stops & Staff
www.jackson-stops.co.uk

John D Wood
www.johndwood.co.uk

King Sturge
www.kingsturge.co.uk

Knight Frank
www.knightfrank.co.uk

London Property Guide
www.londonpropertyguide.co.uk

London Property News
www.lpn.co.uk

National Homes Network
www.nhn.co.uk

National Property Register
www.national-property-register.co.uk

Richard Ellis
www.richardellis.co.uk

Savills
www.fpdsavills.co.uk

Spicer McColl
www.spicer.co.uk

Strettons
www.strettons.co.uk

Strutt & Parker
www.struttandparker.co.uk

Winkworth
www.winkworth.co.uk

Heating

Baxi Heating
www.baxi.com

British Gas
www.gas.co.uk

Calor Gas
www.calorgas.co.uk

Corgi
www.corgi-gas.co.uk

Energy Saving Trust
www.est.org.uk

Energy Shop
www.energyshop-plc.co.uk

Potterton
www.potterton.co.uk

Robinson Willey
www.robinson-willey.co.uk

Valor
www.valor.co.uk

House Builders

Alfred McAlpine
www.alfred-mcalpine.co.uk

Antler Homes
www.antlerhomes.co.uk

Anville Homes
www.anvilleconstruction.co.uk

Ashwood Homes
www.ashwoodhomes.co.uk

Banner Homes
www.banner-homes.co.uk

Barratt Homes
www.barratthomes.co.uk

Beechwood Homes
www.beechwood.co.uk

Bellway
www.bellway.co.uk

Bewley Homes
www.bewley.co.uk

Bloor Homes
www.bloorhomes.com

Bryant Homes
www.bryant.co.uk

Charles Church
www.charles-church.co.uk

Country Life
www.countrylife.demon.co.uk

Countryside Residential
www.countrysideresidential.co.uk

Crownwood Developments
www.crownwooddevelopments.co.uk

David Wilson Homes
www.dwh.co.uk

Fairview
www.fairview.co.uk

Fordy Homes
www.fordyhomes.co.uk

Gainsborough
www.gainsbc.co.uk

George Wimpey
www.wimpey.co.uk

Goldcrest Homes
www.goldcresthomes.plc.uk

Hazelmere
www.hazelmerehomes.co.uk

Laing
www.laing.co.uk

Linden Homes
www.lindenhomes.co.uk

McAlpine
www.alfred-mcalpine.co.uk

McLean Homes
www.wimpey.co.uk/mclean

Persimmon Homes
www.persimmon.plc.uk

Rialto Homes
www.rialtohomes.co.uk

Robertson Residential
www.robertson.co.uk

St James Homes
www.stjameshomes.co.uk

Tarmac
www.tarmac.co.uk

Taylor Woodrow
www.taywood.co.uk

Thirlstone Home Development
www.thirlstone.co.uk

Ward Homes
www.ward-homes.co.uk

Westbury Homes
www.westbury-homes.co.uk

Wilcon
www.wilcon.co.uk

Wimpey Homes
www.wimpey.co.uk

Housekeeping

GH Institute
http://homearts.com/gh/toc/osinstit.htm

Professional Bodies & Trade Associations

Advisory Service (Windows & Conservatories)
www.advisoryservice.co.uk

Association of Electrical & Mechanical Trades
www.aemt.co.uk

Association of Master Upholsterers & Soft Furnishers
www.upholsterers.co.uk

British Standards Institute
www.bsi.org.uk

British Water
www.britishwater.co.uk

British Woodworkers Federation
www.bwf.org.uk

Chartered Institute of Building
www.ciob.org.uk

Confederation of Roofing Contractors
www.corc.co.uk

Construction Employers Federation
www.cefni.co.uk

CORGI (Gas Installers)
www.corgi-gas.co.uk

Electricity Association
www.electricity.org.uk

Federation of Master Builders
www.fmb.org.uk

Glass and Glazing Federation
www.ggf.org.uk

Guild of Architectural Ironmongers
www.martex.co.uk/gai

Housebuilders Federation
www.hbf.co.uk

Incorporated Society of Valuers &
Auctioneers
www.isva.co.uk

Institute of Plumbing
www.plumbers.org.uk

Institution of Structural Engineers
www.istructe.org.uk

Motor Schools Association
www.msagb.co.uk

National Association of Estate Agents
www.naea.co.uk

National Federation of Builders
www.builders.org.uk

National Hairdressers Federation
www.the-nhf.org

National Housebuliders Council (NHBC)
www.nhbc.co.uk

Replacement Window Advisory Service
www.ggf.org.uk

Royal Institution of Chartered Surveyors
www.rics.org.uk

Water UK
www.water.org.uk

Removals & Storage

Abbey Self-Storage
www.abbey-self-storage.co.uk

Association of Relocation Agents
www.relocationagents.com

Baggage Express
www.baggage-express.com

Bishops Move
www.bishops-move.co.uk

Capital Movers
www.capital-worldwide.com

Cargo Forwarding International
www.cargoforwarding.co.uk

House Removals.com
www.houseremovals.com

Interpac
www.interpac.co.uk

Moves
www.moves.co.uk

Pickfords
www.pickfords.co.uk

Teacrate
www.teacrate.com

Transeuro
www.transeuro.com

Safety & Security

Ability Security Systems
www.ability-security.co.uk

ADT
www.adt.co.uk

Banham
www.banham.com

Bates Alams
www.batesalarms.co.uk

Health & Safety Executive
www.open.gov.uk/hse/hsehome.htm

Ingersoll
www.nt-architectural-products.co.uk

Institute of Home Safety
www.homesafe.dircon.co.uk

National Inspection Council for Electrical
Installation Contracting
www.niceic.org.uk

Neighbourhood Watch
www.nwatch.org.uk

RoSPA
www.rospa.co.uk

Safety Systems & Alarm Inspection Board
www.ssaib.co.uk

Secom
www.secom-plc.com

Utilities

Amerada
www.amerada.co.uk

British Energy
www.british-energy.com

British Gas
www.gas.co.uk

Centrica
www.centrica.co.uk

Eastern Energy
www.easternenergy.co.uk

Eastern Group
www.eastern.co.uk

London Electricity
www.london-electricity.co.uk

MEB
www.meb.co.uk

National Grid
www.ngc.co.uk

National Power
www.national-power.com

North West Water
www.nww.co.uk

Northern Ireland Electricity
www.nie.co.uk

Scottish Hydro Electric
www.hydro.co.uk

Scottish Nuclear
www.snl.co.uk

ScottishPower
www.scottishpower.co.uk

Servowarm
www.servowarm.co.uk

Severn Trent
www.severn-trent.com

South West Water
www.swwater.co.uk

Sutton & East Surrey Water
www.waterplc.com

SWALEC
www.swalec.com

Transco
www.transco-bgplc.com

Wessex Water
www.wessexwater.plc.uk

Yorkshire Utilities
www.yorkutil.syol.com

magazines & websites

Antiques Trade Gazette
www.atg-online.com

Baby Directory
www.babydirectory.com

Babyworld
www.babyworld.co.uk

BBC Good Homes
www.goodhomes.beeb.com

Beeb.com
www.beeb.com

Beme
www.beme.com

Big Issue
www.bigissue.com

Charlotte Street
www.charlottestreet.com

Cosmopolitan
www.cosmopolitan.co.uk

Country Life
www.countrylife.co.uk

Docklands & City
www.docklandsandcity.com

Elle
www.ellemag.com

Esquire
www.esquiremag.com

FHM
www.fhm.co.uk

Good Housekeeping
www.goodhousekeeping.co.uk

GQ
www.gq-magazine.co.uk

Handbag.com
www.handbag.com

Hello!
www.hello-magazine.co.uk

House & Garden
www.houseandgarden.co.uk

House Beautiful
http://housebeautiful.women.com/hb

Jewish Online
www.jewishonline.org.uk

Jewish.net
www.jewish.net

Kitchen Specialists Association
www.ksa.co.uk/consumer

Kitchens, Bedrooms & Bathrooms Magazine
www.dmg.co.uk/kbbmag

Life
www.pathfinder.com/life

Loaded
www.loaded.co.uk

Magazine Shop
www.magazineshop.com

Maxim
www.maximmag.com

Men's Health
www.menshealth.com

Mother & Baby
www.motherandbaby.co.uk

National Enquirer
www.nationalenquirer.com

New Woman
www.newwomanonline.co.uk

Parent News
www.parents-news.co.uk

Playboy
www.playboy.com

Private Eye
www.private-eye.co.uk

Readers' Digest
www.readersdigest.co.uk

Shout
www.dcthomson.co.uk/mags/shout

Spectator
www.spectator.co.uk

Tatler
www.tatler.co.uk

Totally Jewish
www.totallyjewish.com

UFO
www.ufomag.co.uk

Vanity Fair
www.vanityfair.co.uk

Viz
www.viz.co.uk

Vogue
www.vogue.co.uk

World of Interiors
www.worldofinteriors.co.uk

Zoom
www.zoom.co.uk

military associations

American Legion
www.legion.org

Army Catering Corps Association
/www.regiments.org/milhist/uk/corps/ACC.htm

Bomber Command Historical Society
www.hellzapoppin.demon.co.uk

Far East Prisoners of War
www.fepow.org.uk

Friends of War Memorials
www.war-memorials.com

Home Service Force Association
www.hsf-association.freeserve.co.uk

Officers' Pensions Society
www.officerspensionsoc.co.uk

Radio Officers' Association
www.btinternet.com/~roae

RAF Benevolent Fund
www.raf-benfund.org.uk

Royal Air Forces Association
www.rafa.org.uk

Royal Auxiliary Air Force
www.rauxaf.mod.uk

Royal Canadian Legion
www.legion.ca

Scottish National War Memorial
www.snwm.org

motorcycles

Autocom
www.autocom.co.uk

Benelli

www.benelli.co.uk

Bikenet Magazine
www.bikenet.co.uk

Bike Trader Interactive
www.biketrader.co.uk

BMW
www.bmw.co.uk

British Motor Racing Circuits
www.bmrc.co.uk

British Motorcyclists Federation
www.bmf.co.uk

British Speedway Promoters
www.british-speedway.co.uk

BSA Owners' Club UK
www.bsaoc.demon.co.uk

CSM Motorcycle Training
www.csm.uk.com

Ducati
www.ducati.com

Ducati Owners Club GB
http://homepages.enterprise.net/dtempleton

Federation of European Motorcyclists'
Associations
www.mag-uk.org/fema/

Harley-Davidson
www.harley-davidson.co.uk

Honda
www.honda.co.uk

Honda Owners Club GB
www.hoc.org.uk

Kawasaki
www.kawasaki.com

Moto Guzzi
www.motoguzzi.it

Moto Guzzi Club GB
http://freespace.virgin.net/motoguzzi.clubgb/

Motorbikes Online
www.motorbikes-online.com

163

Motorcycle Industry Association
www.mcia.co.uk

Motorcycle Sport
www.motorcyclesportandleisure.co.uk

Motorcycle UK
www.motorcycle-uk.com

Motorcycle World Magazine
www.motorcycleworld.co.uk

Norton Owner Club GB
www.noc.co.uk

Piaggio
www.piaggio.com

Scootering Magazine
www.scootering.com

Suzuki
www.suzuki.co.uk

Suzuki Owners Club
www.suzuki-club.co.uk

Triumph
www.triumph.co.uk

Triumph Owners Motorcycle Club
www.tomcc.demon.co.uk

TVR
www.tvr-eng.co.uk

Vespa
www.vespa.com

Yamaha
www.yamaha-motor.co.uk

new age

British Feng Shui Society
www.fengshuisociety.org.uk

Findhorn Foundation
www.findhorn.org

Foundation for International Spiritual
Unfoldment
www.fisu.org

International Centre for Reiki Training
www.reiki.org

Raven Lodge of Shamanism
www.shamana.co.uk

religion

Buddhist

Buddhist Society (UK)
www.buddsoc.org.uk

Centre for Buddhist Studies
www.bris.ac.uk

International Zen Association
www.zen-izauk.org

Journal of Buddhist Ethics
http://jbe.gold.ac.uk

Middle Way Journal
www.buddsoc.org.uk/mw.htm

Christian

Anglican
www.anglican.org/online

Archbishop of Canterbury
www.archbishopofcanterbury.org

Baptist Church
www.baptist.org.uk

Carmelite Friars UK
www.carmelite.org

Catholic Church (in England & Wales)
www.catholic-ew.org.uk

Catholic Church (Scotland)
www.catholic-scotland.org.uk

Christadelphian
www.christadelphian.org.uk

Christian Fellowship Church
www.cfc-net.org

Church of England
www.church-of-england.org

Church of Jesus Christ Latter Day Saints
www.ldscn.com

Church of Scotland
www.cofs.org.uk

Church Society
www.churchsociety.org

Free Church of Scotland
www.freechurch.org

Jehovah's Witnesses
www.watchtower.org

Jesus Army
www.jesus.org.uk

Mennonite Church
www.mennlink.org

Methodist Church
www.methodist.org.uk

Mormons
www.mormon.net

Order of St Benedict
www.osb.org

Orthodox
www.orthodox.co.uk

Religious Society of Friends (Quakers)
www.quaker.org

Retreat Association
www.retreats.org.uk

Salvation Army
www.salvationarmy.org.uk

Scientology
www.scientology.org.uk

Scripture Union
www.scripture.org.uk

Seventh Day Adventist
www.adventist.org.uk

Unitarian
www.unitarian.org.uk

United Free Church of Scotland
www.ufcos.org.uk

United Pentecostal Church
www.upcogbi.freeserve.co.uk

Vatican
www.vatican.va

World Council of Churches
www.wcc-coe.org

Islam

Federation of Students Islamic Societies
www.fosis.org.uk

Islamic Centre England
www.ic-el.org

Islamic Foundation
www.islamic-foundation.org.uk

Islamic Unity Society
www.ius.org.uk

Muslim Council of Britain
www.mcb.org.uk

World Assembly of Muslim Youth
www.wamy.co.uk

Young Muslims UK
www.ymuk.com

Islamic

Islam
www.islamic.org.uk

Jewish

International Council of Jewish Women
www.icjw.org.uk

Jewish Board of Deputies
www.bod.org.uk

Judaism
www.jewish.co.uk

Maccabi Union
www.maccabi.org.uk

Reform Synagogues
www.refsyn.org.uk

Union of Liberal & Progressive Synagogues
www.ulps.org

Minority Faiths

Bahai Faith
www.bahai.com

British Humanist Association
www.humanism.org.uk

Hare Krishna UK
www.iskcon.org.uk

International Society for Krishna Consciousness
www.religioustolerance.org/hare.htm

Order of Bards, Ovates & Druids
www.druidry.org

Pagan Federation
www.paganfed.demon.co.uk

Spiritualists' National Union
www.snu.org.uk

Sikh

British Organization of Sikh Students
www.boss-uk.org

Sikh Arts & Cultural Association
www.saca.co.uk

Sikh Spirit
www.demon.co.uk/charities/sikh

Sikhism UK
www.sikhism.org.uk

retirement

Anchor Homes
www.anchor.org.uk

Association of Retired & Persons over 50
www.arp.org.uk

weddings

Confetti
www.confetti.co.uk

Guild of Wedding Photographers
www.gwp-uk.co.uk

Pronuptia
www.pronuptia.co.uk

Wedding Store UK
www.weddingstore.co.uk

encyclopaedias •

history •

libraries •

maps •

museums •

opinion polls & market research •

phone numbers •

professional bodies & associations •

reference •

weather •

museums, libraries & information

encyclopaedias

Britannica
www.britannica.co.uk

Encarta
www.encarta.msn.com

Encyclopedia
www.encyclopedia.com

Grolier
www.grolier.com

Hutchinson
www.hme.co.uk

Probert
www.probert-encyclopaedia.co.uk

history

Anne Frank Educational Trust
www.afet.org.uk

Britannia History
http://britannia.com/history

British Association of Paper Historians
www.baph.freeserve.co.uk

Economic History Society
www.ehs.org.uk

English Civil War Society
http://english-civil-war-society.org/public_html/index.html

English Heritage
www.english-heritage.org.uk

First Empire Magazine
www.firstempire.ltd.uk

Galpin Society
www.music.ed.ac.uk/euchmi/galpin

Historical Association
www.history.org.uk

History - BBC Online
www.bbc.co.uk/history

History Today Magazine
www.historytoday.com

Institute of Historical Research
www.ihrinfo.ac.uk

Journal of Design History
www.oup.co.uk/design

Journal of Victorian Culture
www.indiana.edu/~victoria/jvc.html

Local History Magazine
www.local-history.co.uk

Making History (BBC)
www.bbc.co.uk/education/archive/makinghistory

Manorial Society of Great Britain
www.msgb.co.uk

Oral History Society
www.essex.ac.uk/sociology/oralhis.htm

Society for History of Mathematics
www.dcs.warwick.ac.uk/bshm

Society for the Promotion of Roman Studies
www.sas.ac.uk/icls/roman/default.htm

libraries

Aberdeen University Library
www.abdn.ac.uk/library

Balliol College Library
www.balliol.ox.ac.uk/library/library.html

Barbican
www.barbican.co.uk

Bodleian Library, Oxford
www.bodley.ox.ac.uk

British Film Institute National Library
www.bfi.org.uk/nationallibrary

British Library
www.bl.uk

Cambridge University Library
www.lib.cam.ac.uk

Corporation of London Records Office (CLRO)
www.corpoflondon.gov.uk

Edinburgh University Library
http://datalib.ed.ac.uk

John Rylands Library
http://rylibweb.man.ac.uk

Library of Congress
www.loc.gov

London Library
http://webpac.londonlibrary.co.uk

National Archives of Ireland
www.nationalarchives.ie

National Art Library (Victoria & Albert Museum)
www.nal.vam.ac.uk

National Library of Scotland
www.nls.uk

National Library of Wales
www.llgc.org.uk

National Library of Women
www.lgu.ac.uk/fawcett/main.htm

Natural History Museum Library
www.nhm.ac.uk/info/library/index.html

Public Record Office of England & Wales
www.pro.gov.uk

Science Museum Library
www.nmsi.ac.uk/library

maps

Association for Geographic Information (AGI)
www.agi.org.uk

Australian National Mapping Agency
www.auslig.gov.au

British Cartographic Society
www.cartography.org.uk

British Geological Survey
www.bgs.ac.uk

Committee of the National Mapping Agencies of Europe
www.cerco.org

Geomatics Canada
www.geocan.nrcan.gc.ca

Harvey
www.harveymaps.co.uk

Land Information New Zealand
www.linz.govt.nz

Mapblast
www.mapblast.com

Multi-purpose European Ground-Related Information Network
www.megrin.org

Multimap
www.multimap.com

National Map Centre
www.mapstore.co.uk

Ordnance Survey
www.ordsvy.gov.uk

Ordnance Survey Ireland
www.irlgov.ie/osi

Ordnance Survey of Northern Ireland
www.nics.gov.uk/doe/ordnance

Shell Geostar
www.shellgeostar.com

Society of Cartographers
www.soc.org.uk

Stanfords
www.stanfords.co.uk

Street Map
www.streetmap.co.uk

3D Atlas Online
www.3datlas.com

US Geological Survey
www.usgs.gov

museums

Aerospace Museum
www.rafmuseum.org.uk/flat/cosford

Andrew Carnegie Birthplace Museum
www.carnegiemuseum.co.uk

Armed Forces Museum
www.nms.ac.uk

Ashmolean Museum
www.ashmol.ox.ac.uk

Bank of England Museum
www.bankofengland.co.uk

Bass Museum
www.bass-museum.com

Beamish Open Air Museum
www.merlins.demon.co.uk/beamish

Bear Museum, Petersfield
www.bearmuseum.co.uk

Birmingham & Midland Transport Museum
www.bammot.org.uk

Birmingham Railway Museum
www.vintagetrains.co.uk/brm.htm

Black Country Living Museum
www.bclm.co.uk

Bletchley Park
www.bletchleypark.org.uk

Brewers Quay & The Timewalk
www.brewers-quay.co.uk

Bristol City Museum & Art Gallery
www.bristol-city.gov.uk/cgi-bin

Britain At War Experience
www.britain-at-war.co.uk

British Lawnmower Museum
www.dspace.dial.pipex.com/town/square/gf86

British Museum
www.british-museum.ac.uk

British Road Transport Museum
www.mbrt.co.uk

Broadfield House Glass Museum
www.dudley.gov.uk

Bronte Parsonage Museum
www.bronte.org.uk

Brooklands Museum
www.brooklands.org.uk

Cabinet War Rooms
www.iwm.org.uk/cabinet.htm

Caernarfon Air Park
www.users.globalnet.co.uk/~airworld

Cambridge Museum of Technology
www.cam.net.uk/home/steam

Chertsey Museum
www.surreycmc.gov.uk/chermus

Clan Cameron Museum
www.clan-cameron.org/museum.html

Clan Donnachaidh Museum
www.donnachaidh.com

Clink Prison Museum
www.clink.co.uk

Cobbaton Combat Collection
www.cobbatoncombat.co.uk

Cowper & Newton Museum
www.cowperandnewtonmuseum.org

Creetown Gem and Rock Museum
www.gemrock.net

Cutty Sark
www.cuttysark.org.uk

Design Museum
www.southwark.gov.uk/tourism

Dickens House Museum
www.dickensmuseum.com

Dinosaur Museum
www.dinosaur-museum.org.uk

Discovery Point
www.rrs-discovery.co.uk

Dover Museum
www.designmuseum.org

Dunaskin Open Air Museum
www.dunaskin.org.uk

Eastleigh Museum
www.hants.gov.uk/museum/eastlmus

Eden Camp Modern History Museum
www.edencamp.co.uk

Elgin Museum
www.elginmuseum.demon.co.uk

Elmbridge Museum
www.surrey-online.co.uk

Eureka The Museum For Children
www.eureka.org.uk

Fitzwilliam Museum
www.fitzmuseum.cam.ac.uk

Florence Nightingale
www.florence-nightingale.co.uk

Fort Grey
www.museum.guernsey.net

Freud Museum
www.freud.org.uk

Galleries of Justice
www.galleriesofjustice.org.uk

Geffrye Museum
www.geffrye-museum.org.uk

Gracie Fields Museum
www.rochdale.gov.uk/gracie

Grampian Transport Museum
www.craigandsuttar.co.uk/gtm

Grantown Museum
www.grantown-on-spey.co.uk/museum.htm

Green Howards Regimental Museum
www.greenhowards.org.uk

Gressenhall Norfolk Rural Life Museum
www.museums.norfolk.gov.uk

Hancock Museum
www.ncl.ac.uk/hancock

Haynes Motor Museum
www.haynesmotormuseum.co.uk

Heritage Motor Centre
www.heritage.org.uk

HMS Belfast
www.iwm.org.uk/belfast.htm

HMS Victory
www.flagship.org.uk/victory.htm

HMS Warrior
www.flagship.org.uk/hmswarrior1860.htm

Horniman Museum
www.horniman.demon.co.uk

Hunterian Museum & Art Gallery
www.gla.ac.uk/museum

Imperial War Museum
www.iwm.org.uk

Ironbridge Museum Trust, Telford
www.ironbridge.org.uk

Jane Austen Museum
www.janeaustenmuseum.org.uk

Jersey Museum
www.jerseyheritagetrust.org/museums

Jewish Museum
www.jewmusm.ort.org

Kew Bridge Steam Museum
www.kbsm.org

London Toy & Model Museum
www.londontoy.com

London Transport Museum
www.ltmuseum.co.uk

Macclesfield Silk Museum
www.silk-macclesfield.org

Mackintosh House
www.gla.ac.uk/museum/machouse

Maidstone Museum
www.museum.maidstone.gov.uk

Manchester Museum
www.mcc.ac.uk/museum

Manchester Museum of Science & Industry
www.msim.org.uk

Mangapps Farm Railway Museum
www.mangapps.co.uk

Mary Rose
www.maryrose.org

Michael Faraday's Museum
www.ri.ac.uk

Midland Air Museum
www.discover.co.uk/~mam

Museum of Army Flying
www.flying-museum.org.uk

Museum of British Road Transport
www.mbrt.co.uk

Museum of Childhood Memories
www.nwi.co.uk/museumofchildhood

Museum of Classical Archaeology
www.classics.cam.ac.uk/ark.html

Museum of Costume
www.museumofcostume.co.uk

Museum of East Anglian Life
www.suffolkcc.gov.uk/central/meal

Museum of East Asian Art
www.east-asian-art.co.uk

Museum of Garden History
www.museumgardenhistory.org

Museum of London
www.museum-london.org.uk

Museum of Scotland
www.museum.scotland.net

Museum of the History of Science
www.mhs.ox.ac.uk

Museum of the Moving Image
www.bfi.org.uk/momi

Museum of the Royal College of Surgeons
www.rcseng.ac.uk/public/museums.htm

Museum of Welsh Life
www.nmgw.ac.uk

Museums of the Potteries
www.stoke.gov.uk/museums

National Army Museum
www.national-army-museum.ac.uk

National Coal Mining Museum
www.clanvis.com/coalmine

National Maritime Museum
www.nmm.ac.uk

National Motor Museum
www.beaulieu.co.uk

National Museum of Cartoon Art
www.pavilion.co.uk/cartoonet

National Museum of Photography, Film & TV
www.nmpft.org.uk

National Museums & Galleries on Merseyside
www.nmgm.org.uk

National Museums of Scotland
www.nms.ac.uk

National Railway Museum
www.nmsi.ac.uk/nrm

National Tramways Museum
www.tramway.co.uk

National Waterways Museum at Gloucester
www.nwm.org.uk

Natural History Museum
www.nhm.ac.uk

Pitt Rivers Museum, Oxford
www.units.ox.ac.uk/departments/prm

Portland Museum
www.weymouth.gov.uk/portmus.htm

Potteries Museum & Art Gallery
www.stoke.gov.uk/museums/pmag

Ragged School Museum
www.ics-london.co.uk/rsm

River & Rowing Museum
www.rrm.co.uk

Roman Baths Museum
www.romanbaths.co.uk

Royal Airforce Museum
www.rafmuseum.org.uk

Royal Albert Memorial Museum & Art Gallery, Exeter
www.exeter.gov.uk/tourism

Royal Armouries Museum, Leeds
www.armouries.org.uk

Royal Cornwall Museum
www.royalcornwallmuseum.org.uk

Royal Naval Museum
www.flagship.org.uk/rnm.htm

Royal Navy Submarine Museum
www.rnsubmus.co.uk

Royal Ulster Constabulary Museum, Belfast
www.ruc.police.uk

Royal Yacht Britannia
www.royalyachtbritannia.co.uk

Science Museum
www.nmsi.ac.uk

Second World War Experience Centre
www.war-experience.org

Sedgwick Museum of Geology
www.esc.cam.ac.uk

Sherlock Holmes Museum
www.sherlock-holmes.co.uk

Shetland Museum
www.shetland-museum.org.uk

Sikh Museum
www.sikhmuseum.org

Sir John Soane's Museum
www.soane.org

Somerset House
www.somerset-house.org.uk

Southampton Maritime Museum
www.southampton.gov.uk/leisure/visitguide/he.htm

Spitfire & Hurricane Memorial
www.spitfire-museum.com

St Albans Museum
www.stalbans.gov.uk/tourism

St Barbe Museum
www.st-barbe-museum.demon.co.uk

St Helens Transport Museum
www.sthtm.freeserve.co.uk

Tank Museum
www.tankmuseum.co.uk

Tank Museum, Bovington
www.tankmuseum.co.uk

Techniquest
www.tquest.org.uk

Thackray Medical Museum
www.thackraymuseum.org

Tunbridge Wells Museum
www.tunbridgewells.gov.uk/museum

Verdant Works
www.verdant-works.co.uk

Victoria & Albert Museum
www.vam.ac.uk

Whitby Museum
www.durain.demon.co.uk

Windermere Steamboat Museum
www.steamboat.co.uk

Wordsworth Museum
www.wordsworth.org.uk

Working Silk Museum
www.humphriesweaving.co.uk

York Castle Museum
www.york.gov.uk/heritage/museums

York Dungeon
www.yorkshirenet.co.uk/yorkdungeon

Yorkshire Museum
www.york.gov.uk/heritage/museums/yorkshire

opinion polls & market research

Audit Bureau of Circulation
www.abc.org.uk

British Market Research Association
www.bmra.org.uk

Gallup Organisation
www.gallup.com

Mintel.com
www.mintel.co.uk

Mori
www.mori.com

NOP Research
www.nopres.co.uk

phone numbers

BT Online Phonebook
www.bt.com/phonenetuk

Business Pages
www.businesspages.co.uk

192.com
www.192.com

Phonenumbers.net
www.phonenumbers.net

Telephone Code Changes
www.numberchange.org

Telephone Directories on the Web
www.teldir.com

Thomson Directories

www.thomweb.co.uk

Yellow Pages
www.yell.co.uk

professional bodies & associations

British Association for Information & Library
Education & Research
www.bailer.ac.uk

Council for Museums, Archives and
Libraries
www.resource.gov.uk

Library & Information Commission
www.lic.gov.uk

Library Association
www.la-hq.org.uk

Museums Association
www.museumsassociation.org

Society of Archivists
www.archives.org.uk

reference

Book Industry Communications
www.bic.org.uk

BUBL Information Service
www.bubl.ac.uk

FTSE
www.ftse.com

Jane's
www.janes.com

Kelly's Guide
www.kellysonline.net

Oxford English Dictionary
www.oed.com

Reference Centre
www.freeserve.net/reference

Roget's Thesaurus
www.thesaurus.com

Scoot
www.scoot.co.uk

Whitakers Almanack
www.whitakersalmanack.co.uk

weather

BBC Weather Centre
www.bbc.co.uk/weather

Belgium
www.meteo.oma.be

France
www.meteo.fr

Germany
www.dwd.de

ITN
www.itn.co.uk/weather

Meteorological Office
www.met-office.gov.uk

Netherlands
www.knmi.nl

Online Weather
www.onlineweather.com

Royal Meteorological Society
www.itu.rdg.ac.uk/rms

Ski Club of Great Britain (Snow Reports)
www.skiclub.co.uk

USA
www.nws.noaa.gov

Weathercall
www.weathercall.co.uk

World Meteorological Organisation
www.wmo.ch

news ●
newspapers ●
professional bodies & associations ●

news

BBC
www.bbc.co.uk/news

CNN
www.cnn.com

IRN
www.irn.co.uk

ITN
www.itn.co.uk

News Unlimited
www.newsunlimited.co.uk

NewsNow
www.newsnow.co.uk

PA News
www.pa.press.net

PR Newswire
www.prnewswire.com

Reuters
www.reuters.com

Sky
www.sky.com/news

Tass
www.tass.ru/english

Teletext
www.teletext.co.uk

Universal Press Syndicate
www.uexpress.com

newspapers

British Local

Aberdeen & District Independent
www.aberdeen-indy.co.uk

Aberdeen Evening Express
www.thisisnorthscotland.co.uk

Andover Advertiser
www.andoveradvertiser.co.uk

Ascot Express
www.ascotexpress.co.uk

Ayrshire Post
www.inside-scotland.co.uk/ayrshire

Ballyclare Gazette
www.ulsternet-ni.co.uk

Banbury Guardian
www.banburyguardian.co.uk

Bangor Caernarfon Chronicle
www.nwn.co.uk/nwninternetpages/chroniclehome.html

Banstead Herald
www.bansteadherald.co.uk

Barnoldswick & Earby Times
www.eastlancsnews.co.uk

Barnsley Chronicle
www.barnsley-chronicle.co.uk

Barry & District News
www.newscom.co.uk

Basildon Evening Echo
www.thisisessex.co.uk

Basingstoke Gazette
www.basingstokegazette.co.uk

Bath Chronicle
www.thisisbath.com

Belfast Telegraph
www.belfasttelegraph.co.uk

Belper News
www.belpernews.co.uk

Bexhill Observer
www.bexhillobserver.co.uk

Bexley News Shopper
www.newsshopper.co.uk

Bicester Advertiser
www.thisisoxfordshire.co.uk

Birmingham Post and Mail
www.go2birmingham.co.uk

Blackburn Citizen
www.thisislancashire.co.uk

Blackpool & Fylde Citizen
www.thisislancashire.co.uk

Blackpool Gazette
www.blackpool.com

Blairgowrie Advertiser
www.inside-scotland.co.uk/pertshire/index.html

Bognor Regis Journal & Guardian
www.jandg.co.uk

Bolton Evening News
www.thisislancashire.co.uk

Bournemouth Daily Echo
www.daily-echo.co.uk

Bradford Star
www.thisisbradford.co.uk

Bradford Telegraph & Argus
www.telegraph-and-argus.co.uk

Braintree Witham & Dunmow Times
www.thisisessex.co.uk

Brentwood Weekly News
www.thisisessex.co.uk

Brighton Evening Argus
www.argus-btn.co.uk

Bristol Evening Post
www.thisisbristol.com

Bristol Journal
www.newscom.co.uk

Bristol Western Daily Press
www.westpress.co.uk

Bromley New Shopper
www.newsshopper.co.uk

Bromsgrove Standard
www.bromsgrovenow.com

Buckingham Advertiser
www.buckinghamonline.co.uk

Bucks Free Press
www.thisisbuckinghamshire.co.uk

Bucks Herald
www.bucksherald.co.uk

Burnley Citizen Group
www.thisislancashire.co.uk

Burnley Express
www.eastlancsnews.co.uk

Bury Free Press
www.buryfreepress.co.uk

Bury Times
www.thisislancashire.co.uk

Business Gazette
www.businessgazette.co.uk

Cambridge Evening News
www.cambridge-news.co.uk

Carlisle News & Star
www.news-and-star.co.uk

Carrickfergus Advertiser
www.ulsternet-ni.co.uk

Castle-Point Rayleigh Standard
www.thisisessex.co.uk

Chelmsford Woodham Weekly News
www.thisisessex.co.uk

Cheltenham Independent
www.thisisgloucestershire.co.uk

Cheltenham News
www.newscom.co.uk

Cheshire Guardian Series
www.thisischeshire.co.uk

Chester Chronicle Newspapers
www.cheshirenews.co.uk

Chichester Observer
www.chiobserver.co.uk

Chorley Citizen
www.thisislancashire.co.uk

Citizen (Gloucester)
www.thisisgloucestershire.co.uk

Clacton, Frinton & Walton Gazette
www.thisisessex.co.uk

Colchester Coastal Express
www.thisisessex.co.uk

Congleton Guardian
www.thisischeshire.co.uk

Consett & Stanley Advertiser
www.thisisthenortheast.co.uk

Cornish Guardian
www.thisiscornwall.co.uk

Cornishman
www.thisiscornwall.co.uk

Courier (Dundee)
www.thecourier.co.uk

Coventry Evening Telegraph
www.go2coventry.co.uk

Craven Herald & Pioneer
www.thisisbradford.co.uk

Crawley News
www.crawleynews.co.uk

Crewe & Nantwich Guardian
www.thisischeshire.co.uk

Cumberland News (Carlisle)
www.cumberland-news.co.uk

Cumbria Life
www.cumbrialife.co.uk

Daily Express
www.express.co.uk

Darlington & Stockton Times
www.thisisthenortheast.co.uk

Darlington Northern Echo
www.thisisthenortheast.co.uk

Daventry Express
www.daventryonline.co.uk

Derby Evening Telegraph
www.thisisderbyshire.co.uk

Derbyshire Times
www.derbyshiretimes.co.uk

Dorking & Leatherhead Advertiser
www.dorkingadvertiser.co.uk

Dundee Courier
www.thecourier.co.uk

Dundee Evening Telegraph
www.dcthomson.co.uk/mags/tele

Dundee Weekly News
www.dcthomson.co.uk/mags/weekly

East Anglian Daily Times
www.eadt.co.uk

East Grinstead Courier
www.thisiskentandsussex.co.uk

East Grinstead Observer
www.eastgrinsteadobserver.co.uk

East London Advertiser
www.leevalley.co.uk/ela

Eastbourne Herald
www.eastbourneherald.co.uk

Eastwood Advertiser
www.eastwoodadvertiser.co.uk

Edinburgh Echo
www.edinburghecho.co.uk

Epsom & Banstead Herald
www.epsomherald.co.uk

Essex Chronicle Series
www.thisisessex.co.uk

Essex County Newspapers
www.essex-news.co.uk

Essex County Standard
www.essex-news.co.uk

Essex Weekly News
www.essex-news.co.uk

Evening Argus (Brighton)
www.argus-btn.co.uk

Evening Herald (Plymouth)
www.plymouth-online.co.uk

Evening Press (York)
www.thisisyork.co.uk

Evening Standard
www.thisislondon.co.uk

Evening Telegraph (Peterborough)
www.peterboroughet.co.uk

Evesham, Cotswold, Stratford Journal
www.newsquestmidlands.co.uk

Express and Star Online (West Midlands)
www.westmidlands.com

Falkirk Herald
www.falkirkherald.co.uk

Gateshead Post
www.gateshead-post.co.uk

Gazette Series
www.gazetteseries.co.uk

Glasgow Evening Times
www.eveningtimes.co.uk

Glasgow Herald
www.theherald.co.uk

Gloucestershire Citizen
www.thisisgloucestershire.co.uk

Gloucestershire Echo
www.thisisgloucestershire.co.uk

Goole Times
www.btinternet.com/~gooletimes

Grimsby Evening Telegraph
www.thisisgrimsby.co.uk

Guardian Series Newspapers
www.thisischeshire.co.uk

Guernsey Press (Guernsey Evening and Weekly Press)
www.guernsey-press.com

Halstead Gazette & Advertiser
www.thisiseesex.co.uk

Hampshire Chronicle
www.hampshirechronicle.co.uk

Hampstead & Highgate Gazette
www.hamhigh.co.uk

Harborough Mail
www.harborough.co.uk

Harlow Star
www.herts-essex-news.co.uk

Harrogate Advertiser
www.harrogate-advertiser-series.co.uk

Hartlepool Mail
www.hartlepool-mail.co.uk

Harwich & Manningtree Standard
www.thisiseesex.co.uk

Hastings Observer
www.observeronline.co.uk

Hemel Hempstead Gazette
www.hemelonline.co.uk

Hendon Times Group
www.thisislocallondon.co.uk/london.html

Herald & Post (Newcastle upon Tyne)
www.herald-and-post.co.uk

Hereford Times
www.herefordshire.com/hereford-times

Hertfordshire Mercury
www.herts-essex-news.co.uk

Herts & Essex News
www.herts-essex-news.co.uk

Herts & Essex Observer
www.herts-essex-news.co.uk

Hinckley Times
www.hinckley-times.co.uk

Hitchin & Stevenage Advertiser
www.theadvertiser.demon.co.uk

Horncastle News
www.horncastlenews.co.uk

Hornsea Post
www.hornseapost.co.uk

Hucknall Dispatch
www.hucknall-dispatch.co.uk

Huddersfield Daily Examiner
www.ichuddersfield.co.uk

Hull Daily Mail
www.hulldailymail.co.uk

Hunts Post
www.huntspost.co.uk

Isle of Man Independent
www.isle-of-man-newspapers.com

Jersey Evening Post
www.jerseyeveningpost.com

Jewish Telegraph
www.jewishtelegraph.com

Johnston Press
www.johnstonpress.co.uk

Keighley News
www.keighleynews.co.uk

Kenilworth Weekly News
www.kenilworthonline.co.uk

Kent & Sussex Courier
www.thisiskentandeastsussex.co.uk

Kent Messenger
www.kent-online.co.uk

Kilmarnock Standard
www.inside-scotland.co.uk

Knutsford Guardian
www.thisischeshire.co.uk

Lancashire Evening Post
www.prestononline.co.uk

Lancashire Evening Telegraph
www.thisislancashire.co.uk

Lancaster & Morecambe Citizen
www.thisislancashire.co.uk

Lancaster Guardian Series
www.thisislancashire.co.uk

Larne Gazette
www.ulsternet-ni.co.uk

Leamington Observer
www.leamington-now.com

Leamington Spa Courier
www.leamingtononline.co.uk

Leatherhead Advertiser
www.leatherheadadvertiser.co.uk

Leicester Mail
www.thisisleicestershire.co.uk

Leigh Reporter
http://wiganonline.co.uk

Leigh, Tyldesley & Atherton Journal
www.thisislancashire.co.uk

Lewisham News Shopper
www.newsshopper.co.uk

Lincolnshire Echo
www.lincolnshire-live.co.uk

Lincolnshire Independent
www.mortons.co.uk/lin

Lincolnshire Target
www.thisislincolnshire.co.uk

Liverpool Daily Post
www.liverpool.com/post

Liverpool Echo
www.liverpool.com/echo

London Evening Standard
www.thisislondon.co.uk/dynamic/index.html

London Jewish News
www.ljn.co.uk

Louth Leader
www.louthleader.co.uk

Luton Herald & Post
www.lutononline.co.uk

Lynn News
www.lynnnews.co.uk

Maidenhead Advertiser
www.maidenhead-advertiser.co.uk

Maldon & Burnham Standard
www.thisisessex.co.uk

Manchester Evening News
www.manchesteronline.co.uk

Mansfield Chad/Chronicle and Advertiser
www.chad.co.uk

Market Rasen Mail
www.mortons.co.uk/lin/mrm

MegaStar
www.megastar.co.uk

Metro
www.metro.co.uk

Mid Devon Gazette
www.middevongazette.co.uk

Milton Keynes Citizen
www.miltonkeynes.co.uk

Morecambe Visitor
http://morecambeonline.co.uk

Nelson Times
http://eastlancashireonline.co.uk

New Zealand News UK
www.nznewsuk.co.uk

Newark Advertiser
www.newarkadvertiser.co.uk

Newbury Weekly News
www.newburynews.co.uk

Newcastle Evening Chronicle
www.evening-chronicle.co.uk

Newcastle Herald & Post
www.herald-and-post.co.uk

Newcastle Journal
www.the-journal.co.uk

Newcastle Sunday Sun
www.sundaysun.co.uk

News & Star (Carlisle)
www.news-and-star.co.uk

Newton & Goldborne Guardian
www.thisischeshire.co.uk

North Devon Journal
www.northdevonjournal.co.uk

North East Evening Gazette (Middlesbroug
www.tees.net

North Eastern Evening Gazette
www.tees.net

North Wales Newspapers
www.nwnews.co.uk

North West Evening Mail
www.nwemail.co.uk

Northampton Chronicle & Echo
www.northamptonchronicleecho.co.uk

Northants Evening Telegraph
www.northamptonshireeveningtelegraph.co.uk

Northern Echo
www.thisisthenortheast.co.uk

Northern Echo (Darlington)
www.northern-echo.co.uk

Northwich & District Guardian
www.thisischeshire.co.uk/cheshire/northwich

Nottingham Evening Post
www.thisisnottingham.co.uk

Ormskirk Advertiser
www.ormskirkadvertiser.co.uk

Oxford Mail
www.thisisoxfordshire.co.uk

Oxford Star
www.thisisoxfordshire.co.uk

Petersfield Post
www.thepost.co.uk

Plymouth Evening Herald
www.thisisplymouth.co.uk

Plymouth Western Morning News
www.thisisplymouth.co.uk

Portsmouth Journal
www.journal.co.uk

Portsmouth News
www.thenews.co.uk

Reading Chronicle
www.readingchronicle.co.uk

Reading Evening Post
www.getreading.co.uk

Reading Newspaper Company
www.rnc.co.uk

Redditch Advertiser/Alcester Chronicle
www.redditch-now.com

Rhyl, Prestatyn & Abergele Journal
www.nwn.co.uk

Rochdale Observer
www.rochdale-observer-group.co.uk

Rugby Advertiser
www.rugbyonline.com

Rugby Observer
www.rugby-now.com

Runcorn & Widnes World
www.thisiswirral.co.uk

Rye & Battle Observer
www.ryeandbattleobserver.co.uk

Sale & Altrincham Messenger
www.thisistrafford.co.uk

Salisbury Journal
www.salisburyjournal.co.uk

Scotland on Sunday (Edinburgh)
www.scotlandonsunday.com

Scunthorpe Evening Telegraph
www.thisisscunthorpe.co.uk

Sentinel (Stoke)
www.thisisstaffordshire.co.uk

Sevenoaks Chronicle
www.thisiskentandeastsussex.co.uk

Sheffield Star & Telegraph
http://thisissheffield.net

Shetland News
www.shetland-news.co.uk

Shetland Times
www.shetland-times.co.uk

Shetland Today
www.shetlandtoday.co.uk

Shields Gazette
www.shields-gazette.co.uk

Shropshire Star
www.shropshirestar.com

Shropshire Star Online
http://shropshire-online.com

Skegness News
www.mortons.co.uk/lin/sn

Slough Express
www.sloughexpress.co.uk

Slough Observer
www.thisisslough.com

Somerset County Gazette
www.countygazette.co.uk

South Bucks Express
www.southbucksexpress.co.uk

South Wales Argus
www.southwalesargus.co.uk

South Wales Evening Post
www.thisissouthwales.co.uk

Southend Evening Echo
www.thisisessex.co.uk

Southend Observer
www.thisisessex.co.uk

Southern Daily Echo (Southampton)
www.dailyecho.co.uk

Southport Visitor
www.southportvisiter.co.uk

St Albans & District Review
www.thisishertfordshire.co.uk

St Albans Observer
www.thisishertfordshire.co.uk

St Helen's Reporter
www.wiganonline.co.uk

St Helen's Star
www.thisislancashire.co.uk

Star (Sheffield)
www.sheffweb.co.uk

Stoke Evening Sentinel
www.thisisstaffordshire.co.uk

Stornoway Gazette
www.stornoway-gazette.com

Stratford Herald
www.stratford-herald.co.uk

Stratford Standard
www.stratford-now.com

Stretford & Urmston Messenger
www.thisistrafford.co.uk

Stroud News & Journal
www.newscom.co.uk

Suffolk Now
www.suffolk-now.co.uk

Sunday Mercury
www.go2birmingham.co.uk

Sunderland Echo
www.sunderland-echo.co.uk

Surrey Advertiser
www.surreyad.co.uk

Surrey Mirror Series
www.surreymirror.co.uk

Sussex Express
www.sussexexpress.co.uk

Swindon Evening Advertiser
www.adver.co.uk

Swindon Messenger
www.newscom.co.uk

Swindon Star
www.adver.co.uk

Torquay Herald Express
www.torquay-online.co.uk

Tyrone Courier
www.ulsternet-ni.co.uk

Ulster Gazette
www.ulsternet-ni.co.uk

Warrington Mercury
www.thisischeshire.co.uk

Warwick Courier
www.warwickonline.co.uk

Worcester Evening News
www.thisisworcestershire.co.uk

British National

Daily Mail
www.dailymail.co.uk

Daily Record
www.record-mail.co.uk

Daily Star
www.megastar.co.uk

Daily Telegraph
www.telegraph.co.uk

Financial Mail on Sunday
www.thisismoney.com

Financial Times
www.ft.com

Guardian
www.guardian.co.uk

Independent
www.independent.co.uk

Mirror
www.mirror.co.uk

News of the World
www.newsoftheworld.com

Observer
www.observer.co.uk

Racing Post
www.racingpost.co.uk

Scotsman
www.scotsman.com

Sun
www.thesun.co.uk

Sunday Herald
www.sundayherald.com

Sunday Mail
www.record-mail.co.uk

Sunday Mirror
www.sundaymirror.co.uk

Sunday People
www.people.co.uk

Sunday Times
www.sunday-times.co.uk

Times
www.the-times.co.uk

Foreign

Asahi Shinbun (Japan)
www.asahi.com/english

Budapest Sun (Hungary)
www.centraleurope.com

China Times (Taiwan)
www.chinatimes.com.tw/english

Copenhagen Post (Denmark)
www.cphpost.dk

Cyprus News (Cyprus)
www.cynews.com

Daily Star (Bangaladesh)
www.dailystarnews.com

Daily Star (Lebanon)
www.dailystar.com.lb

East African Standard (Kenya)
www.eastandard.net

Express (Tanzania)
www.theexpress.com

Gibraltar Chronicle (Gibraltar)
www.gibnet.com/chron

Good Morning (Belgium)
www.yweb.com/goodmorningnews

Guardian (Nigeria)
www.ngrguardiannews.com

Hellenic Star (Greece)
www.hellenicstar.net

Herald (Pakistan)
www.dawn.com

Hindu (India)
www.the-hindu.com

Hollywood Reporter (USA)
www.hollywoodreporter.com

Hurriyet (Turkey)
www.hurriyet.com.tr

Indonesian Observer (Indonesia)
www.indoexchange.com/indonesian-observer

International Herald Tribune (USA)
www.iht.com

Iran Daily
www.iran-daily.com

Irish News (Eire)
www.irishnews.com

Irish Times (Eire)
www.irish-times.com

Island (Sri Lanka)
www.island.lk

Jerusalem Post (Israel)
www.jpost.co.il

Jordan Times (Jordan)
www.arabia.com/jordan/english

Korea Herald (Korea)
www.koreaherald.co.kr

Kurier (Austria)
www.kurier.at

Kuwait Times (Kuwait)
www.paaet.edu.kw/ktimes

Los Angeles Times (USA)
www.latimes.com

Middle East Times (Egypt)
www.metimes.com

Monitor (Uganda)
www.africanews.com/monitor

Nation (Thailand)
www.nationgroup.com

Nederlander (Holland)
www.netherlander.com

New York Times (USA)
www.nytimes.com

Norway Post
www.norwaypost.no

Paris Match
www.parismatch.com

Peoples Daily (China)
http://english.peopledaily.com.cn/index.htm

Philippine Star (Philippines)
www.philstar.com

Pravda (Russia)
www.pravda.ru

Saigon Times (Vietnam)
www.saigon-news.com

South China Morning Post (Hong Kong)
www.scmp.com

Times of India (India)
www.timesofindia.com

USA Today (USA)
www.usatoday.com

Wall Street Journal (USA)
www.wsj.com

Washington Post (USA)
www.washingtonpost.com

WOZA (South Africa)
www.woza.co.za

Zaobao (Singapore)
www.zaobao.com

professional bodies & associations

European Newspaper Publishers Association
www.enpa.be

Press Association
www.pa.press.net

Society of Editors
www.ukeditors.com

banks & building societies ●

credit cards ●

insurance ●

investment funds ●

magazines & websites ●

mortgages ●

professional bodies ●

stockbrokers ●

personal finance

banks & building societies

Abbey National
www.abbeynational.co.uk

Alliance & Leicester
www.alliance-leicester.co.uk

Allied Irish
www.aib.ie

Banc Cymru
www.bankofwales.co.uk

Bank of Ireland
www.bank-of-ireland.co.uk

Bank of Scotland
www.bankofscotland.co.uk

Bank of Wales
www.bankofwales.co.uk

BankNet
www.orders.mkn.co.uk/bank

Barclaycard
www.barclaycard.co.uk

Barclays
www.barclays.co.uk

Bath
www.bibs.co.uk

Beneficial Bank
www.bankbeneficial.com

Birmingham Midshires
www.birmingham-midshires.co.uk

Bradford & Bingley
www.bradford-bingley.co.uk

Bristol & West
www.bristol-west.co.uk

Cahoot
www.cahoot.com

Cambridge
www.cambridge-building-society.co.uk

Capital
www.capitalbank.co.uk

Cash Centres
www.cashcentres.co.uk

Cater Allen (Isle of Man)
www.caterallen-bank.com

Cheltenham & Gloucester
www.cheltglos.co.uk

Chesham
www.cheshambsoc.co.uk

Co-op
www.co-operativebank.co.uk

Darlington
www.darlington.co.uk

ECU
www.ecu.co.uk/group

Egg
www.egg.com

Express Finance
www.express-finance.co.uk

First Active
www.firstactive.co.uk

First Direct
www.firstdirect.co.uk

First Trust
www.ftbni.co.uk/ft

First-e
www.first-e.com

Fleming
www.fleming.co.uk/premier

Forexia
www.forexia.com

Granville
www.granville.co.uk

Grindlays
www.pb.grindlays.com

Halifax
www.halifax.co.uk

Hambros
www.hambrosbank.com

Hamilton
www.hdb.co.uk

Hays
www.hays-banking.co.uk

HFC
www.hfcbank.co.uk

Home & Capital Trust
www.homecapital.co.uk

HSBC
www.hsbc.com

HSBC
www.banking.hsbc.co.uk

ICC
www.icc.ie

Jyske
www.jbpb.com

Lambeth
www.lambeth.co.uk

Leeds & Holbeck
www.leeds-holbeck.co.uk

Leek
www.leek-united.co.uk

Legal & General
www.landg.com

Lloyds TSB
www.lloydstsb.co.uk

Lombard
www.lombard.co.uk/banking

Market Harborough
www.mhbs.co.uk

Marsden
www.marsdenbs.co.uk

Nationwide
www.nationwide.co.uk

NatWest
www.natwest.co.uk

Northern
www.northern-bank.co.uk

Northern Rock
www.northernrock.co.uk

Norwich & Peterborough
www.npbs.co.uk

Personal Loan Corporation
www.loancorp.co.uk

Prudential
www.pru.co.uk

Rea Brothers
www.reabrothers.co.uk

Royal Bank of Canada (Channel Islands)
www.royalbankci.com

Royal Bank of Scotland
www.rbs.co.uk

Save & Prosper
www.prosper.co.uk

Scottish Financial Enterprise
www.sfe.org.uk

Secure Trust
www.securetrustbank.com

Skipton
www.skipton.co.uk

Smile
www.smile.co.uk

Staffordshire
www.staffordshirebuildingsociety.co.uk

Standard
www.sbl.co.uk

Standard Life
www.standardlifebank.com

Stroud & Swindon
www.stroudandswindon.co.uk

Sunbank
www.sunbank.co.uk

Teachers'
www.teachersbs.co.uk

Triodos
www.triodos.co.uk

Universal
www.universal.uk.com

Virgin Direct
www.virgin-direct.co.uk

Woolwich
www.woolwich.co.uk

Yorkshire
www.ybs.co.uk

credit cards

Advanta
www.rbsadvanta.co.uk

American Express
www.americanexpress.co.uk

Barclaycard
www.barclaycard.co.uk

Capital One
www.capitalone.co.uk

CharityCard
www.charitycard.org

Diners Club
www.dinersclub.com

Football Club Credit Cards
www.footballcard.co.uk

Goldfish
www.goldfish.com

Marbles
www.marbles.com

Mastercard
www.mastercard.com

MBNA
www.mbnanetaccess.co.uk

People's Bank
www.peoples.com/ukcreditcards

Scottish Widows
www.scottishwidows.co.uk

Switch
www.switch.co.uk

Visa
www.visa.com

insurance

A1 Insurance
www.a1insurance.co.uk

AA Insurance
www.aainsurance.co.uk

Abacus Direct
www.abacusdirect.co.uk

Abbey Online
www.abbey-online.co.uk

Admiral
www.admiral.co.uk

Allied Dunbar
www.allieddunbar.co.uk

Anglia Countrywide
www.anglia-countrywide.co.uk

Annuity Direct

www.annuitydirect.co.uk

AXA
www.axa.co.uk

Britannic Assurance
www.britannic.co.uk

BUPA
www.bupa.co.uk

Canada Life
www.canadalife.com

Carquote
www.carquote.co.uk

Central Direct
www.central-insurance.co.uk

CGU
www.cgu-direct.co.uk

Chubb
www.chubb.com

Churchill
www.churchill.co.uk

Co-op
www.cis.co.uk

Columbus
www.columbusdirect.co.uk

Commercial Union
www.commercialunion.co.uk

Cornhill
www.cornhill.co.uk

County
www.county-insurance.co.uk

DAS
www.das.co.uk

Denplan
www.denplan.co.uk

Dial Direct
www.ddirect.co.uk

Direct
www.digs.co.uk

Direct Line
www.directline.com

Eagle Star
www.eaglestar.co.uk

Elephant
www.elephant.co.uk

Endsleigh
www.endsleigh.co.uk

Equitable Life
www.equitable.co.uk

General Accident
www.ga.co.uk

Guardian
www.gre.co.uk

Heath Group
www.heathgroup.com

Hibernian Group
www.hibernian.ie

Hiscox
www.hiscox.com

Hogg Robinson
www.hoggrobinson.com

Home Quote
www.home.quote.co.uk

InterSure
www.intersure.co.uk

Ironsure
www.ironsure.com

Lancaster
www.lancaster-ins.co.uk

Legal & General
www.legal-and-general.co.uk

MCM Group
www.mcmgroup.co.uk

Midland Direct
www.midlanddirect.co.uk

National Mutual
www.nationalmutual.co.uk

NFU Mutual
www.nfumutual.co.uk

Norwich Union
www.norwich-union.co.uk

Old Mutual
www.oldmutual.com

Pearl
www.pearl.co.uk

Pet Plan
www.petplan.co.uk

PPP/Columbia
www.columbiahealthcare.co.uk

Preferential
www.preferential.co.uk

Preferred Direct
www.pdinsure.co.uk

Privilege Cars
www.privilege.co.uk

Prospero Direct
www.prospero.co.uk

Prudential
www.pru.co.uk

Royal & Sun Alliance
www.royal-and-sunalliance.com

Royal Liver
www.royal-liver.com

Saga
www.saga.co.uk

Scottish Amicable
www.scottishamicable.com

Scottish Widows
www.scottishwidows.co.uk

Screentrade
www.screentrade.com

Sedgwick Group
www.sedgwick.com

Skandia Life
www.skandia.co.uk

Sportscover
www.sportscover.co.uk

Standard Life
www.standardlife.co.uk

Sun Life
www.sunlife.co.uk

Sun Life of Canada
www.sunbank.co.uk

Swinton
www.swinton.co.uk

Swiss Life (UK)
www.swisslife.co.uk

Trade Indemnity
www.tradeindemnity.com

UK Friendly
www.ukfriendly.co.uk

Western Provident
www.wpahealth.co.uk

Willis Corroon Group
www.williscorroon.com

Woolwich Insurance Services
www.woolwich-insurance.co.uk

World Cover Direct
www.worldcover.co.uk

World Trekker
www.worldtrekker.com

Worldwide Travel
www.wwtis.co.uk

Zurich
www.zurich.com

investment funds

Aberdeen Asset Management
www.aberdeen-asset.com

Aberdeen Unit Trust Managers
www.aberdeen-knowhow.com

ABN AMRO Asset Management
www.invweek.co.uk/abn

AIB Asset Management
www.aibgovett.com

Baring Asset Management
www.baring-asset.com

Capel Cure Sharp
www.capelcuresharp.co.uk

Cazenove Fund Management
www.cazenove.co.uk/cfm

City of London Investment Group
www.citlon.co.uk

Credit Suisse Asset Management
www.csamfunds.co.uk

Edinburgh Fund Managers
www.edfd.com

Ely Fund Managers
www.ely.uk.com

Fidelity
www.fidelity.co.uk

Finsbury Asset Management
www.finsbury-asset.co.uk

Flemings
www.fleming.co.uk

Foreign & Colonial
www.fandc.co.uk

Framlington
www.framlington.com

Friends Provident
www.friendsprovident.co.uk

Gartmore Investment Management
www.gartmore.iii.co.uk

Gerrard Group
www.gerrard.com

Global Asset Management
www.ukinfo.gam.com

GNI Fund Management
www.gnifm.com

Henderson
www.henderson.co.uk

Herald Investment Management
www.heralduk.com

Hill Samuel
www.hillsamuel.co.uk

Invesco
www.invesco.co.uk

Investec Guinness Flight
www.investecguinnessflight.com

ISA Shop
www.isa-shop.co.uk

ITS Investment Trusts
www.itsonline.co.uk

Jupiter
www.jupiteronline.co.uk

M&G Group
www.mandg.co.uk

Mercury Asset Management
www.mam.com/uksite

National Savings
www.nationalsavings.co.uk

Norwich Union
www.norwich-union.co.uk

Perpetual Investment
www.perpetual.co.uk

Pictet Group
www.pictet.com

Pinnacle Investments
www.pinnacle.co.uk/investments

PPM UK
www.ppm-uk.com

Premier Asset Management
www.premierfunds.co.uk

Royal Skandia
www.royalskandia.com

Sabre Fund Management
www.sabrefund.com

Save & Prosper
www.prosper.co.uk

Schroders
www.schroder.co.uk

Scottish Amicable
www.scottishamicable.com

Scottish Investment Trust
www.sit.co.uk

Scottish Life International
www.sli.co.im

Scottish Mutual International
www.smi.ie

Scottish Provident
www.scotprov.co.uk

Scottish Value Management
www.scottish-value.co.uk

Threadneedle Investments
www.threadneedle.co.uk

Virgin
www.virginisa.com

magazines & websites

Bloomberg
www.bloomberg.com

Business Money
www.business-money.com

CAROL
www.carol.co.uk

Citywatch
www.citywatch.co.uk

Direct Debit
www.directdebit.co.uk

Egg-Free Zone
www.eggfreezone.com

Euromoney Online
www.euromoney.com

Hemmington Scott
www.hemscott.co.uk

Interactive Investor International
www.iii.co.uk

International Fund Investment
www.ifiglobal.com

Investment & Pensions Europe
www.ipeurope.co.uk

Investment Trust Newsletter
www.trustnews.co.uk

Investors Chronicle
www.investorschronicle.co.uk

Investors Internet Journal
www.iij.co.uk

Line One Money Zone
www.lineone.net/moneyzone

Money Money Money
www.moneymoneymoney.co.uk

Moneyweb
www.moneyweb.co.uk

MoneyWorld UK
www.moneyworld.co.uk

Motley Fool
www.fool.co.uk

Mrs Cohen
www.mrscohen.com

Offshore Investor
www.offshore-investor.com

Pensions World
www.pensionsworld.co.uk

Quicken.com
www.quicken.com

TheStreet.co.uk
www.thestreet.co.uk

mortgages

Chase De Vere
www.cdvmortgage.co.uk

Home & Capital Trust
www.homecapital.co.uk

John Charcol
www.johncharcol.co.uk

Midlands Insurance Services
www.midlandsinsurance.freeserve.co.uk

Moneynet
www.moneynet.co.uk

Mortgage Alliance
www.magreen.demon.co.uk

Mortgage Help Desk UK
www.mortgage.u-net.com

Mortgage Intelligence
www.mortgage-intelligence.co.uk

Mortgage Shop
www.mortgage-shop.co.uk

MTS Mortgage Company
www.mtsmortgage.co.uk

Royal & Sun Alliance Investments
www.rsa-investments.co.uk

professional bodies

Arson Prevention Bureau
www.arsonpreventionbureau.org.uk

Association of British Insurers
www.abi.org.uk

Association of Consulting Actuaries
www.aca.org.uk

Association of Independent Financial Advisers
www.aifa.net

Association of Unit Trusts and Investment Funds
www.investmentfunds.org.uk

British Bankers' Association
www.bankfacts.org.uk

British Insurance & Investment Brokers Association
www.biiba.org.uk

Building Societies Association
www.bsa.org.uk

Cambridge Building Society
www.cambridge-building-society.co.uk

Chartered Insurance Institute
www.cii.co.uk

Cornhill Direct
www.cornhilldirect.co.uk

Council of Mortgage Lenders
www.cml.org.uk

Countryside
www.cwide.co.uk

Financial Services Authority
www.fsa.gov.uk

Financial Services Consumer Panel
www.fs-cp.org.uk

Gartmore Investment
www.gartmore.iii.co.uk

Guernsey Financial Services Commission
www.gfsc.guernseyci.com

IMRO
www.imro.co.uk

Independent Financial Advisers Associatic
www.ifaa.org.uk

Institute of Actuaries
www.actuaries.org.uk

Insurance Institute of London
www.iilondon.co.uk

International Underwriting Association of London
www.iua.co.uk

Investors Compensation Scheme (ICS)
www.the-ics.org.uk

Jersey Financial Services Commission
www.jerseyfsc.org

Liverpool Victoria Friendly Society
www.lvbestbond.co.uk

Loss Prevention Council
www.lpc.co.uk

M&G Group
www.mandg.co.uk

Mercury Asset Management
www.mam.com

National Association of Bank & Insurance Customers
http://freespace.virgin.net/bank.help

National Association of Pension Funds
www.napf.co.uk

United Kingdom Shareholders' Associatio
www.uksa.org.uk

United Kingdom Shareholders' Associatio (Scotland)
http://members.aol.com/uksascot

stockbrokers

Barclays Stockbrokers
www.barclays-stockbrokers.com

Brewin Dolphin
www.brewin.co.uk

Capel Cure Sharp
www.capelcuresharp.co.uk

Cazenove & Co
www.cazenove.co.uk

Charles Schwab Europe
www.schwab-worldwide.com

Charles Stanley & Co
www.charles-stanley.co.uk

CMC Group
www.cmcplc.com

Credit Suisse First Boston de Zoete & Bevan
www.csamfunds.co.uk

Durlacher Corporation
www.durlacher.co.uk

E*TRADE United Kingdom
www.etrade.co.uk

Edward Jones
www.edwardjones.com

European Stockbrokers
www.europeanstockbrokers.co.uk

GNI
www.gni.co.uk

Greig Middleton
www.greigmiddleton.co.uk

James Brearley & Sons
www.jbrearley.co.uk

Killik & Co.
www.killik.co.uk

Mercury Asset Management
www.mercury-asset-management.co.uk

Rudolf Wolff
www.rwolff.com

Salomon Smith Barney
www.sbil.co.uk

Selftrade
www.selftrade.co.uk

TD Waterhouse
www.tdwaterhouse.co.uk

angola ●	hungary ●	norway ●
argentina ●	iceland ●	pacific islands ●
australia ●	india ●	pakistan ●
austria ●	ireland ●	philippines ●
bangladesh ●	israel ●	portugal ●
belgium ●	italy ●	romania ●
brazil ●	japan ●	russia ●
britain ●	jordan ●	serbia ●
cameroon ●	kenya ●	seychelles ●
canada ●	korea ●	singapore ●
caribbean ●	kuwait ●	south africa ●
channel islands ●	lebanon ●	spain ●
china ●	liechtenstein ●	sweden ●
cyprus ●	luxembourg ●	switzerland ●
denmark ●	malaysia ●	thailand ●
egypt ●	maldives ●	tibet ●
falkland islands ●	malta ●	tunisia ●
finland ●	mauritius ●	turkey ●
france ●	mexico ●	uganda ●
gambia ●	monaco ●	united arab emirates ●
germany ●	morocco ●	usa ●
ghana ●	nepal ●	venezuela ●
gibraltar ●	netherlands ●	web cams ●
greece ●	new zealand ●	

angola

Media
Angolan National Radio
www.rna.ao

Tourist Information
Angola
www.angola.org

Towns & Cities
Luanda
www.luanda.com

argentina

Tourist Information
Argentina
www.info.gov.ar

Towns & Cities
Buenos Aires
www.gba.gov.ar

australia

Media
Australian Broadcasting Corporation
www.abc.net.au

The Australian Newspaper
www.theaustralian.com.au

Sydney Morning Herald
www.smh.com.au

Regions
Western Australia
www.westernaustralia.net

Tourist Attractions
Art Gallery of New South Wales
www.artgallery.nsw.gov.au

Australian Museum
www.austmus.gov.au

Australian National Parks
www.atn.com.au/parks

Museum of Contemporary Art
www.mca.com.au

National Gallery of Australia
www.nga.gov.au

National Gallery of Victoria
www.ngv.vic.gov.au

Powerhouse Museum
www.phm.gov.au

Sydney Opera House
www.soh.nsw.gov.au

Tourist Information
National Tourist Office
www.australia-online.com

Towns & Cities
Canberra
www.nationalcapital.gov.au

Melbourne
www.melbourne.vic.gov.au

Sydney
www.sydney.visitorsbureau.com.au

Victoria
www.tourism.vic.gov.au

austria

Tourist Attractions
Schönbrunn Palace
www.schoenbrunn.at

Vienna Boys Choir
www.wsk.at

Vienna Kunsthistorisches Museum
www.khm.at

Tourist Information
National Tourist Office
www.austria-tourism.at

Towns & Cities
Graz
www.graztourism.at

Innsbruck
www.tiscover.com/innsbruck

Klagenfurt
www.info.klagenfurt.at

Salzburg
www.salzburginfo.at

Vienna
http://info.wien.at

bangladesh

Tourist Information
Bangladesh
www.bangladesh.com

Towns & Cities
Dhaka
www.dhaka.com

belgium

Media
Radio Vlaanderen International
www.rvi.be

Tourist Attractions
Brussels Expo
www.bruexpo.be

Flanders Fields
www.inflandersfields.be/english/home

Flanders Opera
www.vlaamseopera.be

Royal Museums of Fine Arts
www.fine-arts-museum.be

Tourist Information
National Tourist Office
www.belgium-tourism.com

Towns & Cities
Antwerp
www.antwerpen.be

Bruges
www.brugge.be

Brussels
www.brussel.irisnet.be

Gent
www.gent.be

Ostend
www.oostende.be

Travel
Belgian Railways
www.sncb.be

brazil

Tourist Information
Brazil
www.brazilinfo.com

Towns & Cities
Sao Paulo
www.saopaulo.sp.gov.br

britain

Castles
Alnwick Castle
www.alnwickcastle.com

Auckland Castle
www.auckland-castle.co.uk

Balmoral
www.balmoral-castle.co.uk

Caerlaverock Castle
www.aboutscotland.com/caer/caer.html

Castle Cornet
www.museum.guernsey.net

Dundas Castle
www.dundascastle.co.uk

Glamis Castle
www.great-houses-scotland.co.uk/glamis

Hedingham Castle
www.hedinghamcastle.co.uk

Kelburn Castle
www.kelburncountrycentre.com

Leeds Castle
www.leeds-castle.co.uk

Lulworth Castle
www.lulworth.com

Muncaster Castle
www.muncastercastle.co.uk

Powderham Castle
www.powderham.co.uk

Sherborne Castle
www.sherbornecastle.com

Skipton Castle
www.skiptoncastle.co.uk

Thirlestane Castle
www.thirlestanecastle.co.uk

Tower of London
www.camelot-group.com/tower

Warwick Castle
www.warwick-castle.co.uk

Windsor Castle
www.royal.gov.uk/palaces/windsor.htm

Historic Railways
Aberystwyth Electric Cliff
http://westwales.co.uk/cliffrwy.htm

Alford Valley
www.alford.org.uk/avr.htm

Aln Valley
www.avrs.co.uk

Avon Valley
www.avonvalleyrailway.co.uk

Beamish
www.countydurham.com/beamish

Bowes
www.bowesrailway.co.uk

Bridgnorth Cliff
www.pendry.demon.co.uk

Bure Valley
www.bvrw.co.uk

Chinnor & Princes Risborough
www.cprra.co.uk

Churnet
www.churnet-valley-railway.co.uk

Colne Valley
www.cvr.org.uk

Dartmoor
www.dartmoorrailway.freeserve.co.uk

East Lancashire Light
www.east-lancs-rly.co.uk

Eastleigh Lakeside
www.steamtrain.co.uk

Ffestiniog
www.festrail.co.uk

Flying Scotsman
www.flyingscotsman.com

Foxfield
www.foxfieldrailway.co.uk

Gloucestershire Warwickshire Steam
www.gwsr.plc.uk

Great Central
www.gcrailway.co.uk

Great Northern & East Lincolnshire
www.greatnorthernrailway.co.uk

Isle of Wight Steam Railway
www.iwsteamrailway.co.uk

Keighley & Worth Valley
www.kwvr.co.uk

Lappa Valley
www.lappa-railway.co.uk

Leighton Buzzard
www.buzzrail.co.uk

Llangollen
www.llangollen-railway.co.uk

Lynton & Barnstaple
www.lyntonbarnstaple.ndirect.co.uk

Mid Norfolk
www.mnr.org.uk

Mid-Hants 'Watercress'
www.watercressline.co.uk

Middleton
www.middletonrailway.org.uk

Nene Valley
www.internetlink.co.uk/nvr.htm

North Norfolk
www.nnrailway.co.uk

North Yorkshire Moors
www.nymr.demon.co.uk

Northampton & Lamport
www.nlr.org.uk

Peak Rail
www.peakrail.co.uk

Ravenglass
www.ravenglass-railway.co.uk

Ribble
www.dockrail.org.uk

Romney Hythe & Dymchurch
www.rhdr.demon.co.uk/rhdr.html

Royal Scotsman
www.royalscotsman.com

Severn Valley
www.svr.co.uk

Snowdon
www.snowdonrailway.force9.co.uk

South Devon
www.southdevonrailway.org

Swanage
www.swanrail.demon.co.uk

Talyllyn
www.talyllyn.co.uk

Tanfield
www.tanfield-railway.co.uk

Welshpool & Llanfair
www.wllr.org.uk

West Somerset
www.west-somerset-railway.co.uk

Wyvernrail
www.wyvernrail.co.uk

Monuments, Churches & Historic Buildings

Albert Dock
www.merseyworld.com/albert

Althorp
www.althorp.com

Auckland Castle
www.auckland-castle.co.uk

Baden Powell House
www.scoutbase.org.uk

Banqueting House
www.hrp.org.uk/bh/indexbh.htm

Beaulieu
www.beaulieu.co.uk

Blenheim
www.blenheimpalace.com

Bolton Abbey
www.yorkshirenet.co.uk/boltonabbey

Bowood House
www.bowood-estate.co.uk

Broadlands
www.broadlands.net

Buckingham Palace
www.royal.gov.uk/palaces/bp.htm

Burghley House
www.stamford.co.uk/burghley

Callendar House
www.falkirkmuseums.demon.co.uk

Castle Howard
www.castlehoward.co.uk

Chatsworth House
www.chatsworth-house.co.uk

Coventry Cathedral
www.coventrycathedral.org

Cutty Sark
www.cuttysark.org.uk

Duncombe Park
www.duncombepark.com

Durham Cathedral
www.dur.ac.uk/~dla0www/c_tour/tour.html

Ely Cathedral
www.ely.org.uk

Exeter Cathedral
www.exeter-cathedral.org.uk

Fountains Abbey
www.fountainsabbey.org.uk

Fursdon House
www.eclipse.co.uk/fursdon

Glastonbury Abbey
www.glastonburyabbey.com

Hadrian's Wall
www.northumbria-tourist-board.org.uk/hadrian

Hampton Court Palace
www.hrp.org.uk/hcp

Harewood
www.harewood.org

Historic Royal Palaces
www.hrp.org.uk

Houses of Parliament
www.parliament.uk

Kensington Palace
www.hrp.org.uk

Kentwell
www.kentwell.co.uk

Kilmartin House
www.kht.org.uk

Longleat
www.longleat.co.uk

Manderston
www.manderston.co.uk

Mount Stuart
www.mountstuart.com

Newby Hall
www.newbyhall.co.uk

Owlpen Manor
www.owlpen.com

Penshurst Place
www.penshurstplace.com

Port Lympne
www.howletts.net

Royal Mews
www.royal.gov.uk/palaces/bp.htm

Salisbury Cathedral
www.salisburycathedral.org.uk

Sewerby Hall
www.bridlington.net/sewerby

Somerleyton Hall
www.somerleyton.co.uk

St Paul's Cathedral
www.stpauls.co.uk

Stanford Hall
www.stanfordhall.co.uk

Stonehenge
www.stonehenge.co.uk

Sulgrave Manor
www.stratford.co.uk/sulgrave

10 Downing Street
www.number-10.gov.uk

Tower Bridge
www.towerbridge.org.uk

Traquair House
www.traquair.co.uk

Westminster Abbey
www.westminster-abbey.org

Wilton House
www.wiltonhouse.com

York Minster
www.yorkminster.org

Parks & Gardens

Athelhampton
www.athelhampton.co.uk

Birmingham Botanical Gardens
www.bham-bot-gdns.demon.co.uk

Bowood House
www.bowood-estate.co.uk

Bramham Park
www.yorkshirenet.co.uk/bramham

Castle Bromwich Gardens
www.cbhgt.swinternet.co.uk

Castle Howard
www.castlehoward.co.uk

Chatsworth House
www.chatsworth-house.co.uk

Duncombe Park
www.duncombepark.com

Elsham Hall Country & Wildlife Park
www.brigg.com/elsham.htm

Exbury Gardens
www.exbury.co.uk

Finlaystone Country Estate
www.finlaystone.co.uk

Fishers Farm Park
www.fishersfarmpark.co.uk

Garden Visit & Travel Guide
www.gardenvisit.com

Harewood
www.harewood.org

Kelburn Castle & Country Centre
www.kelburncountrycentre.com

Kew Gardens
www.rbgkew.org.uk

Knoll Gardens
www.knollgardens.co.uk

Lulworth Castle
www.lulworth.com

Mount Stuart House & Gardens
www.mountstuart.com

North Devon Farm Park
www.farmpark.co.uk

Odds Farm Park
www.oddsfarm.co.uk

Painswick Rococo Gardens
www.beta.co.uk/painswick

Penshurst Place & Gardens
www.penshurstplace.com

Royal Parks of London
www.open.gov.uk/rp

Somerleyton Hall & Gardens
www.somerleyton.co.uk

Regions

About Scotland
www.aboutscotland.com

Ambleside
www.ambleside.u-k.org

Ayrshire
www.ayr2000.com

Brecon Beacons
www.breconbeacons.org

Chilterns
www.chilterns.net

Cumbria
www.cumbria.com

Dartmoor
www.dartmoor-npa.gov.uk

Derbyshire
www.thisisderbyshire.co.uk

Devon
www.devon-cc.gov.uk/tourism

Durham
www.durham2000.co.uk

Edinburgh and Lothians
www.edinburgh.org

Exmoor
www.apgate.com/exmoor/index.htm

Fort William & Lochabar
www.fort-william.net

Hebrides
www.hebrides.com

Highlands of Scotland
www.host.co.uk

Isle of Bute
www.isle-of-bute.com

Isle of Skye
www.skye.co.uk

Isle of Wight
www.isle-of-wight-tourism.gov.uk

Isles of Scilly
www.rosevear.demon.co.uk

Jersey
www.jersey.co.uk

Lake District
www.lake-district.gov.uk

Merseyside
www.merseyside.org.uk

Norfolk
www.broadland.com

North York Moors
www.northyorkmoors-npa.gov.uk

Northumbria
www.northumbria-tourist-board.co.uk

Orkney
www.orknet.co.uk/tourism

Pembrokeshire Coast
www.pembrokeshirecoast.org

Pembrokeshire Coast National Park
www.pembrokeshirecoast.org

South Devon
www.southdevon.org.uk

South East England
www.southeastengland.uk.com

Southern England
www.gosouth.co.uk

West Country
www.westcountry.net

Wookey Hole
www.wookey.co.uk

Yorkshire
www.yorkshire.ytb.org.uk

Yorkshire Dales
www.yorkshirenet.co.uk/visinfo/ydales

Tourist Attractions

Anglesey Sea Zoo
www.nwi.co.uk/seazoo

BBC Experience
www.bbc.co.uk/experience

Bekonscot
www.bekonscot.org.uk

Cadbury World
www.cadbury.co.uk/cadworld

Deep Sea World
www.deepseaworld.com

Hall of Fame
www.hall-of-fame.co.uk

Jorvik Viking Centre
www.jorvik-viking-centre.co.uk

Kielder Water Bird of Prey Centre
www.discoverit.co.uk/falconry

London Aquarium
www.londonaquarium.co.uk

London Dungeon
www.thedungeons.com

London Eye
www.londoneye.com

Madame Tussaud's
www.madame-tussauds.com

Millennium Bridge
www.mbridge.ft.com

Monkey World
www.monkeyworld.co.uk

Mother Shipton's Cave
www.mothershipton.co.uk

Original Bus Tour Company
www.theoriginaltour.com

World of Beatrix Potter
www.hop-skip-jump.com

Tourist Information

Blue Badge Guides
www.blue-badge.org.uk

British Hotel Reservations Centre
www.bhrc.co.uk

British Tourist Authority
www.visitbritain.com

Edinburgh and Lothians Tourist Board
www.edinburgh.org

English Tourism Council
www.englishtourism.co.uk

Evening Standard
www.thisislondon.com

Good Guide to Britain
www.goodguides.com

Highlands of Scotland Tourist Board
www.host.co.uk

Information Britain
www.information-britain.co.uk

London Tourist Board
www.londontown.com

Northern Ireland Tourist Board
www.ni-tourism.com

Northumbria Tourist Board
www.northumbria-tourist-board.org.uk

Perthshire Tourist Board
www.perthshire.co.uk

Scottish Tourist Board
www.holiday.scotland.net

South East England Tourist Board
www.southeastengland.uk.com

Travel England
www.travelengland.org.uk

24 Hour Museum
www.24hourmuseum.org.uk

Wales Tourist Board
www.tourism.wales.gov.uk

West Country Tourist Board
www.westcountryholidays.com

York
www.york-tourism.co.uk

Yorkshire Tourist Board
www.ytb.org.uk

Towns & Cities

Abergavenny
www.abergavenny.co.uk

Aberystwyth
www.dewin.net/aberystwyth

Abingdon & District
www.oxlink.co.uk/abingdon

Ashbourne
www.ashbourne-town.com

Aylesbury
www.aylesburyvale.net

Ballymena
www.ballymena.gov.uk

Bath
www.bath.co.uk

Beaconsfield
www.beaconsfield.co.uk

Bedford
www.bedfordonline.com

Bicester
www.bicester.net

Biggin Hill
www.bigginhill.co.uk

Blackpool
www.blackpooltourism.com

Blackpool Southshore
www.southshore.co.uk

Bournemouth
www.bournemouth-info.com

Bradford
www.bradford-net.com

Brighton
www.brighton.co.uk

Bristol
www.brisindex.co.uk/tourism

Bury St Edmunds
www.stedmunds.co.uk

Buxton
www.buxtonuk.com

Cambridge
www.cambridge.gov.uk/leisure

Canterbury
www.canterbury.co.uk

Cardiff
www.totalcardiff.com

Chelmsford
www.chelmsfordcityinthemaking.co.uk

Cheltenham
www.cheltenham.uk.com

Chepstow
www.chepstow.co.uk

Chesham
www.chesham.org

Chester
www.chester.org

Chichester
www.chichesteruk.co.uk

Chinatown London
www.fresco-web.co.uk/chinatown

Cirencester
www.cirencester.co.uk

Colchester
www.qlink.co.uk/colchester

Coventry
www.cwn.org.uk

Derby
www.derbycity.com

Didcot
www.didcot.com

Donington
www.donington.com

Dover
www.dover.uk.com

East Grinstead
www.egnet.co.uk

Edinburgh
www.edinburghonline.org.uk

Egham
www.egham.co.uk

Epsom
www.epsom.townpage.co.uk

Exeter
www.thisisexeter.co.uk

Fakenham
www.fakenham.org.uk

Falkirk
www.falkirkweb.co.uk

Farham
www.farham.co.uk

Filey
www.filey.co.uk

Fort William
www.fort-william.net

Glastonbury
www.glastonbury.co.uk

Glossop
www.glossop.com

Guildford
www.guildford.org.uk

Henley-on-Thames
www.henley-on-thames.org.uk

Kidderminster
www.kidderminster.org.uk

Leominster
www.leominster.co.uk

Lindisfarne
www.lindisfarne.org.uk

London
www.londontown.com

Manchester
www.manchesteronline.co.uk

Mansfield
www.mansfieldpages.co.uk

Morpeth
www.morpethnet.co.uk

Plymouth
www.plymouthcity.co.uk

Portmerion
www.virtualportmeirion.com

Redditch
www.redditch.com

Rugby
www.rugbytown.co.uk

Rye
www.rye-tourism.co.uk

Scarborough
www.scarborough.co.uk

Sheffield
www.sheffieldcity.co.uk

Southport
www.visitsouthport.org.uk

Stratford
www.stratford.co.uk

Swansea
www.swansea.com

Thames Ditton
www.thamesditton.com

Virginia Water
www.virginiawater.co.uk

Ware
www.ware-herts.co.uk

West Wickham
www.west-wickam.com

Whitby
www.whitby.co.uk

York
www.yorkgateway.co.uk

cameroon

Tourist Information

Cameroon
www.compufix.demon.co.uk/camweb

Towns & Cities

Douala
www.douala.com

canada

Regions

Alberta
www.travelalberta.com

British Columbia
www.hellobc.com

Manitoba
www.gov.mb.ca/itt/travel

New Brunswick
www.tourismnewbrunswick.ca

Newfoundland & Labrador
www.gov.nf.ca/tourism

Northwest Territories
www.northernfrontier.com

Nova Scotia
http://destination-ns.com

Nunavut
www.nunatour.nt.ca

Ontario
www.ontario-canada.com

Prince Edward Island
www.peiplay.com

Quebec
www.tourisme.gouv/mag/en

Saskatchewan
www.sasktourism.com

Toronto
www.tourism-toronto.com

Yukon
www.touryukon.com

Tourist Information

Canada
www.travelcanada.ca

caribbean

Antigua
www.antigua-barbuda.com

Bahamas
www.bahama.com

Bermuda
www.bermudatourism.com

Cayman Islands
www.caymanislands.ky

Dominican Republic
www.ios.uk.com/domrep

Grenada
www.grenada.org

Jamaica
www.jamaicatravel.com

Puerto Rico
www.prtourism.com

St Kitts & Nevis
www.interknowledge.com/stkitts-nevis

St Vincent & The Grenadines
www.stvincentandgrenadines.com

channel islands

Services

Jersey Post
www.jerseypost.com

Tourist Information

Alderney
www.alderney.gov.gg

Guernsey
www.guernseymap.com/tourism.htm

Herm Island
www.herm-island.com

Jersey
www.jtourism.com

Jersey Battle of Flowers
www.battleofflowers.com

Jersey Heritage Trust
www.jerseyheritagetrust.org

china

Media
China Post
www.chinapost.gov.cn

China Today
www.chinatoday.com

Tourist Information
China
www.cnto.org

China Internet Information Center
www.china.org.cn

Hong Kong
www.hkta.org

National Administration for Cultural Heritage
www.nach.gov.cn

Towns & Cities
Beijing
www.beijing.gov.cn/english/index.htm

Shanghai
www.shanghai.gov.cn/english/index.htm

cyprus

Tourist Information
Cyprus
www.cyprustourism.org

Turkish Republic of Northern Cyprus
www.trncwashdc.org

Towns & Cities
Limassaol
www.limassolmunicipal.com.cy

Nicosia
www.nicosia.org.cy

denmark

Regions
Copenhagen
http://copenhagen.now.dk/english.html

Greenland
www.greenland-guide.gl

Tourist Attractions
Legoland
www.legoland.dk

Tivoli
www.tivoligardens.com

Tourist Information
National Tourist Office
www.dt.dk

egypt

Media
Egyptian Gazette
www.egy.com

Tourist Attractions
Coptic Museum
www.sis.gov.eg/egyptinf/culture/html
/copt001.htm

Egyptian Museum
www.tourism.egnet.net/Attractions_Detail.asp?
code=6

Museum of Mohamed Mahmoud Khalil
www.mkhalilmuseum.gov.eg

Suez Canal
www.suezcanal.com

Tourist Information
Egypt
www.touregypt.net

State Information Service
www.sis.gov.eg

Towns & Cities
Alexandria
www.alexandria2000.com

falkland islands

Tourist Information
Falkland Islands
www.tourism.org.fk

finland

Finland
www.mek.fi

Towns & Cities
Helsinki
www.helsinki.fi

Oulu
www.oulutourism.fi

france

Regions
Brittany
www.brittanytourism.com

Tourist Attractions
Cannes Film Festival
www.festival-cannes.org

Disneyland Paris
www.disneylandparis.com.uk

Eiffel Tower, Paris
www.tour-eiffel.com

Festival de Marseille
www.festivaldemarseille.com

Louvre
www.mistral.culture.fr/louvre

National Museum of Modern Art
www.cnac-gp.fr

Palace of Versailles
www.smartweb.fr/versailles

Parc Asterix
www.parcasterix.com

Pompidou Centre
www.centrepompidou.fr/english

Tourist Information
National Tourist Office
www.franceguide.com

Towns & Cities
Cannes
www.ville-cannes.fr

Cote d'Azur
www.coteazur.com

Courchevel
www.courchevel.com

Lyon
www.lyon-france.com

Nice
www.nice-coteazur.org

Paris
www.paris-france.org

gambia

Tourist Information
Gambia
www.gambia.com

germany

Tourist Attractions
Phantasialand
www.phantasia.de

Tourist Information
National Tourist Office
www.gnm.de

Towns & Cities
Berlin
www.berlin.de/home/english

Cologne
www.colognc.dc

Frankfurt
www.frankfurt-online.de

Munich
www.muenchen.de

Nuremberg
www.nuernberg.de

Stuttgart
www.stuttgart.de

ghana

Tourist Information
Ghana
www.ghana.com/republic

gibraltar

Gibraltar
www.gibraltar.gov.gi

greece

Tourist Attractions
Acropolis
www.culture.gr/2/21/211/21101a/e211aa01.htm

Tourist Information
Greece
www.gnto.gr

hungary

National Tourist Office
www.hungarytourism.hu

Towns & Cities
Budapest
www.budapest.hu

iceland

Tourist Information
National Tourist Office
www.icetourist.is

india

Regions
Assam
http://assamgovt.nic.in

Himachal Pradesh
http://himachal.nic.in

Jammu & Kashmir
www.jammu-kashmir-facts.com

Punjab
http://punjabgovt.nic.in

Rajasthan
www.rajgovt.org

Uttar Pradesh
www.upindia.org

West Bengal
www.westbengal.gov.in

Tourist Information
India
www.indiatouristoffice.org

Towns & Cities
Delhi
http://delhigovt.nic.in

Goa
www.nic.in/goa

Gujarat
www.gujaratindia.com

ireland

Tourist Information
National Tourist Office
www.shamrock.org

Towns & Cities
Cork
www.corkcoco.com

Donegal
www.donegal.ie

Dublin
www.visitdublin.com

Galway
www.galwaycoco.ie

Kerry
www.kerrycoco.ie

Limerick
www.limerickcorp.ie

Waterford
www.waterfordcorp.ie

israel

Tourist Information
Israel
www.infotour.co.il

Towns & Cities
Haifa
www.haifa.gov.il

Jerusalem
www.jerusalem.muni.il

Tel-Aviv
www.tel-aviv.gov.il

italy

Tourist Attractions
Christian Catacombs, Rome
www.catacombe.roma.it/welcome

Gardaland
www.gardaland.it

Sistine Chapel
www.christusrex.org

Teatro alla Scala
www.lascala.milano.it

Uffizi Gallery, Florence
www.uffizi.firenze.it

Tourist Information
National Tourist Office
www.enit.it

japan

Tourist Attractions
Disneyland
www.tokyodisneyland.co.jp

Tourist Information
Japan
www.jnto.go.jp

Towns & Cities
Expoland
www.expoland.co.jp/eng

Hiroshima
www.city.hiroshima.jp/index-e.html

Okinawa
www.virtualokinawa.com

Osaka
www.kanko-osaka.or.jp

Sapporo
www.global.city.sapporo.jp

Yokohama
www.city.yokohama.jp

jordan

Media

Jordan Radio & Television Corp.
www.jrtv.gov.jo

Jordan Times
www.jordantimes.com

Tourist Information

Jordan
www.nic.gov.jo

Jordan
www.see-jordan.com

kenya

Tourist Attractions

National Museums of Kenya
www.museums.or.ke

Tourist Information

Kenya
www.kenyatourism.org

korea

Korea
www.knto.or.kr

Towns & Cities

Seoul
www.metro.seoul.kr

kuwait

Tourist Information

Kuwait
www.moc.kw/english

lebanon

Lebanon
www.lebanon-tourism.gov.lb

Towns & Cities

Beirut
www.bse.com.lb

liechtenstein

Tourist Information

Liechtenstein
www.news.li/touri/index.htm

Towns & cities

Schaan
www.schaan.li

Vaduz
www.vaduz.li

luxembourg

Tourist Information

Luxembourg
www.luxembourg.co.uk

Towns & Cities

Beaufort
www.beaufort.lu

Grosbous
www.grosbous.lu

Larochette
www.larochette.lu

Luxembourg City
www.luxembourg-city.lu/touristinfo

malaysia

Tourist Information

Malaysia
www.tourism.gov.my

Towns & Cities

Kuala Lumpur
www.klse.com.my

maldives

Tourist Information

Maldives
www.visitmaldives.com

malta

Malta
www.tourism.org.mt

mauritius

Mauritius
www.mauritius.net

mexico

Mexico
www.mexico-travel.com

monaco

Monaco
www.monaco.mc

Towns & Cities
Monte-Carlo
www.monaco.monte-carlo.mc

morocco

Tourist Information
Morocco
www.mincom.gov.ma

nepal

Nepal
www.welcomenepal.com

netherlands

Tourist Attractions
Efteling
www.efteling.nl

Van Gogh Museum
www.vangoghmuseum.nl

Tourist Information
National Tourist Office
www.goholland.co.uk

Towns & Cities
Amsterdam
www.visitamsterdam.nl

Arnhem
www.arnhem.nl

Eindhoven
www.eindhoven.nl

Groningen
www.groningen.nl

Hague
www.denhaag.nl

Leiden
www.leiden.nl

Maastricht
www.maastricht.nl

Rotterdam
www.stadhuis.rotterdam.nl

Tilburg
www.tilburg.nl

Utrecht
www.utrecht.nl

Venlo
www.venlo.nl

new zealand

Tourist Information
New Zealand
www.nz.com

Towns & Cities
Auckland
www.akcity.govt.nz

Christchurch
www.ccc.govt.nz

Gisborne
www.gisborne.govt.nz

Rotorua
www.rotoruanz.com

Wellington
www.wcc.govt.nz

norway

Media
Norway Post
www.norwaypost.no

Tourist attractions
Museumnet Norway
www.museumsnett.no/engelsk

Oslo Opera House
www.mnal.no/opera.html

Tourist Information
National Tourist Office
www.norway.org.uk

pacific islands

Fiji
www.fiji-online.com.fj

Solomon Islands
www.solomons.com

Tahiti
www.tahiti-tourisme.com

pakistan

Pakistan
www.tourism.gov.pk

philippines

Philippines
www.tourism.gov.ph

portugal

Portugal
www.portugal.org

Towns & Cities

Faro
www.cm-faro.pt

Lisbon
www.cm-lisboa.pt

romania

Tourist Information

Romania
www.rezq.com/ronto

russia

Tourist Attractions

Russian National Museums
www.museum.ru/defengl.htm

Tourist Information

Russia
www.russia-travel.com

Towns & Cities

Moscow
www.moscowcity.com

St Petersburg
www.stpete.org

serbia

Tourist Information

Serbia
www.serbia-info.com/ntos

seychelles

Seychelles
www.seychelles.demon.co.uk

singapore

Singapore
www.travel.com.sg/sog

south africa

Tourist Attractions

South African National Parks
www.ecoafrica.com/saparks

Tourist Information

National Tourist Office
http://satour.com

Towns & Cities

Cape Town
www.ctcc.gov.za

Durban
www.durban.gov.za

Johannesburg
www.joburg.org.za

Pietermaritzburg
www.pmbcc.gov.za

Pretoria
www.pretoria.co.za

spain

Tourist Information

Spain
www.tourspain.co.uk

Towns & Cities

Barcelona
www.bcn.es

Bilbao
www.bilbao.net

Cadiz
www.cadizayto.es

Madrid
www.munimadrid.es

Palma
www.a-palma.es

Seville
www.sevilla.org

Toledo
www.diputoledo.es

Valencia
www.ayto-valencia.es

sweden

Events

Galaxen, Arvika
www.galaxen.se

Hultsfredsfestivalen
www.rockparty.se

Stockholm Water Festival
www.waterfestival.se

Media

Radio Sweden
www.stfturist.se

Services

Post Office
www.posten.se/03/03a.htm

Tourist Attractions

Astrid Lindgren's World
www.alv.se

Grona Lund, Stockholm
www.grunalund.com

Historiska Museet, Stockholm
www.sshm.se

Kolmarden Zoo, Norrkoping
www.kolmarden.com

Lisebergs Nojespark, Gothenberg
www.tivoli.se

Medeltidsmuseum, Stockholm
www.medeltidsmuseet.kif.stockholm.se

Moderna Museet, Stockholm
www.modernamuseet.se

Nationalmuseum, Stockholm
www.nationalmuseum.se

Nordiska Museet, Stockholm
www.nordm.se

Postmuseum, Stockholm
www.posten.se/museum

Rooseum, Malmo
www.rooseum.se

Royal Palace, Stockholm
www.royalcourt.se

Skansen, Stockholm
www.skansen.se

Sommarland Centres
www.sommarland.se

Strindbergsmuseet
www.strindbergsmuseet.se

Vasa Museet, Stockholm
www.vasamuseet.se

Tourist Information

Culture Net
www.kulturnat.org

SwedNet
www.swetourism.org.uk

Towns, Cities & Regions

Gothenberg
www.goteborg.com

Malmo
www.malmo.com

Stockholm
www2.stockholm.se/english

Torsby
www.torsby.se

Varmlands
www.varmland.org

Travel

Inland Railway
www.inlandsbanan.se/england.html

State Railway
www.sj.se

Stromma Kanalbolaget
www.strommakanalbolaget.com

switzerland

Events

Art Basel
www.art.ch

Montreux Jazz Festival
www.montreuxjazz.com

Services

Swiss Federal Railways
www.sbb.ch

Tourist Attractions

Olympic Museum
www.museum.olympic.org

Tourist Information
Switzerland
www.myswitzerland.com

Towns & Cities
Basel
www.baseltourismus.ch

Geneva
www.geneva-tourism.ch

Zurich
www.zurichtourism.ch

thailand

Tourist Information
Thailand
www.tourismthailand.org

tibet

Tibet
www.tibet.com

tunisia

Tunisia
www.tourismtunisia.co.uk

turkey

Turkey
www.turkey.org/turkey

Towns & Cities
Ankara
www.ankara-bel.gov.tr

Istanbul
www.ibb.gov.tr

uganda

Tourist Information
Uganda
www.ugandaweb.com

united arab emirates

Dubai
http://dubaitourism.co.ao

usa

Tourist Attractions
Andy Warhol Museum, Pittsburgh
www.warhol.org

Busch Gardens
www.buschgardens.com

Disneyland California
www.disney.go.com/disneyland

Disneyworld Florida
www.disneyland.disney.go.com/disneylandresc
index

Dollywood
www.dollywood.com

Empire State Building, New York City
www.esbnyc.com

Guggenheim, New York
www.guggenheim.org

J Paul Getty Museum, California
www.getty.edu

Knotts Berry Farm
www.knotts.com

Library of Congress, Washington
www.loc.gov

Los Angeles Museum of Art
www.lacma.org

Metropolitan Museum of Art, New York
www.metmuseum.org

Mount Rushmore
www.nps.gov/moru

Museum of Fine Arts, Boston
www.mfa.org

Museum of Modern Art, New York
www.moma.org

National Museum of American Art,
Washington
www.nmaa.si.edu

Norman Rockwell Museum, Massachuse
www.nrm.org

Seaworld, Florida
www.seaworld.org

Smithsonian Institution, United States
www.si.edu

Space Needle
www.spaceneedle.com

Statue of Liberty, New York
www.nps.gov/stli

Universal Studios
www.universalstudios.com

Wet 'n' Wild
www.wetnwild.com

Yellowstone National Park
www.nps.gov/yel

Yosemite National Park
www.nps.gov/yose

Tourist Information

Go-United States
www.go-unitedstates.com

Massachusetts
www.mass-vacation.com

Orlando
www.go2orlando.com

Utah
www.utah.com

Virgin Islands
www.usvi.net

Towns & Cities

Boston
www.ci.boston.ma.us

Chicago
www.ci.chicago.il.us

Dallas
www.ci.dallas.tx.us

Denver
www.denvergov.org

Detroit
www.ci.detroit.mi.us

Honolulu
www.co.honolulu.hi.us

Houston
www.ci.houston.tx.us

Las Vegas
www.ci.las-vegas.nv.us

Los Angeles
www.ci.la.ca.us

Memphis
www.ci.memphis.tn.us

Miami
www.ci.miami.fl.us

Minneapolis St Paul
www.ci.minneapolis.mn.us

New York
www.ci.nyc.ny.us

Philadelphia
www.phila.gov

Salt Lake City
www.ci.slc.ut.us

San Francisco
www.ci.sf.ca.us

Seattle
www.ci.seattle.wa.us

St Louis
http://stlouis.missouri.org

venezuela

Tourist Information

Venezuela
www.venezuela.com

web cams

Ben Nevis & Lochaber
www.lochaber.com/neviscam

Dublin
www.nci.ie/ispy

Oxford Circus, London
www.fujiint.co.uk/street/index.html

Snowdon
www.fhc.co.uk/weather/live

Sydney
www.viewsydney.com.au

astronomy ●

conservation ●

magazines & websites ●

societies & institutions ●

zoos ●

science & nature

astronomy

American Astronomical Society
www.aas.org

Armagh Observatory
http://star.arm.ac.uk

Armagh Planetarium
www.armagh-planetarium.co.uk

Astronomy Now
www.astronomynow.com

British Astronomical Society
www.ast.cam.ac.uk/~baa

British National Space Centre
www.bnsc.gov.uk

Buzz Aldrin
www.buzzaldrin.com

Consortium for European Research on
Extragalactic Surveys
www.jb.man.ac.uk/~ceres1

European Space Agency
www.esrin.esa.it

Greenwich Mean Time
www.time.greenwich2000.com

Hubble Space Telescope
www.stsci.edu

International Astronomical Union
www.intastun.org

International Meteor Organisation
www.imo.net

Jodrell Bank
www.jb.man.ac.uk

Kennedy Space Centre
www.ksc.nasa.gov

NASA
www.nasa.gov

National Space Science Centre
www.nssc.co.uk

Royal Astronomical Society
www.ras.org.uk

Royal Observatory Edinburgh
www.roe.ac.uk

Royal Observatory, Greenwich
www.rog.nmm.ac.uk

Sky at Night
www.bbc.co.uk/skyatnight

Society for Popular Astronomy
www.u-net.com/ph/spa

Starchaser Foundation
www.starchaser.co.uk

State Research Centres of Russian
Federation
www.extech.msk.su/english/src

University of London Observatory
www.ulo.ucl.ac.uk

conservation

Advisory Committee on Protection of the
Sea
www.acops.org

Animal Aid
www.animalaid.org.uk

Atlantic Salmon Trust
www.atlanticsalmontrust.org

Bat Conservation Trust
www.bats.org.uk

Bird Life International
www.birdlife.net

Born Free Foundation
www.bornfree.org.uk

British Deer Society
www.bds.org.uk

British Dragonfly Society
www.dragonflysoc.org.uk

British Hedgehog Preservation Society
www.software-technics.co.uk/bhps

British Wildlife Rehabilitation Council
www.nimini.demon.co.uk/bwrc

Fauna & Flora International
www.ffi.org.uk

Flora Locale
www.floralocale.org

Game Conservancy Trust
www.game-conservancy.org.uk

Hawk & Owl Trust
www.mycenae.demon.co.uk/hawkandowl

International Wildlife Coalition
www.iwc.org

Marine Conservation Society
www.goodbeachguide.co.uk

National Birds of Prey Centre
www.nbpc.co.uk

National Federation of Badger Groups
www.badger.org.uk/nfbg

National Ferret Welfare Society
http://homepage.ntlworld.com/ferreter

National Seal Sanctuary
www.sealsanctuary.co.uk

Nature Conservation Bureau
www.naturebureau.co.uk

Orangutan Foundation UK
www.orangutan.org.uk

Parrot Line
www.parrotline.org

Rainforest Action Network
www.ran.org

Raptor Conservation
www.raptor.uk.com

Scottish Natural Heritage
www.snh.org.uk

Tusk Force
www.tusk.force.org.uk

Whale & Dolphin Conservation Society
www.wdcs.org.uk

Whale Foundation
www.whale-foundation.org

Wildfowl & Wetlands Trust
www.greenchannel.com/wwt

Wildlife Trust
www.wildlifetrust.org.uk

World Society for the Protection of Animals
www.wspa.org.uk

World Wide Fund for Nature
www.panda.org

WWF - UK
www.wwf-uk.org

WWF International
www.panda.org

Young People's Trust for the Environment &
Nature Conservation
www.yptenc.org.uk

magazines & websites

Alpha Galileo
www.alphagalileo.org

Astronomy
www.astronomy.com

Birds of Britain
www.birdsofbritain.co.uk

Birdwatch
www.birdwatch.co.uk

Chemistry & Industry Magazine
http://enviro.mond.org

Chemistry UK
www.u-net.com/ukchem

Delphi Magazine
www.itecuk.com/delmag

Developers Review
www.itecuk.com/devrev

Ecologist
www.gn.apc.org/ecologist

Elemental Discoveries
www.camsoft.com/elemental

Journal Of Natural History
www.catchword.com/titles/tandf/00222933
/contp1-1.htm

National Geographic
www.nationalgeographic.com

Nature
www.nature.com

Naturenet
www.naturenet.net

New Civil Engineer
www.nceplus.co.uk

New Electronics
www.neon.co.uk

New Scientist
www.newscientist.co.uk

Physics World
http://physicsweb.org/toc

Planet Ark
www.planetark.org

Science Frontiers
www.science-frontiers.com

Science News
www.sciencenews.org

Science Online
www.scienceonline.org

Stephen Hawking
www.damtp.cam.ac.uk/user/hawking

Tomorrow's World (BBC)
www.bbc.co.uk/tw

Uri Geller
www.urigeller.com

Walking with Dinosaurs
www.bbc.co.uk/dinosaurs

societies & institutions

Amateur Entomologists' Society
www.theaes.org

Association for Science Education
www.ase.org.uk

Association for Women in Science &
Engineering
www.awise.org

British Antarctic Survey
www.antartica.ac.uk

British Aquatic Resource Centre
www.cfkc.demon.co.uk

British Association for the Advancement of
Science
www.britassoc.org.uk

British Bee Keepers Association
www.bbka.demon.co.uk

British Geological Survey
www.bgs.ac.uk

British Horological Institute
www.bhi.co.uk

British Ornithologists' Union
www.bou.org.uk

British UFO Research Association
www.bufora.org.uk

Central Science Laboratory
www.csl.gov.uk

Council for Science & Technology
www.cst.gov.uk

Engineering & Physical Sciences Research Council
www.epsrc.ac.uk

Field Studies Council
www.field-studies-council.org

Forensic Science Society
www.forensic-science-society.org.uk

Geological Society
www.geolsoc.org.uk

Human Cloning Foundation
www.humancloning.org

Human Genetic Advisory Commission
www.dti.gov.uk/hgac

Independent Cat Society
www.welcome.to/tipcs

Institute of Biology
www.iob.org

Institute of Biomedical Sciences
www.ibms.org

Institute of Broadcast Sound
www.ibs.org.uk

Institute of Hydrology
www.nwl.ac.uk/ih

Isaac Newton Institute
www.newton.cam.ac.uk

Jane Goodall Institute
www.janegoodall.org

Linnean Society of London
www.linnean.org.uk

Mammal Society
www.abdn.ac.uk/mammal

National Bird of Prey Centre
www.appsearch.com/nbpc

National Institute of Agricultural Botany
www.niab.com

National NDT Centre
www.aeat.co.uk/ndt

Natural Resources Institute
www.nri.org

Office of Science & Technology
www.dti.gov.uk/ost

Palaeontological Association
www.nhm.ac.uk/hosted_sites/paleonet/palass/index.html

Paleontological Society
http://paleosoc.org

Plantlife
www.plantlife.org.uk

Primate Society of Great Britain
www.psgb.org

Roslin Institute
www.ri.bbsrc.ac.uk

Royal Academy of Engineering
www.raeng.org.uk

Royal Botanic Gardens
www.rbgkew.org.uk

Royal Entomological Society
www.royensoc.demon.co.uk

Royal Geographical Society
www.rgs.org

Royal Society
www.royalsoc.ac.uk

Royal Society of Chemistry
www.rsc.org

Scientists of Global Responsibility
www.sgr.org.uk

Scottish Ornithologists' Club
www.the-soc.org.uk

Society for Experimental Biology
www.sebiology.com

Society for Interdisciplinary Studies
www.knowledge.co.uk/sis

Society for Underwater Exploration
www.underwaterdiscovery.org

Tree Register
www.tree-register.org

UK Science Park Association
www.ukspa.org.uk

UK Scientific Research Councils
www.nas.edu/nrc

Uranium Institute
www.uilondon.org

Zoological Society of London
www.zsl.org

ZOOS

Banham Zoo
www.banhamzoo.co.uk

Blackpool
www.blackpool.gov.uk/zoo

Bristol
www.bristolzoo.org.uk

Chester
www.demon.co.uk/chesterzoo

Colchester
www.colchester-zoo.co.uk

Dublin
www.dublinzoo.ie

Dudley
www.dudleyzoo.org.uk

Edinburgh
www.edinburghzoo.org.uk

Glasgow
www.glasgowzoo.inyourcity.com

Howletts Wild Animal Park
www.howletts.net

Knowsley Safari Park
www.knowsley.com

London
www.londonzoo.co.uk

Longleat Safari Park
www.longleat.co.uk

Marwell
www.marwell.org.uk

Mole Hall Wildlife Park
www.molehall.co.uk

National Sea Life Centre
www.sealife.co.uk

Paignton
www.paigntonzoo.demon.co.uk

Paradise Wildlife Park
www.pwpark.com

Twycross
www.twycrosszoo.com

West Midlands Safari Park
www.wmsp.co.uk

Whipsnade
www.londonzoo.co.uk/whipsnade

Willersmill Wildlife Park
www.sprout.demon.co.uk/Willersmill.html

antiques & auctions •

beds & bedding •

books •

china & glass •

clothes •

computers & electrical •

cosmetics & perfumes •

department stores •

flooring •

flowers •

furniture & upholstery •

gifts & stationery •

healthcare, beauty
& personal hygiene •

home entertainment •

home improvements
& products •

jewellers •

kitchens & appliances •

lighting •

luggage •

magazines & websites •

markets & malls •

mother & baby •

music, games & video •

photography •

shoes & accessories •

specialist •

sports & outdoor •

tobacco •

toys •

trade associations •

wallcovering •

watches •

antiques & auctions

Antique Dealers Directory
www.antique-dealers-directory.co.uk

Antiques Roadshow
www.bbc.co.uk/antiques

Antiques Trade Gazette
www.atg-online.com

Association of Art and Antique Dealers
(LAPADA)
www.lapada.co.uk

Bonhams
www.bonhams.com

British Horological Institute
www.bhi.co.uk

Christie's
www.christies.com

Daltons Antiques
www.daltons.com

Lots Road Galleries
www.thesaurus-co.uk/lotsroad

Olympia Fine Art & Antiques Fairs
www.olympia-antiques.co.uk

Philips
www.philips-auctions.com

Portobello Antiques Market
www.portobelloroad.co.uk

QXL.com
www.qxl.com

Sothebys
www.sothebys.com

Stanley Gibbons
www.stangib.com

Wallis & Wallis
www.wallisandwallis.co.uk

beds & bedding

Dunlopillo
www.dunlopillo.co.uk

Relyon
www.relyon.co.uk

Rest Assured
www.rest-assured.co.uk

Sealy
www.sealyuk.co.uk

Silent Night
www.silentnight.co.uk

Sleep Council
www.sleepcouncil.org.uk

Slumberland
www.slumberland.co.uk

books

AlphabetStreet
www.alphabetstreet.co.uk

Amazon
www.amazon.co.uk

Barnes & Noble
www.barnesandnoble.com

BBC Shop
www.bbcshop.com

Blackwell's
www.blackwells.co.uk

Bol
www.bol.co.uk

Borders
www.borders.com

Cook Book Shop
www.cooks-book-shop.co.uk

Dillons
www.dillons.co.uk

Dorling Kindersley
www.dk.com/uk

Express Bookshop
www.bvcd.net/express

Hammicks
www.thebookplace.com

Heffers
www.heffers.co.uk

Internet Bookshop
www.bookshop.co.uk

John Menzies
www.john-menzies.co.uk

John Smith
www.johnsmith.co.uk

Penguin
www.penguin.co.uk

Waterstones
www.waterstones.co.uk

WH Smith
www.whsmith.co.uk

World Books
www.worldbooks.co.uk

Zwemmer
www.zwemmer.co.uk

china & glass

Chinacraft
www.chinacraft.co.uk

Dartington Crystal
www.dartington.co.uk

Lladro
http://lladrogib.hypermart.net

Poole Pottery
www.poolepottery.co.uk

Portmeirion
www.portmeirion.com

Royal Doulton
www.royal-doulton.com

Spode China
www.spode.co.uk

Wedgwood
www.wedgwood.co.uk

clothes

Alexandra
www.alexandra.co.uk

Aquascutum
www.aquascutum.co.uk

Armani
www.armaniexchange.com

Artigiano
www.artigiano.co.uk

Austin Reed
www.austinreed.co.uk

Ben Sherman
www.bensherman.co.uk

Benetton
www.benetton.com

Bernini
www.bernini.co.uk

Betty Barclay
www.bettybarclay.co.uk

Boden
www.boden.co.uk

Brooks Brothers
www.brooks-brothers.net

Browns
http://global-m.com/browns/browns.html

Burtons
www.burtonmenswear.co.uk

C & A
www.c-and-a.co.uk

Caractere
www.vestebene.com

Charles Tyrwhitt
www.ctshirts.co.uk

Ciro Citterio
www.cirocitterio.com

Contessa
www.contessa.org.uk

Coppernob
www.coppernob.com

Cotswold
www.cotswold-outdoor.co.uk

Cotton Moon
www.cottonmoon.co.uk

Cyrillus
www.cyrillus.co.uk

Damart
www.damartonline.co.uk

Diesel
www.diesel.co.uk

DKNY
www.donnakaran.com

Dockers
www.dockers.com

Donaldson
www.donaldson.be

Dorothy Perkins
www.dorothyperkins.co.uk

Dressmart.com
www.dressmart.com

Eddie Bauer
www.eddiebauer.co.uk

Elvi
www.elvi.co.uk

Empire Stores
www.empirestores.co.uk

Evans
www.evans.ltd.uk

Fat Face
www.fatface.co.uk

Fenn Wright & Manson
www.fwm.co.uk

Frank Usher
www.frankusher.co.uk

Freemans
www.freemans.co.uk

French Connection
www.frenchconnection.com

French Sole
www.frenchsole.com

Gap
www.gap.com

Gap Kids
www.gapkids.com

Georgina von Etzdorf
www.georginavonetzdorf.co.uk

Ghost
www.ghost.ltd.uk

Gianfranco Ferre
www.gianfrancoferre.com

Givenchy
www.givenchy.com

MARKS & SPENCER

- shop online
  24 hours a day,
  7 days a week
- 48 hour delivery
- secure online payment
- easy returns and refunds
- simple search facility
  for enjoyable browsing

did you know?

over 3,000 of

your favourite

Marks & Spencer

products are available

to buy online @

www.marksandspencer.com

Grattan
www.grattan.co.uk

GUS
www.shoppersuniverse.com

Gymboree
www.gymboree.com

H & M Hennes
www.hm.com

Hackett
www.hackett.co.uk

Harvie & Hudson
www.harvieandhudson.com

Hawkeshead
www.hawkshead.com

Henri Lloyd
www.henrilloyd.com

High & Mighty
www.highandmighty.co.uk

Jaeger
www.jaeger.co.uk

James Meade
www.jamesmeade.com

Janet Reger
www.janetreger.com

Kaleidescope
www.kaleidoscope.co.uk

Kays
www.kaysnet.com

Kelsey Tailors
www.kelseytailors.co.uk

Kingshill
www.kingshilldirect.co.uk

L L Bean
www.llbean.com

La Redoute
www.redoute.co.uk

Laetitia Allen
www.laetitiaallenco.uk

Lands' End
www.landsend.co.uk

Laura Ashley
www.laura-ashley.com

Levis
www.eu.levi.com

Liberty
www.liberty-of-london.com

Look Again
www.lookagain.co.uk

Lycra
www.lycra.com

Madhouse
www.madhouse.co.uk

Marks & Spencer

www.marksandspencer.com

Marshalls
www.marshalls.co.uk

Monsoon
www.monsoon.co.uk

Morgan
www.morgan.fr

Moschino
www.moschino.it

Moss Bros
www.mossbros.co.uk

Muji
www.muji.co.jp

Next
www.next.co.uk

Oilily
www.oililyusa.com

Osh Kosh B'Gosh
www.oshkoshbgosh.com

Paul Smith
www.paulsmith.co.uk

Pepe Jeans
www.pepejeans.com

Peruvian Connection
www.peruvianconnection.com

Prada
www.prada.com

Pretty Polly
www.prettypolly.co.uk

Principles
www.principles.co.uk

Pringle
www.pringle-of-scotland.co.uk

QS
www.qsgroup.co.uk

Racing Green
www.racinggreen.co.uk

Red or Dead
www.redordead.co.uk

Reiss
www.reiss.co.uk

River Island
www.riverisland.com

Only The Best Is Good Enough

www.beststuff.co.uk™

- ☑ TV
- ☑ Video
- ☑ Audio
- ☑ Vacuum Cleaner
- ☑ Ice Cream Maker
- ☑ Telephone
- ☑ Food Processor
- ☑ Shaver
- ☑ Dehumidifier
- ☑ Coffee Machine
- ☑ Toaster
- ☑ DVD Player
- ☑ Fax Machine
- ☑ Food Mixer
- ☑ Hair Clippers
- ☑ Juicer
- ☑ MP3 Player
- ☑ Radar Detector
- ☑ Percolator
- ☑ Waffle Maker
- ☑ Kettle
- ☑ Wireless Phone Extension
- ☑ Digital Camera
- ☑ Headphones

And Tons Of Other Stuff

We Stock One Item In Any One Category...

...The Best One!

**Members Of
Which? WebTrader**

Scotch Corner
www.scotch-corner.co.uk

Sophia Swire
www.sophiaswire.com

Ted Baker
www.tedbaker.co.uk

Thomas Pink
www.thomaspink.co.uk

Tie Rack
www.tie-rack.co.uk

Timberland
www.timberland.com

Tommy Hilfiger
www.tommypr.com

Top Man
www.topman.co.uk

Top Shop
www.topshop.co.uk

Van Heusen
www.vanheusendirect.com

Victoria's Secret
www.victoriassecret.com

Virgin Clothing Company
www.virginclothing.co.uk

Wealth of Nations
www.wealthofnations.co.uk

Wonderbra
www.wonderbra.com

Wrangler
www.wrangler.com

Youngs
www.youngs-hire.co.uk

computers & electrical

Best Stuff
www.beststuff.co.uk

Carphone Warehouse
www.carphonewarehouse.com

Comet
www.comet.co.uk

Currys
www.dixons.com/about_currys.html

Dixons
www.dixons.co.uk

Duracell
www.duracell.com

Ever Ready
www.everready.co.uk

Granada
www.box-clever.com

Hewlett Packard
www.hp.com

Hi-Fidelity
www.hi-fidelity.co.uk

Let's Buy It

www.letsbuyit.com

Link
www.the-link.co.uk

PC World
www.pcworld.co.uk

Powerhouse
www.powerhouse-retail.co.uk

Roberts Radios Direct
www.wesellradios.co.uk

Simply
www.simply.co.uk

Tempo
www.tempo.co.uk

Time
www.timecomputers.com

cosmetics & perfumes

Avon
www.uk.avon.com

BeneFit
www.benefitcosmetics.com

Bobbi Brown
www.bobbibrowncosmetics.com

Body Shop
www.thebodyshop.co.uk

Bonne Bell
www.bonnebell.com

Boots
www.boots.co.uk

Cacharel
www.cacharel.com

Chanel
www.chanel.com

Clarins
www.clarins-paris.com

Clinique
www.clinique.com

Color Me Beautiful
www.colorme.com

Colorlab
www.colorlab-cosmetics.com

Coty
www.cotyusine.com

Cover Girl
www.covergirl.com

Crabtree & Evelyn
www.crabtree-evelyn.com

Culpeper
www.culpeper.co.uk

Dior
www.dior.com

Elizabeth Arden
www.elizabetharden.com

Givenchy
www.givenchy.com

Gucci
www.gucci.com

Hard Candy
www.hardcandy.com

Hugo Boss
www.hugo.com

Issey Miyake
www.isseymiyake.com

Jean Paul Gaultier
www.jpgaultier.fr

L'Oreal
www.loreal.com

Lacoste
www.lacoste.com/index_uk.htm

Lancaster
www.lancaster-beauty.com

Lancome
www.lancome.com

Lush
www.lush.co.uk

Mary Kay
www.marykay.com

Max Factor
www.maxfactor.com

MUM Roll On
www.mum-online.co.uk

Oil of Olay
www.olay.com

Paco Rabanne
www.pacorabanne.com

Profaces
www.profaces.com

Revlon
www.revlon.com

Shiseido
www.shiseido.co.uk

Sisley
www.sisley.tm.fr

Tommy Hilfiger
www.tommypr.com

Yves Saint Laurent
www.yslonline.com

department stores

Allders
www.allders.co.uk

Argos
www.argos.co.uk

Bentalls
www.bentalls.co.uk

Bhs
www.bhs.co.uk

Debenhams
www.debenhams.co.uk

Fortnum & Mason
www.fortnumandmason.co.uk

Harrods
www.harrods.com

House of Fraser
www.houseoffraser.co.uk

Index
www.indexshop.com

John Lewis
www.johnlewis.co.uk

Liberty
www.liberty-of-london.com

Marks & Spencer

www.marksandspencer.com

Selfridges
www.selfridges.co.uk

Woolworths
www.woolworths.co.uk

flooring

Allied Carpets
www.alliedcarpets.co.uk

Amtico
www.amtico.co.uk

Axminster
www.axminster-carpets.co.uk

Brintons
www.brintons.co.uk

British Wool Marketing Board
www.i-i.net/britishwool

Carpet Information Centre
www.carpetinfo.co.uk

Carpetright
www.carpetright.co.uk

Duralay
www.duralay.co.uk

Marley
www.marley.co.uk

Ryalux
www.ryalux.com

Stoddard
www.stoddardintl.co.uk

Weston Carpets
www.weston-carpets.co.uk

Wilton
www.wiltoncarpets.com

flowers

Flowers Direct
www.flowersdirect.co.uk

Interflora
www.interflora.co.uk

Jane Packer
www.jane-packer.co.uk

Teleflorist
www.teleflorist.co.uk

William Hayford
www.william-hayford.co.uk

furniture & upholstery

Chaplins
www.chaplins.co.uk

Conran Shop
www.conran.co.uk

Designers Guild
www.designersguild.com

Domain Furniture
www.domainfurniture.com

Ducal
www.ducal-furniture.co.uk

Ercol
www.ercol.com

Fogarty
www.fogarty.co.uk

G Plan
www.morrisfurniture.co.uk/gplan

The Garden Shop
www.thegardenshop.co.uk

General Trading Company
www.general-trading.co.uk

Habitat
www.habitat.net

Harris Carpets
www.harriscarpets.co.uk

The Holding Company
www.theholdingcompany.co.uk

Holding Company
www.theholdingcompany.co.uk

Ikea
www.ikea.com

Indian Ocean Trading Company
www.indian-ocean.co.uk

Iron Bed Company
www.ironbed.co.uk

Kingdom of Leather
www.kingdomofleather.co.uk

Laura Ashley
www.laura-ashley.com

Ligne Roset
www.ligneroset.com

Marks & Spencer

www.marks-and-spencer.co.uk

McCord
www.mccord.uk.com

MFI Homeworks
www.mfi.co.uk

Multiyork
www.multiyork.co.uk

Parker Knoll
www.parkerknoll.co.uk

Purves & Purves
www.purves.co.uk

Sharps
www.sharps.co.uk

Uno
www.uno.co.uk

Wesley Barrell
www.wesley-barrell.co.uk

World of Leather
www.worldofleather.co.uk

gifts & stationery

Birthdays
www.birthdays.co.uk

Cards Galore
www.cardsgalore.com

Charles Letts
www.letts.co.uk

Charles Rennie Mackintosh Store
www.rennie-mackintosh.co.uk

Choc Express
www.chocexpress.com

Hallmark Cards
www.hallmark.com

Lastminute.com
www.lastminute.com

Links
www.linksoflondon.com

Moon Estates
www.moonestates.com

Papermate
www.papermate.co.uk

Past Times
www.past-times.com

Pen Shop
www.penshop.co.uk

Prince's Trust Shop
www.princestrustshop.co.uk

Red Letter Days
www.redletterdays.co.uk

Smythson of Bond Street
www.smythson.com

Thorntons
www.thorntons.co.uk

Victorinox
www.victorinox.com

Voucher Express
www.voucherexpress.com

healthcare, beauty & personal hygiene

Alka Seltzer
www.alka-seltzer.com

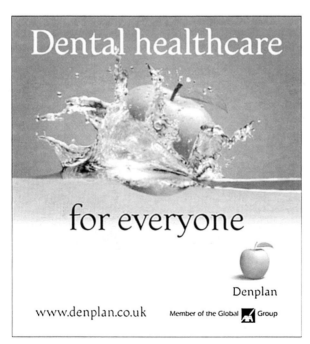

BaByliss
www.babyliss.co.uk

Bic
www.bicworld.com

Bioforce
www.bioforce.co.uk

Bodyform
www.bodyform.co.uk

Braun
www.braun.com

Cibavision
www.cibavision.co.uk

Colgate
www.colgate.com

Denman Brushes
www.denmanbrush.com

Durex
www.durex.com

Gillette
www.gillette.com

Kimberly Clark
www.kimberly-clark.com

L'Oreal
www.loreal.com

Lanes
www.laneshealth.com

Listerine
www.listerine.com

Macleans
www.macleans.co.uk

Nelsons
www.nelsons.co.uk

Nicorette
www.nicorette.co.uk

Nicotinell
www.nicotinell.co.uk

Nivea
www.nivea.co.uk

Nurofen
www.nurofen.com

Oral B
www.oralb.com

Palmers Cocoa Butter
www.palmerscocoabutter.com

Potter's Herbal Medicines
www.pottersherbals.co.uk

Rennies
www.rennie.co.uk

Seven Seas
www.seven-seas.ltd.uk

Slendertone
www.slendertone.co.uk

Solgar
www.solgar.com

Strepsils
www.strepsils.com

Tampax
www.tampax.com

Tisserand
www.tisserand.com

Vitabiotics
www.vitabiotics.com

Wella
www.wella.co.uk

Wilkinson Sword
www.wilkinson-sword.co.uk

home entertainment

Aiwa
www.aiwa.co.uk

Akai
www.akai.com

Alpine
www.alpine-europe.com

Astra
www.ses-astra.com/uk

Bang & Olufsen
www.bang-olufsen.com

Hitachi
www.hitachi.com

JVC
www.jvc-europe.com

Marantz
www.marrantz.com

Naim
www.naim-audio.com

Phillips
www.phillips.com

Richer Sounds
www.richersounds.com

Sharp
www.sharp.co.uk

Sony
www.sony.com

TAG McLaren Audio
www.tagmclarenaudio.com

Technics

www.technics.com

home improvements & products

Amway
www.amway.com

Anglian Home Improvements
www.anglianhome.co.uk

Aqualisa
www.aqualisa.co.uk

Axminster Power Tools
www.axminster.co.uk

B&Q
www.diy.co.uk

BAC Windows
www.bacwindows.co.uk

Ballingers
www.ballingers.co.uk

Black & Decker
www.blackanddecker.com

Bostik
www.bostik.com

British Bathroom Council
www.british-bathrooms.org.uk

British Coatings Federation
www.coatings.org.uk

British Stone
www.british-stone.com

Coldshield
www.coldshield.com

Cookson's Tools
www.cooksons.com

Crown
www.crownpaints.co.uk

De Walt
www.dewalt.com

Dolphin
www.dolphin-fitted-bathrooms.co.uk

Draper Tools
www.draper.co.uk

Dulux
www.dulux.co.uk

Duwit
www.duwit.com

Everest
www.everest.co.uk

Expelair
www.expelair.co.uk

Focus Do-it-All
www.focusdoitall.co.uk

Graham & Brown
www.grahambrown.com

Great Mills
www.greatmills.co.uk

Hammerite
www.hammerite.com

Harris
www.lgharris.co.uk

Homebase
www.homebase.co.uk

Ideal Standard
www.ideal-standard.co.uk

Jewson
www.jewson.co.uk

Makita
www.ukindustry.co.uk/makita

Meddings Machine Tools
www.meddings.co.uk

Mica Hardware
www.micahardware.co.uk

National Tile Association
www.nta.org.uk

Osram
www.osram.co.uk

Paint Research Association
www.pra.org.uk

Polycell
www.polycell.co.uk

Potterton
www.potterton.co.uk

Quickgrip
www.quickgrip.com

Rawlplug
www.rawlplug.co.uk

Rytons Building Products
www.rytons.com

Scott & Sargeant
www.scosarg.co.uk

Screwfix
www.screwfix.com

Showerlux
www.showerlux.com

Spring Ram
www.ultrastyl.com

Stanley Tools
www.stanleyworks.com

Stannah Stairlifts
www.stannah.co.uk

Travis Perkins
www.travisperkins.co.uk

Trend
www.trendm.co.uk

Unibond
www.unibond.co.uk

Universal Fittings
www.universal-fittings.co.uk

Vent Axia
www.vent-axia.com

Weatherseal
www.weatherseal.co.uk

Wickes
www.wickes.com

Wilkinsons
www.wilko.co.uk

jewellers

Adler
www.adler.ch

Alexanders
www.alexanders-the-jewellers.co.uk

Asprey & Garrard
www.asprey-garrard.com

Bogaert
www.bogaertjewellery.com

Boodle & Dunthorne
www.boodles.co.uk

Cartier
www.cartier.com

De Beers
www.adiamondisforever.com

Ernest Jones
www.ernestjones.co.uk

Goldsmiths
www.goldsmiths.co.uk

Graff
www.graff-uk.com

H Samuel
www.hsamuel.co.uk

Hirsh
www.hirsh.co.uk

Lladro
www.lladro.com

Longines
www.longines.com

N Bloom & Son
www.nbloom.co.uk

Theo Fennell
www.theofennell.com

Tiffany
www.tiffany.com

Wright & Teague
www.wrightandteague.com

kitchens & appliances

AEG
www.aeg.com

Aga Rayburn
www.aga-rayburn.co.uk

Atag
www.atag.co.uk

Baumatic
www.baumatic.co.uk

Belling
www.belling.co.uk

Betterwear
www.betterwear.co.uk

Bosch
www.boschappliances.co.uk

Brabantia
www.brabantia.com

Breville
www.breville.co.uk

Cannon
www.cannongas.co.uk

Creda
www.creda.co.uk

Cucina Direct
www.cucinadirect.co.uk

De Dietrich
www.dedietrich.co.uk

Divertimenti
www.divertimenti.co.uk

Dualit
www.dualit.com

Dyson
www.dyson.com

Electrolux
www.electrolux.co.uk

Gaggia
www.gaggia.it

GEC
www.gec.co.uk

Hoover
www.hoover.co.uk

Hotpoint
www.hotpoint.co.uk

Indesit
www.indesit.co.uk

Intoto
www.intoto.co.uk

Lakeland
www.mos.lakelandlimited.co.uk

Le Creuset
www.lecreuset.com

Magnet
www.magnet.co.uk

Miele
www.miele.co.uk

Mitsubishi Electric
www.meuk.mee.com/consumer

Moben
www.moben.co.uk

Moulinex
www.moulinex.co.uk

Neff
www.neff.co.uk

Ocean
www.oceancatalogue.co.uk

Panasonic
www.panasonic.co.uk

Paula Rosa
www.paularosa.com

Philips
www.philips.com

Redring
www.redring.co.uk

Russell Hobbs
www.russell-hobbs.com

Scott & Sargeant Cookshop
www.scottsargeant.com

Servis
www.servis.co.uk

Sheffield Steel
www.made-in-sheffield.com

Siemens
www.siemensappliances.co.uk

Smeg
www.smeguk.com

Stoves
www.stoves.co.uk

Technics
www.technics.co.uk

Tefal
www.tefal.co.uk

Toshiba
www.toshiba.co.uk

Vax
www.vax.co.uk

Whirlpool
www.whirlpool.co.uk

Zanussi
www.zanussi.co.uk

lighting

Abacus
www.abacus-lighting.com

Anglepoise
www.anglepoise.co.uk

Christopher Wray
www.christopher-wray.com

Mathmos
www.mathmos.co.uk

luggage

Antler
www.antler.co.uk

Carlton
www.carlton-luggage-direct.com

Louis Vuitton
www.vuitton.co.uk

Samsonite
www.samsonite.com

Tanner Krolle
www.tannerkrolle.com

magazines & websites

Daltons Weekly
www.daltons.co.uk

Dressmart.com
www.dressmart.com

Empire Direct
www.empiredirect.co.uk

Exchange & Mart
www.exchangeandmart.co.uk

FranceInLondon
www.franceinlondon.co.uk

Goldfish Guide
www.goldfishguide.com

Loot
www.loot.com

Shops on the Net
www.sotn.co.uk

ShopSmart
www.shopsmart.com

Which?
www.which.net

markets & malls

Barclaysquare
www.barclaysquare.co.uk

Bicester Village
www.bicester-village.co.uk

Bluewater
www.bluewater.freeserve.co.uk

Central Milton Keynes
www.cmkshop.co.uk

Covent Garden
www.coventgardenmarket.com

Freeport
www.freeportplc.com

Galleria Outlet Centre
www.factory-outlets.co.uk

Jermyn Street
www.jermynstreet.com

Meadowhall Centre
www.meadowhall.co.uk

Outlet Centres International
www.outletcentres.com

Shops on the Net
www.sotn.co.uk

ShopSmart
www.shopsmart.com

Whitgift
www.whitgiftshopping.co.uk

mother & baby

Avent
www.avent.co.uk

Babies R Us
www.babiesrus.co.uk

Baby Gap
www.babygap.com

Bebe Confort
www.bebeconfort.com

Blooming Marvellous
www.bloomingmarvellous.co.uk

Britax
www.britax.co.uk

Bumpsadaisy
www.covent-gardenlife.com/shopping/shops/bumpsadaisy

Chicco
www.chiccousa.com

Cosatto
www.cosatto.com

Formes
www.formes.com

Graco
www.graco.co.uk or www.gracobaby.com

Huggies
www.huggies.com

Johnson's
www.yourbaby.com

JoJo Maman Bebe
www.jojomamanbebe.co.uk

Klippan
www.klippan.co.uk

Mamas & Papas
www.mamasandpapas.co.uk

Mothercare
www.mothercare.com

Nappies Direct
www.nappies-direct.co.uk

National Childbirth Trust
www.nct-online.org

Pampers
www.pampers.com

Pegasus Pushchairs
www.allterrain.co.uk

Real Nappy Association
www.realnappy.com

Urchin
www.urchin.co.uk

music, games & video

Blackstar
www.blackstar.co.uk

Blockbuster
www.blockbuster.co.uk

Boxman
www.boxman.co.uk

Britannia Music Club
www.britmusic.co.uk

Carlton Video
www.carltonvideo.co.uk

CD Now
www.cdnow.com

CD Wow

www.cd-wow.com

Computer Exchange
www.cex.co.uk

DVDplus
www.dvdplus.co.uk

Game
www.game-retail.co.uk

Gameplay
www.gameplay.com

HMV
www.hmv.com

Jungle.com
www.jungle.com

Music & Games
www.musicandgames.com

Nice Price
www.niceprice.net

Odeon Filmstore
www.filmstore.com

Odeon Videostore
www.filmstore.co.uk

Our Price
www.ourprice.co.uk

Tower Records
www.towerrecords.co.uk

Virgin Megastore
www.virginmega.com

WH Smith
www.whsmithonline.co.uk

Yalplay
www.yalplay.com

photography

Dixons
www.dixons.co.uk

Jessops
www.jessops.co.uk

Olan Mills
www.olanmills.com

Photo Me
www.photo-me.co.uk

shoes & accessories

Accessorize
www.accessorize.co.uk

Barratts
www.barratts.co.uk

Birkenstock
www.birkenstock.co.uk

Cheaney
www.cheaney.co.uk

Church and Co
www.buckinghamgate.com/bgate

Claire's Accessories
www.claires.com

Clarks
www.clarks.co.uk

DASCO
www.shoeworld.co.uk/dasco

Dolcis
www.dolcis.co.uk

Dr Martens
www.drmartens.com

Ecco
www.ecco-shoes.co.uk

Faith
www.faith.co.uk

Gordon Scott
www.gordonscott.co.uk

Gucci
www.gucci.com

Hush Puppies
www.hushpuppiesshoes.com

James Lock
www.lockhatters.co.uk

Jones Bootmaker
www.jonesbootmaker.com

Lulu Guiness
www.luluguinness.com

Mulberry
www.mulberry-england.co.uk

Oakley
www.oakley.com

Office
www.office.co.uk

Ray-Ban
www.rayban.com

Rockport Shoes
www.walking-shoes.com

Sak
www.thesak.com

Skechers
www.skechers.com

Timberland
www.timberland.com

Timpson
www.timpson.com

Whitehouse & Cox
www.whitehouse-cox.co.uk

Wolford
www.wolfordboutique-kenmode-kensington.co.uk

specialist

Ann Summers
www.annsummers.co.uk

Anything Left Handed
www.anythingleft-handed.co.uk

Innovations
www.innovations.co.uk

The Left Hand
www.thelefthand.com

sports & outdoor

Allsports
www.allsportsretail.co.uk

Altberg Boots
www.altberg.co.uk

Barbour
www.barbour.com

Berghaus
www.berghaus.com

Blacks
www.blacks.co.uk

Edge2Edge
www.edge2edge.co.uk

Ellis Brigham
www.ellis-brigham.com

Farlows
www.farlows.co.uk

Fila
www.fila.com

Hawkeshead
www.hawkshead.com

Intersport
www.intersport.co.uk

James Lock
www.lockhatters.co.uk

JD Sports
www.jdsports.co.uk

JJB Sports
www.jjb.co.uk

Kitbag.com
www.kitbag.com

ProLine
www.proline-sports.co.uk

Rohan
www.rohan.co.uk

Snow+Rock
www.snowandrock.co.uk

Sports Connection
www.sportsconnection.co.uk

Sports Division
www.sports-division.com

Sweatshop
www.sweatshop.co.uk

tobacco

Davidoff
www.davidoff.com

Rizla
www.rizla.co.uk

toys

Action Man
www.actionman.com

Barbie
www.barbie.com

Beanie Babies
www.eurobeenie.co.uk

Brio
www.brio.co.uk

Corgi
www.corgi.co.uk

Crayola
www.crayola.com

Dawson & Son
www.dawson-and-son.com

E-Toys
www.etoys.co.uk

Early Learning Centre
www.earlylearningcentre.co.uk

English Teddy Bear Company
www.teddy.co.uk

FAO Schwartz
www.faoschwarz.com

Fisher Price
www.fisher-price.com

Game Store
www.tgs.co.uk/games

Hamleys
www.hamleys.co.uk

Hasbro
www.hasbro.com

Hobbycraft
www.hobbycraft.co.uk

Hornby
www.hornby.co.uk

Knex
www.knex.co.uk

Lego
www.lego.com

Little Tikes
www.rubbermaid.com/littletikes

Matchbox
www.matchboxtoys.com

Mattel
www.mattel.com

Meccano
www.dircon.co.uk-meccano

Paddington Bear
www.paddingtonbear.co.uk

Playmobil
www.playmobil.de

Pokemon
www.pokemon.com

Polly Pocket
www.pollypocket.co.uk

Quadro
www.quadro-toys.co.uk

Scalextric
www.scalextric.co.uk

Tiger Toys
www.tigertoys.co.uk

Tomy
www.tomy.co.uk

Toy City
www.toycity.com

Toys R Us
www.toysrus.co.uk

TP Activity Toys
www.tptoys.com

Wicksteed
www.wicksteed.co.uk

Woolworths
www.woolies.co.uk

trade associations

Alliance of Independent Retailers
www.indretailer.co.uk

Booksellers Association of Great Britain and
Northern Ireland
www.booksellers.org.uk

British Antique Dealers Association
www.bada.org

British Association of Toy Retailers
www.batr.co.uk

British Footwear Association
www.shoeworld.co.uk

British Toy and Hobby Association
www.btha.co.uk

Company of Master Jewellers
www.company-of-master-jewellers.co.uk

Independent Footwear Retailers Association
www.shoeshop.org.uk

LAPADA: Association of Art and Antique
Dealers
www.lapada.co.uk

wallcovering

Armourcoat
www.armourcoat.co.uk

Coleman Brothers
www.colemanbros.co.uk

Coloroll
www.coloroll.co.uk

Farrow & Ball
www.farrow-ball.co.uk

Graham & Brown Wallcoverings
www.grahambrown.com

Monkwell
www.monkwell.com

watches

Baume & Mercier
www.baume-et-mercier.com

Breitling
www.breitling.com

Casio
www.casio.co.uk

Citizen
www.citizenwatch.com

Jaeger le coultre
www.jaeger-lecoultre.com

Longines
www.longines.com

Omega
www.omega.ch

Panerai
www.panerai.com

Patek Philippe
www.patek.com

Rado
www.rado.ch

Rotary
www.rotarywatches.com

Seiko
www.seiko.co.uk

Sekonda
www.sekonda.com

Swatch
www.swatch.com

TAG Heuer
www.tagheuer.com

Timex
www.timex.com

Tissot
www.bme.es/tissot

sport

american football •
athletics •
badminton •
baseball •
basketball •
bowls •
boxing •
canoeing •
combat •
cricket •
cycling •
darts •
fencing •
football •
golf •
gymnastics •
handball •
hockey •
horseracing •
inline & roller skating •
international games •
korfball •
magazines & websites •

• motor racing
• netball
• personalities
• polo
• promotion & education
• rounders
• rowing
• rugby
• sailing & watersports
• show jumping
• snooker & billiards
• softball
• sportswear & equipment
• squash
• sub-aqua
• swimming
• table tennis
• target sports
• tennis
• volleyball
• weightlifting & strength
• winter sports
• wrestling

american football

British Collegiate American Football League
www.bcafl.org

National Football League
www.nfl.com

Sky Sports American Football
www.sky.co.uk/sports/nfl

Super Bowl
www.superbowl.com

athletics

Amateur Athletics Association
www.englandathletics.demon.co.uk

Athletics Board of Ireland
www.athleticsireland.ie

British Athletics Federation
www.british-athletics.co.uk

British Triathlon Association
www.cycling.uk.com/organs/triath.htm

British Wheelchair Sports Foundation
www.britishwheelchairsports.org

English Federation Of Disability Sport
www.efds.co.uk

English Schools Athletics Association
www.esaa.net

European Athletic Federation
www.eaa-athletics.ch

Health Development Agency
www.hea.org.uk

International Amateur Athletics Federation
www.iaaf.org

International Paralympic Committee
www.paralympic.org

International Pentathlon Union
www.pentathlon.org

International Triathlon Union
www.triathlon.org

London Marathon
www.london-marathon.co.uk

National Coaching Foundation
www.ncf.org.uk

Runner's World
www.runnersworld.co.uk

Scottish Athletics Federation
www.saf.org.uk

Sports Aid
www.sportsaid.org.uk

Sydney 2000 Olympics
www.sydney.olympic.org

Youth Sport Trust
www.youthsport.net

badminton

Badminton Association of England
www.baofe.co.uk

Badminton UK
www.badmintonuk.ndo.co.uk

English Schools' Badminton Association
www.esba.co.uk

International Badminton Federation
www.intbadfed.org

Scottish Badminton Union
www.scotbadminton.demon.co.uk

baseball

International Baseball Federation
www.baseball.ch

basketball

Basketball Players Association
www.woods.demon.co.uk/bpa

Budweiser Basketball League UK
www.basketball-league.co.uk

English Basketball Association
www.basketballengland.org.uk

Global Basketball News
www.eurobasket.com

International Basketball Federation
www.fiba.com

National Basketball Association
www.nba.com

Scottish Basketball League
www.basketball-scotland.com

XXL Basketball
www.xxl.co.uk

bowls

English Bowling Association
www.bowlsengland.com

International Bowling Federation
www.fiq.org

Lawn Bowls
www.lawnbowls.com

Official Lawn Bowls
www.lawnbowls.co.uk

boxing

Boxing Monthly Magazine
www.boxing-monthly.co.uk

International Amateur Boxing Association
www.aiba.net

International Boxing Organisation
www.iboboxing.com

World Boxing Association
www.wbaonline.com

canoeing

British Canoe Union
www.bcu.org.uk

European Canoe Association
www.canoe-europe.org

International Canoe Federation
www.canoeicf.com

Irish Canoe Union
www.irishcanoeunion.com

Scottish Canoe Association
www.scot-canoe.org

Welsh Canoeing Association
www.welsh-canoeing.org.uk

combat

British Aikido Association
www.aikido-baa.org.uk

British Council for Chinese Martial Arts
www.bccma.demon.co.uk

British United Taekwon-do Federation
www.butf.com

International Judo Federation
www.ijf.org

UK Taekwon-do Association
www.ukta.com

World Judo Organisation
www.worldjudo.org

World Karate Federation
www.wkf.net

World Kickboxing Association
www.worldkickboxing.com

cricket

Clubs

Derbyshire
www.dccc.org.uk

Durham
www.durham-ccc.org.uk

Essex
www.essexcricket.org.uk

Hampshire
www.hampshire.cricket.org

Kent
www.kentcountycricket.co.uk

Lancashire
www.lccc.co.uk

Leicestershire
www.leicestershireccc.com

Lincolnshire
www.btinternet.com/~lincs.cricket

Melbourne
www.mcc.org.au

Middlesex
www.middlesexccc.co.uk

Northamptonshire
www.nccc.co.uk

Nottinghamshire
www.trentbridge.co.uk

Somerset
www.somerset.cricket.org

Surrey
www.surreyccc.co.uk

Sussex
www.sccc.demon.co.uk

Warwickshire
www.warwickccc.org.uk

Worcestershire
www.wccc.co.uk

Yorkshire
www.yorkshireccc.org.uk

Grounds

Lord's
www.lords.org

Sydney
www.scgt.oz.au

Organisations

Australian Cricket Board
www.acb.com.au

English Cricket Board
www.ecb.co.uk

Federation of International Cricketers
www.ficahof.com

International Cricket Council
www.cricket.org/link_to_database/national/icc

Minor Cricket Counties Association
www.mcca.cricket.org

New Zealand Cricket Board
www.nzcricket.co.nz

Sri Lanka Cricket Board
www.lanka.net/cricket

United Cricket Board of South Africa
www.rsa3.cricket.org

Trophies

NatWest Trophy
www.natwest.co.uk/cricket

World Cup
www.ecb.co.uk/worldcup

Websites & Magazines

BBC Cricket
http://news.bbc.co.uk/hi/english/sport/cricket

CNN Cricket
www.cnnsi.com/cricket

Cric Info
www.cricket.org

Cricketer International Magazine
www.cricketer.com

Live from Lord's Webcam
www.lords.org/mcc/camview

Sky Sports Cricket
www.sky.co.uk/sports/cricket

Wisden
www.wisden.com

cycling

Association of Cycle Traders
www.cyclesource.co.uk

Batavus
www.batavus.com

Beastway MTB
www.londonmtb-x.demon.co.uk/beastway
/index.html

BMX
www.ebmx.com

British Cycling Federation
www.bcf.uk.com

British Cyclo-Cross Association
www.cyclo-cross.co.uk

British Mountain Biking
www.bmb.org

British Pedal Car Championship
www.bpcc2000.freeserve.co.uk

Cycling UK Directory
www.cycling.uk.com

Cyclists Touring Club
www.ctc.org.uk

E-cycles
www.ecycles.uk.com

Falcon
www.falconcycles.co.uk

London Cycling Campaign
www.lcc.org.uk

Mountain Biking UK
www.bikinguk.net

National Cycle Network
www.nationalcyclenetwork.org.uk

On Your Bike
www.onyourbike.com

Orbit
www.orbit-cycles.co.uk

Prutour
www.prutour.co.uk

Raleigh
www.raleighbikes.com

Road Time Trials Council
www.rttc.org.uk

Scottish Cyclists' Union
www.scottish.cycling.btinternet.co.uk

Sturmey Archer
www.sturmey-archer.com

Tour de France
www.letour.fr

Trail Cyclists Association
www.trailquest.co.uk

Union Cycliste Internationale
www.uci.ch

Wheelie Serious
www.wheelie-serious.com

darts

American Darts Organization
www.cyberdarts.com

Bulls Eye Magazine
www.bullsinet.com

Embassy World Darts
www.embassydarts.com

Planet Darts
www.planetdarts.co.uk

fencing

British Academy of Fencing
www.baf-fencing.com

British Fencing Association
www.britishfencing.com

Irish Amateur Fencing Federation
http://homepage.tinet.ie/~iaff

Scottish Fencing
www.britsport.com/fencing

football

Clubs

Aberdeen
www.afc.co.uk

AC Fiorentina
www.acfiorentina.it

AC Milan
www.acmilan.com

Arsenal
www.arsenal.co.uk

AS Roma
www.asromacalcio.it

Aston Villa
www.astonvilla-fc.co.uk

Barcelona
www.fcbarcelona.com/select_language.sps

Barnsley
www.barnsleyfc.co.uk

Berwick Rangers
www.brfc.mcmail.com

Birmingham City
www.bcfc.com

Blackburn Rovers
www.rovers.co.uk

Blackpool
www.blackpoolfc.co.uk

Bolton Wanderers
www.boltonwfc.co.uk

Bournemouth
www.afcb.demon.co.uk

Bradford City
www.bradfordcityfc.co.uk

Bristol City
www.bcfc.co.uk

Burnley
www.clarets.co.uk

Cambridge United
www.cambridge-united.co.uk

Carlisle
www.cufconline.org.uk

Celtic
www.celticfc.co.uk

Charlton Athletic
www.charlton-athletic.co.uk

Chelsea
www.chelseafc.co.uk

Cheltenham Town
www.cheltenhamtown.co.uk

Chester City
www.chester-city.co.uk

Colchester United
www.cufc.co.uk

Coventry City
www.ccfc.co.uk

Crewe Alexandra
www.crewealex.net

Crystal Palace
www.palace-eagles.com

Darlington
www.darlingtonfc.co.uk

Derby County
www.dcfc.co.uk

Dunfermline Athletic
www.dunfermline-athletic.com

England
www.englandfc.com

Everton
www.evertonfc.com

Fulham
www.fulhamfc.co.uk

Glasgow Rangers
www.rangers.co.uk

Heart of Midlothian
www.heartsfc.co.uk

Huddersfield Town
www.huddersfield-town.co.uk

Hull City
www.hullcity.demon.co.uk

Ipswich Town
www.itfc.co.uk

Leeds United
www.lufc.co.uk

Leicester City
www.lcfc.com

Lincoln City
www.redimps.com

Liverpool
www.liverpoolfc.tv

Macclesfield Town
www.mtfc.co.uk

Manchester City
www.mcfc.co.uk

Manchester United
www.manutd.co.uk

Middlesbrough
www.mfc.co.uk

Millwall
www.millwallonline.co.uk

Motherwell
www.motherwellfc.co.uk

Newcastle United
www.nufc.co.uk

Northampton Town
www.ntfc.co.uk

Norwich City
www.canaries.co.uk

Nottingham Forest
www.nottingham-forest.co.uk

Notts County
www.nottscounty.net

Parma AC
www.acparma.it

Peterborough United
www.theposh.com

Plymouth Argyll
www.argyll.org.uk

Queens Park Rangers
www.qpr.co.uk

Rangers
www.rangers.co.uk

Reading
www.readingfc.co.uk

Scunthorpe United
www.scunthorpe-united.co.uk

Sheffield United
www.sufc.co.uk

Sheffield Wednesday
www.swfc.co.uk

Shrewsbury Town
www.shrewsburytown.co.uk

Southampton
www.saintsfc.co.uk

Sunderland
www.sunderland-afc.com

Tottenham Hotspur
www.spurs.co.uk

Watford
www.watfordfc.com

West Bromwich Albion
www.wba.co.uk

West Ham United
www.westhamunited.co.uk

Wimbledon
www.wimbledon-fc.co.uk

Wolverhampton Wanderers
www.wolves.co.uk

York City
www.yorkcityfc.co.uk

Magazines & Websites

Fanzine
www.soccer-fanzine.co.uk

Football 365
www.football365.com

Nationwide League
www.football.nationwide.co.uk

Planet Football
www.planetfootball.com

Roy of the Rovers
www.royoftherovers.com

Soccernet
www.soccernet.com

Organisations

FIFA
www.fifa.com

Football Association
www.the-fa.org

Football Supporters' Association
www.fsa.org.uk

League Managers Association
www.leaguemanagers.com

Scottish Football Association
www.scottishfa.co.uk

UEFA
www.uefa.com

Tournaments

England 2006
www.fa2006.org

FA Carling Premiership
www.fa-carling.com

golf

Associations

English Golf Union
www.englishgolfunion.org

Golf Foundation of Britain
www.golf-foundation.org

Golfing Union of Ireland
www.gui.ie

Ladies' Professional Golf Association
www.lpga.com

Professional Golf Association of America
www.pga.com

Scottish Golf
www.scottishgolf.com

Scottish Golf Schools
www.golfscotland.co.uk

US Golf Association
www.usga.org

World Amateur Golf Council
www.wagc.org

Courses

Carnoustie Golf Course Hotel & Resort
www.carnoustie-hotel.com

Gleneagles
www.gleneagles.com

Royal Birkdale
www.royalbirkdale.com

Royal Troon
www.royaltroon.co.uk

St Andrews
www.standrews.org.uk

Magazines, Websites & TV

Fore Magazine
www.scga.org/fore

Golf
www.golfonline.com

Golf Channel
www.thegolfchannel.com

Golf Digest
www.golfdigest.com

Golf Monthly
www.nexusinternet.co.uk/gm

Golf Today
www.golftoday.co.uk

Golf.com
www.golf.com

UK Golf
www.uk-golf.com

Tournaments

British Open
www.opengolf.com

European Masters
www.golf.european-masters.com

LPGA Classic
www.lpgaclassic.com

Open Championship
www.opengolf.com

PGA European Tour
www.europeantour.com

Times MeesPierson Corporate Golf
Challenge
www.timescorpgolf.com

US Masters
www.masters.org

US Open
www.usopen.org

gymnastics

British Amateur Gymnastics Association
www.baga.co.uk

International Gymnastics Federation
www.fig-gymnastics.com

handball

International Handball Federation
www.ihf.ch

hockey

Field Hockey
www.fieldhockey.com

Field Hockey Foundation
www.fieldhockeytournament.com

Hockey Network
www.hockey-net.co.uk

International Hockey Federation
www.fihockey.org

horseracing

Betting

Barry Dennis
www.barrydennis.co.uk

Blue Sq
www.bluesq.com

IG Index
www.igindex.co.uk

InterBet
www.inter-bet.com

Ladbrokes
www.bet.co.uk

Sean Graham
www.seangraham.com

Sporting Index
www.sportingindex.com

Sportingbet.com
www.sportingbet.com

Sunderlands
www.sunderlands.co.uk

Surrey Racing
www.surreyracing.co.uk

Totalbet.com
www.totalbet.com

Victor Chandler
www.victorchandler.com

William Hill
www.willhill.com

Magazines & Websites

Channel 4 Racing
www.channel4.com/sport/racing

Irish Racing
www.irish-racing.com

Race Horses.com
www.race-horses.com

Racenews
www.racenews.co.uk

Sporting Life

www.sportinglife.co.uk

Organisations

British Betting Office Association
www.bboa.co.uk

British Bloodstock Agency
www.bba.co.uk

British Horseracing Board
www.bhb.co.uk

Horserace Betting Levy Board
www.hblb.org.uk

Irish Horseracing Authority
www.iha.ie

Irish Turf Club
www.turfclub.ie

Jockey Club
www.jockeyclub.com

National Trainers Federation
www.martex.co.uk/racehorsetrainers

Racecourse Association
www.comeracing.co.uk

Tattersalls
www.tattersalls.com

Weatherbys
www.weatherbys-group.com

Racecourses

Aintree
www.aintree.co.uk

Ascot
www.ascot.co.uk

Ayr
www.ayr-racecourse.co.uk

Catterick
www.catterick.com

Cheltenham
www.cheltenham.co.uk

Chepstow
www.chepstow-racecourse.co.uk

Chester
www.chester-races.co.uk

Cork
www.aardvark.ie/cork-racecourse

Curragh
www.curragh.ie

Doncaster
www.britishracing.com

Down Royal
www.downroyal.com

Epsom
www.epsomderby.co.uk

Galway
www.iol.ie/galway-races

Goodwood
www.goodwood.co.uk

Hamilton Park
www.hamilton-park.co.uk

Haydock Park
www.haydock-park.com

Huntingdon
www.huntingdonracing.co.uk

Kelso
www.kelso-races.co.uk

Kempton Park
www.kempton.co.uk

Market Rasen
www.demon.co.uk/racenews/marketrasen

Musselburgh
www.musselburgh-racecourse.co.uk

Newbury
www.raceweb.com/newbury

Newmarket
www.newmarketracecourses.co.uk

Newton Abbot
www.eclipse.co.uk/naracecourse

Nottingham
www.nottinghamracecourse.co.uk

Perth
www.perth-races.co.uk

Punchestown
www.punchestown.com

Sandown Park
www.sandown.co.uk

Stratford on Avon
www.stratfordracecourse.net

Towcester
www.demon.co.uk/racenews/towcester

Tramore
www.tramore-racecourse.com

Uttoxeter
www.uttoxeterracecourse.co.uk

Warwick
www.warwickracecourse.co.uk

Wetherby
www.wetherby.co.uk

Wincanton
www.wincantonracecourse.co.uk

Windsor
www.windsorracing.co.uk

Wolverhampton
www.parkuk.freeserve.co.uk

inline & roller skating

Federation of Roller Skating
www.bfrs.org.uk

Inliners
www.inliners.co.uk

International Roller Skating Federation
www.rollersports.org

international games

Athens 2004 Olympics
www.athens.olympic.org/gr

British Olympic Association
www.olympics.org.uk

International Olympic Committee
www.olympic.org

International Paralympic Committee
www.paralympic.org

Manchester 2002 Sport XVII
Commonwealth Games
www.commonwealthgames2002.org.uk

Olympic Games
www.olympics.com

Sydney 2000 Olympics
www.sydney2000.co.uk

World Anti-Doping Association
www.wada-ama.org

korfball

International Korfball Federation
www.ikf.org

magazines & websites

BAA Millennium Youth Games
www.baamyg.org.uk

SportLive
www.sportlive.co.uk

Sports.com
www.sports.com

motor racing

Automobile Club de l'Ouest
www.lemans.org

Circuits

Anglesey
www.anglesey-race-circuit.co.uk

Brands Hatch
www.brands-hatch.co.uk

Castle Combe
www.castlecombecircuit.co.uk

Donington Park
www.donington-park.co.uk

Knockhill
www.knockhill.co.uk

Le Mans
www.24h-le-mans.com

Mallory Park
www.mallorypark.co.uk

Monaco
www.monaco.mc/monaco/gprix

Monza
www.monzanet.it

Nürburgring
www.nuerburgring.de

Oulton Park
www.oultonpark.co.uk

Pembrey
www.barc.net/pembrey.htm

Silverstone
www.silverstone-circuit.co.uk

Events

British Touring Car Championship
www.btcc.co.uk

Grand Prix

America
www.usgpindy.com

Austria
www.a1ring.at

Belgium
www.spa-francorchamps.be

Canada
www.grandprix.ca

France
www.magnyf1.com

Germany
www.hockenheimring.de

Italy
www.monzanet.it

Japan
www.suzukacircuit.co.jp

Malaysia
www.malaysiangp.com.my

Monaco
www.f1-monaco.com

San Marino
www.formula1.sm

Magazines & Websites

Autosport
www.autosport.com

F1 Today
www.f1today.com

F1-Live
www.f1-live.com

ITV
www.itv-f1.com

Motor Sport
www.motorsport.com

Manufacturers

Lola Cars International
www.lolacars.com

Organisations

British Trials and Rally Drivers Association
http://freespace.virgin.net/liz.cox/BTRDA2/Entry/
indexSS.htm

Federation Internationale de l'Automobile
(FIA)
www.fia.com

Teams

Arrows
www.arrows.com

BAR
www.britishamericanracing.com

Ferrari
www.shell-ferrari.com

Jaguar
www.jaguar-racing.com

Jordan
www.jordangp.com

McLaren
www.mclaren.co.uk

Minardi
www.minardi.it

Prost
www.prostgp.com

Sauber
www.sauber.ch

Williams
www.williamsf1.co.uk

netball

All England Netball Association
www.england-netball.co.uk

International Federation of Netball
Associations
www.netball.org

personalities

Alan Shearer
www.fly.to/shearer

Andre Agassi
www.andresite.com

Anna Kournikova (Fan Club)
www.annak.org

Ayrton Senna
www.ayrton-senna.com

Babe Ruth
www.baberuth.com

Chris Bonington
www.bonington.com

Damon Hill
www.damonhill.co.uk

David Coulthard
www.davidcoulthard.com

David Ginola
www.ginola.net

David Leadbetter
www.leadbetter.com

Diego Maradona
www.diegomaradona.com

Don Bradman
www.bradman.sa.com.au

Eddie Irvine (Fan Club)
www.exclusively-irvine.com

Evander Holyfield
www.evanderholyfield.com

Evel Knieval
www.evel.com

Gary Player
www.garyplayer.com

Geoff Billington
www.geoff-billington.com

Heinz-Harald Frentzen
www.frentzen.de

Jack Nicklaus
www.nicklaus.com

Jacques Villeneuve
www.jacques.villeneuve.com

John Whitaker
www.john-whitaker.com

Johnny Herbert
www.johnnyherbert.co.uk

Lee Westwood
www.westy.com

Lennox Lewis
www.lennox-lewis.com

Lionel Dunning
www.lionel-dunning.com

Mark Spitz
www.cmgww.com/sports/spitz

Michael Jordan
www.jordan.sportsline.com

Michael Schumacher
www.michael-schumacher.com

Mika Hakklnen
www.mikahakkinen.net

Mika Salo
www.micasalo.net

Mohammed Ali
www.ali.com

Nadia Comaneci (Fan Club)
www.nadiacomaneci.com

Pedro De La Rosa
www.pedrodelarosa.com

Pele
www.pele.net

Pete Sampras
www.sampras.com

Phil Mickelson
www.phil-mickelson.com

Prince Naseem Hamed
www.princenaseem.com

Ralf Schumacher
www.ralf-schumacher.de

Ronaldo
www.ronaldinho.com

Steffi Graf
www.steffi-graf.com

Steffi Graf (Fan Club)
www.cgo.wave.ca/~cskelton

Steve Waugh
www.stevewaugh.com.au

Tiger Woods
www.tigerwoods.com

Tim Henman
www.henmagic.freeserve.co.uk

polo

Federation of International Polo
www.fippolo.com

Hurlingham Polo Association
www.hpa-polo.co.uk

International Women's Polo Association
www.polo.co.uk/forum

Polo World Cup on Snow
www.polostmoritz.com

promotion & education

British Association of Sport & Exercise Sciences
www.bases.co.uk

Central Council of Physical Recreation
www.thebritishsporttrust.org.uk

Lilleshall National Sports Centre
www.lilleshall.co.uk

National Coaching Foundation
www.ncf.org.uk

Scottish Sports Association
www.scotsport.co.uk

Sports Council (England)
www.english.sports.gov.uk

Sports Council (Northern Ireland)
www.sportscouncil-ni.org.uk

Sports Council (Scotland)
www.ssc.org.uk

Sports Council (United Kingdom)
www.uksport.gov.uk

Sports Industries Federation
www.sportslife.org.uk

SPRITO
www.sprito.org.uk

Women's Sports Foundation
www.wsf.org.uk

Youth Sport Trust
www.youthsport.net

rounders

National Rounders Association
http://rounders.punters.co.uk

rowing

Amateur Rowing Association
www.ara-rowing.org

Boat Race
www.boatrace.co.uk

Coxless Fours
www.coxless4.com

FISA
www.fisa.org

Henley Royal Regatta
www.hrr.co.uk

International Rowing Federation
www.worldrowing.com

Ocean Rowing Society
www.oceanrowing.com

Regatta Magazine
www.regatta.rowing.org.uk

rugby

Clubs

Aberdeen
www.aberdeenrfc.com

Avondale
www.avonvalerfc.freeserve.co.uk

Ayr
www.netsavvy.co.uk/ayrrfc

Bath
www.bathrugby.co.uk

Bedford
www.bedfordrugby.co.uk

Belfast Harlequins
www.belfastharlequins.com

Bristol Rugby
www.bristolrugby.co.uk

Cardiff
www.cardiffrfc.com

Coventry
www.coventryrugby.co.uk

Dungannon
www.dungannon-rugby.co.uk

Gloucester
www.kingsholm-chronicle.org.uk

Harlequins
www.quins.co.uk

Henley
www.henleyrugbyclub.org.uk

Leeds
www.leedsrugby.co.uk

Leicester
www.tigers.co.uk

Llanelli
www.scarlets.co.uk

London Irish
www.london-irish-rugby.com

London Welsh
www.london-welsh.co.uk

Manchester
www.manchester-rugby.co.uk

Moseley
www.moseleyrugby.co.uk

Neath
www.k-c.co.uk/neathrfc

Newcastle Falcons
www.newcastle-falcons.co.uk

Nothampton Saints
www.northamptonsaints.co.uk

Pontypridd
www.pontypriddrfc.co.uk

Richmond
www.richmondrugby.com

Sale
www.salerugby.com

Saracens
www.saracens.com

Shannon
www.shannonrfc.com

Swansea
www.swansearfc.co.uk

Vulcan
www.vulcanrufc.co.uk

Wakefield
www.wakefieldrugby.com

Wasps
www.wasps.co.uk

West Hartlepool
www.west-rugby.org.uk

Worcester
www.wrfc.co.uk

Magazines & Websites

Rugby World
www.rugbyworld.com

Scrum.com
www.scrum.com

Organisations

English Rugby Union
www.rfu.com

International Rugby Board
www.irb.org

Irish Rugby Union
www.irfu.ie

Rugby World
www.rugbyworld.com

Scottish Rugby Union
www.sru.org.uk

Welsh Rugby Union
www.wru.co.uk

Tournaments

Allied Dunbar Premiership
www.rugbyclub.co.uk

Rugby League
www.rleague.com

Rugby World Cup
www.rwc99.com

sailing & watersports

Boats & Equipment

Banks Sails
www.banks.co.uk

Corsair Marine
www.corsairuk.com

Garmin
www.garmin.com

International Coatings
www.yachtpaint.com

Laser
www.lasersailing.com

Moody
www.moody.co.uk

Nauquip
www.nauquip.com

Online Marine
www.on-line-marine.com

Raytheon Marine
www.raymarine.com

Sobstad Sailmakers
www.sobstad.co.uk

Suzuki Marine
www.suzukimarine.co.uk

Tenrag
www.tenrag.com

Yamaha Motor
www.yamaha-motor.co.uk

Clubs & Organisations

Association of Sea Training Organisations
www.asto.org.uk

British Disabled Water Ski Association
www.bdwsa.org.uk

British Universities Sailing Association
www.busa.co.uk

British Water Ski Federation
www.bwsf.co.uk

Coastguard Agency
www.coastguard.gov.uk

International Sailing Federation
www.sailing.org

International Surfing Association
www.surfing.worldsport.com

International Water Ski Federation
www.iwsf.com

Jubilee Sailing Trust
www.jst.org.uk

National Federation of Sea Schools
www.nfss.co.uk

Ocean Youth Club
www.oyc.org.uk

Royal Institute of Navigation
www.rin.org.uk

Royal Yachting Association
www.rya.org.uk

Team Philips
www.teamphilips.com

Trinity House
www.trinityhouse.co.uk

UK Team Racing Association
www.teamracing.org

World Underwater Federation
www.cmas.org

Yacht Charter Association
www.yca.co.uk

Events, Regattas & Trophies

America's Cup
www.americascup.org

America's Cup Jubilee
www.amcup2001.com

BT Global Challenge
www.btchallenge.com

Champagne Mumm Admiral's Cup
www.admiralscup.org

Cowes Week
www.cowesweek.co.uk

Fastnet Race
www.fastnet.org

Hamble Week
www.hamble-week.org.uk

Millennium Round the World Yacht Race
www.millennium-rtw.co.uk

Royal & Sun Alliance Challenge
www.rsachallenge.com

Sail for Gold 2000
www.sailforgold.co.uk

Holidays

Intersail
www.intersail.co.uk

Moorings
www.moorings.co.uk

Nautilus
www.nautilus-yachting.co.uk

Neilson Holidays
www.neilson.co.uk

Sunsail Holidays
www.sunsail.com

Sunvil Activity Holidays
www.activity-holidays.co.uk

Magazines & Websites

Boat Exchange
www.btx.co.uk

British Waterskiing
www.waterski-uk.com

Classic Boat Magazine
www.classicboat.co.uk

Cruising Association
www.cruising.org.uk

Dinghy Trader
www.dinghytrader.co.uk

Motor Boat & Yachting
www.ybw.co.uk

Sailing Now
www.sailingnow.com

Sailing Today
www.sailingnet.co.uk

UK Harbours Guide
www.harbours.co.uk

UK Sailing Index
www.uksail.com

Yachting & Boating World
www.ybw.co.uk

Yachting World
www.yachting-world.com

show jumping

Events

Badminton Horse Trials
www.badminton-horse.co.uk

Hickstead
www.hickstead.co.uk

Horse of the Year Show
www.hoys.co.uk

Windsor Horse Trials
www.windsor-horse-trials.co.uk

Magazines & Websites

British Dressage
www.britishdressage.co.uk

Jump Magazine
www.jumpmagazine.com

Organisations

British Endurance Riding Association
www.british-endurance.org.uk

British Equestrian Federation
www.bef.co.uk

British Horse Driving Trials Association
www.horsedrivingtrials.co.uk

British Horse Society
www.bhs.org.uk

British Horse Trials Association
www.bhta.co.uk

British Show Jumping Association
www.bsja.co.uk

International Equestrian Federation
www.horsesport.org

Pony Club
www.pony-club.org.uk

snooker & billiards

Billiards Congress of America
www.bca-pool.com

Crucible Theatre
www.shef.ac.uk/city/theatres/crucible

EJ Riley
www.ejriley.com

Embassy World Snooker
www.embassysnooker.com

English Pool Association
www.epa.org.uk

International Billiards & Snooker Federation
www.ibsf.org.uk

Peradon
www.peradon.co.uk

Pot Black Magazine
www.potblack.co.uk

Snooker Market
www.snookermarket.co.uk

Snooker Nations Cup
www.snooker.forceg.co.uk

Snooker Net
www.snookernet.com

Snooker Scene
www.rileyleisure.com/sscene.htm

World Snooker Association
www.wpbsa.com

softball

International Softball Federation
www.internationalsoftball.com

sportswear & equipment

Adidas
www.adidas.com

American Golf Discount
www.americangolf.co.uk

Armour
www.armourgolf.com

Belfe
www.belfe.com

Berghaus
www.berghaus.com

Bogner
www.bogner.com

Chase Sport
www.chase-sport.co.uk

Columbia
www.columbia.com

Couloir
www.couloir.com

Crag Hoppers
www.craghoppers.com

Fat Shaft
www.wilsonsports.com/golf

Footjoy
www.footjoy.com

Golf Pride Grips
www.golfpride.com

Gryphon
www.gryphonhockey.com

Head
www.head.com

Helly Hansen
www.hellyhansen.com

Hi-Tec
www.hi-tecsports.com

Hill Billy Powered Golf Trolleys
www.hillbilly.co.uk

JJB Sports
www.jjb.co.uk

Luhta
www.luhta.com

Maxfli
www.maxfli.com

Mitre
www.mitre.com

Mizuno
www.mizunoeurope.com

Monarch
www.monarch-hockey.com

National Golf Show
www.golflive.co.uk

Nevada Bob Golf Superstores
www.nevadabob.co.uk

Nike
www.nike.com

North Face
www.thenorthface.com

O'Neill
www.oneilleurope.com

Oakley
www.oakley.com

Ping
www.pingeurope.com

Pinnacle
www.pinnaclegolf.com

Powakaddy
www.powakaddy.com

Proline
www.proline-sports.co.uk

Puma
www.puma.com

Reebok
www.europe.reebok.com

Riley Leisure
www.rileyleisure.com

Salomon
www.salomonsport.com

Schoffel
www.schoffel.com

Slazenger
www.slazenger.co.uk

Speedo
www.speedo.com

Taylor Made
www.taylormadegolf.com

TearDrop
www.teardropgolf.com

Tenson
www.tenson.com

Titleist
www.titleist.com

Top Flite
www.topflight.com

Umbro
www.umbro.com

Wilson
www.wilsonsports.com

Zevo
www.zevoeurope.com

Zoppo Hockey Sticks
www.hippo-zoppo.demon.co.uk

squash

British Squash Open Championship
www.britishopensquash.com

International Racquetball Federation
www.racquetball.org

Internet Squash Federation
www.squash.org

Scottish Squash
www.sportuk.com/ssquash

Squash Player
www.squashplayer.co.uk

Squash Rackets Association
www.sportuk.com/sra

World Squash Federation
www.squash.org/wsf

sub-aqua

British Sub-Aqua Club
www.bsac.com

Diver Magazine
www.divernet.com

Historical Diving Society
www.thehds.dircon.co.uk

Scottish Sub-Aqua Club
www.ssac.demon.co.uk

Sub-Aqua Association
www.saa.org.uk

swimming

Federation Internationale de Natation
Amateur (FINA)
www.fina.org

International Life Saving Federation
www.ilsf.org

Speedo
www.speedo.com

Swimming Teachers' Association
www.sta.co.uk

table tennis

English Table Tennis Association
www.etta.co.uk

European Table Tennis Union
www.ettu.org

International Table Tennis Federation
www.ittf.com

Irish Table Tennis Association
www.ttireland.com

Scottish Table Tennis Association
www.sol.co.uk/t/tabletennis

target sports

Airgun UK
www.airgun.org

British Shooting Sports Council
www.bssc.org.uk

Clay Pigeon Shooting Association
www.cpsa.co.uk

Clay Shooting Magazine
www.clubclayshooting.com

European & Mediterranean Archery Union
www.emau.com

Firearms News
http://firearms-news.webjump.com

Grand National Archery Society
www.gnas.org

Gun Trade News
www.brucepub.com

International Archery Federation
www.archery.org

International Practical Shooting
Confederation
www.ipsc.org

International Shooting Sport Federation
www.issf-shooting.org

Muzzle Loaders' Association of Great Britain
www.mlagb.com

National Rifle Association
www.nra.org.uk

National Small-bore Rifle Association
www.nsra.co.uk

Practical Shooting Association
www.ukpsa.co.uk

Scottish Archery
www.scottisharchery.org.uk

Scottish Rifle Association
www.hugon.demon.co.uk/sra

Scottish Smallbore Rifle Association
www.ssra.co.uk

Shooters' Rights Association
www.tsra.demon.co.uk

tennis

ATP Tour
www.atptour.com

AXA Cup
www.axatenniscup.com

Champions Tennis
www.championstennis.com

International Tennis Federation
www.itftennis.com

Lawn Tennis Association
www.lta.org.uk

Real Tennis
www.real-tennis.com

Royal Tennis Court, Hampton Court Palace
www.realtennis.gbrit.com

Tennis Organisation UK
www.tennis.org.uk

US Open
www.usopen.org

Wimbledon
www.wimbledon.org

WTA Tour
www.wtatour.com

volleyball

Association of Volleyball Professionals
www.volleyball.org

International Volleyball Federation
www.fivb.ch

weightlifting & strength

British Amateur Weightlifters' Association
www.olympics.org.uk/weightlifting.htm

British Tug of War Association
www.tugofwar.co.uk

International Weightlifting Federation
www.iwf.net

winter sports

Alpine World Cup Skiing 2000
www.irisco.net/ski

Aviemore & Cairngorms Experience
www.aviemore.co.uk

British Association of Ski Instructors
www.basi.org.uk

British Ski & Snowboard Federation
www.complete-skier.com

Cross Country Skier Magazine
www.crosscountryskier.com

English Ice Hockey Association
www.eiha.co.uk

Great Britain Luge Association
www.gbla.org.uk

Hockey Player Magazine
www.hockeyplayer.com

Ice Hockey UK
www.icehockeyuk.co.uk

International Biathlon Union
www.ibu.at

International Bobsleigh & Tobogganing Federation
www.bobsleigh.com

International Ice Hockey Federation
www.iihf.com

International Luge Federation
www.fil-luge.org

International Skating Union
www.isu.org

International Ski Federation
www.fis-ski.com

National Hockey League
www.nhl.com

Salt Lake City Winter Olympics 2002
www.saltlake2002.com

Scottish National Ski Council
www.snsc.demon.co.uk

Sekonda Ice Hockey Superleague
www.iceweb.co.uk

Ski Club of Great Britain
www.skiclub.co.uk

Ski Magazine
www.skinet.com/ski

Ski World Cup
www.skiworldcup.org

Skier & Snowboarder Magazine
www.ski.co.uk/skimag

Tamworth Snowdome
www.snowdome.co.uk

Torino Winter Olympics 2006
www.torino2006.it

Torvill & Dean (Fan Club)
users.aol.com/tanddfanp

US Figure Skating Association
www.usfsa.org

wrestling

International Federation of Associated Wrestling Styles
www.fila-wrestling.org

International Sumo Federation
www.amateursumo.com

NWO Wrestling
www.nwowrestling.com

WCW Wrestling
www.wcwwrestling.com

World Wrestling Federation
www.wwf.com

cable ●

computers ●

internet companies ●

internet service providers ●

magazines & websites ●

search engines ●

telecommunications ●

web censors ●

technology

cable

Birmingham Cable
www.birmcable.co.uk

Cable Communications Association
www.cable.co.uk

Cable London
www.cablelondon.co.uk

Cable Net
www.cablenet.net

Cable Tel
www.cabletel.co.uk

Cambridge Cable
www.camcable.co.uk

Channel One TV
www.channel-onetv.co.uk

Crimptech National
www.crimptech.co.uk

Diamond Cable
www.diamond.co.uk

Inside Cable
www.inside-cable.co.uk

Peninsula Networks
www.peninsula.co.uk

Power Check
www.powercheck.demon.co.uk

computers

ACER
www.acer.com

Acorn
www.acorn.co.uk

ACT
www.act.org.uk

Adobe
www.adobe.com

AMEC
www.amec.co.uk

Amiga
www.amiga.com

Amstrad
www.amstrad.com

Apple
www.apple.com

AST
www.astcomputer.com

Broderbund Europe
www.broderbund.com

Bull
www.bull.co.uk

Canon
www.canon.com

Claris
www.claris.com

Commodore
www.commodore.net

Compaq
www.compaq.co.uk

DEC
www.dec.com

Dell
www.dell.com/uk

Demon
www.demon.net

Digital
www.digital.co.uk

Eidos
www.eidos.co.uk

Elonex
www.elonex.co.uk

Epson
www.epson.com

Ericsson
www.ericsson.com

Eudora
www.eudora.com

Fujitsu
www.fujitsu-pc.com

Gateway
www.gw2k.co.uk

Hewlett Packard
www.hp.com

Hitachi
www.hds.co.uk

Honeywell
www.honeywell.com

IBM
www.ibm.com

Intel
www.intel.co.uk

Iomega
www.iomega-europe.com

Lexmark
www.lexmark.co.uk

Lotus
www.lotus.com

Mesh
www.meshplc.co.uk

Microlease
www.microlease.com

Microsoft
www.microsoft.com

Misys
www.misysinc.com

Mitel
www.mitel.com

NEC
www.nec-global.com

Netcom
www.netcom.net.uk

Netscape
www.netscape.com

Nintendo
www.nintendodirect.com

Nokia
www.nokia.com

Novell
www.novell.com

Olivetti
www.olivetti.com

Open Universal Software
www.universal.com

Oracle
www.oracle.co.uk

Packard Bell
www.packardbell.com

Playstation
www.playstation-europe.com

Psion
www.psion.com

Racal
www.racalworld.com

Sibelius (Music Software)
www.sibelius.com

Siemens
www.siemens.com

Silicon Graphics
www.sgi.com

Sony
www.sony.com

Sunsoft
www.sunsoft.com

Texas Instruments
www.ti.com

Tiny
www.tiny.com/uk

Toshiba
www.toshiba.com

Tulip
www.tulip.com

Unisys
www.unisys.com

Universal
www.universal.com

Viglen
www.viglen.co.uk

Vitech
www.vitech.net

Vodafone
www.vodafone.co.uk

Wang
www.wang.com

Widget Software
www.widgetsoftware.com

internet companies

Cisco
www.cisco.com

Freeserve
www.freeserve.net

Jellyworks
www.jellyworks.com

Morse
www.morse.com

Netbenefit
www.netbenefit.com

NicNames
www.nicnames.co.uk

internet service providers

Aardvaak
www.aardvaak.co.uk

Abel Gratis
www.abelgratis.com

AOL
www.aol.co.uk

Barclays
www.is.barclays.co.uk

Bigwig
www.bigwig.net

Breathe
www.breathe.com

BT Click
www.btclick.com

BT Internet
www.btinternet.com

Cable & Wireless
www.cwcom.net

ClaraNet
www.clara.net

Demon
www.demon.net

Direct Connection
www.dircon.net

Enterprise
www.enterprise.net

Free UK
www.freeuk.com

Free4All
www.free4all.co.uk

FreeNet
www.freenet.co.uk

Freenetname
www.freenetname.co.uk

Freeserve
www.freeserve.co.uk

Freewire
www.freewire.net

FreeZone
www.freezone.co.uk

Genie
www.genie.co.uk

Global
www.global.net.uk

LineOne
www.lineone.net

Madasafish
www.madasafish.com

NetDirect
www.netdirect.net.uk

Nildram
www.nildram.net

Pipemedia
www.pipemedia.co.uk

Prestel
www.prestel.co.uk

Supanet
www.supanet.com

Talk 21
www.talk21.com

TescoNet
www.tesco.net

Tiny
www.tinyonline.net

UK Online
www.ukonline.co.uk

Virgin
www.virgin.net

WH Smith
www.whsmith.co.uk

X-Stream
www.x-stream.com

Yahoo! Online
www.yahoo.co.uk

magazines & websites

Acorn Gaming
www.acorn-gaming.org.uk

Bluetooth
www.bluetooth.com

British Computer Society
www.bcs.org.uk

Computer & Video Games
www.game-online.com

Computer Shopper
www.compshopper.co.uk

Computer Weekly
www.computerweekly.co.uk

Computeractive
www.computeractive.co.uk

Computing
www.vnunet.com

Future Gamer
www.futurenet.com/futuregamer

GameSpot UK
www.gamespot.co.uk/pcgw

IT Weekly
www.itweek.co.uk

Lara Croft
www.laracroft.com

MacUser
www.macuser.co.uk

Macworld
www.macworld.com

Net
www.thenetmag.co.uk

The Net
www.thenetmag.co.uk

PC Advisor
www.pcadvisor.co.uk

PC Plus
www.pcplus.co.uk

PC Zone OnLine
www.pczone.co.uk

Total Games
www.totalgames.net

search engines

About
www.about.com

Alta Vista
www.altavista.co.uk

Ask Jeeves
www.ask.co.uk

DejaNews
www.dejanews.com

Direct Hit
www.directhit.com

Dogpile
www.dogpile.com

Electric Library
www.elibrary.com

Excite
www.excite.co.uk

Fish4
www.fish4.co.uk

Galaxy
http://galaxy.einet.net

Go To
www.go2.com

Google
www.google.com

HotBot
www.hotbot.com

Infoseek
www.infoseek.co.uk

LookSmart
www.looksmart.com

Lycos
www.lycos.co.uk

Magellan
www.mckinley.com

Maxisearch
www.maxisearch.com

Metacrawler
www.metacrawler.com

Mirago
www.mirago.co.uk

MSN
www.msn.co.uk

Northern Light
www.nlsearch.com

Open Text Index
www.index.opentext.net

Search UK
www.searchuk.co.uk

UK Directory
www.ukdirectory.co.uk

UK Max
www.ukmax.co.uk

UK Online
www.ukonline.co.uk

UK Plus
www.ukplus.co.uk

Webcrawler
www.webcrawler.com

Yahoo!
www.yahoo.co.uk

telecommunications

Alcatel
www.alcatel.com

Alpha Telecom
www.alphatelecom.com

BT
www.bt.com

BT Cellnet
www.btcellnet.co.uk

BT Pagers
www.btmobility.com

Cable & Wireless
www.cwcom.co.uk

Cellnet
www.cellnet.co.uk

Com One
www.com1.fr/uk

Dolphin
www.dolphin-telecom.co.uk

Energis
www.energis.co.uk

Ericsson
www.ericsson.co.uk

Esprit
www.esprittelecom.com

Eurobell
www.eurobell.com

First Telecom
www.first-telecom.com

Hagenuk
www.hagenuk.de

Hutchison Telecom
www.orange.co.uk

Maxon
www.maxon.co.uk

MCI Worldcom
www.wcom.co.uk

Mercury
www.mercury.co.uk

Mitsubishi
www.ite.meu.com/mobiles

Mondial
www.mondial-gsm.com

Motorola
www.mot.com

NEC
www.euronec.com

Nokia
www.nokia.co.uk

Nortel
www.nortel.com

Norweb
www.norwebcomms.com

Nynex
www.nynex.co.uk

Odyssey
www.odysseycorp.co.uk

OFTEL
www.oftel.gov.uk

One 2 One
www.one2one.co.uk

One.Tel UK
www.onetel.co.uk

Orange
www.orange.co.uk

Panasonic
www.mcuk.panasonic.co.uk

Philips
www.pcc.philips.com

Planet Talk
www.planet-talk.co.uk

Sagem
www.sagem.com

Samsung
www.samsungelectronics.com

Siemens
www.siemens.co.uk

Sony
www.sony-europe.com/cons/pce

Telecom UK
www.telecom.co.uk

Telewest
www.telewest.co.uk

Torch
www.torch.co.uk

Virgin
www.virgin.com/mobile

Vodafone
www.vodafone.co.uk

World Online
www.worldonline.com

web censors

Cyber Patrol
www.cyberpatrol.com

Cybersnoop
www.pearlsw.com

Net Nanny
www.netnanny.com

Surf Control

www.surfcontrol.com

Surf on the Safe Side
www.surfonthesafeside.com

X-Stop
www.xstop.com

Xcheck
www.xcheck.net

travel

airlines •

airports •

bus companies •

car hire •

ferries •

hotels •

magazines & websites •

parking •

professional bodies & trade associations •

resorts •

trains •

travel agents, tour operators & cruises •

www.thomascook.com

ABTA
20606
AND I HAVEN'T TOLD HER WE'RE LIVING TOGETHER
IT'S TIME TO LEAVE THE COUNTRY
thomas cook.com

airlines

AccessAir
www.accessair.com

Aer Lingus
www.aerlingus.ie

Aeroflot
www.aeroflot.org

Aerolineas Argentinas
www.aerolineas.com.ar

Aeromexico
www.aeromexico.com/ingles

Aeroperu Airlines
www.aeroperu.com

Air 2000
www.air2000.co.uk

Air Afrique
www.airafrique.com

Air ALM
www.airalm.com

Air Aruba
www.interknowledge.com/air-aruba

Air Asia
www.airasia.com

Air Atlanta Icelandic
www.atlanta.is

Air Baltic
www.airbaltic.lv

Air Berlin
www.airberlin.com

Air Canada
www.aircanada.ca

Air Caribbean
www.aircaribbean.com

Air China
www.airchina.u-net.com

Air Fiji
www.airfiji.net

Air France
www.airfrance.co.uk

Air Georgia
www.air-georgia.com

Air India
www.airindia.com

Air Jamaica
www.airjamaica.com

Air Kazakhstan
www.airkaz.com

Air Lithuania
www.airlithuania.lt

Air Madagascar
www.air-mad.com

Air Malawi
www.africaonline.co.ke/airmalawi

Air Malta
www.airmalta.com

Air Mauritius
www.airmauritius.com

Air Moldova
www.ami.md

Air Namibia
www.airnamibia.com.na

Air New Zealand
www.airnz.com

Air Philippines
www.airphilippines.com

Air Portugal
www.tap-airportugal.pt

Air Seychelles
www.airseychelles.it

Air Tahiti
www.airtahiti-nui.com

Air UK
www.airuk.co.uk

Air Zimbabwe
www.airzimbabwe.com

Airlanka
www.airlanka.com

Alaska Airlines
www.alaska-air.com

Alitalia
www.alitalia.co.uk

All Nippon Airways
www.ana.co.uk

American Airlines
www.americanair.com

Ana Europe
www.ana-europe.com

Ansett
www.ansett.com

Ariana Afghan Airlines
www.geocities.com/afghanairlines/Homes.html

Asiana Airlines
www.asiana.co.kr/english

Atlas Air
www.atlasair.com

Austrian Airlines
www.aua.com

Azzurra Airlines
www.azzurraair.it

Bahamasair
www.bahamasair.com

Balkan Airlines
www.balkan.com

Bhoja Air
www.bhojaair.com.pk

Bouraq Indonesia Airlines
www.bouraq.com

Braathens
http://english.braathens.no/default.asp?

Britannia
www.britanniaairways.com

British Airways
www.british-airways.com

British European
www.british-european.com

British Midland
www.britishmidland.co.uk

British World Airlines
www.british-world.co.uk

Buzz
www.buzzaway.com

BWIA
www.bwee.com

Cameroon Airlines
www.camnet.cm/investir/transport/camair
/camair.htm

Cape Air
www.flycapeair.com

Cathay Pacific
www.cathaypacific.com

China Airlines
www.china-airlines.com

Continental
www.flycontinental.com

Corsair
www.corsair-int.com

Croatia Airlines
www.croatiaairlines.hr

Crossair
www.crossair.ch

Cubana Airlines
www.cubana.cu

Cyprus Airways
www.cyprusair.com

Cyprus Turkish Airlines
www.kthy.net

Czech Airlines
www.csa.cz/en

Delta
www.delta-air.com

Dragon Air
www.dragonair.com

Eastern Airways
www.easternairways.com

EasyJet
www.easyjet.com

El Al
www.elal.co.il

Emirates (UAE)
www.emiratesairline.com

EVA Air
www.evaair.com.tw/english

Finnair
www.finnair.co.uk

Garuda Indonesia
www.garudausa.com

Ghana Airways
www.ghana-airways.com

Go
www.go-fly.com

Cronus Airlines
www.cronus.gr

Greenlandair
www.greenland-guide.dk/gla

Gujarat Airways
www.gujaratairways.com

Gulf Air
www.gulfairco.com

Guyana Airways
www.turq.com/guyana/guyanair.html

Hapag-Lloyd Airlines
www.hapag-lloyd.com

Hawaiian Airlines
www.hawaiianair.com

Iberia
www.iberia.com

Icelandair
www.icelandair.co.uk

Indian Airlines
http://indian-airlines.nic.in

Japan Airlines
www.jal.co.jp

JAS Japan Air System
www.jas.co.jp

Jersey European Airways
www.jea.co.uk

Kenya Airways
www.kenyaairways.co.uk

KLM
www.klm.uk.com

Kuwait Airways
www.kuwait-airways.com

Lauda Air
www.laudaair.com

LOT Polish Airlines
www.lot.com

Lufthansa
www.lufthansa.co.uk

Lynx Air International
www.lynxair.com

Malaysia Air
www.malaysiaair.com

Malaysia Airlines
www.malaysiaairlines.com.my

Malev
www.malev.hu

Mandarin Airlines
www.mandarinair.com/english

Manx Airlines
www.manx-airlines.com

Martin Air
www.martinairusa.com

Middle Eastern Airlines
www.mea.com.lb

Monarch
www.monarch-airlines.com

North West Airlines
www.nwa.com

Pakistan International
www.piac.com

Pan Am
www.panam.org

Philippine Airlines
www.philippineair.com

Polynesian Airlines
www.polynesianairlines.co.nz

Portugalia Air
www.pga.pt

Qantas
www.qantas.com.au

Qatar Airways
www.qatarairways.com

Royal Air Maroc
www.royalairmaroc.com

Royal Brunei
www.bruneiair.com

Royal Jordanian Airlines
www.rja.com.jo

Royal Nepal Airlines
www.royalnepal.com

Ryanair
www.ryanair.com

Sabena
www.sabena.com

Saudi Arabian Airlines
www.saudiarabian-airlines.com

Scandanavian Airlines
www.flysas.co.uk

Singapore Airlines
www.singaporeair.com

Solomon Airlines
www.solomonairlines.com.au

South African Airways
www.saa.co.za

SriLankan Airlines
www.lanka.net/airlanka

Star Alliance
www.star-alliance.com

Surinam Airways
www.cqlink.sr/slm

Swiftair
www.swiftair.com

Swissair
www.swissair.ch

Tahiti Airlines
www.airtahitinui-usa.com

Tasmania Airlines
www.tasair.com.au

Thai Airways
www.thaiair.com

Turkish Airlines
www.turkishairlines.com

TWA
www.twa.com

Tyrolean Airways
www.tyrolean.at

Ukraine International Airlines
www.uia.ukrpack.net

United Airlines
www.ual.com

United Airlines Belgium
www.ual.be

Uzbekistan Airways
www.uzbekistanairways.nl

VARIG Brasil
www.varig.com.br/english

Vietnam Airlines
www.vietnamair.com.vn

Virgin Airways
www.fly.virgin.com

Virgin Atlantic
www.fly.virgin.com/atlantic

World Airways
www.worldair.com

Yemen Airways
http://home.earthlink.net/~yemenair

Yugoslav Airlines JAT
www.jat.com

Zimbabwe Express Airlines
http://home.earthlink.net/~airzimbabwe

airports

Foreign

Albuquerque
www.cabq.gov/airport/index.html

Alicante
www.aena.es

Amsterdam
www.schiphol.nl

Atlanta
www.atlanta-airport.com

Auckland
www.auckland-airport.co.nz

Baltimore Washington
http://bwiairport.com

Bangkok
www.airportthai.or.th

Barcelona
www.aena.es/ae/bcn/homepage.htm

Beijing
www.bcia.com.cn

Berlin
www.berlin-airport.de

Boston
www.massport.com

Brisbane
www.brisbaneairport.com.au

Brussels
www.brusselsairport.be

Calgary
www.calgaryairport.com

Cape Town
www.airports.co.za

Charlotte/Douglas
www.charlotteairport.com

Chicago
www.ohare.com

Cincinnati
www.cvgairport.com

Cologne
www.airport-cgn.de

Copenhagen
www.cph.dk

Dallas Fort Worth
www.dfwairport.com

Dehli
www.delhiairport.com

Denver
www.flydenver.com

Detroit
www.metroairport.com

Dubai
www.dubaiairport.com

Dublin
www.dublin-airport.com

Dusseldorf
www.duesseldorf-international.de

Faro
www.ana-aeroportos.pt

Frankfurt
www.frankfurt-airport.de

Geneva
www.gva.ch/en

Gothenburg
www.lfv.se/site/airports/landvetter/eng/index.as

Hannover
www.flughafen.hannover.de

Helsinki
www.ilmailulaitos.com/english/lentoase/mal
/index.htm

Hong Kong
www.hkairport.com

Honolulu
www.hawaii.gov/dot/airports/visitor_info.htm

Ibiza
www.aena.es

Istanbul
www.dhmiata.gov.tr

Johannesburg
www.airports.co.za

Kansas
www.kcairports.com

Kuala Lumpur
www.klia.com.my/klia

Madrid
www.aena.es/ae/mad/homepage.htm

Marseille
www.marseille.aeroport.fr

Melbourne
www.melbourne-airport.com.au

Memphis
www.mscaa.com

Mexico City
www.asa.gob.mx/grupo_aicm/aicm_set.html

Milan
www.sea-aeroportimilano.it

Montreal
www.admtl.com

Moscow
www.sheremetyevo-airport.ru

Munich
www.munich-airport.de

Nashville
www.nashintl.com

New York
www.panynj.gov

Newark
www.newarkairport.com

Nice
www.nice.aeroport.fr

Orlando
http://fcn.state.fl.us/goaa

Osaka
www.kiac.co.jp

Paris
www.adp.fr

Perth
www.perthairport.com

Pusan
www.kimhae-airport.co.kr

Rome
www.adr.it

San Diego
www.portofsandiego.org/sandiego_airport/index.html

San Fransisco
www.sfoairport.com

Seattle
www.portseattle.org

Seoul
www.kimpo-airport.co.kr

Singapore
www.changi.airport.com.sg

Stockholm
www.arlanda.com

Stuttgart
www.stuttgart-airport.de

Sydney
www.sydneyairport.com.au

Taipei
www.cksairport.gov.tw

Tampa
www.tampaairport.com

Tokyo
www.narita-airport.or.jp/airport

Toronto
www.gtaa.com

Vancouver
www.yvr.ca

Venice
www.veniceairport.it

Vienna
www.viennaairport.com

Washington (Dulles)
www.mwaa.com

Zurich
www.zurich-airport.com

UK

Aberdeen
www.baa.co.uk/main/airports/aberdeen

Belfast
www.bial.co.uk

Birmingham
www.bhx.co.uk

British Airports Authority
www.baa.co.uk

British International Airports
www.bia.co.uk

Exeter
www.eclipse.co.uk/exeterair

Gatwick
www.gatwickairport.co.uk

Glasgow Prestwick
www.glasgow.pwk.com

Heathrow
www.heathrow.co.uk

Isle of Man
www.iom-airport.com

Liverpool
www.livairport.com

London City
www.londoncityairport.com

Luton
www.london-luton.com

Manchester
www.manairport.co.uk

Stansted
www.baa.co.uk/stansted

bus companies

Airbus
www.airbus.co.uk

Arriva
www.arriva.co.uk

Big Bus Tours
www.bigbus.co.uk

Blue Line
www.blueline.demon.co.uk

Bus Web
www.busweb.co.uk

Citylink
www.citylink.co.uk

Clarkes of London
www.clarkes.co.uk

Eurolines
www.eurolines.co.uk

First Group
www.firstgroup.com

Go Ahead
www.go-ahead.com

Green Line
www.greenline.co.uk

London Transport
www.londontransport.co.uk

National Express
www.nationalexpress.co.uk

Oxford Bus
www.oxfordbus.co.uk

Speedlink
www.speedlink.co.uk

Stagecoach
www.stagecoachholdings.com

Yellow Buses
www.yellowbuses.co.uk

car hire

Alamo
www.goalamo.com

Avis
www.avis.co.uk

BCR British Car Rental
www.bcvr.co.uk

British Vehicle Rental Association
www.bbi.co.uk/bvrla

Budget
www.budget-rent-a-car.co.uk

Direct Car Hire
www.direct-car-hire.co.uk

Easy Rentacar
www.easyrentacar.com

Enterprise
www.erac.com

Europcar
www.europcar.com

Hertz
www.hertz.co.uk

Holiday Autos
www.holidayautos.co.uk

Kenning
www.kenning.co.uk

National
www.nationalcar-europe.com

Practical Car & Van Rental
www.practical.co.uk

Thrifty
www.thrifty.co.uk

U-Drive
www.udrive.co.uk

Woods Car Rental
www.woods.co.uk

ferries

Brittany
www.brittany-ferries.com

Calais
www.calais-port.com

Calmac
www.calmac.co.uk

Channel Hoppers
www.channelhoppers.com

Color Line
www.colorline.com

Condor
www.condorferries.co.uk

DFDS Seaways
www.dfdsseaways.co.uk

Emeraude Lines
www.emeraudelines.com

Hover Travel
www.hovertravel.co.uk

Hoverspeed
www.hoverspeed.co.uk

Irish Ferries
www.irishferries.com

P & O European
www.poef.com

P & O North Sea
www.ponsf.com

P & O Scottish
www.poscottishferries.co.uk

P & O Stena Line
www.posl.com

Red Funnel
www.redfunnel.co.uk

Scandinavian Seaways
www.scansea.com

Sea France
www.seafrance.co.uk

Seaview
www.seaview.co.uk/ferries

Stena
www.stenaline.co.uk

Swansea Cork Ferries
www.commerce.ie/cs/scf

Wightlink
www.wightlink.co.uk

hotels

Accor
www.accor.com/accor/english

British Hotel Reservation Centre
www.bhrc.co.uk

Choice
www.hotelchoice.com

Crowne Plaza
www.crowneplaza.com

Dan
www.danhotels.co.il

De Vere
www.devereonline.co.uk

Elounda Beach
www.eloundabeach.gr

Forte & Le Meridien
www.forte-hotels.com

Four Seasons
www.fourseasons.com

Gleneagles
www.gleneagles.com

Goodnight Inn
www.thegoodnightinn.com

Grand Heritage
www.grandheritage.com

Hilton
www.hilton.com

Holiday Inn
www.holiday-inn.com

Intercontinental
www.interconti.com

Lanesborough
www.lanesborough.co.uk

Late Rooms.com
www.laterooms.com

Le Meridien
www.lemeridien-hotels.com

LeisureHunt
www.leisurehunt.com

Mandarin Oriental
www.mandarin-oriental.com

Marriott Hotels
www.marriott.com

McDonald
www.mcdonaldhotels.co.uk

MKI Hotels
www.mki.ltd.uk

Novotel
www.novotel.com

Oberoi
www.oberoihotels.com

Orient Express
www.orient-expresshotels.com

Posthouse
www.posthousehotels.com

Queens Moat
www.queensmoat.com

Radisson
www.radisson.com

Raffles Singapore
www.raffles.com

Red Carnation
www.redcarnationhotels.com

Regal
www.regal-hotels.com

Relais & Chateaux
www.relaischateaux.fr

Ritz
www.theritzhotel.co.uk

Savoy
www.savoy-group.co.uk

Shangri-la
www.shangri-la.com

Sheraton
www.sheraton.com

Stakis
www.stakis.co.uk

Swallow
www.swallowhotels.com

Thistle Hotels
www.thistle.co.uk

Travel Inns
www.travelinn.co.uk

Travelodge
www.travelodge.co.uk

Virgin
www.virginhotels.com

Wyndham
www.mki.ltd.uk/wyndham.htm

magazines & websites

Conde Nast Traveller
www.cntraveller.co.uk

Fodor's Guide
www.fodors.com

Go By Coach
www.gobycoach.com

Good Holiday Guide
www.goodholidayguide.com

Good Ski Guide
www.goodskiguide.com

Holiday Which?
www.which.net/holiday

Lonely Planet
www.lonelyplanet.com

National Geographic
www.nationalgeographic.com

Public Transport Information
www.pti.org.uk

Rough Guides
www.roughguides.com

UK Street Map
www.streetmap.co.uk

Virgin Net Travel
www.virgin.net/travel

parking

BAA Parking
www.baa.co.uk

Britannia Parking
www.britannia-parking.co.uk

Flypark
www.flypark.co.uk

National Car Parks
www.ncp.co.uk

Parking Express, APCOA Parking
www.parkingexpress.co.uk

professional bodies & trade associations

ABTA
www.abtanet.com

Association of Independent Tour Operators
www.aito.co.uk

Railway Industry Association
www.riagb.co.uk

resorts

Butlins
www.butlins.co.uk

Center Parcs
www.centerparcs.co.uk

Club Mark Warner
www.markwarner.co.uk

Club Med
www.clubmed.com

Disneyland California
www.disney.co.uk/usa-resorts/disneyland

Disneyland Paris
www.disneylandparis.com

Disneyworld Florida
www.disney.co.uk/usa-resorts/wdw

Sandals
www.sandals.com

trains

Alphaline Regional Railways
www.alphaline.co.uk

Amtrak
www.amtrak.com

Anglia Railways Train Services
www.angliarailways.co.uk

Association of Train Operating Companies
www.rail.co.uk/atoc

C2C
www.c2c-online.co.uk

Central Trains
www.centraltrains.co.uk

Chiltern Railways
www.chilternrailways.co.uk

Connex
www.connex.co.uk

Docklands Light Rail
www.dlr.co.uk

English Welsh and Scottish Railways
www.ews-railway.co.uk

English Welsh Railway
www.ews-railway.co.uk

Eurostar
www.eurostar.com

First Great Western
www.great-western-trains.co.uk

First North Western
www.firstnorthwestern.co.uk

Gatwick Express
www.gatwickexpress.co.uk

Great Eastern Railway
www.ger.co.uk

Great North Eastern Railway
www.gner.co.uk

Heathrow Express
www.heathrowexpress.co.uk

Jubilee Line Extension
www.jle.lul.co.uk

London Transport
www.londontransport.co.uk

London Transport Season Tickets
www.transportforLondon.gov.uk/ftt_home.shtm

London Underground
www.thetube.com

Midland Mainline
www.midlandmainline.com

NI Railways
www.nirailways.co.uk

North Western Trains
www.nwt.rail.co.uk

Northern Spirit
www.northern-spirit.co.uk

Railtrack
www.railtrack.co.uk

Scotrail
www.scotrail.co.uk

Silverlink Train Services
www.silverlink-trains.com

South West Trains
www.swtrains.co.uk

Stansted Express
www.stanstedexpress.com

Thames Trains
www.thamestrains.co.uk

Thameslink Rail
www.thameslink.co.uk

Train Line
www.thetrainline.co.uk

Virgin Trains
www.virgintrains.co.uk

Wales & West
www.walesandwest.co.uk

travel agents, tour operators & cruises

Abercrombie & Kent
www.abercrombiekent.co.uk

Air Miles
www.airmiles.co.uk

Airtours
www.airtours.com

Arctic Experience & Discover the World
www.arctic-discover.co.uk

Austravel
www.austravel.com

British Airways Holidays
www.britishairwaysholidays.co.uk

Cadogan Holidays
www.cadoganholidays.com

Carnival
www.carnival.com

Carribbean Connection
www.carribbean-connection.com

Citalia
www.citalia.co.uk

Club 18-30
www.18-30.co.uk

Club 25
www.club25.ie

Co-op Travel
www.extratravel.co.uk

Cosmos
www.cosmos.co.uk

Cresta Holidays
www.crestaholidays.co.uk

Crystal Holidays
www.crystalholidays.co.uk

Cunard
www.cunardline.com

Deck Chair Com
www.deckchair.com

Destination Group
www.destination-group.com

Direct Holidays
www.directholidays.co.uk

Disney Cruises
www.disney.com/disneycruise

Dream Travel Africa
www.dreamtravelafrica.co.uk

E-Bookers
www.ebookers.com

Eclipse
www.eclipsedirect.com

Elegant Resorts International
www.elegantresorts.com

Erna Low
www.ernalow.co.uk

Expedia
www.expedia.co.uk

First Choice
www.first-choice.com

Going Places
www.going-places.co.uk

Hayes Travel
www.hayes-travel.co.uk

Headwater
www.headwater.com

Hoseasons
www.hoseasons.co.uk

Inghams
www.inghams.com

Internet Travel Services
www.its.net

JMC
www.jmc-holidays.co.uk

Kuoni
www.kuoni.co.uk

Lastminute.com
www.lastminute.com

Lunn Poly
www.lunn-poly.co.uk

Magic Travel Group
www.magictravelgroup.co.uk

Moorings
www.moorings.co.uk

Nautilus
www.nautilus-yachting.co.uk

Neilson Holidays
www.neilson.co.uk

Norwegian Cruise Line
www.ncl.com

Orient Express Trains & Cruises
www.orient-expresstrains.com

P & O Stena Line
www.posl.com

Page & Moy
www.pagemoy.com

Portland
www.portland-holidays.co.uk

Portman Travel
www.portmantravel.co.uk

Powder Byrne
www.powderbyrne.com

Princess
www.princess.com

Royal Carribean Cruise Line
www.royalcaribbean.com

Saga Holidays
www.saga.co.uk

Scantours
www.scantoursuk.com

Silversea
www.silversea.com

Simply Travel
www.simply-travel.com

Skidream
www.skidream.com

Sovereign
www.sovereign.com

STA Travel
www.statravel.co.uk

Sunsail Holidays
www.sunsail.com

Sunvil Activity Holidays
www.activity-holidays.co.uk

Sunworld
www.sunworld.co.uk

Swan Hellenic
www.swan-hellenic.co.uk

Tenrag
www.tenrag.com

Thomas Cook

www.thomascook.com

Thomson
www.thomson.co.uk

Thomson Cruising
www.thomson-holidays.com/cruises

Thomson Holidays
www.thomson-holidays.com

Tradewings
www.tradewings.co.uk

Trailfinders
www.trailfinders.co.uk

Travel for the Arts
www.travelforthearts.co.uk

Tropical Places

www.tropicalplaces.co.uk

Union Castle Line
www.union-castle-line.com

Virgin Holidays
www.virginholidays.co.uk

Voyages Jules Verne
www.vjv.co.uk

Wallace Arnold
www.wallacearnold.com

Windjammer
www.windjammer.com

A

A&M (Record company) 21
A-ha 14
A-levels 66
A1 14
A1 Insurance 188
AA 135
AA Insurance 188
AAF Industries 45
Aardman Animations 27
Aardvaak 266
Abacus 239
Abacus Direct 188
Abba 14
Abbey Ales 89
Abbey Corrugated 47
Abbey National 40-41, 187
Abbey Online 188
Abbey Road Studios 22
Abbey Self-Storage 161
Abbott 47
Abbott & Costello (Fan Club) 6
Abbott Mead Vickers 35
ABC 26
ABC (Cinemas) 9
Abel Gratis 266
Abercrombie & Kent 283
Aberdeen & District
    Independent
    (Newspaper) 177
Aberdeen (Airport) 277
Aberdeen (Chamber of
    Commerce) 35
Aberdeen (FC) 250
Aberdeen (Gov) 111
Aberdeen (Rugby club) 257
Aberdeen (Uni) 75
Aberdeen Art Gallery 5
Aberdeen Asset
    Management 190
Aberdeen Business School 72
Aberdeen Evening Express 177
Aberdeen Exhibition &
    Conference Centre 25
Aberdeen Royal Infirmary 127
Aberdeen Unit Trust
    Managers 190
Aberdeen University
    Library 169
Aberdeenshire (Gov) 111
Abergavenny (Local info) 202
Abertay Dundee (Uni) 75
Aberystwyth (Local info) 202
Aberystwyth (Uni) 75
Aberystwyth Arts Centre 25
Aberystwyth Electric Cliff
    (Railway) 198
Ability 137
Ability Security Systems 161
Abingdon & District (Local
    info) 202
ABN AMRO Asset
    Management 190
ABN AMRO, Netherlands 37
About 267

About Scotland (Local info) 201
ABSA Bank, South Africa 37
Absolut Vodka 90
ABTA 282
AC 156
AC Fiorentina 250
AC Milan 250
AC/DC 14
Academy of Curative
    Hypnotherapists 73, 125
Academy of Experts 49
Academy of Motion Picture Arts
    & Sciences 11
Accenture (Andersen
    Consulting) 52
AccessAir 273
Accessorize 241
Accor 280
Accountancy 44
Accountancy Age 44
Accounting Standards Body 49
ACER 265
Acorn 265
Acorn Gaming 267
Acropolis 206
ACT 265
Action against Breast
    Cancer 137
Action Aid 138
Action for Cancer Trust 137
Action for ME 137
Action for the Environment 84
Action for Tinnitus
    Research 137
Action for Victims of Medical
    Accidents 136
Action Man 242
Action on Pre-eclampsia 137
Active Birth Centre 130
Adam Ant 14
Adam Sandler 3
Adam Smith Institute 108
ADC Theatre, Cambridge 29
Addaction 136
Addenbrooke's 127
Addictive Television 27
Addison Wesley Longman 35
Adecco 51
Adelaide Symphony
    Orchestra 21
Adelphi Distillery 96
Adidas 259
Adjudicator's Office 140
Adler 238
Admiral 188
Adobe 265
Adoption Information Line 135
ADT 161
Adult Learning
    Inspectorate 140
Adur (Gov) 111
Advanta 188
Adventure Balloons 143
Adventure Island 64
Advertising Age 35

Advertising Association 49
Advertising Standards
    Authority 140
Advisory Centre For
    Education 158
Advisory Committee on
    Protection of the Sea 217
Advisory Service (Windows &
    Conservatories) 160
Advisory, Conciliation &
    Arbitration Service 105, 109
AEG 238
Aer Lingus 273
Aeroclub 146
Aeroflot 273
Aerolineas Argentinas 273
Aeromexico 273
Aeroperu Airlines 273
Aerosmith 14
Aerospace Museum 170
African Bird Club 143
African National Congress,
    South Africa 107
After Eights 90
AGA Group 36
Aga Rayburn 238
Age Concern 136
Agfa 151
AgipPetroli 37
Agnes B 8
Agricultural Bank of China 37
Agricultural Credit Bureau 40
Agricultural Engineers
    Association 49
AIB Asset Management 190
AIDS Education & Research
    Trust 131
Aintree (Racecourse) 253
Air 2000 273
Air Accident Investigation
    Branch 109
Air Afrique 273
Air ALM 273
Air Aruba 273
Air Asia 273
Air Atlanta Icelandic 273
Air Baltic 273
Air Berlin 273
Air Canada 273
Air Caribbean 273
Air China 273
Air Fiji 273
Air France 273
Air Georgia 273
Air India 273
Air Jamaica 273
Air Kazakhstan 273
Air Lithuania 273
Air Madagascar 273
Air Malawi 273
Air Malta 273
Air Mauritius 273
Air Miles 283
Air Moldova 273
Air Namibia 273

Air New Zealand 273
Air Philippines 273
Air Portugal 273
Air Seychelles 273
Air Tahiti 273
Air Training Corps (ATC) 101
Air UK 273
Air Zimbabwe 273
Airbus 277
Airfix 149
Airfix Collectors Club 144
Airfix Models 65
Airgun UK 261
Airlanka 273
Airspace Magazine 146
Airtours 43, 283
Aiwa 236
Akai 150, 236
Alamo 278
Alan Partridge 27
Alan Shearer 255
Alanis Morisette 14
Alaska Airlines 273
Albanian (Gov) 102
Albemarle of London 31
Albert Dock 199
Albert Roux 89
Alberta (Local info) 204
Alberta Ferretti 8
Albuquerque (Airport) 276
Alcatel 268
Alcohol Concern 137
Alcoholics Anonymous 137
Aldeburgh Productions 7
Alder Hey Children's Hospital
  (Hospital) 127
Alderney (Tourist info) 204
Aldi 96
Alexander McQueen 8
Alexander Technique 125
Alexanders 238
Alexandra 224
Alexandria (Local info) 205
Alfa Romeo 156
Alford Valley (Railway) 198
Alfred McAlpine 160
Alfy 67
Algerian (Embassy) 102
Algerian (Gov) 102
Alicante (Airport) 276
Alice Cooper 15
Alicia Silverstone 3
Alien Resurrection 9
Alitalia 273
Alka Seltzer 235
All England Netball
  Association 255
All Nippon Airways 273
All Saints 15
Allders 231
Allen & Overy 50
Allergan 47
Alliance & Leicester 40-41, 187
Alliance for Historic Landscape
  Preservation 84

Alliance of Independent
  Retailers 243
Allied Bank, South Africa 37
Allied Brewers Traders
  Association 96
Allied Carpets 231
Allied Domecq 41
Allied Dunbar 189
Allied Dunbar Premiership 257
Allied Irish 187
AlliedSignal 56
Allmake Motor Parts 155
Allsports 242
Ally McBeal 27
Almeida 29
Aln Valley (Railway) 198
Alnwick (Gov) 111
Alnwick Castle 198
Alpha Galileo 218
Alpha Telecom 268
AlphabetStreet 223
Alphaline Regional
  Railways 282
Alpine 236
Alpine Electronics 155
Alpine World Cup Skiing
  2000 262
Alta Vista 267
Altberg Boots 242
Althorp 199
Alton Towers 64
Alyssa Milano 3
Alzheimer's Association 137
Alzheimer's Disease
  Society 137
Amalgamated Engineering &
  Electrical (AEEU) 55
Amateur Athletics
  Association 247
Amateur Entomologists'
  Society 218
Amateur Photography UK 152
Amateur Rowing
  Association 256
Amateur Stage 13
Amazon 223
Ambache 21
Amber Valley (Gov) 111
Ambit Magazine 13
Ambleside (Local info) 201
Ambulance Service
  Association 135
AMEC 265
Amerada 161
Amerada Hess 56
America (Grand Prix) 254
America (Music) 15
America (Stock exchange) 53
America's Cup 258
America's Cup Jubilee 258
American (Chamber of
  Commerce) 50
American (Embassy) 102
American Adventure Theme
  Park 64

American Airlines 273
American Astronomical
  Society 217
American Ballet Theatre 5
American Beauty 10
American Community
  Schools 74
American Contract Bridge
  League 143
American Darts
  Organization 249
American Electric Power 56
American Express 56, 188
American Film Foundation 12
American Film Institute 11
American Golf Discount 259
American Home Products 56
American International
  University 75
American Legion 163
American Medical
  Association 129
American National Bank 37
American Psycho 10
American Savings Bank 38
American Standard 56
Amersham International 47
Amiga 265
Amnesty International 105,
  108, 138
Amoco 56
Ampleforth 74
Amstel 89
Amsterdam (Airport) 276
Amsterdam (Local info) 209
Amsterdam (Stock
  exchange) 53
Amstrad 265
Amtico 231
Amtrak 36, 282
Amvescap 41
Amway 237
Ana Europe 273
Anatomical Society 129
Ancestry Research 147
Anchor Foods 90
Anchor Homes 165
Andorran (Gov) 102
Andover Advertiser 177
Andre Agassi 255
Andrew Carnegie Birthplace
  Museum 170
Andrew Collinge
  Hairdressing 158
Andrew Logan Museum of
  Sculpture 5
Andy Warhol 4
Andy Warhol Museum,
  Pittsburgh 212
Anetstation 23
Angela's Ashes 10
Anglepoise 239
Anglesey (Gov) 111
Anglesey (Motor racing) 254
Anglesey Sea Zoo 202

Anglia (TV) **26**
Anglia Countrywide **189**
Anglia Railways Train
  Services **282**
Anglian Home
  Improvements **237**
Anglian Water **58**
Anglican **164**
Angling Magazine **145**
Angling News **145**
Anglo American (Metals &
  mining) **46**
Angola (Tourist info) **197**
Angolan (Gov) **102**
Angolan National Radio **197**
Angus (Gov) **111**
Animail **151**
Animal Aid **135, 217**
Animal Health Trust **135**
Animal Rescue **135**
Animal Samaritans **135**
Animal Zone **64**
AnimalKind **135**
Animals **15**
Ankara (Local info) **212**
Ann Summers **241**
Anna Friel **3**
Anna Kournikova (Fan
  Club) **255**
Anne Fine **66**
Anne Frank **13**
Anne Frank Educational
  Trust **169**
Anne Murray **15**
Annuity Direct **189**
Anorexia & Bulimia Care **137**
Another Level **15**
Ansett **273**
Anthea Turner **27**
Anthony Hopkins **3**
Anthony Nolan Bone Marrow
  Trust **125, 137**
Anti-Counterfeiting Group **45**
Antigua (Tourist info) **204**
Antiquarian Horological
  Society **144**
Antique Dealers Directory **223**
Antiques Roadshow **223**
Antiques Trade Gazette **162,
  223**
Antiquity Journal **85**
Antler **239**
Antler Homes **160**
Anton Mosiman **90**
Antonio Banderas **3**
Antrim (Gov) **111**
Antwerp (Local info) **198**
Antz **64**
Anville Homes **160**
Anything Left Handed **241**
AOL **266**
AOL UK Kid's Channel **67**
Apollo **9**
Apple **56, 265**
Aqua **15**

Aqualisa **237**
Aquarium **95**
Aquascutum **224**
Arab Bank **38**
Arab Banking Corporation **40**
Arachnoiditis Trust **137**
Arboricultural Association **85**
Arcadia **52**
Archbishop of Canterbury **164**
Archers (Fan Club) **23**
Archinet **83**
Architects Journal **83**
Architectural Association
  School of Architecture **71**
Architectural Heritage **83**
Architectural Heritage Fund **83**
Architectural Heritage Society
  of Scotland **85**
Architectural Review **83**
Architecture Centre, Bristol **83**
Architecture Foundation **83**
Architecture Week **83**
Architecturelink **83**
Arctic Council **105**
Arctic Experience & Discover
  the World **283**
Ardbeg **96**
Ards (Gov) **111**
Argentina (Tourist info) **197**
Argentinian (Embassy) **102**
Argentinian (Gov) **102**
Argos **231**
Argyll & Bute (Gov) **111**
Ariana Afghan Airlines **273**
Arista (Record company) **21**
Arizona State University **77**
Arjo Wiggins Appleton **45**
Armagh (Gov) **111**
Armagh Observatory **217**
Armagh Planetarium **217**
Armani **8, 224**
Armed Forces Museum **170**
Armour **260**
Armourcoat **243**
Armourer Magazine **144**
Army Catering Corps
  Association **163**
Army Records Office **101**
Arnhem (Local info) **209**
Arnold Schwarzenegger **3**
Arran **96**
Arriva **277**
ARRIVA **56**
Arrow Express **36**
Arrows (Motor racing
  teams) **255**
Arsenal **250**
Arson Prevention Bureau **192**
Art **29**
Art Attack **64**
Art Basel **211**
Art Gallery of New South
  Wales **197**
Art Guide **13**
Art Libraries of UK & Ireland **13**

Art Review **13**
Arthritis Care **137**
Arthur Andersen **50**
Arthur C Clarke **13**
Artigiano **224**
Arts Business **14**
Arts Council **4, 109**
Arts Council for England **12**
Arts Council for Wales **4, 12**
Arts Council of Northern
  Ireland **4**
Arts Educational London
  Schools **71**
Arts Worldwide **7**
Arun (Gov) **111**
Arup **37**
Arvon Foundation **13**
As Good As It Gets **10**
AS Roma **250**
Asahi Shinbun (Japan) **182**
Ascot (Racecourse) **253**
Ascot Express
  (Newspaper) **177**
Asda **41, 52, 96**
ASH **108**
Ashbourne (Local info) **202**
Ashfield (Gov) **111**
Ashford (Gov) **111**
Ashmolean Museum **5, 170**
Ashwood Homes **160**
Ashworth (Hospital) **127**
Asian Development Bank **38**
Asian Home Gourmet **90**
Asiana Airlines **273**
Ask Jeeves **267**
Ask Jeeves for Kids **67**
Asprey & Garrard **238**
Assam (Local info) **207**
Assemblage Archaeology
  Journal **85**
Associated Board of the Royal
  Schools of Music **71**
Associated British Foods **41**
Associated British Ports **56**
Associated News **48**
Associated Sheep, Police and
  Army Dog Society **151**
Associated Society of
  Locomotive Engineers &
  Fireman **55**
Association for Consultants &
  Trainers **54**
Association for Environment
  Conscious Building **83**
Association for Families who
  have Adopted from
  Abroad **135**
Association for Geographic
  Information (AGI) **170**
Association for Improvements
  in Maternity Services **130**
Association for Industrial
  Archaeology **85**
Association for Information
  Management **54**

Association for International Cancer Research **137**
Association for Post-Natal Illness **137**
Association for Science Education **218**
Association for Spina Bifida & Hydrocephalus **137**
Association for the Protection of Rural Scotland **85**
Association for Women in Science & Engineering **218**
Association of Accounting Technicians **49**
Association of Archaeological Illustrators & Surveyors **85**
Association of Art and Antique Dealers (LAPADA) **223**
Association of Art Historians **4**
Association of Blind Piano Tuners **150**
Association of Bottled Beer Collectors **144**
Association of Breastfeeding Mothers **158**
Association of British Counties **108**
Association of British Drivers **108**
Association of British Healthcare Industries **126**
Association of British Insurers **192**
Association of British Investigators **49**
Association of British Kart Clubs **149**
Association of British Orchestras **21**
Association of British Pharmaceutical Industry **130**
Association of British Riding Schools **148**
Association of British Theatre Technicians **22**
Association of Car Fleet Operators **54**
Association of Chartered Certified Accountants **49**
Association of Christian Teachers **74**
Association of Clinical Pathologists **129**
Association of Consulting Actuaries **192**
Association of Consulting Engineers **49, 83**
Association of Corporate Treasurers **49**
Association of Cycle Traders **249**
Association of Direct Labour Organisations **54**
Association of Directors of Social Services **109**

Association of Electrical & Mechanical Trades **160**
Association of European Chambers of Commerce **36**
Association of European Travel Agents International **54**
Association of Exhibition Organisers **52**
Association of Field Ornithologists **143**
Association of First Day Cover Collectors **144**
Association of First Division Civil Servants **109**
Association of Fundraising Consultants **49**
Association of Gardens Trusts **85**
Association of Guilds of Weavers, Spinners and Dyers **148**
Association of Illustrators **4**
Association of Independent Financial Advisers **192**
Association of Independent Tour Operators **282**
Association of Independent Tour Operators **54**
Association of Inland Navigation Authorities **143**
Association of Insurers & Risk Managers **43**
Association of International Accountants **49**
Association of Investment Trust Companies **49**
Association of Local Government Archaeological Officers **85**
Association of Master Upholsters & Soft Furnishers **54, 160**
Association of Motion Picture Sound **11**
Association of Mouth & Foot Painting Artists Worldwide **22**
Association of National Park and Countryside Voluntary Wardens **85**
Association of National Tourist Offices **54**
Association of Operating Department Practitioners **129**
Association of Personal Injury Lawyers **49**
Association of Plastic Manufacturers **54**
Association of Play Industries **54**
Association of Police Authorities **139**
Association of Police Surgeons **129**
Association of Private Client Investment Managers &

Stockbrokers **49**
Association of Professional Ambulance Personnel **125**
Association of Professional Theatre for Children and Young People **12**
Association of Project Management **83**
Association of Psychological Therapists **130**
Association of Qualitative Research Practitioners **49**
Association of Racing Kart Schools **149**
Association of Radical Midwives **130**
Association of Recognised English Language Schools **73**
Association of Reflexologists **125**
Association of Relocation Agents **161**
Association of Residential Letting Agents **54**
Association of Retired & Persons over 50 **165**
Association of Sea Training Organisations **258**
Association of Suppliers to the British Clothing Industry **54**
Association of Suppliers to the Furniture Industry **54**
Association of the British Pharmaceutical Industry **13**
Association of Train Operating Companies **282**
Association of Unit Trusts & Investment Funds (AUTIF) **4**
Association of Unit Trusts and Investment Funds **192**
Association of University Administrators **74**
Association of University Teachers **55**
Association of Volleyball Professionals **262**
Association of Waterways Cruising Clubs **143**
Association of Woodturners of Great Britain **149**
AST **265**
Asta Medica **47**
Asterix **63**
Aston (Uni) **75**
Aston Martin **156-157**
Aston Villa **250**
Astra **236**
AstraZeneca **41, 47**
Astrid Lindgren's World **211**
Astrological Association of Great Britain **143**
Astronomy **218**
Astronomy Now **217**
AT&T **56**

Atag **238**
Atco **147**
Athelhampton **200**
Athens 2004 Olympics **254**
Athletics Board of Ireland **247**
Atlanta (Airport) **276**
Atlantic (Radio) **23**
Atlantic (Record company) **22**
Atlantic Salmon Trust **217**
Atlas Air **273**
Atomic Kitten **15**
Atomic Rooster **15**
ATP Tour **261**
atSchool **72**
Attila the Stockbroker **6**
Auckland (Airport) **276**
Auckland (Local info) **209**
Auckland Castle **198-199**
Auckland University of
 Technology **77**
Audi **156**
Audioseek **155**
Audit Bureau of Circulation **173**
Audit Commission **109**
Audrey Hepburn **3**
Austin Powers **10**
Austin Reed **224**
Australia (British embassy) **101**
Australia (Legal
 institutions) **106**
Australia (Stock exchange) **53**
Australia and New Zealand
 Banking Group **38**
Australian (Embassy) **102**
Australian (Gov) **103**
Australian Ballet **6**
Australian Broadcasting
 Corporation **197**
Australian Cricket Board **248**
Australian Museum **197**
Australian National Mapping
 Agency **170**
Australian National Parks **197**
Australian National
 University **77**
Australian Newspaper **197**
Australian Parliament **103**
Austravel **283**
Austria (Grand Prix) **254**
Austrian (Chamber of
 Commerce) **36**
Austrian (Embassy) **102**
Austrian (Gov) **103**
Austrian Airlines **273**
Auto Exchange **155**
Auto Express **155**
Auto Trader **156**
Autobytel **155-156**
Autocom **163**
Autofinder **155-156**
Autogas UK **155**
Autoglass **155**
Automobile Club de
 l'Ouest **254**
Automobile Magazine **156**

Automotive Body Repair
 News **156**
Automotive Online **156**
Autosport **255**
AutoWired **156**
Ava Gardner **3**
Avengers **10**
Avent **240**
Aventis **47**
Aviation Industry Group **35**
Aviation Today **35**
Aviemore & Cairngorms
 Experience **262**
Avis **278**
Avis Europe **52**
Avon **230**
Avon & Somerset (Police) **139**
Avon (Ambulance) **135**
Avon (Health authority) **126**
Avon Rubber **45**
Avon Valley (Railway) **198**
Avondale (Rugby club) **257**
AXA **189**
AXA Cup **261**
Axminster **231**
Axminster Power Tools **237**
Aylesbury (Gov) **111**
Aylesbury (Local info) **202**
Ayr (Racecourse) **253**
Ayr (Rugby club) **257**
Ayrshire (Local info) **201**
Ayrshire Post **177**
Ayrton Senna **255**
Azerbaijan (British
 embassy) **101**
Aztec Camera **15**
Azzurra Airlines **273**

B

B&Q **237**
B*Witched **15**
B-52's **15**
BAA **41, 56**
BAA Millennium Youth
 Games **254**
BAA Parking **282**
Babbacombe Model Village **64**
Babcock International **37**
Babe Ruth **255**
Babergh (Gov) **111**
Babies R Us **240**
Baby Directory **162**
Baby Gap **240**
BaByliss **236**
Babylon 5 **27**
Babyworld **162**
BAC Windows **237**
Bacardi **90**
Bach Flower Essences **125**
Back to the Future **10**
Backstreet Boys **15**
Baden Powell House **199**
Badger **89**
Badminton Association of
 England **247**

Badminton Horse Trials **259**
Badminton UK **247**
BAFTA **7, 11**
Baggage Express **161**
Bahai Faith **165**
Bahamas (Tourist info) **204**
Bahamasair **273**
Bahlsen **90**
Bahrain (British embassy) **101**
Baileys **90**
Baker & McKenzie **50**
Baker Tilly **50**
Balkan Airlines **273**
Ballantines **96**
Ballingers **237**
Balliol College Library **169**
Balloon Association **54**
Ballroom Dancing Times **145**
Balls Brothers **95**
Ballyclare Gazette **177**
Ballymaloe Cookery
 School **145**
Ballymena (Local info) **202**
Ballymoney (Gov) **111**
Balmoral **107, 198**
Baltic Exchange **53**
Baltimore Washington
 (Airport) **276**
Bananarama **15**
Banbridge (Gov) **111**
Banbury (Gov) **111**
Banbury Guardian **177**
Banc Cymru **187**
Banca Commerciale Italiana **38**
Banca d'Italia **38**
Banco Central Do Brasil **38**
Banco de España **38**
Banco de Portugal **38**
Bang & Olufsen **236**
Bangkok (Airport) **276**
Bangkok Bank, Thailand **38**
Bangladesh (Tourist info) **197**
Bangladeshi (Gov) **103**
Bangor (Uni) **75**
Bangor Caernarfon
 Chronicle **177**
Banham **161**
Banham Zoo **219**
Bank **95**
Bank Austria **38**
Bank of America **38**
Bank of Baharian and
 Kuwait **38**
Bank of Baroda **38**
Bank of Canada **38**
Bank of China **38**
Bank of Cyprus **38**
Bank of England **40**
Bank of England Museum **170**
Bank of Estonia **38**
Bank of Finland **38**
Bank of Greece **38**
Bank of Hawaii **38**
Bank of India **38**
Bank of Ireland **38, 187**

Bank of Israel **38**
Bank of Japan **38**
Bank of Kuwait & the Middle East **38**
Bank of Latvia **38**
Bank of Lebanon **38**
Bank of Lithuania **38**
Bank of Mexico **38**
Bank of Montreal **38**
Bank of Moscow **38**
Bank of Mozambique **38**
Bank of New York **38**
Bank of Papua New Guinea **38**
Bank of Portugal **38**
Bank of Russia **38**
Bank of Scotland **40-41, 187**
Bank of Slovenia **38**
Bank of Thailand **38**
Bank of Tokyo **38**
Bank of Wales **38, 187**
Bank of Zambia **38**
BankAmerica Corp. **56**
Banker **44**
Bankers Trust, New York **38**
Bankgesellschaft Berlin **38**
Banking Liaison Group **40**
Banking Ombudsman **140**
BankNet **187**
Banks Music Publications **150**
Banks Sails **258**
Bankside Fishing Tackle **145**
Banner Homes **160**
Banque Centrale du Luxembourg **38**
Banque de France **38**
Banque Nationale de Belgique **38**
Banque Nationale de Paris **38**
Banqueting House **199**
Banstead Herald **177**
Baptist Church **164**
BAR (Motor racing teams) **255**
Bar Council **105**
Barbadan (Gov) **103**
Barbican **25, 169**
Barbie **65, 242**
Barbour **242**
Barbra Streisand **15**
Barcelona (Airport) **276**
Barcelona (FC) **250**
Barcelona (Local info) **210**
Barclay James Harvest **15**
Barclaycard **187-188**
Barclays **41, 187**
Barclays (ISP) **266**
Barclays Stockbrokers **192**
Barclaysquare **239**
Baring Asset Management **190**
Barking & Dagenham (Gov) **111**
Barking & Havering (Health authority) **126**
Barlow Lyde & Gilbert **50**
Barnado's **135**
Barnes & Noble **56, 223**
Barnet (Gov) **111**

Barney **64**
Barnoldswick & Earby Times **177**
Barnsdale Gardens (Geoff Hamilton) **147**
Barnsley (FC) **250**
Barnsley (Gov) **111**
Barnsley Chronicle **177**
Barratt Developments **45**
Barratt Homes **160**
Barratts **241**
Barrow-in-Furness (Gov) **112**
Barry & District News **177**
Barry Dennis **252**
Barry Island Pleasure Park **64**
Barry Manilow **15**
Bartle Bogle Hegarty **35**
Basel (Local info) **212**
BASF **47**
Basildon (Gov) **112**
Basildon Evening Echo **177**
Basingstoke (Gov) **112**
Basingstoke Gazette **177**
Basketball Players Association **247**
Bass **41**
Bass Ale **89**
Bass Brewers **41**
Bass Museum **170**
Bassetlaw (Gov) **112**
Bat Conservation Trust **217**
Batavus **249**
Bates Alams **161**
Bates Dorland **35**
Bath (Building society) **187**
Bath (Gov) **112**
Bath (Local info) **202**
Bath (Rugby club) **257**
Bath (Uni) **75**
Bath Chronicle **177**
Bath FM **23**
Batman **63**
Batman & Robin **10, 64**
Battersea Dogs Home **135, 151**
Baumatic **238**
Baume & Mercier **243**
Baxi Heating **159**
Baxters **90**
Bayer **47**
Baywatch **27**
BB King **15**
BBC **26**
BBC (News) **177**
BBC (Recruitment) **51**
BBC Asian Network **23**
BBC Comedy Zone **6, 27**
BBC Cricket **249**
BBC Education **72**
BBC Essex **23**
BBC Experience **202**
BBC Food & Drink **94, 145**
BBC GMR (Manchester) **23**
BBC Good Homes **162**
BBC Ground Force **147**
BBC Hereford & Worcester **23**

BBC Home Front in the Garden **147**
BBC Local Radio **23**
BBC Music **14**
BBC Music Magazine **14**
BBC News **26**
BBC Parenting Resource **158**
BBC Philharmonic Orchestra **21**
BBC Radio 1 **23**
BBC Radio 2 **23**
BBC Radio 3 **23**
BBC Radio 4 **23**
BBC Radio 5 **23**
BBC Radio Berkshire **23**
BBC Radio Bristol **23**
BBC Radio Cambridgeshire **2**
BBC Radio Cleveland **23**
BBC Radio Cornwall **23**
BBC Radio Coventry and Warwickshire **23**
BBC Radio Cumbria **23**
BBC Radio Cymru **23**
BBC Radio Derby **23**
BBC Radio Devon **23**
BBC Radio Gloucestershire **2**
BBC Radio Guernsey **24**
BBC Radio Humberside **24**
BBC Radio Jersey **24**
BBC Radio Kent **24**
BBC Radio Lancashire **24**
BBC Radio Leeds **24**
BBC Radio Leicester **24**
BBC Radio Lincolnshire **24**
BBC Radio Merseyside **24**
BBC Radio Newcastle **24**
BBC Radio Norfolk **24**
BBC Radio Northampton **24**
BBC Radio Nottingham **24**
BBC Radio Sheffield **24**
BBC Radio Shropshire **24**
BBC Radio Solent **24**
BBC Radio Stoke **24**
BBC Radio Suffolk **24**
BBC Radio Wales **24**
BBC Radio WM **24**
BBC Radio York **24**
BBC Schools **27, 64**
BBC Shop **223**
BBC Somerset Sound **24**
BBC Southern Counties **24**
BBC Symphony **21**
BBC Three Counties Radio **2**
BBC Ticket Unit **31**
BBC Top Gear **156**
BBC Weather Centre **174**
BBC Wiltshire Sound **24**
BBC World Service **24**
BCR British Car Rental **278**
BDO Stoy Hayward **50**
Be-Bop Deluxe **15**
Beach **10**
Beach Boys **15**
Beachcroft Stanleys **50**
Beacon FM (Shropshire) **24**

Beacon FM
(Wolverhampton) 24
Beaconsfield (Local info) 202
Bead Society of Great
Britain 148
Beamish (Railway) 198
Beamish Brewery 89
Beamish Open Air
Museum 170
Beanie Babies 65, 242
Beanie Babies Official Club 67
Beano 66
Bear Museum, Petersfield 170
Beastie Boys 15
Beastway MTB 249
Beatles 15
Beatrix Potter 66
Beatties 149
Beaufort (Local info) 208
Beaulieu 199
Beautiful Game 29
Beautiful South 15
Beavis and Butthead 63
Bebe Confort 240
Beck 15
Beck's 89
Bedford (Gov) 112
Bedford (Local info) 202
Bedford (Rugby club) 257
Bedfordshire (Chamber of
Commerce) 35
Bedfordshire (Gov) 112
Bedfordshire (Police) 139
Bee Gees 15
Beeb.com 162
Beechwood Homes 160
Beefeater 90
Beer Davies 35
Beggars Banquet 22
Beijing (Airport) 276
Beijing (Local info) 205
Beirut (Local info) 208
Bekonscot 202
Bekonscot Model Village 64
Belarussian (Gov) 103
Belfast (Airport) 277
Belfast (Gov) 112
Belfast Harlequins (Rugby
club) 257
Belfast Royal Hospitals 127
Belfast Telegraph 177
Belfe 260
Belgian (Embassy) 102
Belgian (Gov) 103
Belgian Railways 198
Belgium (British embassy) 101
Belgium (Grand Prix) 254
Belgium (Monarchy) 106
Belgium (Weather) 174
Belgo 95
Bell Atlantic 56
Bellamy Brothers 15
Belle & Sebastian 15
Belling 238
Bellway 45, 160

Belper News 177
Beme 162
Ben & Jerry's 90
Ben Affleck 3
Ben Elton 6
Ben Nevis & Lochaber (Web
cam) 213
Ben Sherman 224
Bendicks of Mayfair 90
Beneficial Bank 187
BeneFit 230
Benefits Agency 109
Benelli 163
Benenden (Public school) 74
Benetton 224
Benihana 95
Bensons Crisps 90
Bentalls 231
Bentley 156
BEPAC 84
Berghaus 242, 260
Berisford 45
Berkeley Group 45
Berkshire (Ambulance) 135
Berlin (Airport) 276
Berlin (Local info) 206
Berlin (Stock exchange) 53
Berlin International Film
Festival 7
Berlin Philharmonic 21
Bermuda (Stock exchange) 53
Bermuda (Tourist info) 204
Bermuda Monetary
Authority 38
Bernini 224
Berry Bros & Rudd 98
Berwick Rangers (FC) 250
Berwick-upon-Tweed
(Gov) 112
Berwin Leighton 50
Best Stuff 228
Betterwear 238
Betty Barclay 224
Betty Ford Center 128
Betty's By Post (Harrogate) 94
Beverly Hills 90210 27
Bewitched 27
Bewley Homes 160
Bexhill Observer 177
Bexley (Gov) 112
Bexley News Shopper 177
BG 58
Bhoja Air 274
Bhs 231
Bibendum 95
Bic 236
BICC 45
Bicentennial Man 10
Bicester Village 239
Bicester (Local info) 202
Bicester Advertiser 177
Big Blue Boat Shows 143
Big Blue Dog 51
Big Breakfast 27
Big Brother and the Holding

Company 15
Big Bus Tours 277
Big Country 15
Big Issue 162
Biggin Hill (Local info) 202
Bigron 46
Bigwig 266
Bike Trader Interactive 163
Bikenet Magazine 163
Bilbao (Local info) 210
Bill 27
Bill Nye the Science Guy 64
Billiards Congress of
America 259
Billie Piper 15
Billiton 41
Billy Elliot 10
Billy Idol 15
Billy Joel 15
Bingham's Park Farm 64
Bioforce 236
Biotechnology and Biological
Sciences 109
Bird & Bird 50
Bird Life International 217
Bird On! 143
Birds Eye Walls 90
Birds of Britain 143, 218
Birdwatch 218
Birdwatch Magazine 143
Birkbeck College London 75
Birkenstock 241
Birmingham & Midland
Transport Museum 170
Birmingham (Airport) 277
Birmingham (Chamber of
Commerce) 35
Birmingham (Gov) 112
Birmingham (Health
authority) 126
Birmingham (Uni) 75
Birmingham Botanical
Gardens 200
Birmingham Cable 265
Birmingham City (FC) 250
Birmingham Contemporary
Music Group 21
Birmingham Hippodrome 25
Birmingham International Film
and Television Festival 7
Birmingham Midshires (Building
society) 187
Birmingham Museum & Art
Gallery 5
Birmingham NEC 25
Birmingham Post and Mail 177
Birmingham Railway
Museum 170
Birmingham Royal Ballet 6
Birmingham School of Speech
& Drama 71
Birstall Garden Centre 147
Birthdays 235
Bishops Move 161
Bitesize Revision 66

BJ Pinchbeck Homework Helper 66
Bjork 15
Bjorn Again 15
Blaby (Gov) 112
Black & Decker 56, 237
Black & Decker Online 147
Black Country Living Museum 170
Black Sabbath 15
Blackburn (Gov) 112
Blackburn Citizen 177
Blackburn Rovers (FC) 250
Blackheath Gallery 5
Blackpool & Fylde Citizen 177
Blackpool (FC) 250
Blackpool (Gov) 112
Blackpool (Local info) 203
Blackpool (Zoo) 219
Blackpool Gazette 177
Blackpool Pleasure Beach 64
Blackpool Southshore (Local info) 203
Blackpool Tower 64
Blackpool Victoria 127
Blacks 242
Blacksheep 89
Blackstar 240
Blackwell (Publishing) 48
Blackwell's 223
Blair Witch Project 10
Blairgowrie Advertiser 177
Blenheim 199
Bletchley Park 170
Blick Rothenberg 50
Blind Date 27
Bliss 137
Blockbuster 240
Blondie 15
Bloomberg 191
Blooming Marvellous 240
Bloomsbury 48
Bloomsbury Theatre 29
Bloor Homes 160
Blue Arrow 51
Blue Badge Guides 202
Blue Circle 45
Blue Cross 135
Blue Dragon 90
Blue Elephant 95
Blue Line 277
Blue Peter 64
Blue Print Café 95
Blue Sq 146, 252
Blues & Roots Music Festival 7
Bluetooth 267
Bluewater 239
Blur 15
Bluthners 150
Blyth Valley (Gov) 112
BMI Healthcare 128
BMP DDB 35
BMW (Car manufacturers) 156
BMW (Motorcycles) 163
BMW Car 156

BMX 249
Boat Exchange 259
Boat Race 256
Boaters Coffee 90
Bob Champion Cancer Trust 137
Bob Dylan 15
Bob Hope 3
Bob Marley 15
Bob Seger 15
Bob the Builder 64
Bobbi Brown 230
BOC 36, 41
Boddingtons 89
Bodegas Faustino 98
Boden 224
Bodleian Library, Oxford 169
Body Shop 52, 230
Bodycote International 46
Bodyform 236
Boeing 56
Bogaert 238
Bogner 260
Bognor Regis Journal & Guardian 177
Bol 223
Bolivian (Gov) 103
Bollywood 12
Bolshoi Ballet 6
Bolsover (Gov) 112
Bolton (Gov) 112
Bolton Abbey 199
Bolton Evening News 177
Bolton Hospice 127
Bolton Wanderers (FC) 250
Bomber Command Historical Society 163
Bon Jovi 15
Bone Collector 10
Bonhams 223
Bonne Bell 230
Bonus.com 67
Boodle & Dunthorne 238
Boogie Nights 10
Book Industry Communications 173
Book Trust 13, 73, 137
Booker 41
Booker Prize 7
Booksellers Association 54
Booksellers Association of Great Britain and Northern Ireland 243
Boosey & Hawkes 150
Boost 90
Boots 41, 52, 230
Boots Dental Care 126
Boots Opticians 131
Boots Pharmacists' Association 130
Bordeaux Direct 98
Border 26
Border Collie Trust 151
Borders 223
Born Free Foundation 217

Borrowers 64
Bosch 238
Bostik 237
Boston (Airport) 276
Boston (Gov) 112
Boston (Local info) 213
Boston Symphony 21
Botswanan (Gov) 103
Bottoms Up 94
Bouraq Indonesia Airlines 274
Bournemouth (FC) 250
Bournemouth (Gov) 112
Bournemouth (Local info) 203
Bournemouth (Uni) 75
Bournemouth Daily Echo 177
Bovis Construction 45
Bowes (Railway) 198
Bowmore 98
Bowood House 199-200
Boxing Monthly Magazine 24
Boxman 240
Boy George 15
Boys' Brigade 63
Boyzone 15
BP Amoco 37, 41
BP Marine 52
BPP Law School 72
Braathens (Airline) 274
Brabantia 238
Bracknell Forest (Gov) 112
Bradford & Bingley (Building society) 187
Bradford & Bingley (Estate agents) 159
Bradford (Chamber of Commerce) 35
Bradford (Gov) 112
Bradford (Health authority) 12
Bradford (Local info) 203
Bradford (Uni) 75
Bradford City (FC) 250
Bradford Star 177
Bradford Telegraph & Argus 177
Brain Teaser 67
Brains 89
Braintree (Gov) 112
Braintree Witham & Dunmow Times 177
Bramham Park 200
Brands Hatch 254
Brannigans 90
Braun 236
Bravo 26
Brazil (Legal institutions) 106
Brazil (Tourist info) 198
Brazilian (Embassy) 102
Brazilian (Gov) 103
Breast Cancer Campaign 137
Breast Clinic 137
Breathe 266
Breckland (Gov) 112
Brecon Beacons (Local info) 201
Breitling 243

Brent (Gov) **112**
Brentwood (Gov) **112**
Brentwood Weekly News **177**
Breville **238**
Brewer **95**
Brewers & Licensed Retailers
Association **96**
Brewers Quay & The
Timewalk **170**
Brewin Dolphin **192**
Breworld **148**
Bridge Today **143**
Bridge World **143**
Bridgend (Gov) **112**
Bridgewater Hall,
Manchester **25**
Bridgnorth Cliff (Railway) **198**
Bright Sparks (Junior Mensa
Magazine) **66**
Brighton & Hove (Gov) **112**
Brighton (Local info) **203**
Brighton (Uni) **75**
Brighton Centre **25, 29**
Brighton Evening Argus **177**
Brighton Festival **7**
Brighton Palace Pier **64**
Brigitte Bardot Foundation **135**
Brintons **231**
Brio **65, 242**
Brisbane (Airport) **276**
Bristol & West **187**
Bristol (Car manufacturers) **156**
Bristol (Gov) **112**
Bristol (Local info) **203**
Bristol (Uni) **75**
Bristol (Vet school) **78**
Bristol (Zoo) **219**
Bristol Cancer Help Centre **128**
Bristol City (FC) **250**
Bristol City Museum & Art
Gallery **170**
Bristol Evening Post **177**
Bristol Journal **177**
Bristol Myers Squibb **47**
Bristol Old Vic **29**
Bristol Old Vic Theatre
School **71**
Bristol Rugby (Rugby club) **257**
Bristol Western Daily Press **178**
Brit Awards **7**
Brit School **71**
Britain At War Experience **170**
Britannia (Airline) **274**
Britannia History **169**
Britannia Music Club **240**
Britannia Parking **282**
Britannic Assurance **189**
Britannica **169**
Britax **155, 240**
Britax International **45**
British (Chamber of
Commerce) **35**
British Academy of Dramatic
Combat **12**
British Academy of

Fencing **249**
British Acoustic Neuroma
Association **137**
British Acupuncture
Council **125**
British Aerobatics
Association **146**
British Aerophilatelic
Federation **145**
British Aerosol Manufacturers
Association **54**
British Aerospace **41**
British Agencies for Adoption &
Fostering **135**
British Aikido Association **248**
British Airline Pilots
Association **49**
British Airports Authority **277**
British Airways **41, 56, 274**
British Airways Holidays **283**
British Amateur Gymnastics
Association **252**
British Amateur Weightlifters'
Association **262**
British Antarctic Survey **218**
British Antique Dealers
Association **243**
British Antique Furniture
Restorers Association **54**
British Apparel and Textile
Confederation **54**
British Aquatic Resource
Centre **151, 218**
British Archaeology
Magazine **85**
British Army **101**
British Arthur Ransome
Society **66**
British Arts Festivals
Association **4, 7**
British Association for
Behavioural & Cognitive
Psychotherapies **130**
British Association for
Counselling **136**
British Association for
Information & Library
Education & Research **173**
British Association for Open
Learning **73, 137**
British Association for Shooting
& Conservation **145**
British Association for the
Advancement of Science **218**
British Association of Accident
& Emergency Medicine **129**
British Association of Balloon
Operators **143**
British Association of
Emergency Medical
Technicians **125**
British Association of European
Pharmaceutical
Distributors **130**
British Association of

Numismatic Societies **144**
British Association of Paediatric
Surgeons **129**
British Association of Paper
Historians **169**
British Association of Picture
Libraries **54**
British Association of Plastic
Surgeons **129**
British Association of
Professional Draftsmen **49**
British Association of
Psychotherapists **130**
British Association of Ski
Instructors **262**
British Association of Sport &
Exercise Sciences **256**
British Association of Toy
Retailers **243**
British Astrological & Psychic
Society **143**
British Astronomical
Society **217**
British Athletics Federation **247**
British Bankers'
Association **192**
British Bathroom Council **237**
British Bee Keepers
Association **218**
British Betting Office
Association **253**
British Biotech **36**
British Blood Transfusion
Service **125**
British Bloodstock Agency **253**
British Board of Film
Classification **11**
British Canoe Union **248**
British Car Auctions **156**
British Car Auctions Group **155**
British Cardiac Society **137**
British Cartographic
Society **170**
British Casino Association **146**
British Chess Federation **144**
British Chess Magazine **144**
British Chiropractic
Association **125**
British Cichlid Association **151**
British Coatings
Federation **237**
British College of Naturopathy &
Osteopathy **73**
British Collegiate American
Football League **247**
British Columbia (Local
info) **204**
British Computer Society **267**
British Construction Industry
Awards **84**
British Contract Furnishing
Association **54**
British Copyright Council **12**
British Council **109**
British Council for Chinese

Martial Arts **248**
British Cycling Federation **249**
British Cyclo-Cross
Association **249**
British Deer Society **217**
British Dental Association **126**
British Dental Health
Foundation **126**
British Dental Trade
Association **126**
British Diabetic
Association **137**
British Dietetic Association **125**
British Disabled Flying
Club **146**
British Disabled Water Ski
Association **258**
British Dog Breeders
Council **151**
British Dragonfly Society **151,
217**
British Dressage **259**
British Driving Society **148**
British Dyslexia
Association **137**
British Educational
Communications &
Technology Agency
(BECTA) **73**
British Egg Information
Service **94**
British Electric Flight
Association **149**
British Endodontic Society **126**
British Endurance Riding
Association **259**
British Energy **41, 58, 161**
British Epilepsy
Association **137**
British Equestrian
Federation **259**
British Equestrian Trade
Association **148**
British Equine Veterinary
Association **125**
British European **274**
British Falconers Club **143, 145**
British Federation of Festivals
for Music, Dance and
Speech **7**
British Fencing
Association **249**
British Feng Shui Society **164**
British Fertility Society **129**
British Field Sports Society **145**
British Film Commission **11**
British Film Institute **11**
British Film Institute National
Library **169**
British Films Catalogue **11**
British Fire Service **139**
British Flute Society **150**
British Food Journal **95**
British Footwear
Association **243**

British Franchise
Association **52**
British Furniture
Manufacturers **54**
British Gas **41, 159, 161**
British Geological Survey **170,
218**
British Geriatrics Society **129**
British Gliding Association **146**
British Healthcare Trade
Association **125**
British Healthcare Trades
Association **54**
British Heart Foundation **137**
British Hedgehog Preservation
Society **217**
British Heraldic Archive **147**
British Holiday & Home Parks
Association **150**
British Homeopathic Dental
Association **126**
British Homing World **143**
British Homoeopathic
Library **125**
British Horological
Institute **218, 223**
British Horse Driving Trials
Association **259**
British Horse Society **135, 148,
259**
British Horse Trials
Association **259**
British Horseracing Board **253**
British Hotel Reservations
Centre **202, 280**
British House Rabbit
Association **151**
British Humanist
Association **165**
British Institute of
Embalmers **139**
British Insurance & Investment
Brokers Association **43, 192**
British International
Airports **277**
British Isles Backgammon
Association **147**
British Jewellers
Association **54**
British Journal of General
Practice **128**
British Journal of Healthcare
Management **128**
British Journal of Nursing **128**
British Journal of
Photography **152**
British Killifish Association **151**
British Koi Keepers'
Society **151**
British Lawnmower
Museum **170**
British Library **169**
British Library Philatelic
Collections **145**
British Marine Industries

Federation **54**
British Market Research
Association **173**
British Matchbox Label and
Booklet Society **144, 149**
British Meat **90, 94**
British Medical Acupuncture
Society **125**
British Medical Association **1**
British Medical Journal **128**
British Microlight Aircraft
Association **146**
British Midland **274**
British Model Flying
Association **149**
British Model Soldier
Society **149**
British Motor Racing
Circuits **163**
British Motorcyclists
Federation **163**
British Mountain Biking **249**
British Mountain Guides **144**
British Mountaineering
Council **144**
British Museum **170**
British Music Information
Centre **21**
British National Space
Centre **217**
British Naturist Society **158**
British Nuclear Fuels **58**
British Nursing Agencies **13**
British Nursing Association **1**
British Nursing News **128**
British Nutrition Foundation
British Office Systems and
Stationery Federation **54**
British Olympic
Association **254**
British Open **252**
British Ophthalmic Anaesthe
Society **131**
British Organ Donor
Society **125**
British Organization of Sikh
Students **165**
British Orienteering
Federation **150**
British Ornithologists'
Union **143, 219**
British Osteopathic
Association **125**
British Parachute
Association **150**
British Pedal Car
Championship **249**
British Pharmacopoeia **130**
British Phonographic
Industry **21**
British Potato Council **94**
British Printing Industries
Federation **54**
British Psychological
Society **129-130**

British Railways Board **109**
British Road Transport
Museum **170**
British Safety Council **125**
British Sandwich
Association **96**
British School of
Homeopathy **73, 125**
British Screen Finance **11**
British Security Association **52**
British Shooting Sports
Council **261**
British Show Jumping
Association **259**
British Ski & Snowboard
Federation **262**
British Sky Broadcasting **45**
British Small Animal Veterinary
Association **125**
British Society for Restorative
Dentistry **126**
British Society of Dentistry for
the Handicapped **126**
British Society of Master Glass
Painters **22**
British Speedway
Promoters **163**
British Squash Open
Championship **260**
British Standards Institute **160**
British Standards
Institution **138**
British Stone **237**
British Sub-Aqua Club **261**
British Sugar **41**
British Superkart
Association **149**
British Telecommunications **41,
54**
British Ten Pin Bowling
Association **152**
British Touring Car
Championship **254**
British Tourist Authority **202**
British Toxicology Society **125**
British Toy and Hobby
Association **54, 243**
British Trade International **109**
British Transport Police **139**
British Trials and Rally Drivers
Association **255**
British Triathlon
Association **247**
British Trust for Conservation
Volunteers **85**
British Trust for
Ornithology **143**
British Tug of War
Association **262**
British UFO Research
Association **219**
British United Taekwon-do
Federation **248**
British Universities Film and
Video Council **11**

British Universities Sailing
Association **258**
British Vehicle Rental
Association **278**
British Venture Capital
Association **40**
British Veterinary
Association **125**
British Veterinary Nursing
Association **125**
British Video Association **11**
British Walking Federation **150**
British Watch & Clock
Collectors Association **144**
British Water **160**
British Water Ski
Federation **258**
British Waterskiing **259**
British Waterways **143**
British Waterways Board **109**
British Weights & Measures
Association **138**
British Wheel of Yoga **158**
British Wheelchair Sports
Foundation **247**
British Wildlife Rehabilitation
Council **217**
British Wind Energy
Association **84**
British Women Pilots'
Association **49**
British Women Racing Drivers
Club **49**
British Woodworkers
Federation **160**
British Wool Marketing
Board **231**
British World Airlines **274**
British Youth Council **149**
British-Borneo Oil & Gas **37**
Britney Spears **15**
Brittany (Ferries) **278**
Brittany (Local info) **206**
BRMB FM (Birmingham) **24**
Broadcasting Entertainment
Cinematograph and Theatre
Union (BECTU) **55**
Broadcasting Standards
Commission **12, 140**
Broadfield House Glass
Museum **170**
Broadland (Gov) **112**
Broadlands **199**
Broderbund Europe **265**
Brodies **50**
Bromley (Gov) **112**
Bromley New Shopper **178**
Bromsgrove (Gov) **112**
Bromsgrove Standard **178**
Bronte Parsonage
Museum **170**
Brook Street **51**
Brooklands Museum **170**
Brooks Brothers **224**
Brookside **27**

Browns **224**
Broxbourne (Gov) **112**
Broxtowe (Gov) **112**
Bruce Lee **3**
Bruce Springsteen **15**
Bruges (Local info) **198**
Bruges Group **108**
Brunei (Gov) **103**
Brunei (Monarchy) **106**
Brunel (Uni) **75**
Brussels (Airport) **276**
Brussels (Local info) **198**
Brussels (Stock exchange) **53**
Brussels Expo **198**
Bryant Group **45**
Bryant Homes **160**
BSA Owners' Club UK **163**
BSkyB **41**
BSM **158**
BT **268**
BT Cellnet **268**
BT Click **266**
BT Global Challenge **258**
BT Internet **266**
BT Online Phonebook **173**
BT Pagers **268**
BT Teaching Awards **72**
BUBL Information Service **173**
Bucharest (Stock exchange) **53**
Buckingham Advertiser **178**
Buckingham Palace **107, 199**
Buckinghamshire (Gov) **112**
Buckinghamshire (Health
authority) **126**
Buckinghamshire Chilterns
University College **75**
Bucks Free Press **178**
Bucks Herald **178**
Budapest (Local info) **206**
Budapest Sun (Hungary) **182**
Buddhist Society (UK) **164**
Buddy Holly Story **29**
Budgens **96**
Budgerigar Society **143**
Budgerigar World **143**
Budget **278**
Budweiser **89-90**
Budweiser Basketball League
UK **247**
Budweiser Budvar **89**
Buena Vista International **12**
Buenos Aires (Local info) **197**
Buffy the Vampire Slayer **27**
Bug's Life **64**
Bugs **27**
Bugs Bunny **63**
Building Societies
Association **192**
Buitoni **90**
Bulgaria (British embassy) **101**
Bulgarian (Gov) **103**
Bulgarian National Bank **38**
Bull **265**
Bulls Eye Magazine **249**
Bullying **67, 72**

Bullying (BBC) 67
Bumpsadaisy 240
Bunzl 47
BUPA 128, 189
Bure Valley (Railway) 198
Burger King 94
Burghley House 199
Burkina Faso (Gov) 103
Burl Ives 3
Burmah Castrol 36-37
Burnley (FC) 250
Burnley (Gov) 112
Burnley Citizen Group 178
Burnley Express 178
Burtons 224
Bury (Gov) 112
Bury Free Press 178
Bury St Edmunds (Local
  info) 203
Bury Times 178
Bus Web 277
Busch Gardens 212
Bushells 159
Business Gazette 178
Business in the
  Community 136
Business Money 191
Business Pages 173
Business Post 36
Business Week 44
Butlers Guild 55
Butlins 282
Butterworth Heinemann 48
Butterworths 48
Buxton (Local info) 203
Buxton Festival 7
Buzz 274
Buzz Aldrin 217
Buzzcocks 15
BWIA 274

C

C & A 224
C.Scope 149
C2C 282
Cabinet Office 111
Cabinet War Rooms 170
Cable & Wireless 41, 54, 266,
  268
Cable Communications
  Association 265
Cable Guide 14
Cable London 265
Cable Net 265
Cable Tel 265
Cacharel 230
Cadbury Schweppes 41
Cadbury World 202
Cadbury's 90
Cadillac 156
Cadiz (Local info) 210
Cadogan Holidays 283
Caerlaverock Castle 198
Caernarfon Air Park 170
Caerphilly (Gov) 112

Caffrey's 89
Café Rouge 95
Cagney & Lacey 27
Cahoot 187
Calais (Ferries) 278
Calderdale (Gov) 112
Caledonian (Cinemas) 9
Calgary (Airport) 276
California State University 78
Callendar House 200
Calligraphy & Lettering Arts
  Society 148
Calmac 278
Calor Gas 159
Cambridge & Huntingdon
  (Health authority) 126
Cambridge (Building
  society) 187
Cambridge (Chamber of
  Commerce) 35
Cambridge (Gov) 112
Cambridge (Local info) 203
Cambridge (Uni) 75
Cambridge (Vet school) 78
Cambridge Building
  Society 192
Cambridge Cable 265
Cambridge Diet 158
Cambridge Evening News 178
Cambridge Folk Festival 7
Cambridge Museum of
  Technology 170
Cambridge Red 24
Cambridge United (FC) 250
Cambridge University
  Library 169
Cambridge University Press 48
Cambridgeshire (Gov) 112
Camden (Gov) 112
Camelot Group 43
Cameron Diaz 3
Cameron McKenna 50
Cameroon (British
  embassy) 101
Cameroon (Tourist info) 204
Cameroon Airlines 274
Camp America 75
Campaign 44
Campaign Against Censorship
  of the Internet in Britain 108
Campaign for an English
  Parliament 108
Campaign for Dark Skies 108
Campaign for Freedom of
  Information 108
Campaign for Nuclear
  Disarmament (CND) 108
Campaign for Press &
  Broadcasting Freedom 108
Campaign for Safe E-
  Commerce Legislation 108
Campaign for Shooting 108
Campbell's 90
Camping & Caravanning
  Club 150

Camping & Outdoor Leisure
  Association 150
Camping UK Directory 150
CAMRA (Campaign for Real
  Ale) 90
Can-Do Community
  Recycling 84
Canada (British embassy) 1
Canada (Grand Prix) 254
Canada (Legal institutions) 1
Canada (Tourist info) 204
Canada Life 189
Canada Trust 38
Canadian (Embassy) 102
Canadian (Gov) 103
Canadian Bridge
  Federation 143
Canadian Chiropractic
  Association 125
Canadian Neuro-Optic
  Research Institute 131
Canary Wharf Group 51
Canberra (Local info) 197
Canberra Institute of
  Technology 77
Cancer Bacup 137
Cancer Research Fund 137
Canine World 151
Cannes (Local info) 206
Cannes Film Festival 7, 206
Cannock (Gov) 112
Cannon 238
Cannons Health Clubs 158
Canon (Computers) 265
Canon (Photography) 151
Canterbury (Gov) 112
Canterbury (Local info) 203
Canterbury Christ Church
  University College 75
Cantina Del Ponte 95
Cape Air 274
Cape Town (Airport) 276
Cape Town (Local info) 210
Capel Cure Sharp 190, 193
Capita Group 52
Capital (Bank) 187
Capital FM (London) 24
Capital Gold (London) 24
Capital Movers 161
Capital One 188
Capital Radio 45
Caprice 8
Captain America 63
Captain Marvel 63
Captain Morgan Rum 90
Car 156
Car Parts World 155
Caractere 224
Caradon 45
Caradon (Gov) 112
Carat 45
Caravan Club 150
Cardiff (Gov) 112
Cardiff (Local info) 203
Cardiff (Rugby club) 257

Cardiff (Uni) **75**
Cardigans **15**
Cards Galore **235**
Care for the Wild
 International **135**
Care International **138**
Careers Research & Advisory
 Centre **73**
Careers Services National
 Association **73, 137**
Careers Services Unit **73**
Carers National
 Association **125**
Cargo Forwarding
 International **161**
Carlisle (FC) **250**
Carlisle (Gov) **112**
Carlisle News & Star **178**
Carlsberg **89**
Carlton **26, 41, 239**
Carlton Communications **45**
Carlton Food Network **95**
Carlton Select **26**
Carlton Video **240**
Carmarthenshire (Gov) **112**
Carmelite Friars UK **164**
Carnegie Museum - Discovery
 Room **67**
CarNet **156**
Carnival **283**
Carnoustie Golf Course Hotel &
 Resort **252**
CAROL **191**
Carousel **29**
Carpet Information Centre **231**
Carpetright **231**
Carphone Warehouse **228**
Carquote **189**
Carratu **49**
Carribbean Connection **283**
Carrick (Gov) **112**
Carrickfergus (Gov) **112**
Carrickfergus Advertiser **178**
Carrie Fisher **3**
Carry On **10**
Cartier **8, 238**
Cartoon Network **65**
Cartoonists' Guild **22**
Cartophilic Society of Great
 Britain **144**
Cartridge Company **47**
Cary Grant **3**
Cash Centres **187**
Casio **243**
Casio (Photography) **152**
Casper **63**
Casting Weekly **14**
Castle Bromwich Gardens **200**
Castle Combe (Motor
 racing) **254**
Castle Cornet **198**
Castle Howard **200**
Castle Morpeth (Gov) **112**
Castle Rock **12**
Castle-Point Rayleigh

Standard **178**
Castlereagh (Gov) **112**
Cat Stevens **15**
Cat World **150**
Catatonia **15**
Cater Allen (Isle of Man) **187**
Caterham **156**
Catering Equipment
 Distributors Association **96**
Cathay Pacific **274**
Catholic Church (in England &
 Wales) **164**
Catholic Church (Scotland) **164**
Cats **29**
Cats Protection League **135,
 151**
Catterick (Racecourse) **253**
Cavern **6**
Cayman (Stock exchange) **53**
Cayman Islands (Tourist
 info) **204**
Cazenove & Co **193**
Cazenove Fund
 Management **190**
CBBC **65**
CBS **56**
CD Now **240**
CD Wow **240**
Cedarpoint **64**
Celebrations **90**
Celebrity **10**
Celine Dion **15**
Cellnet **268**
Celltech Chiroscience **36**
Celtic (FC) **250**
Cendant **56**
Center Parcs **282**
Central & West Lancashire
 (Chamber of Commerce) **35**
Central (TV) **26**
Central Bank of Armenia **38**
Central Bank of Barbados **39**
Central Bank of Bosnia **39**
Central Bank of Chile **39**
Central Bank of China **39**
Central Bank of Cyprus **39**
Central Bank of Iceland **39**
Central Bank of India **39**
Central Bank of Ireland **39**
Central Bank of Jordan **39**
Central Bank of Kenya **39**
Central Bank of Malta **39**
Central Bank of Swaziland **39**
Central Bank of the Netherlands
 Antilles **39**
Central Bank of the Republic of
 Indonesia **39**
Central Bank of the Republic of
 Turkey **39**
Central Bank of the Russian
 Federation **39**
Central Bank of Trinidad &
 Tobago **39**
Central Bank of Uruguay **39**
Central Computer &

Telecommunications Agency
 (CCTA) **109**
Central Council for Education
 and Training in Social
 Work **73**
Central Council of Physical
 Recreation **256**
Central Direct **189**
Central Lancashire (Uni) **75**
Central Milton Keynes **239**
Central Office of
 Information **109**
Central Queensland
 University **77**
Central Reserve Bank of El
 Salvador **39**
Central School of Speech &
 Drama **71**
Central Science
 Laboratory **219**
Central Scotland (Chamber of
 Commerce) **35**
Central Trains **282**
Centre for Alternative
 Technology **84**
Centre for Buddhist
 Studies **164**
Centre for Medicines
 Research **129**
Centre for Photographic
 Art **152**
Centre for Policy Studies **109**
Centre for Recovery from Drug
 & Alcohol Abuse **137**
Centrepoint **136**
Centrica **41, 58, 161**
Century 105 (North West) **24**
Century 106 (Nottingham) **24**
Ceramics Monthly **148**
Ceredigion (Gov) **112**
Cerruti **8**
CGU **42-43, 189**
Challenge 2000 **149**
Challenge Anneka **27**
Challenge TV **26**
Chamber of Shipping **56**
Chamberlain Music **150**
Champagne Mumm Admiral's
 Cup **258**
Champions Tennis **261**
Champneys **158**
Chancellors **159**
Chandos (Record company) **22**
Chanel **8, 230**
Changing Rooms **27**
Channel 103FM (Channel
 Islands) **24**
Channel 4 **26**
Channel 4 Racing **252**
Channel 4 Schools **27, 65**
Channel 5 **26**
Channel Hoppers **278**
Channel One TV **265**
Channel Television **26**
Chaplins **231**

297

Chappells 150
Chapter, Cardiff 29
Chard (Gov) 113
Charity Commission 109
CharityCard 188
Charles Barker 35
Charles Church 160
Charles Jourdan 8
Charles Letts 235
Charles Rennie Mackintosh
    Store 235
Charles Schwab Europe 193
Charles Stanley & Co 193
Charles Tyrwhitt 224
Charles Worthington 158
Charlie Parker 15
Charlie's Angels 27
Charlotte Street 162
Charlotte/Douglas (Airport) 276
Charlton Athletic (FC) 250
Charnwood (Gov) 113
Charted Institute of
    Environmental Health
    Officers 49
Charter 88 108
Chartered Institute of
    Building 161
Chartered Institute of
    Environmental Health 129
Chartered Institute of
    Marketing 49, 52
Chartered Institute of Patent
    Agents 49
Chartered Institute of Public
    Finance & Accountancy 49
Chartered Institute of
    Purchasing & Supply 52
Chartered Institute of
    Taxation 49
Chartered Institute of
    Transport 49
Chartered Insurance
    Institute 192
Chartered Society of
    Physiotherapy 125
Charterhouse Bank 40
Chase De Vere 192
Chase Manhattan 39
Chase Manhattan Corp. 56
Chase Sport 260
Chatsworth House 200
Cheaney 241
Cheese Magazine 152
Chelmsford (Gov) 113
Chelmsford (Local info) 203
Chelmsford Woodham Weekly
    News 178
Chelsea (FC) 250
Chelsea Flower Show 147
Cheltenham & Gloucester
    (Building society) 187
Cheltenham (Gov) 113
Cheltenham (Local info) 203
Cheltenham (Racecourse) 253
Cheltenham College 74

Cheltenham Independent 178
Cheltenham News 178
Cheltenham Town (FC) 250
Chemical Brothers 16
Chemistry & Industry
    Magazine 218
Chemistry UK 218
Chepstow (Local info) 203
Chepstow (Racecourse) 253
Cher 16
Chertsey Museum 170
Cherwell (Gov) 113
Cheryl Ladd 3
Chesham (Building
    society) 187
Chesham (Local info) 203
Cheshire (Gov) 113
Cheshire (Police) 139
Cheshire Fire Brigade 139
Cheshire Guardian Series 178
Chessington World of
    Adventure 64
Chester (Gov) 113
Chester (Local info) 203
Chester (Racecourse) 253
Chester (Zoo) 219
Chester Chronicle
    Newspapers 178
Chester City (FC) 250
Chester le Street (Gov) 113
Chesterfield (Gov) 113
Chestertons 159
Chevrolet 156
Chevron 37, 56
Chez Gerard 95
Chicago 16
Chicago (Airport) 276
Chicago (Local info) 213
Chicago (Musical) 29
Chicago (Stock exchange) 53
Chicago Hope 27
Chicago Symphony 21
Chicco 240
Chicester (Gov) 113
Chichester (Local info) 203
Chichester Festival Theatre 29
Chichester Observer 178
Chicken Run 10
Child Accident Prevention
    Trust 135
Child of Achievement 158
Child Support Agency 109
ChildLine 67, 136
Children in Need 136
Children With Aids 136
Children's Book Council 66
Children's Society 136
Chile (Legal institutions) 106
Chilean (Embassy) 102
Chilean (Gov) 103
Chiltern (Gov) 113
Chiltern Hills 90
Chiltern Railways 282
Chilterns (Local info) 201
China (Tourist info) 205

China Airlines 274
China Internet Information
    Center 205
China Post 205
China Radio International
    (Beijing) 23
China Times (Taiwan) 182
China Today 205
Chinacraft 223
Chinatown London (Local
    info) 203
Chinese (Embassy) 102
Chinese (Gov) 103
Chinnor & Princes Risboroug
    (Railway) 199
Chiropractors' Association of
    Australia 125
Chivas 98
CHJS 35
Chloe 8
Choc Express 235
Chocolate Society 90
Choice 280
Chopin 16
Chorley Citizen 178
Chris Bonington 255
Chris De Burgh 16
Chris Isaak 16
Christadelphian 164
Christchurch (Gov) 113
Christchurch (Local info) 20
Christian Aid 138
Christian Bale 3
Christian Catacombs,
    Rome 207
Christian Democratic Party,
    Netherlands 107
Christian Fellowship
    Church 164
Christian Lacroix 8
Christie's 223
Christie's International 52
Christina Aguilera 16
Christopher Wray 239
Chrysler 156
Chubb 56, 189
Church Action on Poverty 14
Church and Co 241
Church of England 164
Church of Jesus Christ Latte
    Day Saints 164
Church of Scotland 164
Church Society 164
Churchill 189
Churnet (Railway) 199
Cibavision 131, 236
Cilla Black 27
Cincinnati (Airport) 276
Cindy Crawford 8
Cindy Margolis 8
Cinema Organ Society 11
Cinema Theatre Association
Cinemark 9
Cineworld 9
Circa 14

Circle 9
Circle of Wine Writers 90
Cirencester (Local info) 203
Ciro Citterio 224
Cisco 266
Citalia 283
Citibank 39-40
Citizen 243
Citizen (Gloucester) 178
Citizens Advice Bureau 136
Citizens Theatre, Glasgow 29
Citizens' Charter 109
Citroen 156
CITV 65
City & Guilds Institute 73
City (Uni) 76
City Art Gallery,
    Southampton 5
City Hospital, Birmingham 127
City Index 146
City Link 36
City of Birmingham Symphony
    Orchestra 21
City of London (Police) 139
City of London Festival 7
City of London Investment
    Group 190
CityLet 159
Citylink 277
Citywatch 191
Civic Trust 83
Civil Aviation Authority 146
Civil Justice Council 105
Civil Service College 73
CLA Game Fair 145
Clackmannan (Gov) 113
Clacton, Frinton & Walton
    Gazette 178
Claire Danes 3
Claire's Accessories 241
Clan Cameron Museum 170
Clan Donnachaidh
    Museum 170
Clangers 65
ClaraNet 266
Clarice Cliff 4
Clarins 230
Claris 265
Clarkes of London 277
Clarks 241
Clash 16
Classic Boat Magazine 259
Classic Camera Magazine 152
Classic Car Directory 156
Classic Car World 156
Classic FM 24
Classic Gold 24
Classic Gold Amber 24
Classic Motor 156
Classic Motor Boat
    Association 143
Classic Stitch 148
Claude Montana 8
Claudia Schiffer 8
Clay Pigeon Shooting

Association 145, 261
Clay Shooting Magazine 261
Cleopatra 16
Cleveland (Police) 139
Cleveland Fire Brigade 139
Cliff Richard 16
Clifford Chance 50
Clinical Trial Managers
    Association 129
Clinique 230
Clink Prison Museum 171
Clint Eastwood 3
Clipper Teas 90
Close Brothers Group 40
Close Shave 65
Club 18-30 283
Club 25 283
Club Mark Warner 282
Club Med 282
Cluedo 65
Cluttons 159
Clyde (Radio) 24
CMC Group 193
CNN 26, 177
CNN Cricket 249
Co-op (Bank) 187
Co-op (Insurance) 189
Co-op (Supermarket) 96
Co-op Travel 283
Co-operative Funeral
    Services 139
Coastguard Agency 139, 258
Coats Viyella 45
Cobbaton Combat
    Collection 171
Cobra 89
Coca-Cola 56, 90
Cocteau Twins 16
Coin Dealer Directory 144
Coin News 144
Coinco International 40
Coins & Antiquities
    Magazine 144
Colchester (Gov) 113
Colchester (Local info) 203
Colchester (Zoo) 219
Colchester Coastal
    Express 178
Colchester United (FC) 250
Cold Feet 27
Coldplay 16
Coldshield 237
Coleman Brothers 243
Coleraine (Gov) 113
Colgate 236
Colgate-Palmolive 56
College of Integrated Chinese
    Medicine 73, 125
College of Law 72
College of Optometrists 131
Collyer Bristow 50
Colne Valley (Railway) 199
Cologne (Airport) 276
Cologne (Local info) 206
Color Line 278

Color Me Beautiful 230
Colorado State University 78
Colorlab 230
Coloroll 243
Colour Craft Needlework 148
Colt 42
COLT Telecom Group 54
Columbia (Record
    company) 22
Columbia (Sports) 260
Columbia Tristar 12
Columbus 189
Com One 268
Comedy Store 6
Comet 228
Comic Relief 6, 136
Commercial Union 189
Commission for Architecture &
    the Built Environment
    (CABE) 83, 109
Commission for Racial
    Equality 109
Committee of the National
    Mapping Agencies of
    Europe 170
Commodore 265
Commonwealth Association of
    Architects 83
Commonwealth Bank of
    Australia 39
Commonwealth
    Secretariat 105
Commonwealth War Graves
    Commission 109
Communicable Disease
    Surveillance Centre 109
Communications Workers
    Union (CWU) 55
Communist Party 107
Communist Party, Russian
    Federation 107
Communist Party, USA 107
Community Development
    Foundation 12
Community Hygiene
    Concern 158
Community Media
    Association 13
Companies House 109
Company of Master
    Jewellers 243
Company of Water
    Conservators 44
Compaq 265
Compass 42
Compass Group 43
Compass Sport Magazine 150
Complainer 138
Compuserve Kids 67
Computer & Video Games 267
Computer Associates 56
Computer Exchange 240
Computer Shopper 267
Computer Weekly 267
Computeractive 267

Computing 267
Concrete Society 84
Conde Nast Traveller 280
Condor 278
Confederation of British
 Industry 52
Confederation of Roofing
 Contractors 161
Confetti 165
Congleton (Gov) 113
Congleton Guardian 178
Connells 159
Connex 282
Conoco 37
Conqueror 47
Conran Shop 231
Conservation Foundation 84
Conservative Party 107
Consett & Stanley
 Advertiser 178
Consignia 108
Console Domain 63
Consortium for European
 Research on Extragalactic
 Surveys 217
Consortium of Caterers and
 Administration in
 Education 96
Construction Employers
 Federation 161
Construction History
 Society 85
Construction Industry Board 84
Construction Industry
 Council 84
Construction Industry Research
 and Information
 Association 84
Consumer Gateway (DTI) 139
Consumers in Europe
 Group 139
Contact a Family 136
Contax 152
Contessa 224
Continental Airlines 56, 274
Continental Ballet 6
Continental Tyres 155
Contributions Agency 109
Conwy (Gov) 113
Cook Book Shop 223
Cooking for Kids 67
Cooking Light 95
Cookson Group 37
Cookson's Tools 237
Cookstown (Gov) 113
Cool FM (Belfast) 24
Cooper Tyre& Rubber
 Company 155
Copeland (Gov) 113
Copenhagen (Airport) 276
Copenhagen (Local info) 205
Copenhagen International
 Ballet 6
Copenhagen Post
 (Denmark) 182

Coppernob 224
Copping Joyce 159
Coptic Museum 205
Copyright Licensing Agency 13
Corby Press 159
Corgi 65, 149, 159, 242
CORGI (Gas Installers) 161
Cork (Local info) 207
Cork (Racecourse) 253
Corn Exchange, Cambridge 29
Corney & Barrow 95
Cornhill 189
Cornhill Direct 192
Cornish Guardian 178
Cornishman 178
Cornwall & Isles of Scilly (Health
 authority) 126
Cornwall (Gov) 113
Corona 89
Coronation Street 27
Corporation of London 113
Corporation of London Records
 Office (CLRO) 169
Corrs 16
Corsair 274
Corsair Marine 258
Corus Group 46
Cosatto 240
Cosmopolitan 162
Cosmos 283
Costa Rican (Embassy) 102
Costa Rican (Gov) 103
Costain 45
Cote d'Azur (Local info) 206
Cotswold 224
Cotswold (Gov) 113
Cotswold Outdoor 150
Cotton Moon 224
Coty 230
Coudert Brothers 50
Couloir 260
Council for British
 Archaeology 85
Council for Disabled
 Children 137
Council for Museums, Archives
 and Libraries 173
Council for Science &
 Technology 219
Council for the Central
 Laboratory 109
Council of Docked Breeds 151
Council of Europe 105
Council of Mortgage
 Lenders 192
Country Gentleman's
 Association 149
Country Landowners
 Association 83, 108
Country Life 160, 162
Countryside 197
Countryside Agency 84
Countryside Alliance 145
Countryside Council for
 Wales 84

Countryside Foundation 84
Countryside Foundation for
 Education 84
Countryside Residential 160
Countryside Watch 84
Countrysports 145
County 189
County Air Ambulance 135
County Needlecraft 148
County Sound (Surrey) 24
Courchevel (Local info) 206
Courier (Dundee) 178
Court Service of England &
 Wales 105
Courtauld Institute 5, 71
Courtaulds 45
Courteney Cox 3
Courvoisier 90
Covent Garden 240
Covent Garden Festival 7
Coventry (Gov) 113
Coventry (Local info) 203
Coventry (Rugby club) 257
Coventry (Uni) 76
Coventry Cathedral 200
Coventry City (FC) 250
Coventry Evening
 Telegraph 178
Cover Girl 230
Cowes Week 258
Cowper & Newton
 Museum 171
Coxless Fours 256
Crabtree & Evelyn 230
Craft Brewing Association 1
Craft Guild of Chefs 90
Craft UK 148
Crafts Council 13, 109
Crag Hoppers 260
Cragganmore 98
Craig Charles 3
Craig David 16
Craigavon (Gov) 113
Cranberries 16
Cranfield (Uni) 76
Cranwick 98
Crash Test Dummies 16
Craven (Gov) 113
Craven Herald & Pioneer 17
Crawley (Gov) 113
Crawley News 178
Crayola 66, 242
Crealy Park 64
Creation (Record company)
Creda 238
Credit Agricole, France 39
Credit Suisse Asset
 Management 190
Credit Suisse First Boston d
 Zoete & Bevan 193
Creditanstalt 39
Creetown Gem and Rock
 Museum 171
Cresta Holidays 283
Crewe & Nantwich (Gov) 11

Crewe & Nantwich Guardian 178
Crewe Alexandra (FC) 250
Cric Info 249
Cricketer International Magazine 249
Crimestoppers 108
Criminal Cases Review Commission 105
Criminal Justice System 105
Crimptech National 265
Crisis 136
Croatia (Legal institutions) 106
Croatia Airlines 274
Croatian (Gov) 103
Croatian National Bank 39
Crochet Design 148
Crocus 147
Cromwell (Hospital) 128
Cronus Airlines 274
Crosby, Stills, Nash & Young 16
Cross Country Skier Magazine 262
Crossair 274
Crossbreed & Mongrel Club 151
Crossflight 36
Crown 237
Crown Estates 106, 111
Crown Prosecution Service (CPS) 105, 109
Crowne Plaza 280
Crownwood Developments 160
Croydon (Gov) 113
Croydon (Health authority) 126
Crucible Theatre 259
Crufts 7, 151
Cruising Association 259
Crunchie 90
Crusaders 63
Crusaid 137
Crystal Holidays 283
Crystal Palace (FC) 250
Crème Egg 90
CSM Motorcycle Training 163
Cubana Airlines 274
Cucina Direct 238
Cucumberman 47
Cuervo 90
Culpeper 90, 230
Culture Club 16
Culture Net 211
Culture, Media & Sport 111
Cumberland News (Carlisle) 178
Cumbria (Gov) 113
Cumbria (Local info) 201
Cumbria Life 178
Cunard 283
Cure 16
Curragh (Racecourse) 253
Current Archaeology Magazine 85
Currys 228

Cutty Sark 171, 200
Cyber Patrol 269
Cybersnoop 269
Cyclamen Society 147
Cycling UK Directory 249
Cyclists Touring Club 249
Cygnet Training Theatre (Exeter) 71
Cynthia Lennon 4
Cypriot (Gov) 103
Cyprus (British embassy) 101
Cyprus (Tourist info) 205
Cyprus Airways 274
Cyprus News (Cyprus) 182
Cyprus Turkish Airlines 274
Cyrillus 224
Czech (Embassy) 102
Czech (Gov) 103
Czech Airlines 274
Czech National Bank 39
Czech Republic (British embassy) 101

D

Dacorum (Gov) 113
Daewoo 156
Daffy Duck 63
Daily Express 178
Daily Mail 42, 182
Daily Mail & General Trust 45
Daily Record 182
Daily Star 182
Daily Star (Bangaladesh) 182
Daily Star (Lebanon) 182
Daily Telegraph 182
Dairy Crest 41
Dalgety Arable 83
Dallas (Local info) 213
Dallas Fort Worth (Airport) 276
Daltons Antiques 223
Daltons Weekly 239
Dalwhinnie 98
Damart 224
Dame Edna 6
Damon Hill 255
Dan 280
Dance School of Scotland 71
Dance Umbrella 7
Dancer in the Dark 10
DanceSport UK 145
Danepak 90
Danger Mouse 63
Daniel Day-Lewis 3
Daniel Galvin 158
Danielle Steel 13
Danish (Embassy) 102
Danish (Gov) 103
Danka Business Systems 37
Danmarks Nationalbank 39
Dannii Minogue 16
Danny La Rue 6
Danone 90
Darlington & Stockton Times 178
Darlington (Building

society) 187
Darlington (FC) 250
Darlington (Gov) 113
Darlington Northern Echo 178
Dartford & Gravesham (Hospital) 127
Dartington Crystal 223
Dartmoor (Local info) 201
Dartmoor (Railway) 199
DAS 189
DASCO 241
Data Protection Registrar 109, 140
Dateline 157
Daventry (Gov) 113
Daventry Express 178
David Boreanaz 3
David Bowie 16
David Cassidy 16
David Clulow 131
David Copperfield 14, 27
David Coulthard 255
David Essex 16
David Ginola 255
David Knopfler 16
David Leadbetter 255
David Lloyd Leisure 158
David S Smith 47
David Schwimmer 3
David Wilson Homes 160
Davidoff 242
Davies Arnold Cooper 50
Dawson & Son 242
Dawson's Creek 27
Daytona 149
DC Comics 66
DC Thomson 48
De Beers 238
De Dietrich 238
De La Rue 52
De Montfort (Uni) 76
De Montfort Hall, Leicester 29
De Montfort University 71
De Nederlandsche Bank 39
De Vere 280
De Walt 237
Dean Friedman 16
Dean Gallery 5
Debenhams 52, 231
DEC 265
Decca 22
Deck Chair Com 283
Deep Purple 16
Deep Sea World 202
Dehli (Airport) 276
DejaNews 268
Del Amitri 16
Delhi (Local info) 207
Delia Smith 90
Delifrance 90
Deliverance 94
Dell 265
Deloitte & Touche 50
Delphi Magazine 218
Delta 274

Delta Airlines 56
Democracy Movement 108
Democratic Party,
   Australia 107
Democratic Party, USA 107
Democratic Unionist Party,
   Northern Ireland 107
Demon 265-266
Dempsey & Makepeace 27
Denbighshire (Gov) 113
Denham Aerodrome 146
Denman Brushes 236
Denmark (British embassy) 101
Dennis 35
Dennis Group 156
Dennis the Menace 65
Denplan 126, 189
Dental Anxiety & Phobia
   Association 126
Dental Practice Board 126
Denton Hall 50
Denver (Airport) 276
Denver (Local info) 213
Department for Culture, Media
   & Sport 13
Department for Work, Family
   and Pensions 111
Department of Education for
   Northern Ireland 111
Department of Environment,
   Transport & the Regions 84
Department of the Environment
   for Northern Ireland 111
Department of Work &
   Pensions 111
Depeche Mode 16
Depression Alliance 137
Derby (Gov) 113
Derby (Local info) 203
Derby (Uni) 76
Derby County (FC) 250
Derby Evening Telegraph 178
Derbyshire (Cricket club) 248
Derbyshire (Gov) 113
Derbyshire (Local info) 201
Derbyshire (Police) 139
Derbyshire Dales (Gov) 113
Derbyshire Times 178
Derngate Theatre,
   Northampton 29
Derry (Gov) 113
Derwentside (Gov) 113
Des O'Connor 27
Des'ree 16
Design Council 109
Design Museum 171
Designers Guild 231
Destination Group 283
Destiny's Child 16
Detecnicks 149
Detroit (Airport) 276
Detroit (Local info) 213
Deutsche Bank 39
Deutsche Bundesbank 39
Developers Review 218

Devizes (Gov) 113
Devon & Cornwall (Police) 139
Devon (Gov) 113
Devon (Local info) 201
Dew of Ben Nevis 98
Dewynters 35
DFDS Seaways 278
Dhaka (Local info) 197
DHL 36
Diabetes Insight 137
Diageo 41-42
Dial Direct 189
Diamond Cable 265
Dian Fossey Gorilla Fund 135
Diana Memorial Fund 136
Diana Ross 16
Diana, Princess of Wales
   (Obituary) 106
Diana, Princess of Wales Centre
   for Reproductive
   Medicine 129
Dibb Lupton Alsop 50
Dick Tracy 63
Dickens House Museum 171
Didcot (Local info) 203
Diego Maradona 255
Diesel 224
Digital 265
Digital Arts Development
   Agency 13
Digital Photography
   Review 152
Dilbert 6, 63
Dillons 223
Dimension Films 12
Diners Club 188
Dinghy Trader 259
Dinosaur Museum 171
Dior 230
Direct 189
Direct Car Hire 278
Direct Connection 267
Direct Debit 191
Direct Hit 268
Direct Holidays 283
Direct Line 189
Directors' Guild of Great
   Britain 11, 22-23
Disability Now 137
Disabled Living
   Foundation 137
Discovery (TV) 26
Discovery Channel 65
Discovery Point 171
Disney 12
Disney Channel 26, 65
Disney Cruises 283
Disney Interactive 67
Disneyland (Japan) 207
Disneyland California 212, 282
Disneyland Paris 206, 282
Disneyworld Florida 212, 282
Diver Magazine 261
Divertimenti 238
Divine Comedy 16

Dixie Chicks 16
Dixons 42, 52, 228, 241
DJ Freeman 50
DKNY 224
DMBB 35
Dockers 224
Docklands & City 162
Docklands Light Rail 282
Doctor Dolittle 29
Dog Club UK 151
Dogpile 268
Dogs Online 151
Dogs Today 151
Dogs Worldwide 151
Dolce & Gabbana 8
Dolcis 241
Dolland & Aitchison 131
Dolly Parton 16
Dollywood 212
Dolphin 237, 268
Domain Furniture 231
Dome 64
Dominican (Gov) 103
Dominican Republic (Tourist
   info) 204
Domino's Pizza 94
Don Bradman 255
Don Johnson 3
Donaldson 224
Doncaster (Gov) 113
Doncaster (Health
   authority) 126
Doncaster (Racecourse) 253
Donegal (Local info) 207
Donington (Local info) 203
Donington Park (Motor
   racing) 254
Donkey Sanctuary 135
Donmar Warehouse 29
Donny & Marie Osmond 16
Doobie Brothers 16
Doonsbury 63
Doors 16
Doris Day 3
Dorking & Leatherhead
   Advertiser 178
Dorling Kindersley 48, 66, 22?
Dorothy Perkins 224
Dorset (Chamber of
   Commerce) 35
Dorset (Gov) 113
Dorset (Health authority) 126
Dotmusic 14
Douala (Local info) 204
Douglas Adams 13
Douwe Egberts 91
Dove Cottage (The Wordswo
   Museum) 5
Dover (Gov) 113
Dover (Local info) 203
Dover Museum 171
Dow Chemical 56
Dow Jones 53
Down (Gov) 113
Down Royal (Racecourse) 2?

Downs Syndrome
  Association **137**
Dr Martens **241**
Dr Pepper **91**
Dr Quinn Medicine Woman **27**
Dr Seuss **67**
Dragon Air **274**
Drama Centre London **71**
Drambuie **91**
Draper Tools **237**
Drawing Down the Moon **158**
Drayton Manor **64**
Dream Travel Africa **283**
Dresdner Kleinwort Benson **39**
Dressmart.com **224, 239**
Drinking Water
  Inspectorate **140**
Drive **156**
Driver & Vehicle Licensing
  Agency (DVLA) **109**
Drivers Jonas **159**
Driving Standards Agency
  (DSA) **110**
Dryden Brown **35**
Du Pont **56**
Dualit **238**
Dubai (Airport) **276**
Dubai (Tourist info) **212**
Dublin (Airport) **276**
Dublin (Local info) **207**
Dublin (Vet school) **78**
Dublin (Web cam) **213**
Dublin (Zoo) **220**
Ducal **231**
Ducati **163**
Ducati Owners Club GB **163**
Duckworth **155**
Duckworth Finn Grub
  Waters **35**
Dudley (Gov) **113**
Dudley (Health authority) **126**
Dudley (Zoo) **220**
Due South **27**
Duke of Edinburgh's Award
  Scheme **63, 150**
Dulux **237**
Dulwich College **74**
Dumbo **63**
Dumfries & Galloway (Gov) **113**
Dun & Bradstreet **49**
Dunaskin Open Air
  Museum **171**
Dunbarton (Gov) **113**
Duncombe Park **200**
Dundas Castle **198**
Dundee (Gov) **113**
Dundee (Uni) **76**
Dundee Courier **178**
Dundee Evening Telegraph **178**
Dundee Weekly News **178**
Dunfermline Athletic (FC) **250**
Dungannon (Gov) **113**
Dungannon (Rugby club) **257**
Dunkin' Donuts **94**
Dunlopillo **223**

Dura **47**
Duracell **228**
Duralay **231**
Duran Duran **16**
Durban (Local info) **210**
Durex **236**
Durham (City) (Gov) **113**
Durham (County) (Gov) **113**
Durham (Cricket club) **248**
Durham (Local info) **201**
Durham (Police) **139**
Durham (Uni) **76**
Durham Cathedral **200**
Durlacher Corporation **193**
Dusseldorf (Airport) **276**
Dutch (Chamber of
  Commerce) **36**
Dutch (Gov) **103**
Duvel **89**
Duwit **237**
DVDplus **240**
Dwight Yoakam **16**
Dyfed & Powys (Police) **139**
Dyson **238**

E

E*TRADE United Kingdom **193**
E-17 **16**
E-Bookers **283**
E-cycles **249**
E-Toys **242**
Eagle Star **189**
Ealing (Gov) **113**
Ealing - NTFS **12**
Ealing, Hammersmith &
  Hounslow (Health
  authority) **126**
Earls Court Olympia **25**
Early Learning Centre **242**
Earthscan **48**
Earthwatch **84**
EASDAQ **53**
Easier **159**
Easington (Gov) **114**
East 15 Acting School **71**
East African Standard
  (Kenya) **183**
East Anglian Daily Times **178**
East Ayrshire (Gov) **114**
East Devon (Gov) **114**
East Dorset (Gov) **114**
East Dunbartonshire (Gov) **114**
East Grinstead (Gov) **114**
East Grinstead (Local info) **203**
East Grinstead Courier **178**
East Grinstead Observer **178**
East Hampshire (Gov) **114**
East Hertfordshire (Gov) **114**
East is East **10**
East Kent (Health
  authority) **126**
East Lancashire Light
  (Railway) **199**
East Lindsey (Gov) **114**
East London & The City (Health

authority) **126**
East London (Uni) **76**
East London Advertiser **178**
East Lothian (Gov) **114**
East Northamptonshire
  (Gov) **114**
East of England (Chamber of
  Commerce) **35**
East of England Agricultural
  Society **83**
East Renfrewshire (Gov) **114**
East Riding (Gov) **114**
East Surrey (Health
  authority) **126**
East Sussex (Gov) **114**
East Sussex, Brighton & Hove
  (Health authority) **126**
Eastbourne (Gov) **114**
Eastbourne Herald **178**
Eastenders **27**
Eastern **58**
Eastern Airways **274**
Eastern Caribbean Bank **39**
Eastern Counties
  Newspapers **48**
Eastern Energy **161**
Eastern Group **162**
Eastleigh (Gov) **114**
Eastleigh Lakeside
  (Railway) **199**
Eastleigh Museum **171**
Eastman Dental Institute **73**
Eastman Kodak **56**
Eastwood Advertiser **178**
Easy Rentacar **278**
EasyJet **274**
Ecclesiological Society **85**
Ecco **241**
Eclipse **283**
ECM **22**
EcoKids **67**
Ecologist **218**
Economic and Social Research
  Council **109**
Economic History Society **169**
Economist **44**
Ectopic Pregnancy Trust **137**
ECU **187**
Eddie Bauer **224**
Eddie Irvine (Fan Club) **255**
Eddie Izzard **6**
Eden (Gov) **114**
Eden Camp Modern History
  Museum **171**
Eden Court Theatre,
  Inverness **29**
Edge & Ellison **50**
Edge2Edge **242**
Edinburgh (Gov) **114**
Edinburgh (Local info) **203**
Edinburgh (Uni) **76**
Edinburgh (Vet school) **78**
Edinburgh (Zoo) **220**
Edinburgh and Lothians (Local
  info) **201**

Edinburgh and Lothians Tourist
  Board **202**
Edinburgh City Art Centre **5**
Edinburgh Echo **179**
Edinburgh Festival **7**
Edinburgh Fringe Festival **7**
Edinburgh Fund Managers **190**
Edinburgh University
  Library **169**
EDME **148**
Edradour **98**
Education & Skills **111**
Education Show **72**
Edward Jones **193**
Efteling **209**
Egerton **159**
Egg **187**
Egg-Free Zone **191**
Egham (Local info) **203**
Egypt (Legal institutions) **106**
Egypt (Tourist info) **205**
Egypt Government Information
  Service **23**
Egyptian (Embassy) **102**
Egyptian (Gov) **103**
Egyptian Gazette **205**
Egyptian Museum **205**
Eidos **37, 265**
Eiffel Tower, Paris **206**
eightseven3 2GB (Sydney) **23**
Eindhoven (Local info) **209**
EJ Riley **259**
El Al **274**
Electoral Reform Society **108**
Electric Library **268**
Electricity Association **161**
Electrolux **238**
Electronic Data Systems **56**
Elegant Resorts
  International **283**
Elemental Discoveries **218**
Elephant **189**
Elgar Society **149**
Elgin Museum **171**
Eli Lilly **47, 56**
Elisabeth Smith **46**
Elite **46**
Elite Registrations **155**
Elizabeth **10**
Elizabeth Arden **230**
Elizabeth Arden Red Door
  Salons **158**
Elizabeth Garrett Anderson **127**
Elle **162**
Ellis Brigham **242**
Elmbridge (Gov) **114**
Elmbridge Museum **171**
Elmhurst School for Dance &
  Performing Arts **71**
Elonex **265**
Elounda Beach **280**
Elsham Hall Country & Wildlife
  Park **200**
Elstree **12**
Elton John **16**

Elvi **224**
Elvis Costello **16**
Elvis Presley **16**
Ely Cathedral **200**
Ely Fund Managers **190**
Emap **42**
Embassy World Darts **249**
Embassy World Snooker **259**
Embroiderers' Guild **148**
Emeraude Lines **278**
Emerson Lake & Palmer **16**
EMI **42**
EMI Chrysalis **22**
Eminem **16**
Emirates (UAE) **274**
Emma Bunton **16**
Emmerdale **27**
Emmys (Academy of Television
  Arts & Sciences) **26**
Empire **9**
Empire Direct **239**
Empire State Building, New
  York City **212**
Empire Stores **224**
Empire Theatre, Sunderland **29**
Employment Appeal
  Tribunal **105**
Employment Service **110**
Encarta **169**
Enchanted Learning **67**
Encyclopedia **169**
End of Days **10**
End of the Affair **10**
Endsleigh **189**
Endurance Horse and Pony
  Society **148**
Energie **8**
Energis **42, 54, 268**
Energy Saving Trust **84, 159**
Energy Shop **160**
Energy-Efficient Building
  Association **84**
Enfield & Haringey (Health
  authority) **126**
Enfield (Gov) **114**
Engineering & Physical
  Sciences Research
  Council **219**
Engineering and Physical
  Sciences **109**
England (FC) **250**
England 2006 **251**
English Basketball
  Association **247**
English Bowling
  Association **247**
English Bridge Union **144**
English Civil War Society **169**
English Cricket Board **248**
English Federation Of Disability
  Sport **247**
English Golf Union **251**
English Heritage **85, 169**
English Ice Hockey
  Association **262**

English Lakeland
  Ramblers **150**
English National Ballet
  School **6, 71**
English National Board for
  Nursing, Midwifery and
  Health Visiting **130**
English National Opera **21**
English Nature **84**
English Playing Card
  Society **144**
English Pool Association **14?**
  259
English Regional Arts Boards
English Rugby Union **257**
English Schools Athletics
  Association **247**
English Schools' Badminton
  Association **247**
English Table Tennis
  Association **261**
English Teddy Bear
  Company **242**
English Tourism Council **202**
English Welsh and Scottish
  Railways **282**
English Welsh Railway **282**
English-Speaking Union **136**
Enid Blyton **67**
Enigma **16**
Enterprise **267, 278**
Enterprise Oil **37**
Enterprise Zone **110**
Entrapment **10**
Enuresis Resource &
  Information Centre **137**
Environment Agency Wales
Environment, Food & Rural
  Affairs **111**
Environmental Transport
  Association **86**
Enya **16**
Epic **22**
Epilepsy Research
  Foundation **137**
Eplay **67**
Epping Forest (Gov) **114**
Epsom & Banstead Herald **1?**
Epsom (Gov) **114**
Epsom (Local info) **203**
Epsom (Racecourse) **253**
Epson **152, 265**
Equal Opportunities
  Commission **110**
Equality Commission for
  Northern Ireland **110**
Equitable Life **189**
Equity British Actors' Union
ER **27**
Ercol **231**
Erewash (Gov) **114**
Eric Carle **67**
Eric Clapton **16**
Ericsson **265, 268**
Erna Low **283**

Ernest Jones **238**
Ernst & Young **50**
Errol Flynn **3**
Escada **8**
Escher **4**
Esporta **43, 158**
Esprit **8, 268**
Esquire **162**
Essex (Ambulance) **135**
Essex (Cricket club) **248**
Essex (Gov) **114**
Essex (Police) **139**
Essex (Uni) **76**
Essex Chronicle Series **179**
Essex County Newspapers **179**
Essex County Standard **179**
Essex FM **24**
Essex Weekly News **179**
Esso **157**
Estate Agents
  Ombudsman **140**
Estonian (Embassy) **102**
Estonian (Gov) **103**
Eton College **74**
Eudora **265**
Eureka The Museum For
  Children **171**
Eureka! **64**
Euro TV **26**
Eurobell **268**
Eurolines **277**
Euromoney **44**
Euromoney Online **191**
Europcar **278**
European Table Tennis
  Union **261**
European & Mediterranean
  Archery Union **261**
European Agency for the
  Evaluation of Medicinal
  products **130**
European Agency of
  Information on Consumer
  Affairs **139**
European Association of
  Archaeologists **85**
European Athletic
  Federation **247**
European Business Forum **44**
European Canoe
  Association **248**
European Central Bank **39, 105**
European Central Securities
  Depositories Association **49**
European Commission **105**
European Construction
  Institute **84**
European Court of Human
  Rights **105**
European Court of Justice **105**
European Festivals
  Association **7**
European Investment Bank **105**
European Masters **252**
European Monetary Union **105**

European Newspaper
  Publishers Association **183**
European Parliament **105**
European Space Agency **217**
European Stockbrokers **193**
European Trade Union
  Confederation **105**
European Union **101, 105**
Eurostar **282**
Eurotunnel **56**
EVA Air **274**
Evander Holyfield **255**
Evans **224**
Evel Knieval **255**
Evening Argus (Brighton) **179**
Evening Herald (Plymouth) **179**
Evening Press (York) **179**
Evening Standard **179, 202**
Evening Telegraph
  (Peterborough) **179**
Ever Ready **228**
Everest **237**
Eversheds **51**
Everton (FC) **250**
Everyman Theatre **29**
Everyman Theatre,
  Cheltenham **29**
Everyman Theatre,
  Liverpool **29**
Everything But The Girl **16**
Evesham, Cotswold, Stratford
  Journal **179**
Evian **91**
Evidence-Based Nursing **128**
Evita **29**
Ewan McGregor **3**
Exbury Gardens **200**
Exchange & Mart **239**
Excite **268**
Executive Club **158**
Exeter (Airport) **277**
Exeter (Chamber of
  Commerce) **35**
Exeter (Gov) **114**
Exeter (Local info) **203**
Exeter (Uni) **76**
Exeter Cathedral **200**
Exmoor (Local info) **201**
Expedia **283**
Expelair **237**
Expoland (Local info) **207**
Express (Tanzania) **183**
Express and Star Online (West
  Midlands) **179**
Express Bookshop **223**
Express Dairies **41**
Express Finance **187**
Express Newspapers **48**
Exxon **56**
Exxon (Esso) **37**
Eye Clinic **131**
Eyes Wide Shut **10**

F

F1 Today **255**

F1-Live **255**
FA Carling Premiership **251**
Fabian Society **108**
Factors & Discounters
  Association **49**
Fairplay **53**
Fairport Convention **16**
Fairview **160**
Fairy Tale **65**
Faith **241**
Faith Hill **16**
Fakenham (Local info) **203**
Falcon **249**
Falkirk (Gov) **114**
Falkirk (Local info) **203**
Falkirk Herald **179**
Falkland Islands (Tourist
  info) **205**
Falklands Islands
  Government **107**
Families Need Fathers **136,
  158**
Family Planning
  Association **158**
Family Records Centre **147**
Family Tree Magazine **147**
Famous Grouse **98**
Fanciers Breeder Referral
  List **151**
Fantasy Island **64**
Fanzine **251**
FAO Schwartz **242**
Far East Prisoners of War **163**
Fareham (Gov) **114**
Farham (Local info) **203**
Farlows **242**
Farmers Weekly **44**
Farmers Weekly Interactive **83**
Farmers' Union of Wales **83**
Faro (Airport) **276**
Faro (Local info) **210**
Farrow & Ball **243**
Fascinating Aida **6**
Fashion Café **8, 95**
Fashion UK **8**
Fast Show **27**
Fastnet Race **258**
Fat Face **224**
Fat Shaft **260**
Fatboy Slim **17**
Fatty Arbuckle's **95**
Fauna & Flora International **217**
Fay Weldon **13**
FCB **35**
Federal Express **36, 56**
Federal Reserve Bank, San
  Francisco **39**
Federation Internationale de
  l'Automobile (FIA) **255**
Federation Internationale de
  Natation Amateur (FINA) **261**
Federation of Bakers **96**
Federation of European
  Motorcyclists'
  Associations **163**

Federation of Family History Societies **147**
Federation of Independent Detectorists **149**
Federation of Independent Nursing Agencies **130**
Federation of International Cricketers **248**
Federation of International Polo **256**
Federation of Master Builders **161**
Federation of Recruitment and Employment Services **55**
Federation of Roller Skating **254**
Federation of Small Business **52**
Federation of Students Islamic Societies **165**
Federation of the Electronics Industry **55**
Felicity J Lord **159**
Feline Advisory Bureau **151**
Felinfoel **89**
Felix the Cat **63**
Felixstowe (Gov) **114**
Fell Runners Association **150**
Fender **150**
Fenland (Gov) **114**
Fenn Wright & Manson **224**
Fenwick Elliot **51**
Fermanagh (Gov) **114**
Ferodo **155**
Ferragamo **8**
Ferrari **156**
Ferrari (Motor racing teams) **255**
Festival de Marseille **206**
Festival Theatre, Chichester **29**
Festival Theatre, Edinburgh **29**
Ffestiniog (Railway) **199**
FHM **162**
Fiat **156**
Fidelity **190**
Fidelity Federal Savings Bank **39**
Field & Trek **150**
Field Fisher Waterhouse **51**
Field Hockey **252**
Field Hockey Foundation **252**
Field Magazine **85, 145**
Field Studies Council **219**
FIFA **251**
Fife (Gov) **114**
Fiji (British embassy) **101**
Fiji (Tourist info) **210**
Fila **242**
Filey (Local info) **203**
Film & Video Umbrella **13**
FilmFour **12, 26**
Filofax **47**
Financial Accounting Standards Board **49**
Financial Mail on Sunday **182**

Financial Reporting Council **49**
Financial Services Authority **192**
Financial Services Consumer Panel **192**
Financial Times **182**
Findhorn Foundation **164**
Fine Art Trade Guild **22**
Fine Line Features **12**
Finelist **155**
Finish **159**
Finland (British embassy) **101**
Finland (Tourist info) **205**
Finlandia Vodka **91**
Finlaystone Country Estate **201**
Finnair **274**
Finnish (Embassy) **102**
Finnish (Gov) **103**
Finsbury Asset Management **190**
Fiorelli **8**
Fiorucci **8**
Fire Brigade Union **139**
Firearms News **261**
Fireworks Safety Campaign **108**
Firkin **89**
First Active **187**
First Call **31**
First Cheque 2000 **136**
First Chicago **39**
First Choice **283**
First Choice Holidays **43**
First Direct **187**
First Empire Magazine **169**
First Great Western **282**
First Group **277**
First North Western **282**
First Technology **45**
First Telecom **268**
First Trust **187**
First-e **187**
FirstGroup **56**
FISA **256**
Fischer **47**
Fish! **95**
Fish4 **268**
Fish4 Cars **155**
Fisher Price **66, 242**
Fishermans Friends **91**
Fishers Farm Park **201**
Fishing UK **145**
Fishing World **146**
Fitzwilliam Museum **171**
Five **17**
Five Ways Express **36**
FKI **45**
Flambards Village **64**
Flanders Fields **198**
Flanders Opera **198**
Flash Gordon **63, 65, 67**
Fleadh Festival **7**
Fleet NewsNet **156**
Fleet Support Group **155**
Fleming **187**

Flemings **190**
Flex Magazine **143**
Flextech **46**
Flintshire (Gov) **114**
Flintstones **63**
Floodlight **72, 75**
Flora Locale **217**
Florajac's **147**
Florence Nightingale **171**
Florence Nightingale Foundation **130**
Florida State University **78**
Flower & Plant Association **1**
Flowers Direct **231**
Fly Dressers' Guild **146**
Fly Fishing UK **146**
Flyer **146**
Flying Scotsman (Railway) **1**
Flymo **147**
Flypark **282**
Focus **152**
Focus Do-it-All **237**
Fodor's Guide **280**
Fogarty **231**
Food from Britain **94**
Football 365 **251**
Football Association **251**
Football Club Credit Cards **1**
Football Football **95**
Football Supporters' Association **251**
Football World **64**
Footjoy **260**
Forbes **44**
Ford **156**
Ford Motor **56**
Fordy Homes **160**
Fore Magazine **252**
Foreign & Colonial **190**
Foreign & Commonwealth Office **111**
ForeningsSparbanken (Swedbank) **39**
Forensic Science Society **21**
Forest Heath (Gov) **114**
Forest of Dean (Gov) **114**
Forestmere Health Farm **158**
Forestry Commission of Great Britain **110**
Forever Brandy **17**
Forexia **187**
Formes **240**
Fort Grey **171**
Fort William & Lochabar (Local info) **201**
Fort William (Local info) **203**
Forte & Le Meridien **280**
Forth FM (Edinburgh) **24**
Fortnum & Mason **94, 231**
Fosse the Musical **29**
Foster's **89**
Fostering Information Line **1**
Foundation for Art & Creative Technology **13**
Foundation for International

Spiritual Unfoldment **164**
Foundation for Traditional
 Chinese Medicine **125**
Foundation of Nursing
 Studies **130**
Fountains Abbey **200**
Four Seasons **280**
fourLearning **65**
Fox FM (Oxford) **24**
Fox Kids **65**
Foxfield (Railway) **199**
Foxtons **159**
Framlington **190**
France (British embassy) **101**
France (Grand Prix) **254**
France (Weather) **174**
FranceInLondon **239**
Frank Lloyd Wright **83**
Frank Sinatra **17**
Frank Usher **224**
Frankfurt (Airport) **276**
Frankfurt (Local info) **206**
Frankfurt (Stock exchange) **53**
Frankfurt Ballet **6**
Fraser Williams **50**
Frasier **27**
Fred Basset **63**
Fred Olsen Cruises **283**
Free Britain **108**
Free Church of Scotland **164**
Free UK **267**
Free4All **267**
Freedom **89**
Freeform Arts Trust **13**
Freemans **224**
FreeNet **267**
Freenetname **267**
Freeport **240**
Freeserve **54, 266-267**
Freeserve Revision **66**
Freewire **267**
FreeZone **267**
French (Embassy) **102**
French (Gov) **103**
French and Saunders **6**
French Connection **224**
French Sole **224**
Fresh Air FM **24**
Fresh FM (Adelaide) **23**
Fresh Food Company **91**
Fresh Food Cookbook **145**
Freshfields **51**
Freud Museum **171**
Friend & Falcke **159**
Friends **27**
Friends of the Earth **84, 108**
Friends of the Earth
 Scotland **84**
Friends of War Memorials **163**
Friends Provident **190**
Frogmore House **107**
Frosties **91**
Fruit Of The Loom **8**
FTSE **173**
Fugees **17**

Fuji Bank, Japan **39**
Fuji Film **152**
Fujitsu **265**
Fulham (FC) **250**
Fuller's **89**
Furbys **66**
Fursdon House **200**
Future Gamer **267**
Fyffes **91**
Fylde (Gov) **114**

G

G Plan **234**
G-Wizz **14**
G8 **105**
Gabbitas Guide to Independent
 Schools **74**
Gabrielle **17**
Gaggia **238**
Gaiety Theatre Isle of Man **29**
Gail Porter **3**
Gainsborough **160**
Galaxen, Arvika **211**
Galaxy **268**
Galaxy 105 (Yorkshire) **24**
Galaxy Kids **67**
Galaxy Radio **24**
Gallaher **41**
Galleria Outlet Centre **240**
Galleries Magazine **14**
Galleries of Justice **171**
Gallup Organisation **173**
Galpin Society **169**
Galway (Local info) **207**
Galway (Racecourse) **253**
Gambia (Tourist info) **206**
Gambian (Gov) **103**
Gamblers Anonymous **136**
Game **240**
Game Conservancy Trust **84,
 143, 217**
Game Store **242**
Gameplay **240**
GameSpot UK **267**
Gap **224**
Gap Kids **224**
Garbage **17**
Gardaland **207**
Garden **147**
Garden History Society **147**
Garden Shop **234**
Garden Visit & Travel
 Guide **201**
Gardeners' World **27, 147**
Gardner **146**
Garfield **63, 65**
Garmin **258**
Garry Kasparov **144**
Gartmore Investment **192**
Gartmore Investment
 Management **190**
Garuda Indonesia **274**
Gary Barlow **17**
Gary Player **255**
Gateshead (Gov) **114**

Gateshead Post **179**
Gateway **265**
Gateway Theatre, Chester **29**
Gatwick (Airport) **277**
Gatwick Express **282**
Gazette Series **179**
GB Philatelic Society **145**
GCSE Answers **66**
GCSE Bitesize Revision **66**
GEC **42, 238**
Gedling (Gov) **114**
Geest **41**
Geest Line **53**
Geffen **22**
Geffrye Museum **171**
Gendex Genealogical
 Index **147**
Genealogical Services
 Directory **148**
General Accident **159, 189**
General Chiropractic
 Council **125**
General Dental Council **126**
General Election **120**
General Electric **57**
General Medical Council **129**
General Mills **57**
General Motors **57, 157**
General Register Office,
 Northern Ireland **148**
General Register Office,
 Scotland **148**
General Trading Company **234**
Genesis **17**
Geneva (Airport) **276**
Geneva (Local info) **212**
Genie **267**
Gent (Local info) **198**
GENUKI, UK & Ireland
 Geneology **148**
Geoff Billington **255**
Geological Society **219**
Geomatics Canada **170**
George Benson **17**
George Clooney **3**
George Formby **6**
George Harrison **17**
George Michael **17**
George W Bush **107**
George Wimpey **45, 160**
Georgina von Etzdorf **224**
Gerber Foods **91**
Geri Halliwell **17**
German (Embassy) **102**
German (Gov) **103**
German (Parliament) **103**
Germany (British embassy) **101**
Germany (Grand Prix) **254**
Germany (Weather) **174**
Gerrard Group **190**
Gerry Marsden & the
 Pacemakers **17**
GH Institute **160**
Ghana (Tourist info) **206**
Ghana Airways **274**

Ghost **8, 224**
Gianfranco Ferre **8, 224**
Gibraltar (Tourist info) **206**
Gibraltar Chronicle
 (Gibraltar) **183**
Gibson **150**
Giftware Association **55**
Gilbert & George **4**
Gilded Balloon, Edinburgh **29**
Gillette **236**
Gillian Anderson **3**
Gin & Vodka Association of
 Great Britain **96**
Ginger Media Group **27**
Gingerbread **136**
Ginn **48**
Girl Guides **63**
Girl Talk **67**
Girl's World **67**
Gisborne (Local info) **209**
Give As You Earn **136**
Givenchy **8, 224, 230**
GKN **42, 45**
Gladiators **27**
Glamis Castle **198**
Glamorgan (Uni) **76**
Glasgow (Gov) **114**
Glasgow (Uni) **76**
Glasgow (Vet school) **78**
Glasgow (Zoo) **220**
Glasgow Angling Centre **146**
Glasgow Caledonian
 University **73, 76**
Glasgow Dental School **73**
Glasgow Evening Times **179**
Glasgow Herald **179**
Glasgow International Jazz
 Festival **7**
Glasgow Prestwick
 (Airport) **277**
Glasgow Rangers (FC) **250**
Glasgow School of Art **71**
Glass and Glazing
 Federation **161**
Glass Art Society **148**
Glastonbury (Local info) **203**
Glastonbury Abbey **200**
Glastonbury Festival **7**
Glaucoma Research
 Foundation **137**
Glaxo Wellcome **42, 47**
Glen Campbell **17**
Glen Miller Orchestra **17**
Glen Moray **98**
Glen Ord **98**
Glencoe **98**
Gleneagles (Golf course) **252**
Gleneagles (Hotel) **280**
Glenfarclas **98**
Glenfiddich **98**
Glengoyne **98**
Glenkinchie **98**
Glenlivet **98**
Glenmorangie **98**
Glenturret **98**

Glitter Band **17**
Global **267**
Global Asset Management **190**
Global Basketball News **247**
Global Registrations **155**
Global Tickets **31**
Globalaid **138**
Gloria Estefan **17**
Glossop (Local info) **203**
Gloucester (Gov) **114**
Gloucester (Rugby club) **257**
Gloucestershire (Gov) **114**
Gloucestershire (Health
 authority) **127**
Gloucestershire (Police) **139**
Gloucestershire Citizen **179**
Gloucestershire Echo **179**
Gloucestershire Warwickshire
 Steam (Railway) **199**
Glyndebourne **7**
GMTV **27**
GNI **193**
GNI Fund Management **190**
Go (Airline) **274**
Go Ahead **56, 278**
Go By Coach **280**
Go To **268**
Go-United States **213**
Goa (Local info) **207**
God Channel **26**
Godalming (Gov) **114**
Godiva **91**
Godzilla **10**
Going for Green **84, 108**
Going Places **283**
Goldcrest Homes **160**
Golden Earring **17**
Goldfish **188**
Goldfish Guide **239**
Goldschmidt Howland **159**
Goldsmiths **238**
Goldsmiths College London **76**
Golf **252**
Golf Channel **26, 252**
Golf Digest **252**
Golf Foundation of Britain **251**
Golf Monthly **252**
Golf Pride Grips **260**
Golf Today **252**
Golf.com **252**
Golfing Union of Ireland **251**
Gone in 60 Seconds **10**
Good Guide to Britain **202**
Good Holiday Guide **280**
Good Housekeeping **162**
Good Morning (Belgium) **183**
Good Schools Guide **72**
Good Ski Guide **252**
Goodnight Inn **280**
Goodwood (Racecourse) **253**
Goodyear **57**
Google **268**
Goole Times **179**
Goosebumps **67**
Gordon & MacPhail **98**

Gordon Scott **241**
Gordonstoun **74**
Gosport & Fareham Inshore
 Rescue Service **139**
Gosport (Gov) **114**
Gothenberg (Local info) **211**
Gothenburg (Airport) **276**
Gouldens **51**
Gourmet World **145**
Gourmet World **91**
Governess **10**
Government Communications
 Headquarters (GCHQ) **110**
Government Information
 Service **110**
GQ **162**
Gracie Fields Museum **171**
Graco **240**
Graff **238**
Graham & Brown **237**
Graham & Brown
 Wallcoverings **243**
Graham Norton **6, 27**
Grahams Port **91**
Grain and Feed Trade
 Association (GAFTA) **55**
Gramophone Magazine **14**
Grampian (Health
 authority) **127**
Grampian (TV) **26**
Grampian Transport
 Museum **171**
Granada **42, 230**
Granada (TV) **26**
Granada Group **43**
Granada Plus **26**
Granada Sky Broadcasting **2**
Grand Heritage **280**
Grand Marnier **91**
Grand National Archery
 Society **261**
Grand Opera House,
 Belfast **21, 29**
Grand Theatre, Leeds **30**
Grand Theatre,
 Wolverhampton **30**
Grant & Cutler **41**
Grant Thornton **50**
Grantown Museum **171**
Granville **187**
Grapeland **94**
Grapevine **22**
Graphic and Printworkers Uni
 (GPMU) **55**
Grateful Dead **17**
Grattan **226**
Gravesham (Gov) **114**
Grayling Society **146**
Graz (Local info) **197**
Grease **10, 29**
Great Britain Luge
 Association **262**
Great Central (Railway) **199**
Great Eastern Railway **282**
Great Mills **237**

Great North Eastern Railway **282**
Great Northern & East Lincolnshire (Railway) **199**
Great Ormond Street **127**
Great Portland Estates **51**
Great Universal Stores **52**
Great Yarmouth (Gov) **114**
Great Yarmouth Pleasure Beach **64**
Greater London Assembly & Mayor of London **114**
Greater Manchester (Police) **139**
Greece (British embassy) **101**
Greece (Tourist info) **206**
Greek (Gov) **103**
Green Flag **135**
Green Howards Regimental Museum **171**
Green Line **278**
Green Party, England & Wales **107**
Green Party, Scotland **107**
Green Party, Wales **107**
Greenhouse **95**
Greenland (Local info) **205**
Greenlandair **274**
Greenpeace International **84, 108**
Greens Health & Fitness **158**
Greenwich & Docklands Festival **7**
Greenwich (Gov) **114**
Greenwich (Uni) **76**
Greenwich Maritime Institute **74**
Greenwich Mean Time **217**
Greg Lake **17**
Greig Middleton **193**
Grenada (Tourist info) **204**
Gressenhall Norfolk Rural Life Museum **171**
Grey **35**
Greyhound Racing Board **146**
GRID - Global Resource Information Database (United Nations) **84**
Grimsby Evening Telegraph **179**
Grindlays **187**
Grindlays Private Banking **39**
Grocer **95**
Grolier **169**
Grolsch **89**
Grona Lund, Stockholm **211**
Groningen (Local info) **209**
Grosbous (Local info) **208**
Grosvenor House Art & Antiques Fair **7**
Group Line **31**
Gryphon **260**
Guardian **182**
Guardian **189**
Guardian **51**

Guardian (Nigeria) **183**
Guardian Royal Exchange **42**
Guardian Series Newspapers **179**
Gucci **8, 230, 241**
Guernsey (Chamber of Commerce) **36**
Guernsey (Post office) **108**
Guernsey (Tourist info) **204**
Guernsey Financial Services Commission **192**
Guernsey Museum & Art Gallery **5**
Guernsey Press (Guernsey Evening and Weekly Press) **179**
Guess **8**
Guggenheim, New York **212**
Guide to UK Boarding Schools **72**
Guild of Air Pilots and Air Navigators **44**
Guild of Architectural Ironmongers **83, 161**
Guild of Film Production Accountants & Financial Administrators **22**
Guild of Food Writers **90**
Guild of Silk Painters **148**
Guild of Television Cameramen **22**
Guild of Wedding Photographers **165**
Guildford (Gov) **114**
Guildford (Local info) **203**
Guildhall London **76**
Guildhall School of Music & Drama **71**
Guinness **89**
Gujarat (Local info) **207**
Gujarat Airways **274**
Gulf **37**
Gulf Air **274**
Gulf International Bank **39**
Gun Trade News **261**
Gunpowder Plot Society **149**
Guns N' Roses **17**
GUS **42, 226**
Guyana Airways **274**
Gwent (Health authority) **127**
GWR FM **24**
Gwynedd (Gov) **114**
Gwyneth Paltrow **3**
Gymboree **226**

H

H & M Hennes **226**
H Samuel **238**
Haagen Dazs **91**
Haart **159**
Habitat **234**
Hacker Young **50**
Hackett **226**
Hackney (Gov) **114**
Hackney Empire **25, 30**

Hadrian's Wall **200**
Hagar the Horrible **63, 67**
Hagenuk **268**
Hague (Local info) **209**
Haifa (Local info) **207**
Haines Watts **50**
Hale Clinic **127**
Halfords **155**
Halifax **40, 42, 187**
Hall & Oates **17**
Hall of Fame **202**
Hallam FM (Sheffield) **24**
Hallmark Cards **235**
Hallmark Group **145**
Halstead Gazette & Advertiser **179**
Halton (Gov) **114**
Hamble Week **258**
Hambleton (Gov) **114**
Hambros **187**
Hamburg Ballet **6**
Hamilton **187**
Hamilton Park (Racecourse) **253**
Hamleys **242**
Hamlyns **50**
Hammerite **155, 237**
Hammersmith & Fulham (Gov) **114**
Hammicks **223**
Hampshire (Ambulance) **135**
Hampshire (Cricket club) **248**
Hampshire (Gov) **115**
Hampshire (Police) **139**
Hampshire Chronicle **179**
Hampstead & Highgate Gazette **179**
Hampstead Theatre **30**
Hampton Court Palace **200**
Hampton Court Palace Flower Show **147**
Hamptons **159**
Hancock Museum **171**
Handbag.com **162**
Hannants **150**
Hannibal **10**
Hannover (Airport) **276**
Hanson **17, 42, 45**
Hapag-Lloyd Airlines **274**
Harborough (Gov) **115**
Harborough Mail **179**
Harbottle & Lewis **51**
Harbour Club **158**
Harbour Park **64**
Hard Candy **230**
Hard Rock Café **95**
Hardys **98**
Hare Krishna UK **165**
Harewood **200-201**
Haribo **91**
Haringey (Gov) **115**
Harland and Wolff Holdings PLC **53**
Harlequins (Rugby club) **257**
Harley-Davidson **163**

Harlow (Gov) **115**
Harlow Star **179**
Harmonie **91**
Harold Lloyd **3**
Harper Collins **48**
HarperCollins Childrens
   Books **67**
Harris **237**
Harris Carpets **234**
Harrison Ford **3**
Harrison Line **53**
Harrisons Rods **146**
Harrods **94, 231**
Harrogate (Gov) **115**
Harrogate Advertiser **179**
Harrow (Gov) **115**
Harry Connick Jr **17**
Harry Potter **67**
Harry Ramsden's **95**
Hart (Gov) **115**
Hartland **147**
Hartlepool (Gov) **115**
Hartlepool Mail **179**
Harvard Business Review **44**
Harvard University **78**
Harvey **170**
Harveys of Bristol **91**
Harvie & Hudson **226**
Harwich & Manningtree
   Standard **179**
Hasbro **242**
Hasbro **66**
Hasbro Interactive **66**
Hastings (Gov) **115**
Hastings Observer **179**
Hat Trick Productions **27**
Hatton Gallery, Newcastle-
   upon-Tyne **5**
Hatton Gallery, Tyne & Wear **5**
Havant (Gov) **115**
Have I Got News For You **27**
Havering (Gov) **115**
Hawaii Five-O **27**
Hawaiian Airlines **274**
Hawk & Owl Trust **217**
Hawkeshead **226, 242**
Hawkwind **17**
Haydock Park
   (Racecourse) **253**
Hayes Travel **283**
Haymarket, Basingstoke **30**
Haynes **156**
Haynes Motor Museum **171**
Hays **42, 51-52, 187**
Hays Allan **50**
Hayter **147**
Hayward Gallery **5**
Hazelmere **160**
Hazlewood Foods **41**
HDS **12**
Head **260**
Headwater **283**
Health **111**
Health & Safety Executive **110,
   161**

Health Centre **129**
Health Development
   Agency **247**
Health Education Authority **125**
Health Education Board of
   Scotland **125**
Health Service Journal **129**
Health Service
   Ombudsman **140**
Heart of Midlothian (FC) **250**
Heath Group **189**
Heatherwood & Wexham Park
   Hospitals (NHS Trust) **127**
Heathrow (Airport) **277**
Heathrow Express **282**
Heaven 17 **17**
Hebrides (Local info) **201**
Hedingham Castle **198**
Heffers **223**
Heineken **89**
Heinemann **48**
Heinz **91**
Heinz Direct **94**
Heinz-Harald Frentzen **255**
Helen Keller **13**
Helena Bonham-Carter **3**
Hellenic Star (Greece) **183**
Hello! **162**
Helly Hansen **260**
Helmut Lang **8**
Help the Aged **136**
Helsinki (Airport) **276**
Helsinki (Local info) **205**
Helsinki (Stock exchange) **53**
Hemel Hempstead
   Gazette **179**
Hemmington Scott **191**
Henderson **190**
Hendon Times Group **179**
Henley (Rugby club) **257**
Henley Festival **7**
Henley Royal Regatta **256**
Henley-on-Thames (Local
   info) **203**
Henlow Grange Health
   Farm **158**
Henlys **35**
Henri Lloyd **226**
Henry Moore Foundation **5**
Henry Purcell **17**
Herald & Post (Newcastle upon
   Tyne) **179**
Herald (Pakistan) **183**
Herald Investment
   Management **190**
Herb Society **147**
Herbert Smith **51**
Hercules **65**
Hereford Times **179**
Herefordshire (Gov) **115**
Heriot-Watt (Uni) **76**
Heritage Lottery Fund **13**
Heritage Motor Centre **171**
Heritage Seed Library **147**
Herm Island (Tourist info) **204**

Heron's Brook **64**
Hershey Foods **57**
Hertfordshire (Gov) **115**
Hertfordshire (Police) **139**
Hertfordshire (Uni) **76**
Hertfordshire Mercury **179**
Herts & Essex News **179**
Herts & Essex Observer **179**
Hertsmere (Gov) **115**
Hertz **278**
Hewlett Packard **57, 230, 260**
Hexagon, Reading **30**
HFC **187**
HHCL **35**
Hi-Fidelity **230**
Hi-Tec **260**
Hibernian Group **189**
Hickstead **259**
Hideous Kinky **10**
High & Mighty **226**
High Fidelity **10**
High Peak (Gov) **115**
Higher Education Funding
   Council for England **73**
Higher Education Funding
   Council for Scotland **73**
Higher Education Funding
   Council for Wales **73**
Highland (Gov) **115**
Highland Distillers **41**
Highland Park **98**
Highlands of Scotland (Local
   info) **201**
Highlands of Scotland Tourist
   Board **202**
Highways Agency **110**
Hilary & Jackie **10**
Hill Billy Powered Golf
   Trolleys **260**
Hill Samuel **190**
Hill Street Blues **28**
Hillingdon (Gov) **115**
Hillingdon (Health
   authority) **127**
Hillsdown Holdings **41**
Hilton **280**
Hilton Group **43**
Hilton Hotels **57**
Himachal Pradesh (Local
   info) **207**
Hinckley Times **179**
Hindu (India) (Newspaper) **1**
Hippodrome, Birmingham **3**
Hiroshima (Local info) **208**
Hirsh **238**
Hiscox **43, 189**
Historic Chapels Trust **85**
Historic Gardens
   Foundation **85**
Historic Houses Association
Historic Royal Palaces **200**
Historical Association **169**
Historical Diving Society **26**
Historical Model Railway
   Society **149-150**

Historiska Museet, Stockholm **211**
History - BBC Online **169**
History Today Magazine **169**
Hitachi **236, 265**
Hitchhikers Guide to the Galaxy **14**
Hitchin & Stevenage Advertiser **179**
HM Customs & Excise **110**
HM Land Registry **105, 110**
HM Prison Service **110**
HM Queen Elizabeth **106**
HM Queen Elizabeth, Queen Mother **106**
HM Stationery Office **110**
HM Treasury **111**
HM Treasury Euro Site **110**
HMS Belfast **171**
HMS Victory **171**
HMS Warrior **171**
HMSO **48**
HMV **22, 240**
Hobbycraft **242**
Hockey Network **252**
Hockey Player Magazine **262**
Hodder & Stoughton **48**
Hoechst **47**
Hogg Robinson **189**
Holburne Museum of Art **5**
Holby City **28**
Holding Company **234**
Holiday (TV programme) **28**
Holiday Autos **278**
Holiday Inn **280**
Holiday Which? **282**
Hollies **17**
Hollyoaks **28**
Hollywood **12**
Hollywood Reporter (USA) **183**
Holmes Place **158**
Holsten **89**
Holyroodhouse **107**
Home & Away **28**
Home & Capital Trust **187, 192**
Home Grown Cereals Authority **83**
Home Office **111**
Home Quote **189**
Home Service Force Association **163**
Homebase **237**
Homepride **91**
Homework Elephant **66**
Homework High **66**
Honda **157, 163**
Honda Owners Club GB **163**
Honest **10**
Honeywell **57, 265**
Honeyz **17**
Hong Kong (Airport) **276**
Hong Kong (British embassy) **101**
Hong Kong (Gov) **103**
Hong Kong (Legal

institutions) **106**
Hong Kong (Stock exchange) **53**
Hong Kong (Tourist info) **205**
Hong Kong Ballet **6**
Honolulu (Airport) **276**
Honolulu (Local info) **213**
Hootie & the Blowfish **17**
Hoover **238**
Hope University **128**
Horizon **28**
Horizon Foods **91**
Hornby **66, 150, 242**
Horncastle News **179**
Horniman Museum **171**
Hornsea Post **179**
Horse of the Year Show **259**
Horserace Betting Levy Board **253**
Horsham (Gov) **115**
Horwath Clark Whitehill **50**
Hoseasons **284**
Hospital Broadcasting Association **125**
Hospital Consultants & Specialists Association **129**
Hospital Doctor **129**
Hospital for Tropical Diseases **128**
Hot Tickets Direct **31**
HotBot **268**
Hotel & Catering International Management Association **49**
Hotpoint **238**
Houdini The Musical **29**
Hounslow (Gov) **115**
House & Garden **162**
House Beautiful **162**
House of Colour **158**
House of Commons **120**
House of Fraser **52, 231**
House of Lords **120**
House Removals.com **161**
Housebuilders Federation **161**
Houses of Parliament **200**
Housing Corporation **110**
Housing Forum **84**
Houston (Local info) **213**
Hover Travel **278**
Hovercraft Club of Great Britain **149**
Hoverspeed **278**
How Stuff Works **67**
Howard Jones **17**
Howletts Wild Animal Park **220**
Hoxton Hall **30**
HP Bulmer **89**
HRH Duke of York **106**
HRH Earl of Wessex **106**
HRH Prince of Wales **106**
HRH Prince Philip, Duke of Edinburgh **106**
HRH Princess Alexandra **107**
HRH Princess Margaret **107**
HRH Princess Royal **107**

HSBC **42, 187**
HSBC (Bank) **187**
HTV **26**
Hubble Space Telescope **217**
Hucknall Dispatch **179**
Huddersfield (Uni) **76**
Huddersfield Daily Examiner **179**
Huddersfield Town (FC) **250**
Huggies **240**
Hughes Allen **50**
Hugo Boss **8, 230**
Hula Hoops **91**
Hull (Uni) **76**
Hull City (FC) **250**
Hull Daily Mail **179**
Hull School of Architecture **71**
Hultsfredsfestivalen **211**
Human Cloning Foundation **219**
Human Genetic Advisory Commission **219**
Humberside (Police) **139**
Humberts **159**
Hungarian (Gov) **103**
Hunterian Art Gallery **5**
Hunterian Museum & Art Gallery **171**
Huntingdon (Racecourse) **253**
Huntingdonshire (Gov) **115**
Hunts Post **179**
Hurlingham Polo Association **256**
Hurriyet (Turkey) **183**
Hush Puppies **241**
Husqvarna **148**
Hutchinson (Encyclopaedias) **169**
Hutchison Telecom **268**
Hyndburn (Gov) **115**
Hyperion **22**
Hyperlinks **65**
Hyundai **157**

I

I Can't Believe It's Not Butter **91**
Ian Dury **17**
Ian Fleming **13**
Ian McKellen **3**
Ian St John's Soccer Camps **146**
Iberia (Airline) **274**
Ibiza (Airport) **276**
IBM **265**
ICC **187**
Ice Hockey UK **262**
Iceland (Supermarket) **52, 96**
Icelandair **274**
Icelandic (Gov) **103**
ICI **42**
Ideal Home Show **7**
Ideal Standard **237**
IG Index **146, 252**
Ikea **234**

Ikon 47
Ikon Gallery, Birmingham 5
Iman 9
Imax 9
Imperial Chemical
  Industries 36
Imperial College 76
Imperial College of Science,
  Technology & Medicine 73
Imperial Society of Teachers of
  Dancing (ISTD) 145
Imperial Tobacco 41-42
Imperial War Museum 171
IMRO 192
In-flight Nurses
  Association 130
Inchcape 35
Incorporated Association of
  Preparatory Schools 72, 74
Incorporated Society of British
  Advertisers 49
Incorporated Society of
  Musicians 22
Incorporated Society of Valuers
  & Auctioneers 161
Independence Day 10
Independent (Newspaper) 182
Independent Cat Society 219
Independent Complaints
  Reviewer to HM Land
  Registry 140
Independent Financial Advisers
  Association (IFA
  Association) 55, 192
Independent Footwear
  Retailers Association 243
Independent Insurance 43
Independent Publishers
  Guild 55
Independent Schools
  Directory 72, 74
Independent Schools
  Information Service 72, 74
Independent Television
  Commission 13
Independent Television
  Commission 140
Independent Theatre
  Council 13
Indesit 238
Index 231
India (British embassy) 101
India (Legal institutions) 106
India (Tourist info) 207
Indian (Embassy) 102
Indian Airlines 274
Indian Government 103
Indian Ocean Trading
  Company 234
Indiana University 78
Indonesia (British
  embassy) 101
Indonesian (Gov) 103
Indonesian Observer
  (Indonesia) 183

Infection Control Nurses
  Association 130
Information Britain 202
Infoseek 268
ING Bank, Netherlands 39
Ingersoll 161
Inghams 284
Ingrid Pitt 3
Inland Railway 211
Inland Revenue 110
Inland Waterways
  Association 143
Inliners 254
Innovations 241
Innsbruck (Local info) 197
Insect World 151
Inside Cable 265
Insitute of Export 52
Insolvency Service 110
Inspector Gadget 63
Institut Francais 75
Institute for Animal Health 83
Institute for Fiscal Studies 110
Institute for the Study of Drug
  Dependency 137
Institute of Actuaries 192
Institute of Advanced
  Motoring 158
Institute of Arable Crops
  Research 83
Institute of Biology 219
Institute of Biomedical
  Sciences 219
Institute of Brewing 96
Institute of Broadcast
  Sound 219
Institute of Building Control 55
Institute of Chartered
  Accountants 49
Institute of Chartered
  Accountants of Scotland 49
Institute of Chartered
  Engineers 49
Institute of Chartered
  Shipbrokers 53
Institute of Child Health 129
Institute of Contemporary
  Art 71
Institute of Contemporary
  Arts 4
Institute of Field
  Archaeologists 85
Institute of Financial
  Accountants 49
Institute of Food Research 83,
  96
Institute of Food Science &
  Technology 96, 125
Institute of Health Service
  Management 126
Institute of Heraldic &
  Genealogical Studies 148
Institute of Historical
  Research 169
Institute of Home Safety 161

Institute of Hydrology 219
Institute of Internal Auditors
Institute of Mental Health 13
Institute of Packaging 55
Institute of Paper 55
Institute of Plumbing 161
Institute of Practitioners in
  Advertising 49
Institute of Printing 55
Institute of Professional
  Investigators 49
Institute of Psychiatry 131
Institute of Psychotherapy &
  Social Studies 131
Institute of the Motor
  Industry 55
Institute of World Politics 10
Institution of Civil Engineers
Institution of Historic Building
  Conservation 85
Institution of Professionals
  Managers and Specialists
  (IPMS) 55
Institution of Structural
  Engineers 161
Insurance Institute of
  London 192
Insurance Ombudsman
  Bureau 140
Intel 57, 265
Interactive Investor
  International 191
InterBet 252
Intercontinental 280
Interflora 231
International Albert Schweitz
  Foundation 105
International Amateur Athleti
  Federation 247
International Amateur Boxing
  Association 248
International Animal
  Rescue 135
International Archery
  Federation 261
International Arts Bureau 13
International Association for
  Protection of Industrial
  Property 55
International Association of
  Travel Couriers 36
International Astronomical
  Union 217
International Atomic Energy
  Agency 105
International Badminton
  Federation 247
International Baseball
  Federation 247
International Basketball
  Federation 247
International Biathlon
  Union 262
International Billiards & Snoo
  Federation 259

International Bobsleigh &
Tobogganing Federation 262
International Bowling
Federation 247
International Boxing
Organisation 248
International Brewers' Guild 96
International Bulb Society 147
International Canoe
Federation 248
International Centre for Reiki
Training 164
International Chiropractors
Association 125
International Coatings 258
International Council of Jewish
Women 165
International Court of
Justice 105
International Cricket
Council 248
International Crisis Group 105
International Dance Sport
Federation 145
International Dance Teachers
Association (IDTA) 145
International Development 111
International Directory of Art
Libraries 14
International Equestrian
Federation 259
International Federation of
Accountants 50
International Federation of
Aromatherapists 125
International Federation of
Associated Wrestling
Styles 262
International Federation of
Associations of Private
Investigators 49
International Federation of
Body Builders 143
International Federation of
Chemical, Energy, Mine &
General Workers Unions 55
International Federation of
Netball Associations 255
International Feltmakers
Association 148
International Festival of
Chocolate 7
International Film Festival of
Wales 7
International Fund for Animal
Welfare 135
International Fund
Investment 191
International Gymnastics
Federation 252
International Handball
Federation 252
International Herald Tribune
(USA) 183
International Hockey

Federation 252
International Ice Hockey
Federation 262
International Judo
Federation 248
International Korfball
Federation 254
International League for the
Protection of Horses 135
International Life Saving
Federation 261
International Luge
Federation 262
International Maritime
Organisation 105
International Meteor
Organisation 217
International Monetary
Fund 105
International Movie
Database 14
International Musical
Eisteddfod 7
International Olympic
Committee 254
International Orienteering
Federation 150
International Paralympic
Committee 247, 254
International Pentathlon
Union 247
International Petroleum
Exchange (IPE) 53
International Playing Card
Society 144
International Practical Shooting
Confederation 261
International Racquetball
Federation 260
International Red Cross 105
International Rescue
Corps 139
International Roller Skating
Federation 254
International Rowing
Federation 257
International Rugby Board 257
International Sailing
Federation 258
International Shooting Sport
Federation 261
International Skating Union 262
International Ski
Federation 262
International Socialist
Organisation 107
International Society for Krishna
Consciousness 165
International Society of
Arboriculture 85
International Softball
Federation 259
International Sumo
Federation 262
International Surfing

Association 258
International Table Tennis
Federation 261
International Tennis
Federation 261
International Thespian
Society 13
International Triathlon
Union 247
International Underwriting
Association of London 192
International Union of
Architects 83
International Volleyball
Federation 262
International Water Ski
Federation 258
International Weightlifting
Federation 262
International Wildlife
Coalition 217
International Wine
Challenge 98
International Women's Polo
Association 256
International Workshop
Festival 7
International Zen
Association 164
Internet Bookshop 223
Internet Chess Club 144
Internet Squash
Federation 260
Internet Travel Services 284
Interpac 161
Interpol 139
Intersail 258
Intersport 242
InterSure 189
Intoto 238
Invensys 37, 42
Inverleith House, Edinburgh 5
Invesco 190
Investec Guinness Flight 191
Investment & Pensions
Europe 191
Investment Trust
Newsletter 191
Investment Week 44
Investors Chronicle 191
Investors Compensation
Scheme (ICS) 192
Investors Internet Journal 191
Invicta FM (Kent) 24
Iomega 265
Iowa State University 78
Ipswich (Gov) 115
Ipswich Town (FC) 250
Iran Daily (Newspaper) 183
Iranian (Embassy) 102
Iranian (Gov) 103
Ireland (Legal institutions) 106
Ireland (Post office) 108
Irish (Gov) 103
Irish Amateur Fencing

Federation 249
Irish Canoe Union 248
Irish Family History
  Foundation 148
Irish Ferries 278
Irish Horseracing Authority 253
Irish News (Eire) 183
Irish Racing 253
Irish Rugby Union 257
Irish Table Tennis
  Association 261
Irish Times (Eire) 183
Irish Turf Club 253
IRN 177
Irn Bru 91
Iron Bed Company 234
Iron Maiden 17
Ironbridge Museum Trust,
  Telford 171
Ironsure 189
ISA Shop 191
Isaac Hayes 17
Isaac Newton Institute 219
Islam 165
Islamic Centre England 165
Islamic Foundation 165
Islamic Unity Society 165
Island (Record company) 22
Island (Sri Lanka) 183
Island FM (Guernsey) 24
Islay 98
Isle of Bute (Local info) 201
Isle of Man (Airport) 277
Isle of Man (Parliament) 120
Isle of Man (Post office) 108
Isle of Man Government 107
Isle of Man Independent
  (Newspaper) 179
Isle of Skye (Local info) 201
Isle of Wight (Gov) 115
Isle of Wight (Health
  authority) 127
Isle of Wight (Local info) 201
Isle of Wight Radio 25
Isle of Wight Steam
  Railway 199
Isles of Scilly (Local info) 201
Isley Brothers 17
Islington (Gov) 115
Israel (British embassy) 101
Israel (Legal institutions) 106
Israel (Tourist info) 207
Israel Philharmonic 21
Israeli (Embassy) 102
Israeli (Foreign Affairs) 103
Israeli (Gov) 103
Israeli Bridge Federation 144
Issey Miyake 230
Istanbul (Airport) 276
Istanbul (Local info) 212
Istituto di Credito
  Sammarinese 39
Isuzo 157
IT Weekly 267
Italian (Embassy) 102

Italian (Gov) 103
Italy (British embassy) 101
Italy (Grand Prix) 254
ITN 174, 177
ITS Investment Trusts 191
ITV 26
ITV (Motor racing) 255

J

J & B 98
J C Penney 57
J D Wetherspoon 43
J P Morgan & Co. 39
J Paul Getty Museum,
  California 212
J Sainsbury 52
J Walter Thompson 35
Jack Daniels 98
Jack Nicklaus 255
Jack Ryder 3
Jackie Brown 10
Jackson-Stops & Staff 159
Jacobs Creek 98
Jacques Villeneuve 255
Jaeger 226
Jaeger le coultre 243
Jaffa Cakes 91
Jaguar 157
Jaguar (Motor racing
  teams) 255
Jam Jar 155
Jamaica (Gov) 103
Jamaica (Tourist info) 204
Jamaican (Embassy) 102
Jamba (Carlton TV) 146
James Bond 10
James Brearley & Sons 193
James Lock 241-242
James Meade 226
Jamiroquai 17
Jammu & Kashmir (Local
  info) 207
Jane Asher Party Cakes 94
Jane Austen Museum 171
Jane Goodall Institute 219
Jane Packer 231
Jane's 174
Janet Jackson 17
Janet Reger 226
Japan (British embassy) 101
Japan (Grand Prix) 255
Japan (Legal institutions) 106
Japan (Tourist info) 207
Japan Airlines 274
Japanese (Embassy) 102
Japanese (Gov) 103
Jardine Lloyd Thompson 43
JAS Japan Air System 274
Jasper Griegson (The
  Complainer) 140
Jazz Café 6, 95
Jazz FM (London) 25
JD Sports 242
JD Wetherspoon 89
Jean Michel Jarre 17

Jean Paul Gaultier 9, 230
Jeep 157
Jeff Beck 17
Jeffrey Green Russell 51
Jehovah's Witnesses 164
Jekyll & Hyde 29
Jelly Belly 91
Jellyworks 266
Jennifer Lopez 17
Jensen 157
Jeremy Whelan 71
Jermyn Street 240
Jerry Maguire 10
Jerry Springer Show 28
Jersey (Gov) 115
Jersey (Local info) 201
Jersey (Post office) 108
Jersey (Tourist info) 204
Jersey Battle of Flowers 205
Jersey European Airways 271
Jersey Evening Post 179
Jersey Financial Services
  Commission 192
Jersey Heritage Trust 205
Jersey Museum 171
Jersey Post 204
Jersey Royals 91
Jerusalem (Local info) 207
Jerusalem Post (Israel) 183
Jessops 241
Jesus Army 164
Jethro Tull 17
Jewel 17
Jewish Board of Deputies 16
Jewish Museum 171
Jewish Online 162
Jewish Telegraph 179
Jewish.net 162
Jewson 237
Jim Beam 98
Jim Carrey 3
Jimi Hendrix 17
Jimmy Stewart 3
JJ72 17
JJB Sports 52, 242, 260
JMC 284
Jo Dee Messina 17
Jo Hansford 158
Joan Armatrading 17
Joan Baez 17
Job Hunter 51
Jobs Unlimited 51
Jockey Club 253
Jodrell Bank 217
Joe Brown 17
Joe Diffle 17
Joe Jackson 17
Johannesburg (Airport) 276
Johannesburg (Local info) 21
Johannesburg (Stock
  exchange) 53
John Charcol 192
John D Wood 159
John Galliano 9
John Grisham 13

John Innes Centre 83
John Laing 45
John Lewis 231
John Lewis Partnership 52
John Menzies 223
John Moore's University 71
John Rylands Library 169
John Smith 223
John Steinbeck 13
John Whitaker 255
Johnny Cash 17
Johnny Herbert 256
Johnny Walker 98
Johnson & Johnson 47, 57
Johnson Matthey 46
Johnson's 240
Johnston Press 46, 179
JoJo Maman Bebe 240
Jon Bon Jovi 18
Jonathan Cainer 143
Jonathan Dimbleby 27
Jones Bootmaker 241
Jongleurs 6
Joni Mitchell 18
Joop 9
Jordache 9
Jordan (British embassy) 101
Jordan (Legal institutions) 106
Jordan (Monarchy) 106
Jordan (Motor racing
    teams) 255
Jordan (Tourist info) 208
Jordan National Bank 39
Jordan Radio & Television
    Corp. 208
Jordan Times 208
Jordan Times (Jordan) 183
Jordanian (Embassy) 102
Jordanian (Gov) 103
Jorvik Viking Centre 202
Joseph Smith 3
Joslin Shaw 35
Journal of Buddhist Ethics 164
Journal of Community
    Nursing 129
Journal of Design History 169
Journal Of Natural History 218
Journal of Neonatal
    Nursing 129
Journal of Public Health
    Medicine 129
Journal of the British
    Acupuncture Council 129
Journal of Victorian Culture 169
Joy Division 18
JP Morgan 39, 57
Jubilee Line Extension 282
Jubilee Sailing Trust 258
Judaism 165
Judy Blume 67
Judy Tzuke 18
Julian Cope 18
Julian Lennon 18
Julie Felix 18
Julien Donkey-boy 10

Julio Inglesias 18
Jump Magazine 259
Junction 68
Jungle.com 240
Jupiter 191
Just For Laughs - International
    Comedy Festival (Montreal) 7
JVC 236
Jyske 187

K

KAGE 155
Kajagoogoo 18
Kaleidescope 226
Kall Kwik 47
Kansas (Airport) 276
Kansas University 78
Kate Moss 9
Kate Winslet 3
Kavana 18
Kavanagh QC 28
Kawasaki 163
Kays 226
KC & the Sunshine Band 18
kd lang 18
Keanu Reeves 3
Keele (Uni) 76
Keighley & Worth Valley
    (Railway) 199
Keighley News 180
Keith Prowse 31
Kelburn Castle 198
Kelburn Castle & Country
    Centre 201
Kelda 58
Kellogg's 57, 91
Kelly Brook 3
Kelly's Guide 174
Kelsey Tailors 226
Kelso (Racecourse) 253
Kemble Pianos 150
Kempton Park
    (Racecourse) 253
Ken Follett 13
Kenco 91
Kenilworth Weekly News 180
Kennedy Space Centre 217
Kennel Club 151
Kennet (Gov) 115
Kenneth More Theatre,
    Ilford 30
Kenning 278
Kenny Rogers 18
Kensington & Chelsea
    (Gov) 115
Kensington Palace 107, 200
Kent & Sussex Courier 180
Kent (Cricket club) 248
Kent (Gov) 115
Kent (Uni) 76
Kent Messenger 180
Kentwell 200
Kenwood 155
Kenya (Legal institutions) 106
Kenya (Tourist info) 208

Kenya Airways 274
Kenyian (Gov) 103
Kerrier (Gov) 115
Kerry (Local info) 207
Kerrygold 91
Kettering (Gov) 115
Kevin Spacey 3
Kew Bridge Steam
    Museum 171
Kew Gardens 201
KFC 94
Khalili Collections 5
Kia 157
Kidderminster (Local info) 203
Kids' Almanac 68
Kids' Crosswords 68
Kids' Jokes 68
Kidscape 136
Kidsnet 64
Kidsons Impey 50
Kidstravel 64
Kielder Water Bird of Prey
    Centre 202
KIIS FM (Los Angeles) 25
Killik & Co. 193
Kilmarnock Standard 180
Kilmartin House 200
Kimberly Clark 57, 236
Kinder Surprise 91
King and I 10, 29
King Sturge 159
King's (Public school) 74
King's College London 76
King's College School of
    Medicine & Dentistry 73
King's Fund 138
Kingdom of Leather 234
Kingfisher 42, 52
Kings Lynn & West Norfolk
    (Gov) 115
Kingshill 226
Kingston & Richmond (Health
    authority) 127
Kingston-upon-Hull (Gov) 115
Kingston-upon-Thames
    (Gov) 115
Kingston-upon-Thames
    (Uni) 76
Kinks 18
Kirklees (Gov) 115
Kirov Ballet 6
Kiss 18
Kiss FM (London) 25
Kit-Kat 91
Kitbag.com 242
Kitchen Specialists
    Association 162
Kitchen Specialists
    Association 55
Kitchens, Bedrooms &
    Bathrooms Magazine 162
Klagenfurt (Local info) 197
Klippan 240
KLM 274
Knex 66, 242

Knight Frank **159**
Knight Rider **28**
Knitting Now **148**
Knitting Today **148**
Knitting, Footwear & Textile
    Workers (KFAT) **55**
Knockhill (Motor racing) **254**
Knoll Gardens **201**
Knotts Berry Farm **212**
Knowsley (Gov) **115**
Knowsley Safari Park **220**
Knutsford Guardian **180**
Kodak **152**
Kogan Page **48**
Kolmarden Zoo,
    Norrkoping **211**
Komedia Theatre, Brighton **30**
Konica **152**
Kookai **9**
Korea (Legal institutions) **106**
Korea (Tourist info) **208**
Korea Herald (Korea) **183**
Korean (Gov) **103**
Korn **18**
KPMG **50**
Kraft **91**
Kristen Johnston **3**
Krizia **9**
Kronenbourg **89**
Kuala Lumpur (Airport) **276**
Kuala Lumpur (Local info) **208**
Kula Shaker **18**
Kumon Maths **75**
Kuoni **284**
Kurier (Austria) **183**
Kuwait (Tourist info) **208**
Kuwait Airways **274**
Kuwait Times (Kuwait) **183**
Kuwaiti (Gov) **103**
Kwik-Fit **35, 155**
Kylie Minogue **18**

L

L L Bean **226**
L'Oreal **230, 236**
La Leche League **158**
La Perla **9**
La Redoute **226**
La Scala **21**
Labatt's **89**
Labour Party **107**
Labour Party, Australia **107**
Labour Party, New Zealand **107**
Labour Party, Norway **107**
Lace Guild **148**
Lace Magazine **148**
Lacoste **9, 230**
Ladbroke **42**
Ladbrokes **146, 252**
Ladies' Professional Golf
    Association **251**
Laetitia Allen **226**
Lagavulin **98**
Laing **160**
Laird **45**

Lake District (Local info) **201**
Lakeland **238**
Lambeth **187**
Lambeth (Gov) **115**
Lambeth, Southwark &
    Lewisham (Health
    authority) **127**
Lamborghini **157**
Lancashire (Ambulance) **135**
Lancashire (Cricket club) **248**
Lancashire (Gov) **115**
Lancashire (Police) **139**
Lancashire Evening Post **180**
Lancashire Evening
    Telegraph **180**
Lancaster **189, 230**
Lancaster & Morecambe
    Citizen **180**
Lancaster (Gov) **115**
Lancaster (Uni) **76**
Lancaster Guardian Series **180**
Lancet **129**
Lancome **9, 230**
Land Information New
    Zealand **170**
Land Rover **157**
Land Securities **42, 51**
Landmark Trust **85**
Landmark, Ilfracombe **30**
Lands' End **64, 226**
Landscape Design Trust **85**
Landscape Institute **85**
Landscape Trust **147**
Lanes **236**
Lanesborough **280**
Lantern FM (Devon) **25**
LAPADA: Association of Art and
    Antique Dealers **243**
Laphroaig **98**
Laporte **36**
Lappa Valley (Railway) **199**
Lara Croft **267**
Larne (Gov) **115**
Larne Gazette **180**
Larochette (Local info) **208**
Las Vegas (Local info) **213**
Laser **258**
Lashmars **31**
Lasmo **37**
Last Orders.com **94**
Lastminute.com **31, 235, 284**
Late Rooms.com **280**
Latvian (Gov) **103**
Lauda Air **274**
Laura Ashley **226, 234**
Laurel & Hardy **6**
Laurence Olivier Awards **7**
Lavazza **91**
Law Commission **110**
Law Society **50**
Law Society Gazette **44**
Law Society of England &
    Wales **105**
Law Society of Scotland **105**
Lawn Bowls **247**

Lawn Tennis Association **26**
Lawrence Graham **51**
Laytons **98**
LBC (London) **25**
Le Creuset **238**
Le Gourmet Francais **94**
Le Mans (Motor racing) **254**
Le Meridien **280**
Le Pont de la Tour **95**
League Against Cruel
    Sports **108**
League Managers
    Association **251**
League of Gentlemen **28**
Leamington Observer **180**
Leamington Spa Courier **18**
LeAnn Rimes **18**
Learn **66, 72**
Learn Direct **75**
Learn Free **66**
Learner Drivers UK **156**
Leatherhead Advertiser **180**
Leavesden **12**
Lebanese (Gov) **103**
Lebanon (British embassy)
Lebanon (Tourist info) **208**
Led Zeppelin **18**
Lee & Herring **6**
Lee Strasberg **71**
Lee Westwood **256**
Leeds & Holbeck **187**
Leeds (Gov) **115**
Leeds (Health authority) **12**
Leeds (Rugby club) **257**
Leeds (Uni) **76**
Leeds Castle **198**
Leeds International Film
    Festival **7**
Leeds Metropolitan (Uni) **76**
Leeds United (FC) **250**
Leek **187**
Left Hand **241**
Legacy Recordings **22**
Legal & General **42-43, 18**
    189
Legal Aid **105**
Lego **66, 242**
Legoland **64, 205**
Leica **152**
Leicester (Gov) **115**
Leicester (Rugby club) **257**
Leicester (Uni) **76**
Leicester City (FC) **250**
Leicester Mail **180**
Leicester Royal Infirmary **1**
Leicestershire (Cricket
    club) **248**
Leicestershire (Gov) **115**
Leicestershire (Health
    authority) **127**
Leicestershire (Police) **139**
Leiden (Local info) **209**
Leigh Reporter **180**
Leigh, Tyldesley & Atherton
    Journal **180**

Leighton Buzzard (Railway) **199**
LeisureHunt **280**
Leith's **95**
Leith's School of Food &
Wine **145**
Lennox Lewis **256**
Lenny Kravitz **18**
Leo Burnett **35**
Leominster (Local info) **203**
Leonard Bernstein **18**
Leonard Cheshire
Foundation **136**
Leonard Cohen **18**
Leonard Nimoy **3**
Leonardo di Caprio **3**
Les Miserables **29**
Let's Buy It **230**
Letchworth Museum and Art
Gallery **5**
Leukaemia Research Fund **138**
Level 42 **18**
Levellers **18**
Levington **147**
Levis **226**
Levy Gee **50**
Lewes (Gov) **115**
Lewis Carroll **13**
Lewisham (Gov) **115**
Lewisham News Shopper **180**
Lex Retail **155**
Lex Service **35**
Lexmark **265**
Lexus **157**
Liberal Democratic Party **107**
Liberal Democratic Party,
Japan **108**
Liberal Party, Australia **108**
Liberal Party, Canada **108**
Liberian (Gov) **103**
Liberty **226, 231**
Liberty (National Council for
Civil Liberties) **109**
Library & Information
Commission **173**
Library Association **173**
Library of Congress **169**
Library of Congress,
Washington **212**
Library Theatre, Manchester **30**
Lichfield (Gov) **115**
Lichfield Festival **7**
Liechtenstein (Gov) **103**
Liechtenstein (Monarchy) **106**
Liechtenstein (Tourist info) **208**
Life **162**
Lifelong Learning (DfEE) **75**
Lifespan Healthcare **128**
LIFFE **53**
Lift **91**
Lighthouse Family **18**
Lighthouse Society of Great
Britain **149**
Lightning Seeds **18**
Lightwater Valley **64**
Ligne Roset **234**

Lilleshall National Sports
Centre **256**
Limahl **18**
Limassaol (Local info) **205**
Limerick (Local info) **207**
Limp Bizkit **18**
Lincoln (Gov) **115**
Lincoln City (FC) **250**
Lincolnshire & Humberside
(Uni) **76**
Lincolnshire (Cricket club) **248**
Lincolnshire (Gov) **115**
Lincolnshire (Police) **139**
Lincolnshire Echo **180**
Lincolnshire Independent **180**
Lincolnshire Target **180**
Lincs FM (Lincolnshire) **25**
Lindemans **98**
Linden Homes **160**
Lindisfarne (Local info) **203**
Lindsay Bareham **90**
Line One Money Zone **191**
LineOne **267**
LineOne Learning **66**
Linguaphone **75**
Link **230**
Linklaters **51**
Links **235**
Linnean Society of London **219**
Lionel Dunning **256**
Lisbon (Local info) **210**
Lisbon (Stock exchange) **53**
Lisburn (Gov) **115**
Lisebergs Nojespark,
Gothenberg **211**
Listerine **236**
Litchfield (Gov) **115**
Little Chef **94**
Little Mermaid **65**
Little Tikes **66, 242**
Littlewoods Pools **146**
Live & Kicking **65**
Live Art Magazine **14**
Live from Lord's Webcam **249**
Liverpool (Airport) **277**
Liverpool (Chamber of
Commerce) **36**
Liverpool (FC) **250**
Liverpool (Gov) **115**
Liverpool (Health authority) **127**
Liverpool (Uni) **76**
Liverpool (Vet school) **79**
Liverpool Daily Post **180**
Liverpool Echo **180**
Liverpool Institute for
Performing Arts **71**
Liverpool Philharmonic **21**
Liverpool School of Tropical
Medicine **73**
Liverpool Victoria Friendly
Society **192**
Living **26**
Lladro **224, 238**
Llanelli (Rugby club) **257**
Llangollen (Railway) **199**

Llewelyn Zietman **51**
Lloyd's List **44**
Lloyd's of London **43**
Lloyds Register **56**
Lloyds TSB **42, 187**
Lloyds TSB Group **40**
Loaded **162**
Local Authorities Co-ordinating
Body on Food & Trading
Standards **139**
Local Government
Association **110**
Local Government
Ombudsman **140**
Local History Magazine **169**
Loch Fyne **91**
Lock, Stock & Two Smoking
Barrels **10**
Lockheed Martin **57**
Logica **37**
Lola Cars International **255**
Lombard **188**
Londis **96**
London (Ambulance) **135**
London (Local info) **203**
London (Stock exchange) **53**
London (Uni) **76**
London (Zoo) **220**
London Academy of Music &
Dramatic Art (LAMDA) **71**
London Aquarium **202**
London Arena **25**
London Art Week **7**
London Arts Board **4**
London Association of Art &
Design Education **22**
London Business School **72,
76**
London Chess Centre **144**
London City (Airport) **277**
London Clearing House **53**
London Clinic **128**
London College of Clinical
Hypnosis **73**
London College of Printing **71**
London College of Traditional
Acupuncture & Oriental
Medicine **73**
London Contemporary Dance
School **71**
London Cycling
Campaign **109, 249**
London Dungeon **202**
London Electricity **162**
London Evening Standard **180**
London Eye **202**
London Fashion Week **7**
London Festival of Literature **7**
London Film and Video
Development Agency **12**
London Film Festival **7**
London Guildhall (Uni) **76**
London Hospital Medical
College **73**
London International Festival of

Theatre 7
London International Film
  School 71
London International Insurance
  and Reinsurance Market
  Association (LIRMA) 43
London International Mime
  Festival 7
London Investment Bank
  Association 50
London Irish (Rugby club) 257
London Jewish News 180
London Junior Ballet 6
London Library 169
London Marathon 247
London Metal Exchange 53
London Metropolitan 21
London Open House 7
London Opera Players 21
London Parade 7
London Philharmonic 21
London Property Guide 159
London Property News 159
London Radiosurgical
  Centre 128
London Review of Books 13
London School of
  Economics 76
London School of Hygiene &
  Tropical Medicine 74
London String of Pearls
  Millennium Festival 7
London Symphony 21
London Taxi 157
London Theatre Bookings 31
London Tonight 28
London Tourist Board 202
London Toy & Model
  Museum 171
London Transport 278, 282
London Transport Museum 171
London Transport Season
  Tickets 282
London Underground 282
London Underground Railway
  Society 149
London Welsh (Rugby
  club) 257
Londonderry (Gov) 115
Lonely Planet 282
Longines 238, 243
Longleat 200
Longleat Safari Park 220
Look Again 226
LookSmart 268
Loot 239
Loquax 147
Lord Chancellor's
  Department 105, 111
Lord Mayor's Show 7
Lord of the Dance 29
Lord's 248
Los Angeles (Local info) 213
Los Angeles Film Festival 7
Los Angeles Museum of

Art 212
Los Angeles Philharmonic
  (Orchestra) 21
Los Angeles Times (USA) 183
Loss Prevention Council 192
Lost in Space 10, 28
LOT Polish Airlines 274
Lothian (Health authority) 127
Lots Road Galleries 223
Lotus 157, 265
Lou Reed 18
Louden Castle 64
Loughborough (Uni) 76
Louis Vuitton 9, 239
Louth Leader 180
Louvre 206
Lovell White Durrant 51
Lowe Howard Spink 35
Lowther Leisure & Wildlife
  Park 64
LPGA Classic 252
Luanda (Local info) 197
Lucas Film 12
Lucozade 91
Lufthansa 274
Luhta 260
Lulu Guiness 241
Lulworth Castle 198, 201
Lunn Poly 284
Lush 230
Luther Vandross 18
Luton (Airport) 277
Luton (Gov) 115
Luton (Uni) 76
Luton Herald & Post 180
Luxembourg (Embassy) 102
Luxembourg (Gov) 103
Luxembourg (Tourist info) 208
Luxembourg City (Local
  info) 208
LWT 26
Lycos 268
Lycra 226
Lynn News 180
Lynton & Barnstaple
  (Railway) 199
Lynx 36
Lynx Air International 275
Lynx Group 37
Lynyrd Skynyrd 18
Lyon (Local info) 206
Lyric Studio Theatre 30
Lyric Theatre, Belfast 30

M

M & G Group 40
M&G Group 191-192
Maastricht (Local info) 209
Macallan 98
Maccabi Union 165
Macclesfield (Gov) 116
Macclesfield Silk Museum 171
Macclesfield Town (FC) 250
MacFarlanes 51
Mackies 91

Mackintosh House 171
Maclay Murray & Spens 51
Maclay Thistle 89
Macleans 236
Macmillan 48
Macmillan Relief 138
MacUser 267
Macworld 267
Macy Gray 18
Madame Tussaud's 202
Madasafish 267
Madhouse 226
Madness 18
Madonna 18
Madrid (Airport) 276
Madrid (Local info) 211
Madrid (Stock exchange) 53
Maersk Company 53
Magazine Shop 162
Magellan 268
Magherafelt (Gov) 116
Magic AM (Yorkshire) 25
Magic Circle 22
Magic Travel Group 284
Magistrates' Association 10
Magnet 239
Maharishi 9
Maidenhead Advertiser 180
Maidstone (Gov) 116
Maidstone Museum 171
Maidstone Museum & Art
  Gallery 5
Making History (BBC) 169
Makita 237
Malaysia (Grand Prix) 255
Malaysia (Legal
  institutions) 106
Malaysia (Tourist info) 208
Malaysia Air 275
Malaysia Airlines 275
Malaysian (Gov) 104
Maldives (Tourist info) 208
Maldon & Burnham
  Standard 180
Maldon (Gov) 116
Malev 275
Malibu 91
Mallory Park (Motor racing)
Malmo (Local info) 211
Malta (Tourist info) 209
Maltese (Gov) 104
Mamas & Papas 240
Mamma Mia! 29
Mammal Society 219
Manchester (Airport) 277
Manchester (Chamber of
  Commerce) 36
Manchester (Gov) 116
Manchester (Health
  authority) 127
Manchester (Local info) 20
Manchester (Rugby club) 2
Manchester (Uni) 76
Manchester 2002 Sport XVI
  Commonwealth Games 2

Manchester Business School 72
Manchester City (FC) 250
Manchester City Art Galleries 5
Manchester Evening News 180
Manchester G-Mex 25
Manchester Grammar 74
Manchester Institute of Psychotherapy 131
Manchester Metropolitan (Uni) 76
Manchester Metropolitan University, School of Theatre 71
Manchester Museum 171
Manchester Museum of Science & Industry 171
Manchester United (FC) 43, 250
Mandarin Airlines 275
Mandarin Oriental 280
Manderston 200
Mandy Moore 18
Mangapps Farm Railway Museum 171
Manic Street Preachers 18
Manitoba (Local info) 204
Manorial Society of Great Britain 169
Manpower 51, 57
Mansfield (Gov) 116
Mansfield (Local info) 203
Mansfield Chad/Chronicle and Advertiser 180
Mansun 18
Manx Airlines 275
Manx Radio 25
Mapblast 170
Marantz 236
Marbles 188
Marc Almond 18
Marconi 54
Margaret Drabble 13
Mariah Carey 18
Marie Curie Cancer Care 138
Marie Stopes Health Clinics 128
Marillion 18
Marilyn Manson 18
Marine Conservation Society 217
Maritime & Coastguard Agency 139
Mark Knofler 18
Mark Spitz 256
Market Harborough (Building society) 188
Market Rasen (Racecourse) 253
Market Rasen Mail 180
Marketing 44
Marks & Spencer 42, 52, 96, 226, 231, 234
Marlborough Fine Art 5
Marley 231

Marmaduke 63
Marquetry Society 148
Marriott Hotels 280
Mars 91
Marsden 188
Marseille (Airport) 276
Marshall Amplification 150
Marshalls 226
Marston's 89
Martin Air 275
Martin Lawrence 3
Martine McCutcheon 18
Marvel Comics 67
Marwell (Zoo) 220
Mary Chapin Carpenter 18
Mary J Blige 18
Mary Kay 230
Mary Rose 171
Maserati 157
Massachusetts (Tourist info) 213
Massachusetts Institute of Technology 78
Massive Attack 18
Mastercard 188
Matchbox 66, 242
Mathmos 239
Maths Maze 72
Matt Damon 3
Mattel 66, 242
Mauritanian (Gov) 104
Mauritius (Tourist info) 209
Maver 146
Mavericks 18
Max Factor 230
Maxfli 260
Maxim 162
Maxisearch 268
Maxon 268
Mayflower 31
Mayo Clinic 128
Mazars Neville Russell 50
Mazda 157
MBNA 188
MCA 22
MCA Universal 12
McAlpine 160
McCann Erickson 35
McCord 234
McDonald 280
McDonald's 57, 94
McGraw-Hill 48, 57
McGrigor Donald 51
MCI Worldcom 268
McLaren (Motor racing teams) 255
McLean Homes 160
MCM Group 189
McVities Jaffa Cakes 68
Meadowhall Centre 240
Mean Fiddler 25
Meat Loaf 18
MEB 162
Mecca Bingo Online 146
Meccano 66, 242

Meddings Machine Tools 237
Medeltidsmuseum, Stockholm 211
Medeva 47
Media Trust 13
Media Week 14, 44
Medic Direct 129
Medical 109
Medical Advisory Services for Travellers Abroad (MASTA) 125
Medical Defence Union 129
Medical Devices Agency 110, 126
Medical Protection Society 129
Medical Research Council 129
Medicines Control Agency 110, 126, 130
Medisearch 129
Medway (Gov) 116
Medway FM (Kent) 25
Medway Ports 53
Meg Ryan 4
MegaStar 180
Melanie C 18
Melanie Griffith (Fan Club) 4
Melbourne (Airport) 276
Melbourne (Cricket club) 248
Melbourne (Local info) 197
Melissa Joan Hart 4
Melton (Gov) 116
Memphis (Airport) 276
Memphis (Local info) 213
Men Behaving Badly 28
Men In Black 10
Men's Health 162
Mencap 138
Mendip (Gov) 116
Meningitis Research Foundation 138
Mennonite Church 164
Mens Fitness Magazine 143
Mensa 149
Mensa Foundation for Gifted Children 136
Mentorn 27
Mercedes Benz 157
Mercer's Company 44
Merck 47, 57
Mercury (Couriers) 36
Mercury (Record company) 22
Mercury (Telecom) 268
Mercury Asset Management 191-193
Meridian 26
Merrill Lynch 57
Merrydown 89
Mersey Docks & Harbour Company 56
Mersey Television Company 27
Mersey Young Peoples Theatre 67
Merseyside (Local info) 201
Merseyside (Police) 139
Merthyr Tydfil (Gov) 116

Merton (Gov) **116**
Mesh **265**
Metacrawler **268**
Metal Bulletin **46**
Metallica **18**
Meteorological Office **174**
Methodist Church **164**
Metro **48, 180**
Metro FM (Newcastle) **25**
Metropolitan Museum of Art,
New York **212**
Metropolitan Police
(Police) **139**
Mexican (Embassy) **102**
Mexican (Gov) **104**
Mexico (British embassy) **101**
Mexico (Legal institutions) **106**
Mexico (Tourist info) **209**
Mexico City (Airport) **276**
MFI Furniture **52**
MFI Homeworks **234**
MG **157**
MG Enthusiast **156**
MGM **12**
MI5 **110**
Miami (Local info) **213**
Mica Hardware **237**
Michael Bolton **19**
Michael Faraday's
Museum **171**
Michael Jackson **19**
Michael Jordan **256**
Michael Nyman **19**
Michael Page **51**
Michael Schumacher **256**
Michelin **155**
Michigan State University **78**
Microlease **265**
Microsoft **265**
Microsoft **57**
Microsoft Kids **68**
Mid Bedfordshire (Gov) **116**
Mid Devon (Gov) **116**
Mid Devon Gazette **180**
Mid Norfolk (Railway) **199**
Mid Suffolk (Gov) **116**
Mid-Hants 'Watercress'
(Railway) **199**
Mid-Sussex (Gov) **116**
Middle East Times (Egypt) **183**
Middle Eastern Airlines **275**
Middle Way Journal **164**
Middlesbrough (FC) **250**
Middlesbrough (Gov) **116**
Middlesbrough General **128**
Middlesex (Cricket club) **248**
Middlesex (Hospital) **128**
Middlesex (Uni) **76**
Middleton (Railway) **199**
Midland Air Museum **171**
Midland Direct **189**
Midland Mainline **283**
Midlands Insurance
Services **192**
Midlothian (Gov) **116**

Midsummer Night's Dream **10**
Miele **239**
Miffy **67**
Mighty Morphin' Power
Rangers **65**
Mika Hakkinen **256**
Mika Salo **256**
Mike Oldfield **19**
Milan (Airport) **276**
Miles Davis **19**
Milk Marque **83**
Millennium Bridge **202**
Millennium Commission **13**
Millennium Experience **8**
Millennium Round the World
Yacht Race **258**
Miller Freeman **48**
Miller Lite **89**
Millfield (Public school) **74**
Millwall (FC) **250**
Milton Keynes (Gov) **116**
Milton Keynes Citizen **180**
Milton Keynes Theatre and
Gallery **30**
Minack Theatre, Porthcurno **30**
Minardi (Motor racing
teams) **255**
Mind **138**
Minerva Press **48**
Mini **157**
Mini Heroes **91**
Minimus **66**
Ministry of Agriculture, Fisheries
& Food **84**
Ministry of Defence **111**
Ministry of Sound **6, 22**
Minneapolis St Paul (Local
info) **213**
Minnesota State University **78**
Minolta **152**
Minor Cricket Counties
Association **248**
Mintel.com **173**
Miracle-Gro Online **147**
Mirago **268**
Miramax **12**
Mirror **182**
Miscarriage Association **138**
Miss Saigon **29**
Missing Kids **136**
Mission Impossible **10**
Mississippi State University **78**
Misys **37, 42, 266**
Mitel **266**
Mitre **260**
Mitsubishi **157, 268**
Mitsubishi Electric **239**
Mizuno **260**
MKI Hotels **280**
Moben **239**
Mobil **37, 157**
Model Yachting
Association **150**
Models 1 **46**
Moderna Museet,

Stockholm **211**
Moet & Chandon **91**
Mohammed Ali **256**
Mole Hall Wildlife Park **220**
Mole Valley (Gov) **116**
Molson **89**
Monaco (Grand Prix) **255**
Monaco (Monarchy) **106**
Monaco (Motor racing) **254**
Monaco (Tourist info) **209**
Monarch (Airline) **275**
Monarch (Sportswear &
equipment) **260**
Mondial **268**
Money Money Money **191**
Moneynet **192**
Moneyweb **191**
MoneyWorld UK **191**
Mongolian (Gov) **104**
Monitor (Uganda) **183**
Monkey World **202**
Monkwell **243**
Monmouthshire (Gov) **116**
Monopoly **66, 147**
Monsanto **47, 57**
Monsoon **226**
Monster **51**
Monte-Carlo (Local info) **209**
Montessori Foundation **74**
Montreal (Airport) **276**
Montreal (Stock exchange) **●**
Montreux Jazz Festival **8, 2●**
Monty Python **28**
Monty Python Online **6**
Monza (Motor racing) **254**
Moody **258**
Moody Blues **19**
Moon Estates **235**
Moores Rowland **50**
Moorfields (Hospital) **128**
Moorings **258, 284**
Moorland Association **85**
Moray (Gov) **116**
Morecambe & Wise **6**
Morecambe Bay (Health
authority) **127**
Morecambe Visitor **180**
Morgan **157, 226**
Morgan Crucible **45**
Morgan Stanley Dean Witte●
Discover **57**
Mori **173**
Morland **89**
Mormons **164**
Mormons Family Search **14●**
Morocco (Tourist info) **209**
Morpeth (Local info) **203**
Morrells **89**
Morrisons **96**
Morrissey **19**
Morse **266**
Mortgage Alliance **192**
Mortgage Help Desk UK **19●**
Mortgage Intelligence **192**
Mortgage Shop **192**

Moschino **226**
Moscow (Airport) **276**
Moscow (Local info) **210**
Moscow Flying Ballet **6**
Moscow State Circus **8**
Moseley (Rugby club) **257**
Moshi Moshi **95**
Mosiman Academy **145**
Moss Bros **226**
Mother & Baby **162**
Mother Shipton's Cave **202**
Mothercare **240**
Motherwell (FC) **250**
Motley Fool **191**
Moto Guzzi **163**
Moto Guzzi Club GB **163**
Motor Auction Consortium **155**
Motor Boat & Yachting **259**
Motor Schools Association **161**
Motor Show **8**
Motor Sport **255**
Motor Vehicle Repairers'
  Association **35**
Motor World **155-156**
Motorbikes Online **163**
Motorcycle Industry
  Association **164**
Motorcycle Sport **164**
Motorcycle UK **164**
Motorcycle World
  Magazine **164**
Motoring UK **156**
Motorola **155, 268**
MotorTrader **156**
Moulinex **239**
Mount Rushmore **212**
Mount Stuart **200**
Mount Stuart House &
  Gardens **201**
Mountain 103.7
  (Washington) **25**
Mountain Biking UK **249**
Mountain Rescue **139, 144**
Mountain Sports Guide **144**
Mountaineering Council for
  Scotland **144**
Mountview Theatre School **71**
Moves **36, 161**
Moving Image Society **12**
Moy Park **91**
Moyle (Gov) **116**
Mozambiqui (Gov) **104**
MP3 **14**
Mr Bean **28**
Mr Men **67**
Mr Potato Head **66**
Mr Python **9**
Mrs Cohen **191**
MSN **268**
MTS Mortgage Company **192**
MTV **26**
Muji **226**
Mulan **65**
Mulberry **241**
Muller **91**

Multi-purpose European
  Ground-Related Information
  Network **170**
Multimap **170**
Multiple Births Foundation **138**
Multiple Sclerosis Society **138**
Multiyork **234**
MUM Roll On **230**
Mummy **10**
Muncaster Castle **198**
Munich (Airport) **276**
Munich (Local info) **206**
Munsters **65**
Muppets **65**
Muppets from Space **65**
Muscle & Fitness
  Magazine **143**
Muscular Dystrophy
  Campaign **138**
Museum of Army Flying **172**
Museum of British Road
  Transport **172**
Museum of Childhood
  Memories **172**
Museum of Classical
  Archaeology **172**
Museum of Contemporary
  Art **197**
Museum of Costume **172**
Museum of East Anglian
  Life **172**
Museum of East Asian Art **172**
Museum of Fine Arts,
  Boston **212**
Museum of Garden History **172**
Museum of London **172**
Museum of London
  Archaeology Service **85**
Museum of Modern Art, New
  York **212**
Museum of Modern Art,
  Oxford **5**
Museum of Mohamed
  Mahmoud Khalil **205**
Museum of Scotland **172**
Museum of the History of
  Science **172**
Museum of the Moving
  Image **172**
Museum of the Royal College of
  Surgeons **172**
Museum of Welsh Life **172**
Museumnet Norway **209**
Museums & Galleries
  Commission **13, 110**
Museums Association **173**
Museums of the Potteries **172**
Music & Games **241**
Music Festivals UK **8**
Music Festivals Worldwide **8**
Music Industries
  Association **21**
Musicians Union **55**
Muslim Commercial Bank,
  Pakistan **39**

Muslim Council of Britain **165**
Musselburgh (Racecourse) **253**
Muzzle Loaders' Association of
  Great Britain **261**
My Dog Skip **10**
My Fair Lady **29**

N

N Bloom & Son **238**
Nabarro Nathanson **51**
NACC **138**
Nadia Comaneci (Fan
  Club) **256**
Naim **236**
Nando's Chickenland UK **95**
Napier (Uni) **76**
Nappies Direct **240**
NASA **217**
NASDAQ **54**
Nashville (Airport) **276**
Natalie Imbruglia **19**
Natco Spices **91**
Nation (Thailand) **183**
National (Car hire) **278**
National Acrylic Painters
  Association **4**
National Addiction Centre **138**
National Administration for
  Cultural Heritage **205**
National AIDS Trust **138**
National Anti-Vivisection
  Society **135**
National Arborist
  Association **85**
National Archives of
  Ireland **169**
National Army Museum **172**
National Art Library **4-5**
National Art Library (Victoria &
  Albert Museum) **169**
National Association for
  Premenstrual Syndrome **138**
National Association of Bank &
  Insurance Customers **192**
National Association of Boat
  Owners **143**
National Association of
  Catering Butchers **96**
National Association of Citizens
  Advice Bureaux **110, 139**
National Association of Estate
  Agents **161**
National Association of
  Goldsmiths **55**
National Association of Health
  Authorities & Trusts **125**
National Association of Master
  Bakers **96**
National Association of
  Memorial Masons **139**
National Association of Paper
  Merchants **55**
National Association of Pension
  Funds **192**
National Association of

Regional Game Councils **145**
National Association of School Masters Union of Women Teachers (NASUWT) **55**
National Association of Specialist Anglers **145**
National Association of Theatre Nurses UK **130**
National Association of Youth Orchestras **21**
National Association of Youth Theatre **67**
National Asthma Campaign **138**
National Audit Office **110**
National Australia Bank **39**
National Autistic Society **138**
National Back Pain Association **138**
National Ballet of Canada **6**
National Bank of Bahrain **39**
National Bank of Egypt **39**
National Bank of Moldova **39**
National Bank of New Zealand **39**
National Bank of the Republic of Macedonia **39**
National Basketball Association **247**
National Bird of Prey Centre **143, 217, 219**
National Blood Service **125**
National Board for Nursing, Midwifery and Health Visiting for Northern Ireland **130**
National Board of Nursing, Midwifery and Health Visiting in Scotland **130**
National Campaign for the Arts **13**
National Canine Defence League **135, 151**
National Car Auctions **155**
National Car Parks **282**
National Caving Association **150**
National Childbirth Trust **158, 240**
National Coaching Foundation **247, 256**
National Coal Mining Museum **172**
National Commercial Bank, Saudi Arabia **40**
National Congress, India **108**
National Council for Drama Training **71, 73**
National Council for Metal Detecting **149**
National Council for the Training of Journalists **73**
National Council for Voluntary Organisations **13**
National Countryside Show **85**
National Crime Squad **140**

National Criminal Intelligence Service **110**
National Curriculum **72**
National Cycle Network **249**
National Dairy Council **94**
National Deaf Children's Society **138**
National Dentists Directory **126**
National Disability Council **110**
National Dogsitters **151**
National Endometriosis Society **138**
National Endowment for Science, Technology and the Arts (NESTA) **13**
National Enquirer **162**
National Express **56, 278**
National Fancy Rat Society **151**
National Farmers' Union **96**
National Federation of Anglers **146**
National Federation of Badger Groups **217**
National Federation of Builders **161**
National Federation of Fish Friers **96**
National Federation of Sea Schools **258**
National Federation of Young Farmers Clubs **149**
National Ferret Welfare Society **217**
National Fertility Association **138**
National Film & Television School **71**
National Flying Club **143**
National Football League **247**
National Foundation for Youth Music **13, 21**
National Gallery **5**
National Gallery of Australia **197**
National Gallery of Scotland **5**
National Gallery of Victoria **197**
National Garden Scheme **147**
National Geographic **218, 282**
National Geographic for Kids **67**
National Gerbil Society **151**
National Golf Show **260**
National Grid **42, 58, 162**
National Grid for Learning **72, 110**
National Hairdressers Federation **161**
National Hamster Council **151**
National Health Service **110**
National Herb Centre **147**
National Heritage **84, 111**
National HIV Nurses Association **130**
National Hockey League **262**
National Homebuilder

Awards **84**
National Homes Network **15**
National Hospital for Neurolo & Neurosurgery **128**
National Housebuliders Coun (NHBC) **161**
National Housing Federation **55**
National Indoor Arena **25**
National Inspection Council f Electrical Installation Contracting **161**
National Institute for Social Work **110**
National Institute of Adult Continuing Education **73**
National Institute of Agricultu Botany **83, 219**
National Institute of Ayurvedi Medicine **126**
National Kidney Research Fund **138**
National Library of Scotland **169**
National Library of Wales **16**
National Library of Women **1**
National Literacy Trust **73, 7**
National Lotteries Charities Board **136**
National Lottery **146**
National Lottery Charities Board **13**
National Map Centre **170**
National Maritime Museum **1**
National Meningitis Trust **13**
National Motor Museum **172**
National Museum of America Art, Washington **212**
National Museum of Cartoor Art **172**
National Museum of Modern Art **206**
National Museum of Photography, Film & TV **5, 172**
National Museums & Gallerie of Wales **5**
National Museums & Gallerie on Merseyside **172**
National Museums of Kenya **208**
National Museums of Scotland **172**
National Mutual **189**
National NDT Centre **219**
National Office of Animal Health **125**
National Organisation for Ad Learning **75**
National Osteoporosis Society **138**
National Party, New Zealand **108**
National Pasta Association **1**
National Pet Week **135**

National Pharmaceutical
Association **130**
National Playing Fields
Association **110**
National Pork Producers
Council **90**
National Portrait Gallery **5**
National Portraiture
Association **4**
National Postal Museum **145**
National Power **42, 58, 162**
National Property Register **159**
National Puppy Register **151**
National Pure Water
Association **109**
National Radiological
Protection Board **126**
National Railway Museum **172**
National Rifle Association **261**
National Rivers Authority **110**
National Rounders
Association **256**
National Rounders
Association **63**
National Savings **191**
National Sea Life Centre **220**
National Seal Sanctuary **217**
National Small-bore Rifle
Association **261**
National Society for Education
in Art and Design **71**
National Society for the
Prevention of Cruelty to
Children (NSPCC) **136**
National Soft Drink
Association **96**
National Space Science
Centre **217**
National Sports Medicine
Institute **129**
National Sports Medicine
Institute of the UK **129**
National Tile Association **237**
National Tourist Office
(Australia) **197**
National Tourist Office
(Austria) **197**
National Tourist Office
(Belgium) **198**
National Tourist Office
(Denmark) **205**
National Tourist Office
(France) **206**
National Tourist Office
(Germany) **206**
National Tourist Office
(Hungary) **206**
National Tourist Office
(Iceland) **207**
National Tourist Office
(Ireland) **207**
National Tourist Office
(Italy) **207**
National Tourist Office
(Netherlands) **209**

National Tourist Office
(Norway) **209**
National Tourist Office (South
Africa) **210**
National Trails **150**
National Trainers
Federation **253**
National Training Organisation
for Arts and Entertainment
(Metier) **71**
National Tramways
Museum **172**
National Trust **85**
National Trust for Scotland **85**
National Tyre Distributors
Association **155**
National Tyres **155**
National Union of Journalists
(NUJ) **55**
National Union of Students **75**
National Union of Teachers
(NUT) **55**
National Waterways Museum at
Gloucester **172**
National Westminster Bank **40**
Nationalist Party, Vietnam **108**
Nationalmuseum,
Stockholm **211**
Nationwide **188**
Nationwide Investigations
Group **49**
Nationwide League **251**
NATO **105**
Natural Environment Research
Council **84, 109**
Natural History Museum **172**
Natural History Museum
Library **169**
Natural Law Party **107**
Natural Resources Institute **219**
Nature **218**
Nature Conservation
Bureau **217**
Naturenet **218**
NatWest **42, 188**
NatWest Trophy **249**
Nauquip **258**
Nautilus **258, 284**
Naxos & Marco Polo **22**
NBC **26**
NCH **136**
NCH Action for Children **136**
NCR **47, 57**
Neath (Rugby club) **257**
Neath Port Talbot (Gov) **116**
NEC **266, 268**
Nederlander (Holland) **183**
Neff **239**
Neighbourhood Watch **136,
161**
Neighbours **28**
Neil Diamond **19**
Neilson Holidays **258, 284**
Nelson Books **72**
Nelson Times **180**

Nelsons **236**
Nene Valley (Railway) **199**
Neneh Cherry **19**
Nepal (Tourist info) **209**
Nescafe **91**
Nesquik **91**
Nestle **91**
Net **267**
Net Doctor **129**
Net Nanny **269**
Netbenefit **266**
Netcom **266**
NetDirect **267**
Netherlands (British
embassy) **101**
Netherlands (Monarchy) **106**
Netherlands (Weather) **174**
Netscape **266**
Nevada Bob Golf
Superstores **260**
New Atlantic 252 (Radio) **25**
New Brunswick (Local info) **204**
New Civil Engineer **218**
New Deal **110**
New Eden **147**
New Electronics **218**
New Forest (Gov) **116**
New Line **12**
New Musical Express **14**
New Opportunties Fund **13**
New Orleans Channel **25**
New Producer's Alliance **12**
New Reg Personalised
Registration Numbers **155**
New Scientist **218**
New Victoria Theatre, Stoke on
Trent **30**
New Woman **162**
New York (Airport) **277**
New York (Local info) **213**
New York (Stock exchange) **54**
New York City Ballet **6**
New York Philharmonic **21**
New York Times (USA) **183**
New York University **78**
New Zealand (British
embassy) **101**
New Zealand (Embassy) **102**
New Zealand (Gov) **104**
New Zealand (Legal
institutions) **106**
New Zealand (Tourist info) **209**
New Zealand Cricket
Board **248**
New Zealand News UK **180**
New Zealand Symphony
Orchestra **21**
Newark (Airport) **277**
Newark (Gov) **116**
Newark Advertiser **180**
Newbury (Racecourse) **253**
Newbury Weekly News **180**
Newby Hall **200**
Newcastle (Uni) **76**
Newcastle Brown **89**

Newcastle Evening Chronicle **180**
Newcastle Falcons (Rugby club) **257**
Newcastle Herald & Post **180**
Newcastle Journal **180**
Newcastle Sunday Sun **180**
Newcastle United (FC) **250**
Newcastle-under-Lyme (Gov) **116**
Newcastle-upon-Tyne (Gov) **116**
Newfoundland & Labrador (Local info) **204**
Newham (Gov) **116**
Newmarket (Racecourse) **253**
Newport (Gov) **116**
News & Star (Carlisle) **180**
News Direct (London) **25**
News International **48**
News of the World **182**
News Unlimited **177**
NewsNow **177**
Newspaper Society **55**
Newsquest **46**
Newsround **65**
Newton & Goldborne Guardian **180**
Newton Abbot (Racecourse) **253**
Newtonabbey (Gov) **116**
Next **52, 226**
NFC **56**
NFU Mutual **189**
NHS Confederation **126**
NHS Digest **129**
NHS Direct **129**
NHS Nursing **130**
NHS Primary Care Group Alliance **129**
NI Railways **283**
Nice (Airport) **277**
Nice (Local info) **206**
Nice Price **241**
Nicholson Graham Jones **51**
Nickelodeon **57, 65**
NicNames **266**
Nicolas Cage **4**
Nicole Kidman (Fan Club) **4**
Nicorette **236**
Nicosia (Local info) **205**
Nicotinell **236**
Nightclub Network **6**
Nightmare on Elm Street **10**
Nike **260**
Nikon **152**
Nildram **267**
Nimble **91**
Nimbus (Record company) **22**
nineoneone **19**
Nintendo **63, 266**
Nirvana Spa **158**
Nissan **157**
Nitty Gritty Dirt Band **19**
Nivea **236**

Noggin The Nog **63**
Nokia **266, 268**
NOP Research **173**
Nordiska Museet, Stockholm **211**
Norfolk (Gov) **116**
Norfolk (Local info) **201**
Norland Nanny School **74**
Norman Greenbaum **19**
Norman Rockwell Museum, Massachusetts **212**
Norman Shipping Group **53**
Nortel **269**
North & Mid Hampshire (Health authority) **127**
North Ayrshire (Gov) **116**
North Cornwall (Gov) **116**
North Cumbria (Health authority) **127**
North Dakota University **78**
North Derbyshire (Chamber of Commerce) **36**
North Devon (Gov) **116**
North Devon Farm Park **201**
North Devon Journal **180**
North Dorset (Gov) **116**
North Down (Gov) **116**
North East Derbyshire (Gov) **116**
North East Evening Gazette (Middlesbrough) **180**
North East Lincolnshire (Gov) **116**
North Eastern Evening Gazette **180**
North Essex (Health authority) **127**
North Face **260**
North Hertfordshire (Gov) **116**
North Kesteven (Gov) **116**
North Lanarkshire (Gov) **116**
North Lincolnshire (Gov) **116**
North London (Uni) **76**
North Norfolk (Gov) **116**
North Norfolk (Railway) **199**
North of England College of Dance **71**
North Riding Infirmary **128**
North Shropshire (Gov) **116**
North Somerset (Gov) **116**
North Staffs Acute Psychiatric Unit **128**
North Tyneside (Gov) **116**
North Wales (Health authority) **127**
North Wales (Police) **140**
North Wales Newspapers **180**
North Wales Theatre, Llandudno **30**
North Warwickshire (Gov) **116**
North West Airlines **275**
North West Arts Board **4**
North West Evening Mail **181**
North West Lancashire (Health authority) **127**

North West Leicestershire (Gov) **116**
North West Water **162**
North Western Trains **283**
North Wiltshire (Gov) **116**
North York Moors (Local info) **201**
North Yorkshire (Gov) **116**
North Yorkshire (Health authority) **127**
North Yorkshire Moors (Railway) **199**
Northampton & Lamport (Railway) **199**
Northampton (Gov) **116**
Northampton Chronicle & Echo **181**
Northampton Town (FC) **251**
Northamptonshire (Cricket club) **248**
Northamptonshire (Gov) **116**
Northamptonshire (Health authority) **127**
Northamptonshire (Police) **1·**
Northants Evening Telegraph **181**
Northern (Bank) **188**
Northern Arts Board **4**
Northern Ballet Theatre **6**
Northern Echo **181**
Northern Echo (Darlington) **1**
Northern Exposure **28**
Northern Foods **41**
Northern Ireland (Ambulance) **135**
Northern Ireland (Chamber c Commerce) **36**
Northern Ireland Assembly **1**
Northern Ireland Bridge Union **144**
Northern Ireland Chest, Hear Stroke Association **138**
Northern Ireland Electricity **1**
Northern Ireland Film Commission **4**
Northern Ireland Office **111**
Northern Ireland Ombudsman **140**
Northern Ireland Tourist Board **202**
Northern Light **268**
Northern Rock **40, 188**
Northern School of Contemporary Dance **71**
Northern Sinfonia **21**
Northern Spirit **283**
Northern Territory University
Northgate Vehicle Hire **278**
Northumberland (Gov) **117**
Northumbria (Ambulance) **1**
Northumbria (Local info) **20·**
Northumbria (Police) **140**
Northumbria (Uni) **76**
Northumbria Tourist Board **2**
Northwest Territories (Local

info) **204**
Northwich & District
  Guardian **181**
Norton Owner Club GB **164**
Norton Rose **51**
Norway (British embassy) **101**
Norway Post **183, 209**
Norweb **269**
Norwegian (Embassy) **102**
Norwegian (Gov) **104**
Norwegian Cruise Line **284**
Norwich & Peterborough
  (Building Society) **188**
Norwich (Gov) **117**
Norwich City (FC) **251**
Norwich Gallery **5**
Norwich Union **42-43, 189, 191**
Nothampton Saints (Rugby
  club) **257**
Notre Dame de Paris **29**
Notting Hill (Film) **10**
Notting Hill Carnival **8**
Nottingham (Gov) **117**
Nottingham (Racecourse) **253**
Nottingham (Uni) **76**
Nottingham Evening Post **181**
Nottingham Forest (FC) **251**
Nottingham Trent (Uni) **76**
Nottinghamshire (Cricket
  club) **248**
Nottinghamshire (Gov) **117**
Notts County (FC) **251**
Nova Scotia (Local info) **204**
Novartis **47**
Novell **266**
Novo Nordisk **47**
Novotel **280**
NRICH Primary Maths
  (University of Cambridge) **66**
NTC Touring Theatre
  Company **28**
Nuffield (Hospital) **128**
Nuffield Theatre, Lancaster **30**
Nuffield Trust **74, 136, 138**
Nunavut (Local info) **204**
Nuremberg (Local info) **206**
Nurofen **236**
Nursing Homes Registry **125**
Nursing Standard **129**
Nursing Times **129**
Nutrasweet **91**
NWO Wrestling **262**
Nycomed Amersham **47**
Nynex **269**
NYPD Blue **28**
Nürburgring (Motor racing) **254**

O

O'Neill **260**
Oadby (Gov) **117**
Oakley **241, 260**
Oakwood Park **64**
Oasis **19**
Oban **98**
Oberoi **280**

Observer **182**
Occidental Petroleum **57**
Occupational Pensions
  Regulatory Authority **110**
Ocean **56, 239**
Ocean Colour Scene **19**
Ocean FM **25**
Ocean Music Venue **25**
Ocean Rowing Society **257**
Ocean Youth Club **258**
Ocean Youth Trust **63**
October Films **12**
Oddbins **94**
Odds Farm Park **201**
Odeon **9**
Odeon Filmstore **241**
Odeon Videostore **241**
Odyssey **269**
Oesterreichische Nationalbank
  (Austria) **40**
OFFER (Electricity) **140**
Office **241**
Office for the Supervision of
  Solicitors **140**
Office of Fair Trading **140**
Office of Science &
  Technology **219**
Office of Technology **110**
Office World **47**
Officers' Pensions Society **163**
Official Lawn Bowls **247**
Official London Theatre **14**
Official Publications **110**
Official Solicitor's
  Department **106**
Offshore **95**
Offshore Investor **191**
OFGAS (Gas) **140**
OFSTED (Teaching) **140**
OFTEL **140, 269**
OFWAT (Water) **140**
Ohio State University **78**
Oil of Olay **230**
Oilily **226**
Okinawa (Local info) **208**
Oklahoma State University **78**
Olan Mills **241**
Old Mutual **189**
Old Speckled Hen **91**
Oldham (Gov) **117**
Olivetti **266**
Olivetum Olive Oil **91**
Olivia Newton John **19**
Olswang **51**
Olympia Fine Art & Antiques
  Fairs **223**
Olympic Games **254**
Olympic Museum **211**
Olympus **152**
Omani (Gov) **104**
Omega **243**
On Course **72-73**
On Your Bike **249**
Oncourse **75**
ONDigital **26**

One 2 One **269**
One.Tel UK **269**
oneninetwo.com **173**
Online Marine **258**
Online Weather **174**
Ontario (Local info) **204**
Opel **157**
Open Air Theatre Regent's
  Park **30**
Open Championship **252**
Open Churches Trust **85**
Open Text Index **268**
Open Universal Software **266**
Open University **76**
Opening Line **14**
Operadio (Radio) **25**
Oprah Winfrey **28**
Oracle **266**
Oral B **236**
Oral History Society **169**
Orange **269**
Orange **42, 54, 269**
Orangutan Foundation UK **217**
Orbit **48, 249**
Orchard FM **25**
Order of Bards, Ovates &
  Druids **165**
Order of St Benedict **164**
Ordnance Survey **110, 150,
  170**
Ordnance Survey Ireland **170**
Ordnance Survey of Northern
  Ireland **170**
Oregon State University **78**
Organics Direct **94**
Organisation for Economic Co-
  operation & Development
  (OECD) **105**
Organisation of Petroleum
  Exporting Countries
  (OPEC) **105**
Organon **47**
Orgasmic Wines **98**
Orient Express **280**
Orient Express Trains &
  Cruises **284**
Oriental Bird Club **143**
Original Bus Tour
  Company **202**
Orion **12**
Orkney (Local info) **201**
Orlando (Airport) **277**
Orlando (Tourist info) **213**
Ormskirk Advertiser **181**
Orthodox **164**
Osaka (Airport) **277**
Osaka (Local info) **208**
Osborne Books **48**
Oscar Wilde **10**
Oscars **8**
Osh Kosh B'Gosh **226**
Oslo Opera House **209**
Osmonds **19**
Osram **237**
Ostend (Local info) **198**

Osteopathic Information
  Service **126**
Ottoman Bank, Turkey **40**
Oulton Park (Motor racing) **254**
Oulu (Local info) **205**
Oundle (Public school) **74**
Our Price **241**
Out-of-Towners **10**
Outlet Centres
  International **240**
Owlpen Manor **200**
Oxfam **138**
Oxford (Chamber of
  Commerce) **36**
Oxford (Gov) **117**
Oxford (Uni) **76**
Oxford Brookes (Uni) **76**
Oxford Bus **278**
Oxford Circus, London (Web
  cam) **213**
Oxford English Dictionary **174**
Oxford Mail **181**
Oxford School of Drama **71**
Oxford Star **181**
Oxford University Press **48**
Oxfordshire (Gov) **117**
Oxygen FM **25**
Oz Clarke **95**
Ozzy Osbourne **19**

P

P & O **42**
P & O European **278**
P & O North Sea **278**
P & O Scottish **278**
P & O Stena Line **278, 284**
PA News **177**
Pablo Picasso **4**
Packard Bell **266**
Paco Rabanne **230**
PACT **136**
Paddington Bear **67, 242**
Pagan Federation **165**
Page & Moy **284**
Paignton (Zoo) **220**
Painswick Rococo
  Gardens **201**
Paint Research
  Association **237**
Paintball Zone **149**
Paisley (Uni) **76**
Paisner & Co **51**
Pakistan (Legal
  institutions) **106**
Pakistan (Tourist info) **210**
Pakistan Bridge
  Federation **144**
Pakistan International **275**
Pakistani (Gov) **104**
Palace of Versailles **206**
Palaeontological
  Association **219**
Paleontological Society **219**
Paling Walters Targis **35**
Palma (Local info) **211**

Palmers Cocoa Butter **236**
Pamela Anderson Lee **4**
Pampers **240**
Pan Am **275**
Panamanian (Gov) **104**
Panasonic **152, 239, 269**
Panerai **243**
Panini **66**
Pannell Kerr Forster **50**
Papermate **235**
Parachute Association of
  Ireland **150**
Paradise Wildlife Park **220**
Paragon **48**
Paralinks **138**
Paramount **12**
Paramount Pictures **57**
Parc Asterix **206**
Parcel Force **36**
Parent News **158, 162**
Parent Soup **158**
Parentline **158**
Pareto Law **51**
Paris (Airport) **277**
Paris (Local info) **206**
Paris (Stock exchange) **54**
Paris Match **183**
Parity Group **37**
Parker Knoll **234**
Parking Express, APCOA
  Parking **282**
Parliament (UK) **120**
Parliamentary Monitoring and
  Information Service **110**
Parliamentary
  Ombudsman **140**
Parlophone **22**
Parma AC **251**
Parrot Line **217**
Parrot Society UK **143**
Particle Physics and
  Astronomy **109**
Partnerships in Care **128**
Parts Direct **155**
Passport Agency **110**
Past Times **235**
Patek Philippe **243**
Pathe **9, 12**
Patriot **10**
Patsy Cline **19**
Paul Daniels **14**
Paul Nicholls **4**
Paul Smith **226**
Paul Smith **9**
Paul Young **19**
Paula Abdul **19**
Paula Rosa **239**
Pavilion Theatre, Glasgow **30**
Paxton & Whitfield **94**
PC Advisor **267**
PC Plus **267**
PC World **230**
PC Zone OnLine **267**
PDSA **135**
Peak Practice **28**

Peak Rail **199**
Pearl **189**
Pearson **42, 48**
Pedigree Petfoods **151**
Pedro De La Rosa **256**
Pegasus Pushchairs **240**
Pele **256**
Pembrey (Motor racing) **254**
Pembrokeshire (Gov) **117**
Pembrokeshire Coast (Local
  info) **201**
Pembrokeshire Coast Nation
  Park **201**
Pen Shop **235**
Pendle (Gov) **117**
Penguin **48, 223**
Peninsula Networks **265**
Penn & Teller **6, 14**
Pennon Group **58**
Pennsylvania State
  University **78**
Penshurst Place **200**
Penshurst Place &
  Gardens **201**
Pensions World **191**
Pentax **152**
Penwith (Gov) **117**
People's Bank **188**
People's Palace **95**
People's Party, Pakistan **10**
Peoples Daily (China) **183**
Pepe Jeans **226**
Peperami **92**
Pepsi **92**
PepsiCo **57**
Peradon **259**
Perfect Pizza **94**
Perfect Storm **10**
Performing Rights Society **2**
Periodical Publishers
  Association **55**
Permaculture Association **1**
Pernod-Ricard **92**
Perpetual **40**
Perpetual Investment **191**
Perrier **92**
Persil **159**
Persimmon **45**
Persimmon Homes **160**
Personal Loan Corporation
Perth & Kinross (Gov) **117**
Perth (Airport) **277**
Perth (Racecourse) **253**
Perthshire Tourist Board **20**
Peruvian (Embassy) **102**
Peruvian (Gov) **104**
Peruvian Connection **226**
Pet Cover **151**
Pet Plan **189**
Pet Plan Insurance **151**
Pet Shop Boys **19**
Pete Sampras **256**
Peter Andre **19**
Peter Gabriel **19**
Peter Tork **19**

Peterborough (Gov) **117**
Peterborough United (FC) **251**
Petersfield Post **181**
Pets Pyjamas.com **151**
Peugeot **157**
Pevsner Architectural
   Guides **83**
Pfizer **47, 57**
PG Wodehouse (Fan Club) **13**
PGA European Tour **252**
Phantasialand **206**
Phantom Menace **11**
Phantom of the Opera **29**
Pharmacia & Upjohn **57**
Pharmacy **95**
Phil Mickelson **256**
Philadelphia (Local info) **213**
Philharmonia **21**
Philip Morris **57**
Philippine Airlines **275**
Philippine National Bank **40**
Philippine Star
   (Philippines) **183**
Philippines (Embassy) **102**
Philippines (Tourist info) **210**
Philippino (Gov) **104**
Philips **223, 239, 269**
Phillipines (Legal
   institutions) **106**
Phillips **236**
Phoenix Arts, Leicester **30**
Phonenumbers.net **173**
Photo Me **241**
Photo-Me International **52**
Photographers' Gallery **5**
Physics World **218**
Physiological Society **129**
Piaggio **164**
Piano Tuners' Association **22**
Pickfords **161**
Pictet Group **191**
Picture House **9**
Picture Palace Productions **12**
Pietermaritzburg (Local
   info) **210**
Pilates Foundation **158**
Pilates.co.uk **159**
Pilkington **45**
Pillsbury **92**
Pilot Magazine **146**
Pilot Pens **47**
Ping **260**
Pinnacle **260**
Pinnacle Investments **191**
Pinsent Curtis **51**
Pioneer (Munich) **23**
Pipemedia **267**
Pirate FM **25**
Pirelli **155**
Pitlochry Festival Theatre **30**
Pitney Bowes **47**
Pitt Rivers Museum,
   Oxford **172**
Pizza Hut **95**
PizzaExpress **43, 95**

PJ Harvey **19**
Placebo **19**
Placido Domingo **19**
Plaid Cymru, Wales **107**
Plan It For Kids **64**
Planet Ark **218**
Planet Darts **249**
Planet Football **251**
Planet Hollywood **95**
Planet of the Apes **28**
Planet Talk **269**
Planning Inspectorate **110**
Plantlife **219**
Playboy **163**
Playhouse Theatre, Derby **30**
Playhouse Theatre, Oxford **30**
Playhouse, Edinburgh **30**
Playhouse, Liverpool **30**
Playhouse, Nottingham **30**
Playmobil **66, 242**
Playstation **63, 266**
Pleasure Island **64**
Pleasureland **64**
Plymouth (Chamber of
   Commerce) **36**
Plymouth (Gov) **117**
Plymouth (Local info) **203**
Plymouth (Uni) **76**
Plymouth Argyll (FC) **251**
Plymouth Evening Herald **181**
Plymouth FM **25**
Plymouth Gin **92**
Plymouth Western Morning
   News **181**
Poetry Book Society **13**
Poetry Review **13**
Pogues **19**
Pokemon **11, 63, 66, 243**
Pokemon the First Movie **65**
Poland (British embassy) **101**
Polaroid **152**
Polish (Embassy) **102**
Polish (Gov) **104**
Polka Children's Theatre **67**
Polly Pocket **243**
Polo World Cup on Snow **256**
Polycell **237**
Polydor **22**
Polygram (Record
   company) **22**
Polygram Video **12**
Polynesian Airlines **275**
Pompidou Centre **206**
Pontypridd (Rugby club) **257**
Pony Club **63, 149, 259**
Pooh Corner **68**
Poole (Gov) **117**
Poole (Hospital) **128**
Poole Pottery **224**
Popcorn **14**
Popeye **63, 65**
Poppets **92**
Porsche **157**
Port of Kawasaki **53**
Port Lympne **200**

Port of Antwerp **53**
Port of Bordeaux **53**
Port of Larne **53**
Port of Liverpool **53**
Port of London **53**
Port of London Authority **110**
Port of Marseilles **53**
Port of Montreal **53**
Port of Oostende **53**
Port of Osaka **53**
Port of Quebec **53**
Port of Reykjavik **53**
Port of Zeebrugge **53**
Porters **95**
Portfolio of British Nursing **129**
Portishead **19**
Portland **284**
Portland Museum **172**
Portman Group **109**
Portman Travel **284**
Portmeirion **224**
Portmerion (Local info) **203**
Portobello Antiques
   Market **223**
Portsmouth & South East
   Hampshire (Health
   authority) **127**
Portsmouth (Gov) **117**
Portsmouth (Uni) **77**
Portsmouth Journal **181**
Portsmouth News **181**
Portugal (Tourist info) **210**
Portugalia Air **275**
Portuguese (Embassy) **102**
Portuguese (Gov) **104**
Positive Health **129**
Post Office **36, 108, 110, 145,
   211**
Post Office Counters **108**
Posthouse **280**
Postman **11**
Postmuseum, Stockholm **211**
Pot Black Magazine **259**
Potter's Herbal Medicines **236**
Potteries Museum & Art
   Gallery **172**
Potterton **160, 237**
Poulter **35**
Powakaddy **260**
Powder Byrne **284**
Powderham Castle **198**
Power Check **265**
Power FM **25**
Power On Wheels **156**
Powergen **42, 58**
Powerhouse **230**
Powerhouse Museum **197**
Powys (Gov) **117**
PPM UK **191**
PPP Healthcare **128**
PPP/Columbia **128, 189**
PR Newswire **177**
Practical Car & Van Rental **278**
Practical Fishkeeping **151**
Practical Shooting

Association 261
Practice Nursing 129
Prada 9, 226
Pravda (Russia) 183
Preferential 189
Preferred Direct 189
Premier Asset
    Management 191
Premier Oil 37
Premier Percussion 150
Press Association 183
Press Complaints
    Commission 140
Prestel 267
Preston (Gov) 117
Pret A Manger 94
Pretoria (Local info) 210
Pretty Polly 226
Price Offers 94
PricewaterhouseCoopers 50
Primary Immunodeficiency
    Association 138
Primate Society of Great
    Britain 219
Primebake 92
Prince 19
Prince Edward Island (Local
    info) 204
Prince Naseem Hamed 256
Prince of Egypt 11
Prince's Trust 136
Prince's Trust Shop 235
Princess 284
Princeton University 78
Principles 226
Pringle 226
Printmakers Council 55
Priory (Hospital) 128
Prism 95
Prisoner 28
Privacy International 109
Private Eye 163
Privilege Cars 190
Pro Plus 92
Probert 169
Proctor & Gamble 57
Prodigy 19
Producers Alliance for Cinema
    & Television 12, 22, 26
Production Managers'
    Association 22
Profaces 230
Professional Golf Association of
    America 251
Progrssive Unionist Party 107
Proline 242, 260
Promenade Concerts 8
Prontaprint 47
Pronuptia 165
Prospero Direct 190
Prost (Motor racing teams) 255
Prostate Cancer 138
Proton 157
Provident Financial 40
Prudential 42-43, 188, 190

Prutour 249
Psion 37, 266
Psycho 11
Pub Guide 95
Public and Commercial
    Services Union 55
Public Enemy 19
Public Record Office 110, 148
Public Record Office of England
    & Wales 169
Public Transport
    Information 282
Puerto Rico (Tourist info) 204
Puff Daddy 19
Puffin 48
Pulp 19
Pulse 129
Puma 260
Punchestown
    (Racecourse) 253
Punjab (Local info) 207
Punjab National Bank, India 40
Pupil Line 68
Puppeteers Company 67
Purves & Purves 234
Pusan (Airport) 277
Puzzle Up 68

Q

Q 14
Qantas 275
Qatar Airways 275
QED Productions 22
QS 226
Quadro 66, 243
Quaker Oats 57, 92
Qualcast 147
Qualifications & Curriculum
    Authority 53, 72
Qualifications for Industry 53
Quebec (Local info) 204
Queen 19
Queen Margaret College,
    School of Drama
    (Edinburgh) 71
Queen Mary & Westfield
    College London 77
Queen Victoria, East
    Grinstead 128
Queen's (Uni) 77
Queen's Film Theatre, Belfast 9
Queens Moat 280
Queens Park Rangers (FC) 251
Quick and Easy Cross Stitch
    Magazine 148
Quicken.com 191
Quickgrip 237
QuickSilver 67
Quicksilver Theatre
    Company 28
Quilters' Guild of the British
    Isles 148
Quilting Directory 148
Quincy Jones 19
Quorn 92

QXL.com 37, 223

R

Rabbits Online 151
Rabbits UK 151
Rabobank, Netherland 40
RAC 135
RAC Trackstar 155
Racal 266
Racal Electronics 37
Race Horses.com 253
Racecourse Association 253
Racenews 253
Racing Green 226
Racing Pigeon Magazine 14
Racing Post 182
Radio Australia (Melbourne)
Radio Authority 140
Radio Caroline 25
Radio City 96.7 (Liverpool) 2
Radio Nepal 23
Radio Officers' Association
Radio Society of Great
    Britain 149
Radio Sweden 211
Radio Times 14
Radio Vlaanderen
    International 198
Radiohead 19
Radisson 280
Rado 243
RAF Benevolent Fund 163
RAF Careers 101
Raffles Singapore 280
RAFT Institute 131
Ragged School Museum 17
Rail Users' Consultative
    Committees 140
Railtrack 42, 56, 283
Railway Children 28
Railway Industry
    Association 282
Raindance Film Showcase
Rainforest Action Network
Rainforest Café 95
Rajasthan (Local info) 207
RAK Recording Studios 22
Raleigh 249
Raleigh International 137
Ralf Schumacher 256
Ralph Vaughan Williams 19
Rambert Dance Company
Rambert School 71
Ramblers Association 150
Ramones 19
Random House 48
Rangers (FC) 251
Rank 43
Rank Hovis 92
Rank Leisure 146
Raptor Conservation 218
Rare Breeding Birds Panel
Raven Lodge of
    Shamanism 164
Ravenglass (Railway) 199

Rawlplug 237
Ray Charles 19
Ray-Ban 241
Raymond Blanc 90
Raymond Gubbay 23
Raytheon Marine 258
RCR International 51
RDW 35
Rea Brothers 188
Reach 138
Reader's Digest Association 57
Readers' Digest 163
Reading (FC) 251
Reading (Gov) 117
Reading (Uni) 77
Reading Chronicle 181
Reading Evening Post 181
Reading Festival 8
Reading Newspaper
  Company 181
Readymix 45
Real Meat Company 94
Real Nappy Association 240
Real Tennis 261
Really Useful Theatres 30-31
Recipe World 145
Reckitt and Colman 42
Reckitt Benckiser 45
Red Arrows 146
Red Carnation 280
Red Cross 138
Red Dragon FM 25
Red Dragon FM (Cardiff) 25
Red Dwarf 28
Red Fort 95
Red Funnel 278
Red Letter Days 235
Red or Dead 226
Redbridge & Waltham Forest
  (Health authority) 127
Redbridge (Gov) 117
Redcar & Cleveland (Gov) 117
Redditch (Gov) 117
Redditch (Local info) 203
Redditch Advertiser/Alcester
  Chronicle 181
Redfern Gallery 5
Redring 239
Reebok 260
Reed 48, 51
Reed Elsevier 46
Reeltime 9
Reeves & Mortimer 6
Reference Centre 174
Reform Party 108
Reform Synagogues 165
Regal 280
Regatta Magazine 257
Regeneration Through
  Heritage 85
Regent, Ipswich 30
Regional Arts Boards of
  England 110
Register of Chinese Herbal
  Medicine 126

Registration Transfers 155
Regus 47
Reigate & Banstead (Gov) 117
Reiss 226
Relais & Chateaux 280
Relate 136
Religious Society of Friends
  (Quakers) 164
Relyon 223
REM 19
Remy Martin 92
Renault 157
Renfrewshire (Gov) 117
Rennies 236
Rentokil 52
Rentokil Initial 42, 52
Replacement Window Advisory
  Service 161
Reptilian Online 151
Republican Movement,
  Australia 108
Republican Party, Ireland 108
Republican Party, USA 108
RESCUE (British Archaeology
  Trust) 85
Reserve Bank of Australia 40
Reserve Bank of India 40
Reserve Bank of New
  Zealand 40
Rest Assured 223
Restaurant Association 96
Retail Motor Industry
  Federation 35
Retail Week 44
Retreat Association 164
Reuters 42, 46, 177
Reuters Health Information 129
Reuters Money Network 45
Revlon 230
Rexam 47
Reykjavík Savings Bank,
  Iceland 40
Rhondda-Cynon-Taff (Gov) 117
Rhyl, Prestatyn & Abergele
  Journal 181
Rialto Homes 160
RIAS, Scotland 83
RIBA Publications 83
Ribble (Railway) 199
Ribble Valley (Gov) 117
Richard Ellis 159
Richer Sounds 236
Richmond (Gov) 117
Richmond (Rugby club) 257
Richmondshire (Gov) 117
Ricky Martin 19
Ricoh 47, 152
Ridgways 92
Ridleys 89
Right Start 67
Riley Leisure 260
Rindal Sparebank, Norway 40
Ringo Starr 19
Rio Tinto 42, 46
Ritz 95, 280

Rivella 92
River & Rowing Museum 172
River Island 226
River Thames Society 85
Riverdance 29
Rizla 242
RJR Nabisco Holdings 57
RM 72
RMC Angling 146
Road Haulage Association 56
Road Runner 63
Road Time Trials Council 249
Road to Eldorado 11
Roadchef 94
Roadhouse 6
Roaduser 155
Roald Dahl 67
Roald Dahl Club 63
Robbie Williams 19
Robert Gordon (Uni) 77
Robert Stigwood
  Organisation 23
Roberts Radios Direct 230
Robertson Residential 160
Robin Hood Stamp
  Company 145
Robins 9
Robinson Willey 160
Robson Green 4
Robson Rhodes 50
Rochdale (Gov) 117
Rochdale Observer 181
Roche 47
Rochester-upon-Medway
  (Gov) 117
Rochford (Gov) 117
Rock Garden 95
Rocket Theatre Company 28
Rockface 144
Rockport Shoes 241
Rockwell International 57
Rockwool 45
Rocky Horror Picture Show 11,
  29
Rod Stewart 19
Rodier 9
Roedean 75
Roehampton Institute of
  Dance 72
Roger Daltrey 19
Roger Waters 19
Roger Whittaker 19
Roget's Thesaurus 174
Rohan 242
Rolf Harris 19
Rollei 152
Rolling Rock 89
Rolling Stone 14
Rolling Stones 19
Rolls Royce 37, 42, 157
Roman Baths Museum 172
Romania (Tourist info) 210
Romanian (Gov) 104
Rombouts 92
Rome (Airport) 277

Romney Hythe & Dymchurch (Railway) **199**
Ronaldo **256**
Ronan Keating **19**
Ronnie Scott's **6**
Room Service **94**
Rooseum, Malmo **211**
Rose Bruford College of Speech & Drama **72**
Roslin Institute **219**
RoSPA **161**
Rotaract Club **149**
Rotary **243**
Rotary International **136**
Rother (Gov) **117**
Rotherham (Chamber of Commerce) **36**
Rotherham (Gov) **117**
Rotorua (Local info) **209**
Rotterdam (Local info) **209**
Rough Guides **48, 282**
Route On-line **14**
Rover **157**
Rowan **148**
Rowan Atkinson **7**
Roxy **9**
Roy Castle Lung Cancer Foundation **138**
Roy of the Rovers **251**
Roy Orbison **20**
Roy Rogers **4**
Roy Wood **20**
Royal Opera House **21, 26**
Royal & Sun Alliance **42-43, 190**
Royal & Sun Alliance Challenge **258**
Royal & Sun Alliance Investments **192**
Royal Academy **5**
Royal Academy of Dramatic Art (RADA) **72**
Royal Academy of Engineering **219**
Royal Academy of Engineers **74**
Royal Academy of Music **72**
Royal Agricultural College **71**
Royal Agricultural Society **83**
Royal Air Force **101**
Royal Air Forces Association **101, 163**
Royal Air Maroc **275**
Royal Airforce Museum **172**
Royal Albert Hall **26**
Royal Albert Memorial Museum & Art Gallery, Exeter **172**
Royal Armouries Museum, Leeds **172**
Royal Astronomical Society **217**
Royal Auxiliary Air Force **101, 163**
Royal Ballet **6**
Royal Ballet School **6, 72**

Royal Bank of Canada (Channel Islands) **188**
Royal Bank of Scotland **40, 42, 188**
Royal Bath & West Society **83**
Royal Birkdale **252**
Royal Botanic Gardens **219**
Royal Bournemouth (Hospital) **128**
Royal British Legion **149**
Royal Brompton (Hospital) **128**
Royal Brunei **275**
Royal Buckinghamshire (Hospital) **128**
Royal Canadian Legion **163**
Royal Carribean Cruise Line **284**
Royal Centre, Nottingham **30**
Royal College of Anaesthetists **129**
Royal College of Art **71**
Royal College of General Practitioners **129**
Royal College of Music **72**
Royal College of Nursing **130**
Royal College of Nursing Scotland **130**
Royal College of Obstetricians & Gynaecologists **130**
Royal College of Paediatrics & Child Health **74**
Royal College of Physicians **74**
Royal College of Physicians, Edinburgh **130**
Royal College of Psychiatrists **74**
Royal College of Speech & Language Therapists **73, 126**
Royal College of Surgeons, Edinburgh **130**
Royal College of Surgeons, England **130**
Royal College of Veterinary Surgeons **125**
Royal College of Veterinary Surgeons (London) **79**
Royal Commission on Historical Manuscripts **84**
Royal Commission on the Ancient and Historical Monuments of Scotland **84**
Royal Commonwealth Society **105**
Royal Cornwall Museum **172**
Royal Court Theatre **30**
Royal Doulton **224**
Royal Entomological Society **219**
Royal Exchange Theatre Company **30**
Royal Exchange Theatre, Manchester **30**
Royal Forestry Society **85**
Royal Free & University College Medical School **74**

Royal Geographical Society **219**
Royal Highland and Agricultu Society of Scotland **83**
Royal Highland Education Trust **85**
Royal Highland Games **8**
Royal Holloway London (Uni) **77**
Royal Horticultural Society **1**
Royal Horticultural Society Shop **147**
Royal Infirmary of Edinburgh **128**
Royal Institute of British Architects **83**
Royal Institute of Internationa Affairs **74**
Royal Institute of Navigation **258**
Royal Institute of Public Hea & Hygiene **125**
Royal Institution of Chartere Surveyors **161**
Royal Institution of Great Britain **73**
Royal Jordanian Airlines **27!**
Royal Liver **190**
Royal Liverpool Philharmoni Orchestra **21**
Royal Lyceum Theatre, Edinburgh **30**
Royal Mail **36**
Royal Mail (Post office) **108**
Royal Marines **101**
Royal Marsden (Hospital) **12**
Royal Meteorological Society **174**
Royal Mews **200**
Royal Mint **110**
Royal Museums of Fine Arts **198**
Royal National Institute for D People (RNID) **136**
Royal National Institute for t Blind (RNIB) **136**
Royal National Lifeboat Institution (RNLI) **136**
Royal National Rose Society **147**
Royal National Theatre **30**
Royal Naval Lifeboat Institution **139**
Royal Naval Museum **172**
Royal Navy **101**
Royal Navy Careers **101**
Royal Navy Submarine Museum **172**
Royal Nepal Airlines **275**
Royal Northern College **72**
Royal Numismatic Society **'**
Royal Observatory Edinburgh **217**
Royal Observatory, Greenwich **217**

Royal Palace, Stockholm **211**
Royal Parks of London **201**
Royal Pharmaceutical Society
  of Great Britain **130**
Royal Philatelic Society
  London **145**
Royal Philharmonic **21**
Royal Photographic
  Society **152**
Royal Pigeon Racing
  Association **143**
Royal School of
  Needlework **148**
Royal Scotsman (Railway) **199**
Royal Scottish Academy of
  Music & Drama **72**
Royal Scottish National **21**
Royal Shakespeare Company
  Theatre **30**
Royal Skandia **191**
Royal Society **219**
Royal Society for Nature
  Conservation **85**
Royal Society for the Prevention
  of Accidents (ROSPA) **136**
Royal Society for the Prevention
  of Cruelty to Animals
  (RSPCA) **135**
Royal Society for the Protection
  of Birds (RSPB) **135**
Royal Society of Chemistry **219**
Royal Society of Medicine **130**
Royal Television Society **26**
Royal Tennis Court, Hampton
  Court Palace **261**
Royal Thai Cookery School **145**
Royal Theatre,
  Northampton **30**
Royal Troon (Golf course) **252**
Royal Ulster Agricultural
  Society **83**
Royal Ulster Constabulary
  (Police) **140**
Royal Ulster Constabulary
  Museum, Belfast **172**
Royal United Hospital Bath **128**
Royal Veterinary College
  (London) **79**
Royal Welsh Agricultural
  Society **83**
Royal Yacht Britannia **172**
Royal Yachting
  Association **258**
Royal, Hanley **30**
RSA **4**
RSPCA Kid's Stuff **68**
RTHK (Hong Kong) **23**
Ruddles **89**
Rudolf Wolff **193**
Rudyard Kipling **13**
Rugby (Local info) **203**
Rugby (Public school) **75**
Rugby Advertiser **181**
Rugby Group **45**
Rugby League **257**

Rugby Observer **181**
Rugby World **257**
Rugby World Cup **257**
Rugrats **65**
Rugrats the Movie **11, 65**
Rules **95**
Rules of Engagement **11**
Runaway Bride **11**
Runcorn & Widnes World **181**
Runner's World **247**
Runnymede (Gov) **117**
Rural Development Council **85**
Rushcliffe (Gov) **117**
Rushmore (Gov) **117**
Ruskin School of Drawing &
  Fine Art **71**
Russell Grant **143**
Russell Hobbs **239**
Russia (Tourist info) **210**
Russian (Embassy) **102**
Russian (Gov) **104**
Russian (Parliament) **104**
Russian National
  Museums **210**
Rutland (Gov) **117**
Ryalux **231**
Ryanair **275**
Rye & Battle Observer **181**
Rye (Local info) **203**
Ryedale (Gov) **117**
Ryman **47**
Rytons Building Products **237**
Ryvita **92**

S

S Club 7 **20**
S-Cool **66**
S4C (Wales) **26**
Saab **157**
Saatchi & Saatchi **35**
Sabena **275**
Sabre Fund Management **191**
Sabrina the Teenage Witch **65**
Sadler's Wells **6, 30**
Safety Systems & Alarm
  Inspection Board **161**
Safeway **52, 96**
SAFM (Johannesburg) **23**
Saga **190**
Saga Holidays **284**
Sage **37**
Sagem **269**
Saigon Times (Vietnam) **183**
Sail for Gold 2000 **258**
Sailing Now **259**
Sailing Today **259**
Sainsburys **42, 96**
Saint **11, 28**
Sak **241**
Sale & Altrincham
  Messenger **181**
Sale (Rugby club) **257**
Salford (Gov) **117**
Salford (Uni) **77**
Salisbury (Gov) **117**

Salisbury Cathedral **200**
Salisbury Journal **181**
Salmon & Trout
  Association **146**
Salomon **260**
Salomon Smith Barney **40, 193**
Salt Lake City (Local info) **213**
Salt Lake City Winter Olympics
  2002 **262**
Salvation Army **136, 164**
Salzburg (Local info) **197**
Samantha Fox **9**
Samaritans **136**
Samson **152**
Samsonite **239**
Samsung **269**
San Diego (Airport) **277**
San Diego State University **78**
San Francisco (Local info) **213**
San Fransisco (Airport) **277**
San Jose State University **78**
San Marino (Grand Prix) **255**
Sandals **282**
Sandown Park
  (Racecourse) **253**
Sandra Bullock **4**
Sandringham House **107**
Sandwell (Gov) **117**
Sao Paulo (Local info) **198**
Sapporo (Local info) **208**
Sara Lee **57, 92**
Saracens (Rugby club) **257**
Sarah McLachlan **20**
Sardis **95**
Saskatchewan (Local info) **204**
Satellite World **14**
Saturday Night Fever **29**
Sauber (Motor racing
  teams) **255**
Saudi Arabian Airlines **275**
Savacentre **96**
Save & Prosper **188, 191**
Save the Children **136**
Save the Rhino **135**
Savills **159**
Saving Private Ryan **11**
Savoy **280**
Savoy Grill **95**
Scala **6**
Scalextric **66, 150, 243**
Scallywags **46**
Scandanavian Airlines **275**
Scandinavian Seaways **278**
Scantours **284**
Scarborough (Gov) **117**
Scarborough (Local info) **203**
Scarlet Theatre **30**
SceneOne **14**
Schaan (Local info) **208**
Schering-Plough **47, 57**
Schofel **260**
Schools Online (Science) **66**
Schroders **40, 42, 191**
Schwartz Herbs **92**
Schweizerische Nationalbank

(Switzerland) 40
Schweppes 92
Schönbrunn Palace 197
Sci-Fi Channel 26
Science Frontiers 218
Science Museum 172
Science Museum Library 169
Science News 218
Science Online 218
Scientists of Global
  Responsibility 219
Scientology 165
Scooby Doo 63
Scoot 174
Scoot.com 37
Scootering Magazine 164
Scope 138
Scotch Corner 228
Scotch Whisky Association 96
Scotch Whisky Heritage
  Centre 98
Scotchcare 159
Scotiabank 40
Scotland (Police) 140
Scotland on Sunday
  (Edinburgh) 181
Scotrail 283
Scotsman 182
Scott 9
Scott & Sargeant 237
Scott & Sargeant
  Cookshop 239
Scottish & Newcastle 41, 43
Scottish & Southern Energy 58
Scottish Agricultural College 71
Scottish Amicable 190-191
Scottish and Newcastle 42
Scottish and Southern
  Energy 42
Scottish Anglers National
  Association (SANA) 146
Scottish Archery 261
Scottish Arts Council 4, 13
Scottish Athletics
  Federation 247
Scottish Badminton Union 247
Scottish Ballet 6
Scottish Basketball
  League 247
Scottish Book Trust 73, 137
Scottish Borders (Gov) 117
Scottish Bridge Union 144
Scottish Canoe
  Association 248
Scottish Car Auctions 155
Scottish Chess
  Association 144
Scottish Council for
  Educational Technology 73
Scottish Council For Research
  In Education 73
Scottish Courts Service 106
Scottish Cyclists' Union 249
Scottish Environment
  Protection Agency 84

Scottish Equestrian
  Magazine 149
Scottish Fencing 249
Scottish Financial
  Enterprise 188
Scottish Football
  Association 251
Scottish Gallery, Edinburgh 5
Scottish Genealogy
  Society 148
Scottish Golf 251
Scottish Golf Schools 251
Scottish Hydro-Electric 162
Scottish Investment Trust 191
Scottish Legal Services
  Ombudsman 140
Scottish Liberal Democratic
  Party 107
Scottish Life International 191
Scottish Media Group 46
Scottish Mountaineering
  Club 144
Scottish Mutual
  International 191
Scottish National Blood
  Transfusion Service 125
Scottish National Ski
  Council 262
Scottish National War
  Memorial 163
Scottish Nationalist Party 107
Scottish Natural Heritage 218
Scottish Newspaper Publishers
  Association 55
Scottish Nuclear 162
Scottish Ornithologists'
  Club 219
Scottish Parliament 120
Scottish Pharmaceutical
  General Council 130
Scottish Power 42, 58
Scottish Provident 191
Scottish Qualifications
  Authority 72
Scottish Rifle Association 261
Scottish Rugby Union 257
Scottish Smallbore Rifle
  Association 261
Scottish Sports
  Association 256
Scottish Squash 261
Scottish Sub-Aqua Club 261
Scottish Table Tennis
  Association 261
Scottish Television 26
Scottish Tourist Board 202
Scottish Value
  Management 191
Scottish Widows 188, 190
ScottishPower 162
ScoutNet 63
Scouts 63
Scrabble 66, 147
Scream 3 11
Screen 9

Screen International 14
Screen Printers Association
Screentrade 190
Screwfix 237
Scripture Union 165
Scrum.com 257
Scrumpy Jack 89
Scunthorpe Evening
  Telegraph 181
Scunthorpe United (FC) 251
Sea Anglers Conservation
  Network 146
Sea Cadets 63
Sea Containers 56
Sea France 278
Seagram 98
Seal 20
Scaly 223
Sean Graham 252
Search UK 268
Searchers 20
Searchlight 109
Searle 48
Sears Roebuck 57
SEAT 157
Seattle (Airport) 277
Seattle (Local info) 213
Seattle Symphony 21
Seaview 278
Seaworld, Florida 212
Secom 161
Second World War Experienc
  Centre 172
Secret Bunker St Andrews 6
Secretts 147
Secure Trust 188
Securicor 42
Securicor-Omega 36
Securities Institute 50
Sedgefield (Gov) 117
Sedgwick Group 190
Sedgwick Museum of
  Geology 172
Sefton (Gov) 117
Sega 63
Sega Dreamcast 64
Seiko 243
Seinfeld 28
Sekonda 243
Sekonda Ice Hockey
  Superleague 262
Selby (Gov) 117
Select Appointments 51
Selfridges 52, 94, 231
Selftrade 193
Sema 43
Sema Group 37
Senegalese (Gov) 104
Sentinel (Stoke) 181
Seoul (Airport) 277
Seoul (Local info) 208
Serbia (Tourist info) 210
Serene 158
Serious Fraud Office 106
Serpentine Gallery 5

Serpents Magazine 151
Servis 239
Servowarm 162
Sesame Street 65
Seven Seas 236
Sevenoaks (Gov) 117
Sevenoaks Chronicle 181
Seventh Day Adventist 165
Severn Trent 43, 58, 162
Severn Valley (Railway) 199
Seville (Local info) 211
Sewerby Hall 200
Seychelles (Tourist info) 210
Shakespeare Birthplace
  Trust 13
Shakespeare in Love 11
Shakespeare's Globe 30
Shanghai (Local info) 205
Shangri-la 280
Shania Twain 20
Shanks 45
Shannon (Rugby club) 257
Sharp 236
Sharps 234
Sharwood's 92
Shaw Trust 158
Sheena Easton 20
Sheet Music Direct 150
Sheffield (Gov) 117
Sheffield (Local info) 204
Sheffield (Uni) 77
Sheffield Arena 26
Sheffield Hallam (Uni) 77
Sheffield Star & Telegraph 181
Sheffield Steel 239
Sheffield United (FC) 251
Sheffield Wednesday (FC) 251
Shell 43, 157
Shell Geostar 170
Shell Transport & Trading
  Company 37
Shelter 136
Shepherd Neame 89
Shepway (Gov) 117
Sheraton 280
Sherborne Castle 198
Sheree J Wilson 4
Sherlock Holmes Museum 172
Sheryl Crow 20
Shetland Islands (Gov) 117
Shetland Museum 172
Shetland News 181
Shetland Times 181
Shetland Today 181
Shields Gazette 181
Shipbuilders and Shiprepairers
  Association 37, 55
Shire Pharmaceuticals
  Group 48
Shiseido 231
Shola Ama 20
Shoosmiths 51
Shooters' Rights
  Association 261
Shooting Gazette 145

ShopQ 156
Shops on the Net 239-240
ShopSmart 239-240
Shout 163
Showcase 9
Showerlux 237
Shrewsbury & Atchham
  (Gov) 117
Shrewsbury (Public school) 75
Shrewsbury Town (FC) 251
Shropshire (Chamber of
  Commerce) 36
Shropshire (Gov) 117
Shropshire (Health
  authority) 127
Shropshire Star 181
Shropshire Star Online 181
Sibelius (Music Software) 266
Side Saddle Association 149
SIDS - Foundation 138
Siemens 239, 266, 269
Sierra Leonian (Gov) 104
Sight Savers 138
Sigma 152
Signal Radio FM 25
Sikh Arts & Cultural
  Association 165
Sikh Museum 172
Sikh Spirit 165
Sikhism UK 165
Silent Majority 109
Silent Night 223
Silicon Graphics 266
Silver Spoon 92
Silverlink Train Services 283
Silversea 284
Silverstone 254
Simkins Partnership 51
Simmons & Simmons 51
Simon & Garfunkel 20
Simon & Schuster 48
Simply 230
Simply Travel 284
Simpsons 63, 65
Sinead O'Connor 20
Singapore (Airport) 277
Singapore (British
  embassy) 101
Singapore (Legal
  institutions) 106
Singapore (Tourist info) 210
Singapore Airlines 275
Singaporean (Chamber of
  Commerce) 36
Singaporean (Gov) 104
Singha 89
Sinn Fein, Northern Ireland 107
Sir John Soane's Museum 172
Sirius 158
Sisley 9, 231
Sistine Chapel 207
Sixpence None the Richer 20
Skandia Life 190
Skansen, Stockholm 211
Skechers 241

Skegness News 181
Sketchley 159
Ski Club of Great Britain 262
Ski Club of Great Britain (Snow
  Reports) 174
Ski Magazine 262
Ski World Cup 262
Skidream 284
Skier & Snowboarder
  Magazine 262
Skipton 188
Skipton Castle 198
Skoda 157
Sky 26, 177
Sky at Night 217
Sky Sports American
  Football 247
Sky Sports Cricket 249
Slade 71
Slaughter & May 51
Slazenger 260
Sleep Council 223
Sleepy Hollow 11
Slendertone 236
Slimming World 159
Slough (Gov) 118
Slough Estates 51
Slough Express 181
Slough Observer 181
Slovakian (Gov) 104
Slovenian (Embassy) 102
Slow Food 90
Slumberland 223
Slush Puppy 92
Smashing Pumpkins 20
Smeg 239
Smile 188
Smint 92
Smirnoff 92
SmithKline Beecham 43, 48
Smiths Industries 37, 43
Smithsonian Institution 78, 105
Smithsonian Institution, United
  States 212
Smokey Robinson & the
  Miracles (Fan Club) 20
Smythson of Bond Street 235
Snatch 11
Snickers 92
Snooker Market 259
Snooker Nations Cup 259
Snooker Net 259
Snooker Scene 259
Snoopy 67
Snow+Rock 242
Snowdon (Railway) 199
Snowdon (Web cam) 213
Sobstad Sailmakers 258
Soccernet 251
Social & Democratic Labour
  Party, Northern Ireland 107
Social Democratic Party,
  Germany 108
Socialist Party 107
Society for Computers &

Law 106
Society for Experimental Biology 219
Society for History of Mathematics 169
Society for Interdisciplinary Studies 219
Society for Popular Astronomy 217
Society for the Promotion of Roman Studies 169
Society for the Protection of Ancient Buildings 85
Society for the Study of Fertility 131
Society for Underwater Exploration 219
Society of Allied & Independent Funeral Directors 139
Society of Antiquaries 74
Society of Architectural Historians of Great Britain 83
Society of Archivists 173
Society of Authors 23, 50
Society of Cartographers 170
Society of Chiropodists & Podiatrists 126
Society of Editors 183
Society of Freelance Editors and Proofreaders 50
Society of Genealogists 148
Society of Indexers 50
Society of Insolvency Practitioners 50
Society of Investment Professionals 50
Society of Practising Veterinary Surgeons 125
Society of Scribes and Illuminators 148
Society of Teachers of the Alexander Technique 126
Society of Television Lighting Directors 23
Society of Ticket Agents & Retailers 31
Soho Theatre Company 28
Soil Association 83
Solgar 236
Solihull (Gov) 118
Solomon Airlines 275
Solomon Islands (Tourist info) 210
Solvay 48
Somerfield 52, 96
Somerleyton Hall 200
Somerleyton Hall & Gardens 201
Somerset (Chamber of Commerce) 36
Somerset (Cricket club) 248
Somerset (Gov) 118
Somerset County Gazette 181
Somerset House 172
Sommarland Centres 211

Sonia Rykiel 9
Sonic Arts Network 21
Sony 236
Sony (Computers) 266
Sony (Record company) 22
Sony (Telecom) 269
Sony Classical 22
Sony Pictures Entertainment 12
Sophia Swire 228
Sopwell House 159
Sothebys 223
South Africa (British embassy) 101
South African (Embassy) 102
South African (Gov) 104
South African Airways 275
South African Breweries 43
South African Bridge Federation 144
South African National Parks 210
South and West Devon (Health authority) 127
South Ayrshire (Gov) 118
South Bank (Uni) 77
South Bank Centre 26
South Bedfordshire (Gov) 118
South Buckinghamshire (Gov) 118
South Bucks Express 181
South Cambridgeshire (Gov) 118
South Cheshire (Health authority) 127
South China Morning Post (Hong Kong) 183
South Cleveland (Hospital) 128
South Devon (Local info) 201
South Devon (Railway) 199
South East England (Local info) 201
South East England Tourist Board 202
South Essex (Health authority) 127
South Gloucestershire (Gov) 118
South Hams (Gov) 118
South Holland (Gov) 118
South Humber (Health authority) 127
South Kesteven (Gov) 118
South Korean (Gov) 104
South Lanarkshire (Gov) 118
South Norfolk (Gov) 118
South Northamptonshire (Gov) 118
South Oxfordshire (Gov) 118
South Park 28
South Park The Movie 11
South Ribble (Gov) 118
South Shropshire (Gov) 118
South Somerset (Gov) 118
South Staffordshire (Gov) 118

South Tyneside (Gov) 118
South Wales (Police) 140
South Wales Argus 181
South Wales Evening Post 181
South West Arts Board 4
South West Trains 283
South West Water 162
South Yorkshire (Police) 140
Southampton & South West Hampshire (Health authority) 127
Southampton (FC) 251
Southampton (Gov) 118
Southampton (Uni) 77
Southampton Maritime Museum 172
Southampton University Hospitals 128
Southend Evening Echo 181
Southend Observer 181
Southend on Sea (Gov) 118
Southend on Sea Pier 64
Southern Arts Board 4
Southern Comfort 92
Southern Daily Echo (Southampton) 181
Southern Derbyshire (Chamber of Commerce) 36
Southern England (Local info) 201
Southern General, Glasgow 128
Southport (Local info) 204
Southport Visitor 181
Southwark (Gov) 118
Sovereign 284
Space 1999 28
Space Needle 212
Spain (Tourist info) 210
Spam 92
Spanish (Embassy) 102
Spanish (Gov) 104
Spar 96
Sparks 20
Spear & Jackson 147
Special Educational Needs 7
Specialist Anglers Conservation Group 146
Specsavers 131
Spectator 163
Speedlink 278
Speedo 260-261
Spelthorne (Gov) 118
Spend, Spend, Spend 29
Spice Girls 20
Spicer McColl 159
Spicers 47
Spider Man 67
Spiderman 63
Spinal Tap 20
Spink & Son 144
Spire FM 25
Spiritualists' National Union 165
Spitfire & Hurricane

Memorial 172
Spode China 224
Sporting Index 146, 252
Sporting Life 253
Sportingbet.com 252
SportLive 254
Sports Aid 247
Sports Connection 242
Sports Council (England) 256
Sports Council (Northern Ireland) 256
Sports Council (Scotland) 256
Sports Council (United Kingdom) 256
Sports Division 242
Sports Industries Federation 256
Sports.com 254
Sportscover 190
Sportsman's Association 145
Spotlight Casting Directory 14
Spring Ram 237
Sprint 36
SPRITO 256
Squash Player 261
Squash Rackets Association 261
Squeeze 20
Sri Lanka Cricket Board 249
SriLankan Airlines 275
Ssang Yong 157
St Albans & District Review 181
St Albans (Gov) 118
St Albans Museum 173
St Albans Observer 181
St Andrews (Golf course) 252
St Andrews (Uni) 77
St Andrews Group 128
St Barbe Museum 173
St Bartholomew's & The Royal London School of Medicine & Dentistry 74
St Edmundsbury (Gov) 118
St George's Hospital Medical School 74
St Helen's Reporter 181
St Helen's Star 182
St Helens & Knowsley (Health authority) 127
St Helens (Gov) 118
St Helens Transport Museum 173
St Ivel 92
St Ives 48
St James Homes 160
St James's Palace 107
St John's Ambulance Brigade 135
St Kitts & Nevis 204
St Louis (Local info) 213
St Mark & St John (Uni) 77
St Martin's Healthcare 128
St Paul's (Public school) 75
St Paul's Cathedral 200
St Petersburg (Local info) 210

St Vincent & The Grenadines (Tourist info) 204
STA Travel 284
Stafford (Gov) 118
Staffordshire (Building society) 188
Staffordshire (Gov) 118
Staffordshire (Police) 140
Staffordshire (Uni) 77
Stage 14
Stagecoach 43, 278
Stagecoach Holdings 56
Stakis 280
Standard 188
Standard Chartered Bank 40, 43
Standard Life 188, 190
Standard Life Assurance Company 43
Stanford Hall 200
Stanford University 78
Stanfords 170
Stanley Gibbons 145
Stanley Gibbons 223
Stanley Tools 237
Stannah Stairlifts 237
Stansted (Airport) 277
Stansted Express 283
Star (Sheffield) 182
Star Alliance 275
Star Trek 28, 65
Star Wars 11, 65
Starbucks 94
Starchaser Foundation 217
Starlight Express 29
Stars In Their Eyes 28
Starsky & Hutch 28
State Bank of India 40
State Information Service 205
State Railway 211
State Research Centres of Russian Federation 217
States of Jersey (Parliament) 120
Stationery Office 110
Statue of Liberty, New York 212
Status Quo 20
Steel Construction Institute 84
Steffi Graf 256
Steffi Graf (Fan Club) 256
Steinway 150
Stena 278
Stephen Berkoff 23
Stephen Collins 4
Stephen Hawking 218
Stephen Joseph Theatre, Scarborough 30
Stephen King 13
Stephen Sondheim 20
Steps 20
Stepstone 52
Stereophonics 20
Sterling (Gov) 118
Steve Waugh 256
Steven Spielberg

Dreamworks 12
Stevenage (Gov) 118
Stevens Shakin 20
Stevie Nicks 20
Sticky Fingers 95
Stillbirth & Neonatal Death Society 138
Sting 20
Stirling (Uni) 77
Stirling Prize 83
Stockholm (Airport) 277
Stockholm (Local info) 211
Stockholm (Stock exchange) 54
Stockholm Water Festival 211
Stockport (Gov) 118
Stockton-on-Tees (Gov) 118
Stoddard 231
Stoke Evening Sentinel 182
Stoke-on-Trent (Gov) 118
Stoll Moss Theatres 30
Stoll UK 148
Stonehenge 200
Storehouse 52
Storm 46
Stornoway Gazette 182
Stoves 239
Stowe (Public school) 75
Strabane (Gov) 118
Stratford (Local info) 204
Stratford Herald 182
Stratford on Avon (Racecourse) 253
Stratford Standard 182
Strathclyde (Uni) 77
Street Map 170
Strepsils 236
Stretford & Urmston Messenger 182
Strettons 159
Strindbergsmuseet 211
Stringfellows 6
Stroke Association 138
Stromma Kanalbolaget 211
Strongbow 89
Stroud & Swindon (Building society) 188
Stroud (Gov) 118
Stroud News & Journal 182
Strutt & Parker 159
Stuart Little 11
Student Life 72
Student Life Magazine 75
Student UK 75
Student World 72
Sturmey Archer 249
Stuttgart (Airport) 277
Stuttgart (Local info) 206
Sub-Aqua Association 261
Subaru 157
Suede 20
Suez Canal 205
Suffolk (Chamber of Commerce) 36
Suffolk (Gov) 118

Suffolk (Police) **140**
Suffolk Now **182**
Sulgrave Manor **200**
Sumitomo Bank **40**
Sun **182**
Sun Life **190**
Sun Life and Provincial
Holdings **43**
Sun Life of Canada **190**
Sunbank **188**
Sundance Film Festival **8**
Sunday Football League
Directory **146**
Sunday Herald **182**
Sunday Mail **182**
Sunday Mercury **182**
Sunday Mirror **182**
Sunday People **182**
Sunday Times **182**
Sunderland (FC) **251**
Sunderland (Gov) **118**
Sunderland (Uni) **77**
Sunderland Echo **182**
Sunderlands (Betting) **252**
Sunny Delight **92**
Sunsail Holidays **284, 258**
Sunsoft **266**
Sunvil Activity Holidays **258,
284**
Sunworld **284**
Suomen Pankki (Finland) **40**
Supanet **267**
Super Bowl (American
football) **247**
SuperBowl (Ten pin
bowling) **152**
Supergrass **20**
Supertramp **20**
Supreme Cat Show **151**
Surf Control **37, 68, 72, 269**
Surf on the Safe Side **269**
Surgicare **128**
Surinam Airways **275**
Surrey (Cricket club) **248**
Surrey (Gov) **118**
Surrey (Police) **140**
Surrey (Uni) **77**
Surrey Advertiser **182**
Surrey Heath (Gov) **118**
Surrey Institute of Art &
Design **71**
Surrey Mirror Series **182**
Surrey Racing **252**
Sussex (Ambulance) **135**
Sussex (Cricket club) **248**
Sussex (Police) **140**
Sussex (Uni) **77**
Sussex Express **182**
Sustrans **86**
Sutton & East Surrey Water **162**
Sutton (Gov) **118**
Suzanne Vega **20**
Suzuki **157, 164**
Suzuki Marine **258**
Suzuki Owners Club **164**

Sveriges Riksbank
(Sweden) **40**
Swale (Gov) **118**
SWALEC **162**
Swallow **280**
Swallow Group **43**
Swan Hellenic **284**
Swanage (Railway) **199**
Swansea (Gov) **118**
Swansea (Local info) **204**
Swansea (Rugby club) **257**
Swansea (Uni) **77**
Swansea Cork Ferries **280**
Swatch **243**
Swaziland (Gov) **104**
Sweatshop **242**
Sweden (British embassy) **101**
Sweden (Monarchy) **106**
Swedish (Embassy) **102**
Swedish (Gov) **104**
SwedNet **211**
Sweeney **28**
Sweet & Maxwell **48**
Sweet Factory **92**
Sweet'N Low **92**
Swiftair **275**
Swimming Teachers'
Association **261**
Swindon (Gov) **118**
Swindon (Hospital) **128**
Swindon Evening
Advertiser **182**
Swindon Messenger **182**
Swindon Star **182**
Swinton (Insurance) **190**
Swiss (Embassy) **102**
Swiss (Gov) **104**
Swiss Federal Railways **211**
Swiss Life (UK) **190**
Swiss National Bank **40**
Swissair **275**
Switch **188**
Switzerland (British
embassy) **101**
Switzerland (Stock
exchange) **54**
Switzerland (Tourist info) **212**
Sydney (Airport) **277**
Sydney (Cricket club) **248**
Sydney (Local info) **197**
Sydney (Web cam) **213**
Sydney 2000 Olympics **247,
254**
Sydney Morning Herald **197**
Sydney Opera House **197**

T

TAG Heuer **243**
TAG McLaren Audio **236**
Tahiti (Tourist info) **210**
Tahiti Airlines **275**
Tai Chi Union of Great
Britain **149**
Taipei (Airport) **277**
Taiwan (Stock exchange) **54**

Takeda **48**
Talented Mr. Ripley **11**
Talisker **98**
Talisman **51**
Talk 21 **267**
Talk Radio **25**
Talk Sport **25**
Talk TV **28**
Talyllyn (Railway) **199**
Tameside (Gov) **118**
Tammy Wynette **20**
Tampa (Airport) **277**
Tampax **236**
Tamworth (Gov) **118**
Tamworth Snowdome **262**
Tandridge (Gov) **118**
Tanfield (Railway) **199**
Tango **92**
Tank Museum **173**
Tank Museum, Bovington **173**
Tanner Krolle **239**
Tante Marie Cookery
School **145**
Tanzanian (Embassy) **102**
Tanzanian (Gov) **104**
Tap Dogs **29**
Tara Arts **29**
Tarmac **45, 160**
Tarzan **65**
Tarzan (Disney's) **11**
Tasmania Airlines **275**
Tass **177**
Tate & Lyle **41, 92**
Tate Gallery **5**
Tate Gallery, St Ives **5**
Tatler **163**
Tattersalls **253**
Taunton Deane (Gov) **118**
Taylor Joynson Garrett **51**
Taylor Made **260**
Taylor Woodrow **45, 160**
TD Waterhouse **193**
Tea Council **94**
Teacher Training Agency **73,
110**
Teachers' (Building
society) **188**
Teacrate **161**
Team Philips **258**
TearDrop **260**
Tears for Fears **20**
Teatro alla Scala **207**
Technics **236, 239**
Techniquest **173**
Ted Baker **9, 228**
Teddington **12**
Teddy Bears **65**
Teenage Mutant Ninja
Turtles **63**
Teesdale (Gov) **118**
Teeside (Uni) **77**
Tefal **239**
Teignbridge (Gov) **118**
Tel-Aviv (Local info) **207**
Telecom UK **269**

Teleflorist **231**
Telephone Code Changes **173**
Telephone Directories on the
  Web **173**
Teletext **14, 177**
Teletubbies **65**
Telewest **43, 269**
Telewest Communications **54**
Telford & Wrekin (Gov) **118**
Telstar **22**
Tempo **230**
Tempus Group **52**
ten Downing Street **200**
Tenant Farmers Association **83**
Tendring (Gov) **118**
Tennis Organisation UK **262**
Tenovus **74, 131**
Tenrag **258, 284**
Tenson **260**
Terence Higgins Trust **138**
Territorial Army **101**
Tesco **43, 52, 96**
TescoNet **267**
Test Valley (Gov) **119**
Tetrapak **47**
Tewksbury (Gov) **119**
Texaco **37, 157**
Texas (Music) **20**
Texas Instruments **57, 266**
TFI Friday **28**
Thackray Medical Museum **173**
Thai (Embassy) **102**
Thai (Gov) **104**
Thai Airways **275**
Thailand (Monarchy) **106**
Thailand (Tourist info) **212**
Thames Ditton (Local info) **204**
Thames Festival **8**
Thames Trains **283**
Thames Valley (Chamber of
  Commerce) **36**
Thames Valley (Police) **140**
Thames Valley (Uni) **77**
Thames Water **43, 58**
Thameslink Rail **283**
Thannet (Gov) **119**
Theatre **14**
Theatre Royal, Bury St
  Edmunds **30**
Theatre Royal, Glasgow **30**
Theatre Tokens **31**
Theo Fennell **238**
Theodore Goddard **51**
There's Something About
  Mary **11**
TheStreet.co.uk **191**
They Think It's All Over **28**
Thin Red Line **11**
Thirlestane Castle **198**
Thirlstone Home
  Development **160**
This Morning **28**
This Week in Chess **144**
Thistle Hotels **44, 280**
Thomas Cook **284**

Thomas Cook Group **44**
Thomas Crown Affair **11**
Thomas Dolby **4**
Thomas Pink **228**
Thomas the Tank Engine **67**
Thomson (Publishing) **48**
Thomson (Travel agents) **284**
Thomson Cruising **284**
Thomson Directories **173**
Thomson Holidays **284**
Thomson Travel Group **44**
Thorntons **92, 235**
Thorpe Park **64**
Thorsons **48**
Threadneedle Investments **191**
Three Mills Island **12**
Three Peaks Challenge **144**
Three Rivers (Gov) **119**
threed Atlas Online **170**
threeiGroup **40, 43**
threeM **48**
Threshers **94**
Thrifty **278**
Thunderbirds **65**
Thunk.com **66**
Thurrock (Gov) **119**
Thwaites **89**
TI **45**
Tia Maria **92**
Tibbett & Britten **47**
Tibet (Tourist info) **212**
Ticketmaster **31**
Tickets Online **31**
Ticketweb **31**
Tie Rack **228**
Tiffany **238**
Tiger Toys **243**
Tiger Woods **256**
Tilburg (Local info) **209**
Tim Henman **256**
Timberland **228, 241**
Time **230**
Time (Magazine) **14**
Time Code **11**
Time Out **14**
Time Warner **48, 57**
Times **182**
Times Educational
  Supplement **72**
Times Higher Educational
  Supplement **72**
Times Literary Supplement **72**
Times MeesPierson Corporate
  Golf Challenge **252**
Times of India (India) **183**
Timex **243**
Timothy Dalton **4**
Timpson **241**
Tina Turner **20**
Tintin **67**
Tiny **266-267**
Tiptree **92**
Tisserand **236**
Tissot **243**
Titanic **11**

Titleist **260**
Tivoli **205**
Tizer **92**
TNT **36**
Tobacco Manufacturers'
  Association **55**
Today's the Day **28**
Togan (Gov) **104**
Tokyo (Airport) **277**
Tokyo (Stock exchange) **54**
Toledo (Local info) **211**
Tom and Jerry **63**
Tom Cruise (Fan Club) **4**
Tom Jones **20**
Tom Petty **20**
Tomkins **45**
Tommy Hilfiger **9, 228, 231**
Tomorrow Never Dies **11**
Tomorrow's World **28**
Tomorrow's World (BBC) **218**
Tomorrow's World Plus **28**
Tomy **66, 243**
Tonbridge & Malling (Gov) **119**
Toni & Guy **158**
Toni Braxton **20**
Tony Awards **8**
Tony Bennett **20**
Tony Curtis **4**
Tony Hancock (Fan Club) **4**
Top Flite **260**
Top Gear **28, 156**
Top Jobs **52**
Top Man **228**
Top of the Pops **28, 65**
Top Shop **228**
Topmarks **66**
Torbay (Gov) **119**
Torch **269**
Torfaen (Gov) **119**
Tori Amos **20**
Tori Spelling **20**
Torino Winter Olympics
  2006 **262**
Toronto (Airport) **277**
Toronto (Local info) **204**
Toronto (Stock exchange) **54**
Toronto International Film
  Festival **8**
Toronto Symphony **21**
Torquay Herald Express **182**
Torridge (Gov) **119**
Torsby (Local info) **211**
Torvill & Dean (Fan Club) **262**
Toshiba **239, 266**
Total **37**
Total Games **267**
Total Jobs **52**
Totalbet.com **252**
TotalFinaElf **157**
Totally Jewish **163**
Tote **146**
Tottenham Hotspur (FC) **251**
Tour de France **249**
Towcester (Racecourse) **253**
Tower (Record company) **22**

Tower Bridge **200**
Tower Hamlets (Gov) **119**
Tower of London **198**
Tower Records **241**
Town & Country Planning
  Association **84**
Toy City **243**
Toy Story 2 **11**
Toyota **157**
Toys R Us **243**
TP Activity Toys **243**
Tracker **155**
Trade & Industry **111**
Trade Card Collector's
  Association **144**
Trade Indemnity **190**
Trade UK **110**
Tradewings **284**
Trading Standards Central **111**
Trading Standards Office **139**
Traffic Committee for
  London **111**
Trafficmaster **155**
Trafford (Gov) **119**
Traidcraft **41**
Traidcraft Exchange **96**
Trail Cyclists Association **249**
Trailfinders **284**
Train Line **283**
Training & Enterprise
  Councils **73**
Trainspotting **11**
Tramore (Racecourse) **253**
Transco **162**
Transeuro **161**
Transport & General Workers
  Union **55**
Transport for London **111**
Transport Salaried Staffs
  Association **55**
Transport, Local Government &
  the Regions **111**
Traquair House **200**
Travel England **202**
Travel for the Arts **284**
Travel Inns **280**
Travelodge **280**
Traverse Theatre, Edinburgh **30**
Travis **20**
Travis Perkins **45, 237**
Tree Register **85, 219**
Trees for Life **85**
Trend **237**
Trepanation Trust **126**
TRH Duke & Duchess of
  Kent **107**
TRH Princess Alice, Duchess of
  Gloucester & the Duke &
  Duchess of Gloucester **107**
Tri-ang Model Railways **149-
  150**
Tricky **20**
Trinidad & Tobagan (Gov) **104**
Trinity College of Music **72**
Trinity House **258**

Trinity Mirror **48**
Triodos **188**
Trisha Yearwood **20**
Triumph **164**
Triumph Owners Motorcycle
  Club **164**
Trivial Pursuit **66, 147**
Tron Theatre, Glasgow **30**
Tropical Places **284**
Trussardi **9**
TT **45**
TUC **55**
Tulip **266**
Tumbletots **63**
Tumbleweeds **11**
Tunbridge Wells (Gov) **119**
Tunbridge Wells Museum **173**
Tunbridge Wells Museum and
  Art Gallery **5**
Tunisia (British embassy) **101**
Tunisia (Tourist info) **212**
Tunisian (Gov) **104**
Turbo: A Power Rangers
  Movie **11**
Turkey (Legal institutions) **106**
Turkey (Tourist info) **212**
Turkish (Embassy) **102**
Turkish (Gov) **104**
Turkish Airlines **275**
Turkish Cypriot (Gov) **104**
Turkish Republic of Northern
  Cyprus **205**
Turner House Gallery **5**
Turtle World **151**
Turtles **20**
Tusk Force **218**
TV Times **14**
TVR **157, 164**
TWA **275**
Tweenies **65**
Twentieth Century Society **83**
twentiethCentury Fox UK **12**
twentyfirst Century Music **22**
twentyfour Hour Museum **202**
twentytwenty Opticians **131**
Twinings Tea **92**
Twix **92**
Twycross (Zoo) **220**
Tyne & Wear Metropolitan Fire
  Brigade **139**
Tynedale (Gov) **119**
Typhoo **92**
Tyre Trade News **156**
Tyres-Online **156**
Tyresave **155**
Tyrolean Airways **275**
Tyrone Courier **182**

U

U-Drive **278**
U2 **20**
UB 40 **20**
UBS **40**
UC Berkeley **78**
UCI **9**

UCL Hospitals **128**
UCL Obstetric **128**
UCLA **78**
UEFA **251**
Uffizi Gallery, Florence **207**
UFO **163**
Uganda (Tourist info) **212**
UK Amateur Photograph **152**
UK Angling Guide **146**
UK Aromatherapy Practitioner
  & Suppliers **55**
UK Betting **146**
UK Clubs **6**
UK Council for Graduate
  Education **73**
UK Cross Stitch Club **148**
UK Detector Net **149**
UK Directory **268**
UK Firework Safety **136**
UK Fly Fishing & Tyers
  Federation **146**
UK Friendly **190**
UK Golf **252**
UK Harbours Guide **259**
UK Independence Party **109**
UK Karting **149**
UK Learner Drivers **158**
UK Max **268**
UK Motor Vehicle Auctions **15**
UK National Workplace Bullyir
  Advice Line **136**
UK Online **267-268**
UK Parrot Society **143**
UK Philatelic Museums &
  Libraries **145**
UK Plus **268**
UK Practical Shooting
  Association **145**
UK Registrations **155**
UK Reptiles Online **151**
UK Sailing Index **259**
UK Science Park
  Association **219**
UK Scientific Research
  Councils **219**
UK Stained Glass News **148**
UK Stamp Fairs **145**
UK Street Map **282**
UK Sucrologists Club **144**
UK Taekwon-do
  Association **248**
UK Team Racing
  Association **258**
UK Waterways Network **143**
Ukraine (British embassy) **10**
Ukraine International
  Airlines **275**
Ukranian (Gov) **104**
Ulster (Uni) **77**
Ulster Democratic Party **107**
Ulster Gazette **182**
Ulster Unionist Party **107**
Ultimate Band List **14**
Ultravox **20**
Umbro **260**

Umbro International Football Festival **146**
Uncle Ben's **92**
UNESCO **105**
Unibank, Denmark **40**
Unibond **237**
UNICEF (United Nations Children's Fund) **105**
UniChem **48**
Unicorn Theatre for Children **30**
Unigate **41, 92**
Unilever **41, 43**
Union Bank of Switzerland **40**
Union Carbide **57**
Union Castle Line **284**
Union Cycliste Internationale **249**
Union of Liberal & Progressive Synagogues **165**
Union of Shop, Distributive & Allied Workers (USDAW) **55**
Union Pacific **57**
Unionamerica Holdings **43**
Unipart **155**
Unison **55, 136**
Unisys **57, 266**
Unitarian **165**
United Airlines **57, 275**
United Airlines Belgium **275**
United Arab Emirates (British embassy) **101**
United Arab Emirates (Gov) **104**
United Biscuits **41**
United Biscuits **92**
United Cricket Board of South Africa **249**
United Democratic Front, Nigeria **108**
United Distillers & Vintners **41**
United Free Church of Scotland **165**
United International Pictures **12**
United Kingdom Central Council for Nursing, Midwifery and Health Visiting **130**
United Kingdom Council for Psychotherapy **131**
United Kingdom Hydrographic Office **111**
United Kingdom Institute for Conservation **85**
United Kingdom Medicines Information Pharmacists Group **130**
United Kingdom Radio Society **149**
United Kingdom Shareholders' Association **192**
United Medical & Dental Schools of King's, Guy's & St Thomas' Hospitals **74**
United National Party, Sri Lanka **108**

United Nations **105**
United Nations (British embassy) **101**
United News & Media **43, 46**
United Parcel Service **57**
United Pentecostal Church **165**
United States Parachute Association **150**
United States Sports Academy **75**
United Technologies **57**
United Utilities **43, 58**
Universal (Bank) **188**
Universal (Computers) **266**
Universal (Film studios) **12**
Universal Fittings **238**
Universal Music Group **22**
Universal Pictures **12**
Universal Press Syndicate **177**
Universal Studios **65, 212**
University & Colleges Admissions Service **75**
University College (Hospital) **128**
University College London **77**
University Gallery, Leeds **5**
University Hospital of Wales **128**
University of Aberdeen **74**
University of Adelaide **77**
University of Alberta **77**
University of Arizona **78**
University of Auckland **77**
University of Birmingham School of Medicine **74**
University of Canterbury **77**
University of Chicago **78**
University of Colorado **78**
University of Delaware **78**
University of Georgia **78**
University of Hull **74**
University of Idaho **78**
University of Illinois **78**
University of Iowa **78**
University of London Careers Service **73**
University of London Observatory **217**
University of Maryland **78**
University of Melbourne **77**
University of Michigan **78**
University of Minnesota **78**
University of Missouri-Columbia **78**
University of New South Wales **77**
University of Nottingham **74**
University of Oregon **78**
University of Otago **77**
University of Pennsylvania **78**
University of Queensland **77**
University of South Australia **77**
University of Southampton **74**
University of Southern California **78**

University of Southern Queensland **77**
University of Surrey **72**
University of Sydney **77**
University of Tasmania **77**
University of Texas **78**
University of the Third Age **75**
University of Utah **78**
University of Virginia **78**
University of Wales, Cardiff **74**
University of Washington **78**
University of Western Australia **77**
University of Wisconsin-Madison **78**
Uno **234**
Uppingham (Public school) **75**
UPS **36**
Uranium Institute **219**
Urban Design Alliance **84**
Urchin **240**
Uri Geller **218**
Uruguayan (Gov) **104**
US Figure Skating Association **262**
US Geological Survey **170**
US Golf Association **251**
US Masters **252**
US Open **252, 262**
USA (British embassy) **102**
USA (Legal institutions) **106**
USA (Weather) **174**
USA - CIA **104**
USA - Congress **104**
USA - FBI **104**
USA - House of Representatives **104**
USA - Republican National Committee **104**
USA - Senate **104**
USA - Supreme Court **104**
USA - White House **104**
USA Today (USA) **183**
Usborne Publishing **48**
Utah (Tourist info) **213**
Utrecht (Local info) **209**
Uttar Pradesh (Local info) **207**
Utterly Butterly **92**
Uttlesford (Gov) **119**
Uttoxeter (Racecourse) **253**
UTV (Ulster) **26**
Uzbekistan Airways **275**
Uzbekistani (Gov) **104**

V

Vaduz (Local info) **208**
Val Kilmer **4**
Vale of Glamorgan (Gov) **119**
Vale Royal (Gov) **119**
Valencia (Local info) **211**
Valor **160**
Van den Bergh Foods **92**
Van Gogh Museum **209**
Van Halen **20**
Van Heusen **228**

Van Tubergen **147**
Vancouver (Airport) **277**
Vancouver (Stock exchange) **54**
Vanessa Mae **20**
Vanity Fair **163**
Variety **14**
Variety Club of Great Britain **136**
VARIG Brasil **275**
Varmlands (Local info) **211**
Vasa Museet, Stockholm **211**
Vatican **165**
Vatican (Gov) **104**
Vatican Radio **23**
Vaux Breweries **89**
Vauxhall **157**
Vax **239**
Veeraswamy **95**
Vegan Society **90**
Vegetarian Society **90, 109**
Vegnet **94**
Vehicle Inspectorate **111**
Venezuela (British embassy) **102**
Venezuela (Tourist info) **213**
Venezuelan (Embassy) **102**
Venezuelan (Gov) **104**
Vengaboys **20**
Venice (Airport) **277**
Venlo (Local info) **209**
Vent Axia **238**
Verdant Works **173**
Verve **20**
Vespa **164**
Veterinary Medicines Directorate **125**
Viacom **57**
Vibroplant **45**
Vichy **92**
Victor Chandler **146, 252**
Victor Lewis-Smith **26**
Victoria & Albert Museum **173**
Victoria (Local info) **197**
Victoria Wine **94**
Victoria's Secret **228**
Victorinox **235**
Victory FM (Portsmouth) **25**
Vidal Sassoon **158**
Vienna (Airport) **277**
Vienna (Local info) **197**
Vienna Boys Choir **197**
Vienna Kunsthistorisches Museum **197**
Vienna Philharmonic **21**
Vienna Symphony **21**
Vietnam Airlines **275**
Viglen **266**
Viking **47**
Village People **20**
Vinopolis **98**
Virgin (Cinemas) **9**
Virgin (Hotels) **280**
Virgin (Investment funds) **191**
Virgin (ISP) **267**

Virgin (Media) **46**
Virgin (Record company) **22**
Virgin (Telecom) **269**
Virgin Airways **275**
Virgin Atlantic **275**
Virgin Challenger **143**
Virgin Clothing Company **228**
Virgin Cola **92**
Virgin Direct **188**
Virgin Holidays **284**
Virgin Islands (Tourist info) **213**
Virgin Megastore **241**
Virgin Net Travel **282**
Virgin Radio **25**
Virgin Trains **283**
Virgin Wines **98**
Virginia Water (Local info) **204**
Viridian Group **58**
Visa **188**
Vision Express **131**
Vitabiotics **236**
Vitech **266**
VIVA **135**
Viva Rock Vegas **11**
Vivarium Magazine **151**
Viz **163**
Vodafone **43, 266, 269**
Vodafone AirTouch **54**
Vogue **163**
Vogue Knitting **148**
Voice of America **25**
Voice of Russia **23**
Volkswagen **157**
Voluntary Euthanasia Society **109**
Volvic **92**
Volvo **157**
Voucher Express **235**
Voyages Jules Verne **284**
VSO **137**
Vulcan (Rugby club) **257**

W

Wagamama **96**
Waitrose **96**
Wakefield (Gov) **119**
Wakefield (Health authority) **127**
Wakefield (Rugby club) **257**
Wal-Mart **57**
Wales & West (Trains) **283**
Wales Information Society **111**
Wales Institute **77**
Wales Tourist Board **202**
Walkers **92**
Walking with Dinosaurs **218**
Wall Street Journal (USA) **183**
Wallace & Gromit **65**
Wallace Arnold **284**
Wallace Collection **5**
Wallis & Wallis **223**
Walsall (Gov) **119**
Walt Disney **12, 57**
Waltham Forest (Gov) **119**
Wandsworth (Gov) **119**

Wang **266**
Wansbeck (Gov) **119**
Ward Homes **160**
Ware (Local info) **204**
Warehouse Theatre, Croydon **30**
Warner (Cinemas) **9**
Warner Bros **12, 65**
Warner Bros (Record company) **22**
Warner Bros Kid's Page **68**
Warner ESP (Music Catalogue) **14**
Warner-Lambert **48, 57**
Warrington (Gov) **119**
Warrington Mercury **182**
Warsaw (Stock exchange) **54**
Warwick (Racecourse) **254**
Warwick (Uni) **77**
Warwick Castle **198**
Warwick Courier **182**
Warwickshire (Cricket club) **248**
Warwickshire (Gov) **119**
Warwickshire (Health authority) **127**
Washington (Dulles) (Airport) **277**
Washington Post (USA) **183**
Washington State University **257**
Wasps (Rugby club) **257**
Waste Watch **84**
Watchdog **139**
Water UK **161**
Water Web **151**
Waterford (Local info) **207**
Watership Down **67**
Waterside Inn **96**
Waterstones **223**
Waterworld: Quest for the Mariner **11**
Watford (FC) **251**
Watford (Gov) **119**
Watford Theatre **30**
Waveney (Gov) **119**
Waverley (Gov) **119**
WCW Wrestling **262**
Wealden (Gov) **119**
Wealth of Nations **228**
Wear Valley (Gov) **119**
Weatherbys **253**
Weathercall **174**
Weatherseal **238**
Web TV **26**
Webber Douglas Academy of Dramatic Art **72**
Webcrawler **268**
Wedding Store UK **165**
Wedgwood **224**
Weider Nutrition **143**
Weightwatchers **159**
Weir **45**
Wella **236**
Wellingborough (Gov) **119**
Wellington (Local info) **209**

Wells Fargo **40**
Wells Fargo Bank, USA **40**
Welsh Assembly **120**
Welsh Blood Transfusion
  Service **125**
Welsh Bridge Union **144**
Welsh Canoeing
  Association **248**
Welsh College of Music &
  Drama **72**
Welsh Fishing & Trout
  Association **145**
Welsh International Film
  Festival **8**
Welsh National Board for
  Nursing, Midwifery and
  Health Visiting **130**
Welsh National Mountain
  Centre **144**
Welsh National Opera **21**
Welsh Rugby Union **257**
Welshpool & Llanfair
  (Railway) **199**
Welwyn Hatfield (Gov) **119**
Wembley **26, 31**
Wensleydale **92**
Wes Craven **4**
Wesley Barrell **235**
Wessex Water **162**
West Bengal (Local info) **207**
West Berkshire (Gov) **119**
West Bromwich Albion
  (FC) **251**
West Coast (Cinemas) **9**
West Country (Local info) **201**
West Country (TV) **26**
West Country Tourist
  Board **202**
West Devon (Gov) **119**
West Dorset (Gov) **119**
West Dunbartonshire (Gov) **119**
West End Theatre Bookings **31**
West Freugh **12**
West Ham United (FC) **251**
West Hartlepool (Rugby
  club) **257**
West Hertfordshire (Health
  authority) **127**
West Mercia (Police) **140**
West Midlands (Police) **140**
West Midlands Safari Park **220**
West of England (Uni) **77**
West Oxfordshire (Gov) **119**
West Somerset (Railway) **199**
West Surrey (Health
  authority) **127**
West Sussex (Gov) **119**
West Sussex (Health
  authority) **127**
West Sussex Fire Brigade **139**
West Wickham (Local info) **204**
West Wiltshire (Gov) **119**
West Yorkshire (Police) **140**
West Yorkshire Playhouse,
  Leeds **30**

Westbury Homes **160**
Western Australia (Local
  info) **197**
Western Isles (Gov) **119**
Western Newspapers **48**
Western Provident **190**
Westfield **157**
Westlife **20**
Westminster (Gov) **119**
Westminster (Public school) **75**
Westminster (Uni) **77**
Westminster Abbey **200**
Weston Carpets **231**
Wet 'n' Wild **212**
Wet Wet Wet **21**
Wetherby (Racecourse) **254**
Weymouth & Portland
  (Gov) **119**
WFNX (Boston) **25**
WH Smith **52, 223, 241, 267**
Whale & Dolphin Conservation
  Society **218**
Whale Foundation **218**
What's On Stage **31**
WhatCar? **156**
Wheelie Serious **249**
Which Camera? **152**
Which? **239**
Which? - Motoring **156**
Whipsnade (Zoo) **220**
Whirlpool **57, 239**
Whiskas Cat Food **151**
Whisky Shop **98**
Whitakers Almanack **174**
Whitbread **43-44**
Whitbread Book Awards **8**
Whitby (Local info) **204**
Whitby Museum **173**
White Cube Gallery **5**
White Knight **159**
Whitehouse & Cox **241**
Whitgift **240**
Whitney Houston **21**
Whittard of Chelsea **92, 94**
Whitworth Art Gallery,
  Manchester **5**
Whitworths **94**
Who Wants to be a
  Millionaire? **28**
Whole Earth **94**
Wickes **238**
Wicksteed **243**
Wicksteed Park **64**
Widget Software **266**
Wigan (Gov) **119**
Wightlink **280**
Wilcon **160**
Wild Wild West **11**
Wildfowl & Wetlands Trust **218**
Wildlife Trust **218**
Wiley **48**
Wilkinson Sword **236**
Wilkinsons **238**
Will Smith **4, 21**
Willersmill Wildlife Park **220**

William Hayford **231**
William Hill **146, 252**
William Morris Gallery **5**
William Shatner **4**
Williams **52**
Williams (Motor racing
  teams) **255**
Willie Nelson **21**
Willie Wonka **67**
Willis Corroon Group **43, 190**
Wilson **260**
Wilton **231**
Wilton House **200**
Wiltons **96**
Wiltshire (Gov) **119**
Wiltshire (Police) **140**
Wimbledon **262**
Wimbledon (FC) **251**
Wimbledon Theatre **31**
Wimpey Homes **160**
Wincanton (Racecourse) **254**
Winchester (Gov) **119**
Winchester College **75**
Windermere Steamboat
  Museum **173**
Windjammer **284**
Windsor & Maidenhead
  (Gov) **119**
Windsor (Racecourse) **254**
Windsor Castle **107, 198**
Windsor Horse Trials **259**
Wine Cellar **94**
Wine Spectator **95**
Wine Today **95**
Winkworth **159**
Winnie the Pooh **67**
Winona Ryder **4**
Wirral (Gov) **119**
Wisden **249**
Wish You Were Here? **28**
Wishbone Ash **21**
Wizard of Oz **11**
Wm. Morrison
  Supermarkets **52**
WNYC (New York) **25**
Woking (Gov) **119**
Wokingham (Gov) **119**
Wolford **241**
Wolsey **52**
Wolverhampton (Chamber of
  Commerce) **36**
Wolverhampton (Gov) **119**
Wolverhampton
  (Racecourse) **254**
Wolverhampton (Uni) **77**
Wolverhampton Wanderers
  (FC) **251**
Womad **8**
Wombats **65**
Women's Aid **137**
Women's Institute **149**
Women's National
  Commission **111**
Women's Sports
  Foundation **256**

Womens Royal Voluntary Service (WRVS) **149**
Wonderbra **228**
Woodfordes **89**
Woods Car Rental **278**
Wookey Hole (Local info) **201**
Woolwich **40, 43, 188**
Woolwich Insurance Services **190**
Woolworths **231, 243**
Worcester (Gov) **119**
Worcester (Rugby club) **257**
Worcester Evening News **182**
Worcestershire (Cricket club) **248**
Worcestershire (Gov) **119**
Worcestershire (Health authority) **127**
Wordflow **47**
Wordsworth Museum **173**
Workers' Educational Association **75**
Working Silk Museum **173**
World Air Sports Federation **146**
World Airways **275**
World Amateur Golf Council **251**
World Anti-Doping Association **254**
World Architecture **83**
World Assembly of Muslim Youth **165**
World at War **28**
World Bank **40, 105**
World Books **223**
World Boxing Association **248**
World Bridge Federation **144**
World Chess Federation **144**
World Council of Churches **165**
World Courier **36**
World Cover Direct **190**
World Cup **249**
World Federation of Haemophilia **138**
World Health Organisation **105**
World in Action **28**
World is Not Enough **11**
World Judo Organisation **248**
World Karate Federation **248**
World Kickboxing Association **248**
World Meteorological Organisation **105, 174**
World of Beatrix Potter **202**
World of Interiors **163**
World of Leather **235**
World of Money **144**
World Off Road **156**
World Online **269**
World Snooker Association **259**
World Society for the Protection of Animals **135, 218**
World Squash Federation **261**
World Trade Organisation **105**

World Trekker **190**
World Underwater Federation **258**
World Wide Arts Resources **14**
World Wide Fund for Nature **218**
World Wrestling Federation **262**
Worldwide Travel **190**
Worshipful Collection of Clock Makers **44**
Worshipful Company of Bakers **44, 96**
Worshipful Company of Barbers **44**
Worshipful Company of Carpenters **44**
Worshipful Company of Curriers **44**
Worshipful Company of Engineers **44**
Worshipful Company of Fan Makers **44**
Worshipful Company of Farriers **44**
Worshipful Company of Framework Knitters **44**
Worshipful Company of Goldsmiths **44**
Worshipful Company of Grocers **44**
Worshipful Company of Information Technologists **44**
Worshipful Company of Ironmongers **44**
Worshipful Company of Makers of Playing Cards **44**
Worshipful Company of Marketors **44**
Worshipful Company of Professional Turners **44**
Worshipful Company of Scientific Instrument Makers **44**
Worshipful Company of Spectaclemakers **44**
Worshipful Company of Stationers and Newspaper Makers **44**
Worshipful Company of Upholders **44**
Worshipful Company of Wax Chandlers **44**
Worshipful Company of World Traders **44**
Worshipful Society of Apothecaries **44**
Worthing (Gov) **119**
Wotsits **94**
WOZA (South Africa) **183**
WPP **43**
Wrangler **228**
Wrekin College **75**
Wrexham (Gov) **119**
Wright & Teague **238**
Wrigley's **94**

Writers' Guild of Great Britain **23, 50**
WTA Tour **262**
WWF - UK **218**
WWF International **218**
Wychavon (Gov) **120**
Wychwood Brewery **89**
Wyclef **21**
Wycombe (Gov) **120**
Wyndham **280**
Wyre (Gov) **120**
Wyre Forest (Gov) **120**
Wyvernrail (Railway) **199**

X

X-Files **28**
X-men **63**
X-Stop **269**
X-Stream **267**
Xcheck **269**
Xena Warrior Princess **65**
Xerox **37, 58**
XFM **25**
XFM (Dublin) **23**
XXL Basketball **247**

Y

Yacht Charter Association **2**
Yachting & Boating World **2**
Yachting World **259**
Yahoo Finance **45**
Yahoo! **268**
Yahoo! Classifieds **52**
Yahoo! Games **68**
Yahoo! Online **267**
Yahooligans! **68**
Yakult **94**
Yale University **78**
Yalplay **241**
Yamaha (Motorcycles) **164**
Yamaha (Music) **150**
Yamaha Motor **258**
Yashica **152**
Yellow Buses **278**
Yellow Pages **173**
Yellowstone National Park **2**
Yemen Airways **275**
Yemenite (Gov) **104**
Yeo Valley **94**
YMCA **149**
Yo! Sushi **96**
Yogz **94**
Yokohama (Local info) **208**
York & North Yorkshire (Chamber of Commerce)
York (Gov) **120**
York (Local info) **204**
York (Tourist info) **202**
York (Uni) **77**
York Archaeological Trust **8**
York Castle Museum **173**
York City (FC) **251**
York City Art Gallery **5**
York Dungeon **173**

York Minster **200**
York Theatre Royal **31**
Yorkshire (Building society) **188**
Yorkshire (Cricket club) **248**
Yorkshire (Local info) **201**
Yorkshire Agricultural
  Society **83**
Yorkshire Dales (Local info) **201**
Yorkshire Museum **173**
Yorkshire Tourist Board **202**
Yorkshire Utilities **162**
Yosemite National Park **213**
You've Got Mail **11**
Young & Rubicam **35**
Young Embroiderers **66**
Young Muslims UK **165**
Young People's Trust for the
  Environment & Nature

Conservation **218**
Young's (Breweries) **89**
Youngs **228**
Youth Clubs UK **149**
Youth Hostelling
  Association **149**
Youth Justice Board **106**
Youth Sport Trust **247, 256**
Yugoslav Airlines JAT **275**
Yugoslavian (Gov) **104**
Yukon (Local info) **204**
Yves Saint Laurent **9, 231**
Yvonne Arnaud Theatre,
  Guildford **31**

Z

Zambian (Gov) **104**

Zandra Rhodes **9**
Zanussi **239**
Zaobao (Singapore) **183**
Zeiss Direct **131**
Zetters **147**
Zevo **260**
Zimbabwe Express Airlines **275**
Zoe Ball **27**
Zoological Society of
  London **219**
Zoom **163**
Zoppo Hockey Sticks **260**
Zurich (Airport) **277**
Zurich (Insurance) **190**
Zurich (Local info) **212**
Zwemmer **223**